Critical Acclaim for this Book

The author's knowledge, understanding and love of the country shine from every page. This will surely become the definitive account of East Timor's most traumatic years.

Fergal Keane, BBC Special Correspondent and author of Season of Blood

If there is another journalist who knows as much about East Timor as Irena Cristalis I haven't met them. *Bitter Dawn* is informative, vividly written, and acutely observed. It is also a thrilling page-turner.

Jonathan Mirsky, ex-East Asia editor, The Times *[London]. Now I.F. Stone Fellow, Graduate School of Journalism, Berkeley, USA*

Irena Cristalis's account of East Timor's final years under Indonesian occupation is a gem of a book. Anyone wishing to know how a tiny nation of 700,000 won eventually their freedom against impossible odds, will find her eyewitness memoir simply riveting. A tale of courage and humanity which will pass into legend.

Peter Carey, Laithwaite Fellow and Tutor in Modern History, Trinity College, Oxford

Irena Cristalis has produced a highly readable, dramatic account of East Timor's last years under Indonesian occupation. She writes as a committed witness who shared the emotions and fears of the East Timorese, while doing what she could to reveal the terrible reality to a largely unconcerned world. She interweaves her own personal experiences, monitoring key events in the people's resistance with a history of the struggle. Her portraits of many of the individuals, high and low, who steered the struggle to its final victory give her account a special feeling of immediacy and warmth.

Carmel Budiardjo, human rights activist and author of Surviving Indonesia's Gulag, *an account of her own years as a prisoner under Suharto*

About the Author

Irena Cristalis, who also writes and broadcasts under the byline Irene Slegt, is a Dutch journalist and photographer who since 1990 has been based in East Asia, including at various times Hong Kong, Beijing and Bangkok, and who has also worked in East Timor and London. She understands three Asian languages – Chinese, Indonesian and Tetum, the indigenous language of the East Timorese. She broadcasts regularly on the BBC, Radio Netherlands and Deutsche Welle, and her reports and photographs have appeared frequently in a wide range of outlets, including *Asiaweek*, *The Economist*, the *Guardian*, the *Independent*, the *Far Eastern Economic Review* and many others. Her connection with East Timor goes back a number of years. She spent time with Falintil in the mountains; she was also one of the three Western journalists to stay on in the besieged UN compound (from where she reported for National Public Radio in the United States) during the ransacking of Dili by the militias and the Indonesian security forces at the time of their impending departure from the island in September 1999.

Bitter Dawn: East Timor, a People's Story

Irena Cristalis

Zed Books
LONDON • NEW YORK

Bitter Dawn: East Timor, a People's History was first published by
Zed Books Ltd, 7 Cynthia Street, London N1 9JF, UK and Room 400,
175 Fifth Avenue, New York, NY 10010, USA in 2002.

Distributed in the USA exclusively by Palgrave, a division of St Martin's
Press, LLC, 175 Fifth Avenue, New York, NY 10010, USA

Supplementary visual and other material relating to each chapter of this
book can be accessed on the following website: http://www.geocities.
com/easttimor_bitterdawn/index.html. The publisher is not responsible
for the content and management of the site.

Set in Monotype Dante by Ewan Smith, London
Printed and bound in Great Britain by Bookcraft Ltd, Midsomer Norton

A catalogue record for this book is available from the British Library
Library of Congress Cataloging-in-Publication Data: available

ISBN 1 84277 144 2 cased
ISBN 1 84277 145 0 limp

Contents

Illustrations

Acknowledgements

First of all I thank the Timorese I have written about, who gave so freely of their stories, trust, hospitality and time, and, especially, their friendship. This book is a tribute to them: their resilience, strength and amazing fighting spirit.

I thank my many friends in London, Amsterdam, Dili and the USA who read the manuscript at different stages and provided invaluable suggestions and encouragement. In particular, Anthony Goldstone, Minka Nijhuis, Catherine Scott and Alison McEwan were exceptionally generous in sharing their insight and wisdom.

My friends and my father have had to put up with my obsession about writing this book and kept me afloat at times when I thought I would drown in the process of finishing it.

Many thanks also to everyone at Zed Books who have been involved in publishing this book for their professionalism and understanding.

And above all my partner for his patience and love and unfaltering confidence in me. For without him and the support he has given me, from near and from afar, this book would never have been written.

Glossary

ABRI	Angkatan Bersenjata Republik Indonesia, Armed Forces of the Republic Indonesia, including the national police, army, navy, marines and air force. In April 1999 ABRI was renamed TNI
Aitarak	Thorn, militia operating in and around Dili
ANP	Associação Nacional Popular, Portugal's ruling party till 1974
Apodeti	Associação Popular Democrática Timorense, Timorese Popular Democratic Association
ASDT	Associação Social Democrática Timorense, Association of Timorese Social Democrats
ASEAN	Association of South East Asian Nations
aspirante	trainee
assimilado	'civilised' native population who could speak Portuguese and had adopted the Catholic faith
Bahasa Indonesia	the official Indonesian language
BAKIN	Badan Kordinasi Intelijen Negara, National Intelligence Coordinating Agency
bemo	small bus
Besi Merah Putih	Red and White Iron, militia operating in Liquiça
bom dia	good morning
Brimob	Brigade Mobil, Police Mobile Brigade
BRTT	Barisan Rakyat Timor Timur, East Timor People's Front
Buibere	female name, see Maubere
bupati	district administrator
capela	chapel
celcom	an underground cell in the clandestine structure
CNRM	Conselho Nacional da Resistência Maubere, National Council of Maubere Resistance, became CNRT in 1998
CNRT	Conselho Nacional da Resistência Timorense, National Council of Timorese Resistance, umbrella organisation of Timorese resistance to Indonesian rule
CPD-RDTL	Conselho Popular pela Defesa da Republica Democratica

	de Timor Leste, Popular Council for the Defence of the Democratic Republic of East Timor
CRTR	Commission for Reception, Truth and Reconciliation
dato	village chief or nobleman (prince) with political power
deportado	(political) deportee
Dom	Sir, Portuguese term of respect to prelates and noblemen
DSMTT	Dewan Solidaritas Mahasiswa Timor Timur – East Timor Student Solidarity Council
estafeta	messenger
ETTA	East Timor Transitional Administration (under UNTAET)
fado	Portuguese song
Falintil	Forças Armadas de Libertação Nacional de Timor Leste, Armed Forces for the National Liberation of East Timor
fazenda	plantation
fazendeiro	plantation owner
FDTL	Força Defensa Timor Leste, East Timor Defence Force (successor to Falintil)
Forçarepetil	Pro-Referendum East Timorese Intellectuals' Forum
FPDK	Forum Persatuan, Demokrasi dan Keadilan, Forum for Unity, Democracy and Justice
FPI	Frente de Politica Interna, Internal Political Front
Fretilin	Frente Revolucionária de Timor Leste Independente, Revolutionary Front for an Independent East Timor
Garda Paksi	Gardu Penegak Integrasi, Youth Guards to Uphold Integration
GFFTL	Grupo Feto Foinsae Timor Lorosae, East Timor Young Women Group
Golkar	Golongan Karya, Functional Group, Indonesia's ruling party under Suharto
GRPRTT	Movement for Reconciliation and Unity of the People of East Timor
Halilintar	Thunderbolt/Lighting militia in Bobonaru
Hansip	Pertahanan Sipil, Civil Defence (under department of Home Affairs)
ICMI	Ikatan Cendekiawan Muslim se Indonesia, organisation of Islamic intellectuals
ICRC	International Committee of the Red Cross
Impettu	Ikatan Mahasiswa dan Pejalar Timor Timur, East Timorese student organisation in Indonesia
intel	Indonesian intelligence (agents)
Interfet	International Force for East Timor
Kamra	Keamanan Raykat, civil defence force

karau	water buffalo
katana	large bladed knife or samurai sword
Kijang	Indonesian-produced four-wheel-drive jeep
knua	hamlet, group of clans
Komnas Ham	Komisi Nasional Hak Asasi Manusia, National Commission on Human Rights (Indonesia)
Kopassus	Komando Pasukan Khusus, Special Forces Command
Kota	Klibur Oan Timor Asuwain, Association of Timorese Heroes
KPS	Komisi Perdamaian dan Stabilitas, Peace and Stability Commission
kretek	clove cigarette
kuku nain	shaman, ritual leader
lia nain	traditional authority and go-between
liurai	king or chief of a kingdom or village
lorosae	east, (literally: where the sun rises)
lulik	sacred, holding spirituality
Madre	Mother, nun
Mahidi	Mati Hidup Demi Integrasi, Life or Death for Integration, militia in Cassa, Ainaro
mercado	market
mana	older sister, also polite form of addressing a woman of the same generation
mandi	bath, shower
Maubere	common name, used derisively by the Portuguese to describe the Timorese. Fretilin adopted it to symbolise the common people they claimed to represent
maun	older brother, also polite form of addressing a man of the same or older generation
Maun Alin Iha Kristo	Brothers and Sisters in Christ
Maun Boot	literally: big elder brother, generally used for someone who is much older and has more power
mestiços	people of mixed race
MPR	Majelis Permusyawaratan Rakyat, People's Consultative Assembly
ninjas	death squads, plain-clothed masked men recruited by the military
nurep	Nucleos Representatives, members of a celcom
OMT	Organização da Mulher Timorense, Timorese women's organisation under the umbrella of the CNRT
Operasi Kikis	Operation 'Scraping' or 'Eliminating'
OPMT	Organização Popular da Mulher Timorense, Timorese women's organisation under the umbrella of Fretilin

Padre	Father, priest
Pak (Bapak)	polite from of addressing older or superior male in Indonesia
PAM Swakarsa	community defence group
Pancasila	the Indonesian state ideology: faith in one God, humanity, nationalism, representative government and social justice
PD	Partido Democrática, Democratic Party
Polda	Police Regional Command, also police regional head-quarters
PPI	Pasukan Pejuang Integrasi Pro-Integration forces
PSD	Partido Social Democrática Timor Lorosae, Social Democrat Party of East Timor
PST	Partido Socialista de Timor, Socialist Party of Timor
rai	land
reformasi	political reformation
Renetil	Resistência Nacional dos Estudantes de Timor Leste, Timorese student organisation under the umbrella of the CNRT
Sagrada Familia	Holy Family, underground organisation
SGI	the intelligence task force of Kopassus
Suara Timor Timur	Voice of East Timor, local newspaper
suco	village
tais	traditional weavings
tauk	afraid
tebe tebe	traditional circle dance
tetum	lingua franca of East Timor
tia	aunt, also a polite form of addressing a woman of an older generation
Tim Alfa	militia operating in Lautem
Tim Saka	paramilitary operating in Baucau
Tim Sera	militia operating in Baucau
Timor Timur	Indonesian name for East Timor
tio	uncle, also a polite form of addressing a man of an older generation
TNI	Tentara Nasional Indonesia, Indonesian National Military
Trabalhista	Timor Labour Party
tua sabu	strong fermented palm wine
UDT	Uniao Democrática Timorense, Timorese Democratic Union
uma lulik	sacred house
Unamet	United Nations Mission in East Timor

UNIF	Front Bersama Pro Otonomi Timor Timur, United Front for East Timor Autonomy
UNTAET	United Nations Transitional Administration in East Timor
Untim	University of East Timor
Wanra	Perlawanan Rakyat, Civil Defence (Army)
wisma	guesthouse, hostel
yayasan	foundation
Yayasan HAK	Foundation for Human Rights and Justice

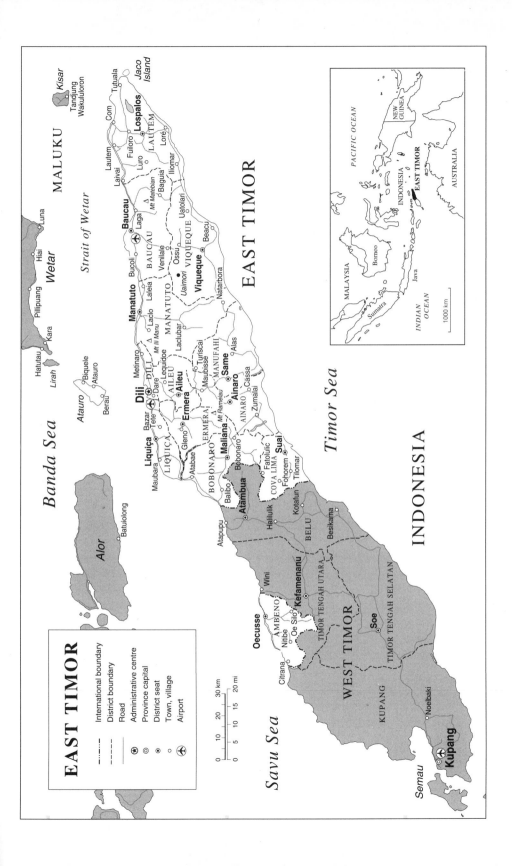

For Simon

Prologue

§ DILI is burning. An unearthly orange glow fills the sky over the town, and thick columns of dark, acrid smoke billow up all around us. The smoke stings my eyes and makes it difficult to breathe. Long bursts of automatic gunfire pierce the air, sounding sometimes far away, sometimes all too close. They echo from the hills, making me feel that I am surrounded on all sides by the shooting.

My vantage point in witnessing this mindless destruction of what will become the capital of a newly independent nation is the balcony of one of the buildings in the compound housing the headquarters of Unamet, the United Nations Mission in East Timor. Below me babies are wailing in their mothers' arms. Squatting between the buildings, hundreds of families are huddled on mats and plastic sheets, around little kerosene stoves. They are cooking rice and whatever other provisions they managed to grab when they fled their homes to escape the violence and took refuge in the compound.

For me, it is like watching a film after having read the book. The scenario Timorese all over the country had predicted is playing out before my eyes. A few days earlier, nearly all of those old enough to vote had done so, in a referendum they had almost lost hope they would ever be allowed. Four-fifths chose to reject Indonesia's offer of greater 'autonomy' to East Timor, a territory it had invaded in 1975 and ruled badly, and often savagely, since. They had chosen independence, and fully expected Indonesia to wreak its revenge. The brutal meanness of that retribution was now unfolding all around us, in an orgy of arson, looting, vandalism and killing. Among the perpetrators were Timorese nationals. But they received their orders from Indonesian commanders, and met no resistance from the Indonesian police and soldiers.

At the time, I felt consumed by anger. Why did it have to go so far? Why was there nothing the UN, or some regional body, or individual foreign countries, or anyone else could have done to prevent this happening, or, now that it was almost too late, to stop it?

I had reached the compound on 6 September 1999, forced to go there by the Indonesian military, who were intent on rounding up every foreigner and frightening us into leaving. They nearly succeeded. Soon after I arrived in the

UN compound a large group of military observers, their duffel bags slung over their shoulders, were marching towards the gate. I was so stunned that they should be leaving now, when the compound was under siege, that I couldn't hold back my tears. An official from the UN's information division scolded me: 'Don't cry in front of the Timorese,' he said, 'it'll upset them.'

What really upset them, I thought, was to see Unamet personnel leaving at such a crucial moment. Most of the people in the compound probably did not know about Srebrenica; about Rwanda; about the other disastrous modern failures of international intervention. But they knew the UN was all that stood between them and Indonesia's spite. The official told me I should not blame the staff for leaving. 'They are given orders to do so; it's hard for them, too.' But I did blame them. 'You can defy your orders!' I shouted at the embarrassed-looking security men. Another journalist, I noticed, was arguing passionately with Unamet's military commander, General Rezaqul Haider. Then, at the last possible moment, after the men had already boarded their cars at the gate, they were called back. The general had concluded: 'It doesn't look good to have UN uniformed staff leaving.'

It would not look good, that is, either to the terrified Timorese refugees, or, more importantly, to those watching from abroad. For so long largely ignored by the outside world, like a sick relative whose afflictions have become a family embarrassment, East Timor was enduring its 15 minutes of international fame. The international press was gripped by the horror, the madness and the sheer, flagrant injustice of what was being done to East Timor. And because virtually every remaining foreigner in the territory had been corralled into this besieged compound, the eyes of the world were on it. The fate of its occupants – local and foreign UN staff, the hundreds of refugees, and a handful of journalists – became the symbol for the world's willingness and ability to rescue East Timor.

All that day the UN's political division was receiving a stream of telephone calls, telling it that the Indonesian army was in the process of rounding up people from the churches and school compounds where they had taken refuge. They were herding them onto buses and bringing them to the port to be ferried out on waiting ships, or onto trucks to the neighbouring Indonesian-ruled territory of West Timor. By the time order was restored to East Timor, at least 300,000 people – nearly half of the population – were in exile. At the time of writing, more than 70,000 remain in squalid camps in West Timor.

The mayhem was presented as some kind of oriental delirium – part of an Indonesian culture of 'running amok'[1] – an unforeseen, even unforeseeable, outburst of incomprehensible and motiveless violence. Yet it was, in truth, all too predictable; many Timorese had indeed expected something very like this. People knew that their long ordeal had not yet ended. The foreigners in the UN and the capitals of the countries most concerned – in South-East Asia,

Australia and the United States – should also have had some idea of what was coming. For many months secret documents had circulated, spelling out detailed plans for the total destruction of East Timor if its people rejected autonomy within Indonesia. Australia, which boasted the best intelligence on East Timor, had known it, but had consistently downplayed the threats. Pro-independence Timorese had repeatedly given dire warnings about what was to come. But their Cassandra cries were dismissed as propaganda, exaggerating the dangers in the hope that this would speed up the arrival of UN peace-keepers.

Even now, as the catastrophe was happening, the UN remained in denial. Those leaving the country, we were told, were those who had supported continued Indonesian rule and feared reprisals. The Indonesian police were doing their best to maintain security, but had lost control. As had happened countless times during Indonesia's occupation, foreigners were giving it the benefit of the doubt, partly out of a squeamish refusal to confront the horror.

One excuse for that refusal, over the years, had been the lack of impartial information about what was happening in East Timor. Indonesia had largely succeeded in sealing the territory off from prying reporters. Occasionally, organised, closely shepherded groups would be taken in. Some journalists managed to sneak in posing as tourists or businessmen – it was in this way that hugely influential film footage of the 'Santa Cruz' massacre in Dili in 1991 reached television screens. Others attempted clandestine visits – I myself had been caught and expelled on one such trip in 1994. Yet now, once again, the Indonesians were doing their utmost to rid East Timor of foreign reporters. And the UN, fearful for the safety of the foreign press, and, perhaps, not wanting it around to witness its abandonment of the East Timorese to their fate, was encouraging us to leave. Almost everybody did.

But along with four colleagues, I defied the threats and entreaties of the UN, the Indonesians, and, at times, the media organisations I worked for, and refused to go. For a week, equipped with a satellite telephone, we broadcast on radio and television stations almost around the clock. By the time we were at last forced to board an aeroplane for Darwin in northern Australia, the refugees in the compound were evacuated as well; and Indonesia had agreed to what had seemed unthinkable even days before: the intervention of an international peacekeeping force.

My decision to stay on was born not just of a journalist's stubborn reluc-tance to be deprived of a story. It was also a result of the months of research I had undertaken in East Timor as a reporter, and to prepare for this book. I was committed to the place and the people and to leave would have felt like betrayal. The Timorese in the compound were not nameless unfortunates. Many were my friends. This is their story.

It also aspires to be the story of how and why East Timor, which is after all far from unique in having endured a dreadful history, should have turned into this unique corner of hell. That story involves far more than simply Indonesian duplicity and brutality. A much more complex mixture of factors was at work: the impact of East Timor's own tribal loyalties and conflicts; the legacy of Portuguese colonial rule; and the fate of a small, seemingly insignificant place caught up in the global strategies of the Cold War. Against this backdrop, a number of institutions and ideas struggled to influence the course of events. They included the Catholic Church and traditional animist beliefs; students and other young people who had grown up under Indonesian rule but became an important engine of the independence movement; the militias sponsored by Indonesia that were to wreak such havoc; and the lonely, heroic and seemingly futile war waged in the mountains by the armed resistance to Indonesian occupation. In the end, these hardened jungle fighters won their war, but only after one of the hardest of all the sacrifices they made in 24 years of resistance: not to fight at all, when their enemies' provocations threatened to destroy the very country whose existence they were fighting for. It was to go to meet them in their hilltop hideouts that I had first visited East Timor.

CHAPTER I

. . . .

The View from the Ditch

§ MY view of the stars was framed by palm leaves, gently swaying in the wind. Lying on my back in the ditch I could see them progressing, ever so slowly, across the moonless sky. Hours after we dived into this drainage ditch to take refuge, a dog started barking at a distant farm. I knew that, soon, other dogs in the neighbourhood would join in. Then the search would be on again, and I would have to keep very still. I could not help but think of my Timorese travel companions. Had they been caught already or had they managed to get away? I prayed they had escaped.

I had a lot of time to think and my thoughts soon wandered back over the journey that had brought me here, to this ditch along the road somewhere on the outskirts of Baucau.

It had begun three weeks earlier, in November 1994, in Jakarta. Jill Jolliffe, an Australian journalist, and a leading authority on East Timor, had hired me to do the camerawork for a documentary she wanted to make about Falintil, the military wing of the Timorese resistance. The assignment had fired my imagination. Falintil's story had become a legendary tale of heroism. They had been fighting a David-and-Goliath battle against the Indonesian army for almost two decades. This tiny army claimed to have inflicted more than 20,000 casualties among Indonesian soldiers. This amounted to a remarkable military success over one of the world's largest armies. But the war had cost Timor many more lives – some 200,000 Timorese, a quarter of the population, are believed to have died as a consequence of it.

Very occasionally, a few photos or a videotape, smuggled out of the mountainous interior, gave a glimpse of what life was like for the guerrillas. Skinny men with emaciated faces, long frizzy hair and beards, dressed in threadbare uniforms, would stare with burning eyes into the camera while proudly brandishing M-16 semi-automatic rifles they had seized from the Indonesian army.

In 1992 the Indonesian army captured their leader, Falintil's commander, Kay Rala Xanana Gusmão. I could still remember the picture in the newspapers:

a handsome, bearded man, greying at the temples, smiling self-confidently while being led into court, chained between two guards.

At first Xanana's capture came as a hard blow for the resistance. But soon they realised they now had a Nelson Mandela: a high-profile political prisoner who, it turned out, was able to work from his cell in the high-security Cipinang prison in Jakarta more effectively than he could from his remote hiding places in Timor. It led to a new era in Timor's fight for independence: the armed struggle in the jungle and the underground resistance in Timor's towns now had a link with the diplomatic struggle in the international arena. Xanana continued to direct the clandestine movement in Timor and Indonesia, while also communicating on the diplomatic front. For example, from his cell in Jakarta, Xanana Gusmão had given his blessing to this film project.

It was also in Jakarta, thousands of miles away, that I had my first contact with the Timorese resistance in Indonesia. The Timorese underground in Jakarta lived like hunted animals. It was impossible for them to melt into the crowds. Their features – frizzy hair, dark skin and prominent noses – made them stand out from the city's majority population of ethnic Malays and Chinese. We had to be very circumspect. Our first meeting with the resistance had taken place under cover of darkness, in an obscure backpackers' guest-house in Jalan Jaksa, the street to which Jakarta's budget travellers gravitate. There we met Avelino de Coelho, code-name 'FF' (pronounced 'Effi Effi'). FF's life as a resistance leader in Jakarta was to be part of the film.

But we also had to meet the *estafetas*, messengers of Falintil, to work out the details of our journey. We would engage in complex subterfuges to meet. Before the first encounter we hung around in a branch of McDonald's in central Jakarta until the appointed time, and then sauntered through the adjacent Sarinah department store, shuffling past the perfume counters, the gentlemen's suits and ties, and the long escalators to the floor with batik, sarongs and souvenirs. There we spotted our contacts. After a brief exchange of codewords, we followed the two Timorese outside onto one of Jakarta's wide avenues where the evening rush-hour traffic crawled through a heavy, tropical downpour. They led us to a yet more luxurious shopping centre, through a labyrinth of shining marble façades with names such as Gucci, Armani and Calvin Klein, to a small Dunkin' Donut outlet tucked away in the basement. As we settled in the orange plastic seats, two Timorese came in. A group of four of them had staked out the route making sure that we were not followed. The other two kept watch outside.

They knew of Jill, as did everyone in the Timorese resistance. She had already made the trip a few months earlier when she had sneaked into East Timor and met Nino Konis Santana, Falintil's vice-commander. After we ordered a few soft drinks I began to realise they had been sent to check me out. They seemed to look me over, as if they were gauging my strength, and trying to assess whether I was up to the task ahead. One of them spoke some Portuguese and another a bit of English. 'You'll have to climb a lot,' they said, 'and eat whatever is available, and that's often not much.' But after a few more questions I seemed to have passed their test, and they changed the subject.

'What is your objective?' one of them asked. This question was a standard one in all dealings with journalists. Their concern, they explained, was that the international media adopted the line of Indonesian propaganda: that Falintil was no more than a group of fifty or so cranky, poorly armed old men. Indonesia had put up a blockade around the island. No journalists or independent foreign observers could enter without permission from Jakarta. Falintil was eager to show the world that it was still a force to be reckoned with.

I had something to discuss, too. Falintil, I knew, had announced, just a few months earlier, a unilateral ceasefire. But Jill had told me that they planned to break it for the film and organise an attack on an Indonesian convoy. I had argued with Jill about this. It seemed to me journalistically and ethically irresponsible and wrong. I did not want to have any deaths, including those of Indonesian soldiers, on my conscience: killed to fit the needs of a film.

I explained this to the envoys, who nodded, and said they saw my point. Perhaps, they suggested, they could organise an attack to commemorate the day of the Indonesian invasion? This was not quite what I had meant but I decided to drop the issue, at least for the moment. They were not the ones who made the decisions anyway.

Jill had worked out an intricate itinerary. As *persona non grata* in Indonesia, she operated with extreme caution. To avoid passport checks at airports and the risk that the omnipresent Indonesian military intelligence – *intel* – might get on her trail, we had to make the long journey over land. It was a journey that would take us by bus, car and boat, covering a far greater distance than the two-thousand-kilometre flight. One of the young men, who had introduced himself as Antonio, was to travel with us on a different bus, to prepare the route and take us, if all went well, to meet the Falintil commanders.

§

It took us two weeks to reach Kupang, the capital of West Timor: an ugly, unpleasant town. Historically it was a recruiting ground for soldiers and mercenaries to fight in East Timor, and the Indonesian army exploited this potential to the full. We had to be careful not to be spotted by one of the many *intel* officers who used to hang around in this nest of spies. It was not one of Indonesia's tourist hot spots. It attracted a few Australians, mainly sex tourists from nearby Darwin, who would pop over for a dirty weekend – not a crowd we could easily melt into.

Jill insisted that we change hotels every other day. I had to pretend to be sick while she would go out to find a safe phone to call Dili to find out why our escorts for the last leg of our journey had failed to show up in the ferry port. That week, there had been a summit of the Asia-Pacific Economic Co-operation forum in Bogor, near Jakarta, attracting foreign dignitaries as well as a large contingent of the international press. This had triggered demonstrations in Jakarta as well as Dili. As a consequence, the Indonesians had blocked all the roads into Dili. We had no other choice than to make our own way to the border.

Hoping to shake off anybody who might be tailing us, we did not make a beeline for the nearest border crossing. Instead, we zig-zagged slowly through the poor, dusty interior of West Timor, before reaching the frontier town of Atambua, another dingy trading and spying post.

More days of waiting in a guesthouse followed, until, at last, in the middle of the siesta, they arrived: four youths in white singlets driving a green army jeep. We tried to jump into the car unnoticed, but the noise of the engine had woken the owner of the guesthouse, a retired army officer. He staggered outside, eyes blinking against the fierce sunlight, to demand the hotel registration forms we were supposed to have given him when we checked in – a bureaucratic necessity I had kept putting off in the hope that he would forget. He looked suspiciously at the scene in front of him. Our hasty and supposedly inconspicuous departure had become very conspicuous indeed.

Our guides seemed not to worry. Their plan was to travel through the central highlands to skirt the military checkpoint at the border. The dirt track led us through fortified hilltop villages, which crawled with children and piglets, all coloured red-brown by the dust they played in.

Passing through one such village, a huge pile of branches blocked the track. The boys jumped out and managed to clear a path just before the villagers, their curiosity aroused, could reach us. I realised that we had crossed the border – a small stream of greenish water that runs in a wide stony riverbed – when the sandy track gave way to a new asphalt road, one of many built by the Indonesians as part of their development strategy for East Timor. The roads also, of course, served the needs of the Indonesian army: not just to move soldiers to control the population, but also, in the case of this stretch, to log the last of East Timor's famous, and extremely valuable, sandalwood trees.

Jill, who had been silent during the journey, perked up as soon as we crossed the border. She pointed at a rock formation. That, she said, was where she had sheltered in 1975, when the Indonesians started to shell East Timor from the sea. What she experienced in those last months before Indonesia invaded East Timor, when she was working as a reporter for news agencies, had changed her life. In October, five of her colleagues had been murdered by Indonesian troops in the town of Balibo.[1] Later many Timorese friends died too. Just days before the Indonesians invaded she left Timor on the last flight. Her friends had convinced her that she could do more for the country overseas. She followed the refugees to Portugal and settled there, remaining close to the Timorese community, while continuing to write about East Timor for anyone who would print it.

Soon we left the road and followed a broad, rocky riverbed that led us safely to the coastal road. Darkness had fallen. Near Dili the Indonesian army had set up a road-block. Fully armed soldiers shone their torches into the car. My heart leapt into my throat. 'Don't worry,' Antonio, who was driving, tried to reassure me. He got out of the car and talked briefly to the soldiers and I saw him handing over an ID card. 'How did you manage to get us out of this?' I asked when we were driving again. 'They know this car, it's one of theirs,' Antonio grinned, 'and I left them my ID card and some money.'

§

The atmosphere was tense in the house. The curtains were drawn. When a car stopped Antonio jumped up and tiptoed to the window. He peered outside through a slit in the curtain. 'What's up?' I asked. He hissed: 'Keep your voice down: the neighbours are Indonesians.'

Even on a less secretive and risky visit it would have been hard not to see the signs of fear and repression in Timor. Hiding out with the resistance, it was unmissable. I had been in East Timor less than 24 hours when I was confronted with its violent past. A friend of the family sheltering us popped in for a visit. He showed me the bullets under his skin. They were clearly visible, one near his shinbone and the other in the inside of his thigh. He said that they hurt but he was too afraid to go to a hospital. Bullet wounds made him a suspect. They dated from 1991. He had been at the Santa Cruz cemetery when the army opened fire. The wounded were pulled out of the hospitals and either thrown into prison or 'disappeared'.

For us, the worst that could happen, I thought, was expulsion. The people who helped us were risking their lives.

We waited for two days. Antonio had made a trip to Baucau on his motor-bike and checked the road. He had returned with bad news. He and the others who had picked us up in Atambua talked for a long time. The police, they said, had arrested 30 students after the recent APEC-prompted demonstrations, and one person had died. The city was teeming with soldiers. They seemed nervous and couldn't agree on whether it was safe enough. Eventually, they reached a decision. We would wait until nightfall and then drive along the north coast to a priest near Baucau. From there we would go into the hills on foot.

§

All had gone according to plan until, not long after we left, the car broke down. I was nervous. 'Keep thinking positive,' I told myself. But then the car broke down a second time and we were stranded on the edge of a high cliff. Our guides warned us to stay inside but I knew the handbrake didn't work and didn't want to risk ending up in the foaming sea below. Jill and I squatted behind the wheels when the third car that passed us stopped. I thought the driver had spotted us and I panicked. But our companions laughed my worries away. 'It's OK, he's a priest,' they said reassuringly.

Back in the jeep I kept glancing out of the rear window. 'Don't worry, everything is OK,' Antonio would repeat every time he saw a worried look on my face. 'Only when we worry, you have to worry.'

I sucked nervously on a *kopico* coffee candy and then it happened. As we drove through the dark deserted streets of Baucau, I saw a Kijang jeep parked at the side of the road. As soon as we passed, it turned on its headlights. Now everybody was nervous. No one said 'Don't worry' any more. Antonio put his foot down and we raced round the bends. They exchanged agitated remarks. Just after one sharp bend one of them opened the back doors. 'Jump!' they shouted. But Antonio was driving much too fast for us to get out safely. We screamed at them to slow down. They did so in front of a fully lit house. We had no choice but jump out.

While the four of them sped off we ran as fast as we could away from the lights, into the fields. We kept running until we stumbled onto the courtyard of a small wooden hut. An old lady grabbed Jill's hand and pleaded with her in Portuguese: 'If you stay here, they'll kill us all,' she said. Jill asked her to direct us to somewhere, anywhere – a tree in a field, a big rock – where we could stay until sunrise. The woman called two children, a boy and a girl. They could not have been older than twelve. They took our hands to guide us and we ran again. It was pitch-black and the fields were covered with razor-sharp stones. I tripped and fell several times and the small girl helped me up and kept her hand in mine. She seemed unperturbed by her adventure. But to our disappointment we found ourselves back on the road again. This was the last place we wanted to be: it would be too dangerous to walk on the road by night. Jill worried that any Indonesian patrol could open fire and no one would have seen what had happened. She suggested hiding in the bushes near the side of the road until daybreak. Then we noticed the flood-channel hidden in the shadow of some trees.

§

So here I was. When we went into the ditch, dogs from the nearby farm had barked. After we had not moved for some time they fell silent, and only the sound of crickets filled the air. But now I heard them again. The barking started in the distance and moved closer, until I saw the light of torches. I covered my face with a thin scarf so that I could still see but my face would not reflect the light, and held my breath. The dogs on the nearest farm started to make a furious noise. I could hear the sound of footsteps and sharp, breathless barks coming from the side of the road. The beam of a torch, or perhaps car headlights, shone over the ditch, lighting up the bushes right above us and coming within centimetres of touching my face. I could hear the breathing of a dog very near to my ear now and imagined I felt its damp breath on my face. It was just a few seconds, then the searchers had moved on.

We lay there for eight hours, until in the grey half-light I could make out the shapes of passers-by on the roadside. I pulled myself up and sat on the edge of the ditch. Amazingly, the first person I saw walking down the road was one of our friends. 'Wait here,' he whispered as he passed us without stopping, 'we'll come back to get you'. Elated, I dived back into the ditch. Not much later I heard a car stop. 'We are friends,' called a voice in Portuguese, 'please come out.' I stuck my head out of the ditch, thinking for a moment that we might make it after all. It was all too good to be true.

It was. I saw a blue *bemo* – a small bus – with an old Timorese standing next to it. Where were our friends? Before I could think any more, the *bemo*'s passengers jumped out: they wore camouflage trousers, T-shirts and the red berets of the elite, and feared, special forces, Kopassus. They pointed their automatic weapons at us, ordering us to get into the *bemo*. We refused. 'We are journalists and my name is Jill Jolliffe. Who are you?' Jill asked defiantly. Their commander pulled out his ID: Edy Matje, Kopassus. In the faint hope it might intimidate him I scribbled it in my notebook. 'We'll have to bring you to our headquarters,' he said in good English. But Jill was afraid that they could take us anywhere, where anything could happen to us. 'We will go to a hotel on foot,' she retorted. 'Your superiors can contact us there.' That way, we thought, we would at least have witnesses if anything happened to us. Reluctantly, they agreed. But the people we passed on the road avoided our eyes. They were too afraid even to look at our strange procession. They made themselves as small as possible, trying to blend into the bushes at the side of the road.

I hauled myself up the hill, a few steps ahead of the soldiers with their guns burning in my back. With every step, hope evaporated further. This was it, the end of our journey. And what about our friends? What had happened to them?

We stopped at a police station near the old market in Baucau. Better to hand ourselves over to the police than to stay in the hands of the Kopassus, we agreed. Most of the policemen were Timorese. One of them politely offered us a seat on a long wooden bench and another hurried to bring us coffee and fresh bread rolls. When we finished our breakfast they took us to the main barracks, a large sprawling building a little above the old town. I wondered if our four friends were there, behind some of the many doors that opened on to the long corridor.

The commander had not arrived yet and we were led into a waiting area: a dark room with wooden benches that swarmed with mosquitoes. I worried about a couple of telephone numbers that I had in my notebook, and asked permission to go to the toilet. While I tore the notepaper into tiny shreds I noticed dark spots on the floor. Blood? Suddenly, I felt sick with worry about our helpers. I knew of course the stories of torture, rape and murder, and had seen the gruesome pictures Indonesian soldiers had taken of the mutilated bodies of their victims. Why torturers seem so intent on documenting their deeds still mystifies me. But they do, all around the world, perhaps for different reasons: to add to the victim's humiliation; out of satisfaction at a job 'well done'; to keep a record in some grotesque filing system; or to have something to brag about with torturer colleagues. 'Avoid taking photographs showing torture in progress,' it says in one of the manuals for Indonesian soldiers.[2] For the Indonesian soldiers there was an additional reason to take photographs: money. They sold the photographs to the resistance movement, which in turn used them as evidence of the human rights violations that went on in Timor.

Back in the waiting room the silence was suddenly broken, by a loud thump, as if a heavy object had fallen against one of the wooden doors. What was going on? I opened the door and looked down the corridor. The noise, I guessed, had come from behind a door near to us. I feared the sound had something to do with our Timorese friends. Were they being beaten and tortured in the room across the corridor? What if we burst in there, would it shame the torturers into stopping? Or would it make them even more cruel? I didn't dare take the risk. Jill and I concentrated on what else we could do to avoid worsening their plight. We decided that the best tactic would be not to give them any evidence that our presence in Baucau had anything to do with the guys in the car. So we resolved not to speak and to refuse to be separated. We would give our passport details, but after that we would insist on seeking assistance from our embassies.

The commander, a lieutenant-colonel – a short, heavily built, gap-toothed man of around fifty with a bristling moustache – possessed the characteristics of his tribe: as a Batak from Sumatra, he loved to talk. He started in Indonesian, while leafing through a fat file that lay in front of him on the desk. I understood some of the questions but thought it best not to show this. He eyed me suspiciously, pointing out that as a Dutch person I was likely to speak Indonesian. Frustrated by our silence, he summoned a Portuguese-speaking Timorese police officer to do the translations.

We gave the agreed answer to every question, 'We want to cooperate but want to call our embassies first,' until the commander got quite annoyed and, eventually, gave up. He called his superior and I heard him spelling out my name. The quality of the telephone connection from Baucau was so bad that he had to repeat every letter several times, and the versions of my name that appeared later in the press reports were still inaccurate.

When his boss left the room the Timorese policeman apologised, saying what was happening to us made him very ashamed of his job. The only work available was for the government. 'I have a wife and children, they have to eat.' Again we heard the sound, a deafening thud. No cries, no voices, a sound of water sluicing. The Timorese policeman fixed his eyes ahead, jaw set, sweat breaking out on his brow. Perhaps he had to steel himself against these sounds every day. I noticed Jill was about to explode in anger and gave her a warning look. The commander came back and gestured to one of his subordinates to get us out of there.

Not much later we were on the road again, this time in a police car. We raced round the hairpin bends. Far below us glittered the cobalt-blue sea. Edy Matje sat next to me with a thick brown envelope on his lap, containing, I presumed, our file. He offered us some bananas. I refused. I didn't want *his* bananas. He ate several and within half an hour he had to hang his head out of the window to vomit. Served him right, I thought, with childish spite.

In the police barracks in Dili the interrogation continued in a similar vein, this time to a bizarre background chorus of Brimob riot troops training in the yard. A group of them posed as rioters shouting abuse and pretending to throw stones; the others were kitted out in full battle gear. Our interrogators read from a large file in front of them. I heard them discussing our itinerary. This added to my suspicion that we had walked into a trap set by Indonesian intelligence. It looked as if they had known about our plans even before we had arrived. Who had given them this information?

Just when I thought that the man leading the questioning was on the point of losing patience with us, the first big storm of the rainy season clattered on the tin roof. The deafening noise made it impossible to understand a word. After a short, half-hearted attempt at a good cop/bad cop routine, and a threat to keep us incommunicado for 21 days, they eventually gave up. One of them disappeared and came back with *nasi-bungkus*, a take-away meal of fried rice with egg and *sate*, wrapped up in brown paper.

Unable to torture or rape us, they seemed to have decided to feed us instead. Our passports seemed to provide some protection against the fate that Timorese women would have met. While we were eating the food with our hands out of the soggy paper an immigration officer entered the room. 'Ha, they will lock you up in their prison,' sneered one of our interrogators when we climbed into the grey Immigration Department van.

The head of immigration was a Javanese from Yogyakarta. He opened his questioning by asking us our religion. According to *pancasila*, Indonesia's state ideology, it is forbidden not to have a religion. I decided that probably the best thing was to say Christian. He looked elated: 'Me too,' he said. 'My name is Johannes and I'm Protestant.' It was as if we had signed a pact. He smiled pleasantly when I repeated our request to contact our embassies. 'Go ahead, but please make it short and ask them to call you back,' he said.

I hesitated with the phone in my hand, feeling slightly awkward. What was I supposed to say? That I had been captured in East Timor? Everyone knew journalists were not allowed to enter without a permit. They would probably think I was a troublemaker and treat me like a naughty schoolgirl.

Within half an hour the political attaché called back, dutifully mumbling something about breaking Indonesian law, but he promised to make some calls. Soon things changed again. Johannes Sri Triswoyo returned from his office, beaming. His boss in Jakarta had called, to tell him to treat us well. 'Now I have his backing, I don't have to lock you up in the immigration cells. Tomorrow you'll be deported, but tonight you are free to go to a hotel.'

'Or,' he continued, 'you can stay in my office. It has only one key and I'll give it to you.' I wanted nothing more than to get away from it all, to take a bath and enjoy a long sleep between clean white sheets. But while Johannes was busy making a hotel reservation, Jill said she thought it would be safer to stay in the office. She saw herself as enemy number one for the Indonesian army, and was afraid that the hawks among them would be able to enter the hotel and take revenge on her.

Johannes seemed pleased at our decision, and promised he would get us some bedding. But first, he said, he wanted to take us home to meet his wife and son. 'Home' was a simple but comfortable bungalow in a leafy neighbourhood where many Indonesian civil servants lived. The Indonesians, as the new rulers, took over the houses left by Portuguese civil servants and built new neighbourhoods. They even relaid the water-supply pipes so that the Indonesian part of town was provided with clean spring water from the hills, while most of Dili's Timorese residents had to make do with polluted wells in their back yards.

His family welcomed us warmly and Johannes's wife gave us towels and new toothbrushes. Without wasting any time I took my much-needed *mandi* bath. I had not often felt so filthy, and in their clean, neat living room I was even more aware of it than in the interrogation rooms.

After our baths Johannes invited us to eat with his family in a Chinese restaurant, one of the few proper restaurants in town. It was all rather bewildering. Why was he treating us so well? Was he a genuinely nice guy, or was it part of a charm offensive designed to find out who had helped us? Although I felt instinctively that I could trust him, I also still felt a 'prisoner' and thought it better not to let my guard down.

It was as pleasant an evening as it could be in the circumstances. Johannes seemed an enlightened civil servant, who hinted several times that he was not pleased with his country's rule in Timor. (Before we left his office he had turned around in the doorway, and, pointing at his chair had said: 'A Timorese should be sitting there, not me.') And he had been very interested to hear our view of Indonesian rule in Timor.

'I will not come back,' he said when he dropped us off at the office and made sure we were comfortable, 'so if anybody knocks on the door in the night it won't be me.' It sounded like a warning. Just after we switched off the light and slid between the clean sheets, there was a knock at the door. I crept over and anxiously asked who it was. A male voice said a name I didn't recognise. 'I need to come in,' he urged. I told him to come back tomorrow: 'It's too late now; we're already asleep.' I never found out who it was.

The next day, after breakfast at Johannes's house, Immigration Department officers escorted us around town. We could buy some socks and underwear and a ticket to Bali. I could even make overseas phone calls from the telecommunications office.

We were transported in an Immigration Department van, accompanied by two of their officers. Johannes, looking worried, followed behind us. The route to the airport was dotted with agents with ear-pieces. Jill thought this was because of our deportation, but it seemed to me more likely that it had to do with a visit of a UN special rapporteur, who had arrived for a fact-finding mission.

I watched the town glide past the window. Only a bit of glass separated me from the world outside but it felt like a steel plate. I felt exhausted and deeply affected by the unhappiness around us.

But then I saw a small miracle: a blue Kijang swung behind us, packed with young men and women. They saluted us with V-signs and by blowing kisses. At the next side road they disappeared again. A mirage in the streets of Dili: a glimpse of the defiance and courage of Timorese youth. I had to swallow back my tears and hoped that our guards had not noticed. For four years tears would well in my eyes again every time I told the story. This sight of the determination of the Timorese against all odds not to submit but to stand up, to keep up a struggle that looked, at that time, to be hopeless, was an image that never left me. I lived at that time in South-East Asia and kept a close eye on the developments in Indonesia. I knew that if, one day, it became possible to return to East Timor, I would be on the first plane back.

CHAPTER 2

. . . .

Distant Glimmers

§ AT the airport Johannes showed us a selection of Indonesian newspapers. The story of our arrest had made the front pages. One of the banner headlines read: 'Two journalists found in ditch.'

'I know that you won't tell me anything,' Johannes had said, 'But one thing I would really like to know, just for myself. How did you end up in a ditch?' And when his question met with silence he had added, 'You do realise that these ditches are used by Falintil to attack our troops?'

It was only when Johannes made that remark about the ditch that I grasped how much danger we had been in, how close to being shot dead in the middle of nowhere by soldiers who would then blame Falintil. Perhaps that was why he said it – he was baffled by our refusal to be rattled. He made me realise that our conviction that deportation was the worst that was likely to happen to us was based on a misunderstanding of just how grim things were in East Timor.

In other ways that short ill-starred trip confirmed the truth of much that I had read and heard about East Timor: notably, of course, about the sheer ruthlessness of Indonesian rule. We had tried to do what we could for our Timorese helpers, through our embassies and the International Committee of the Red Cross.

In some respects, they were lucky: they were freed quite soon. Antonio later managed to escape to Australia on a leaky boat. From him we learnt that they had been interrogated and tortured for four days. In the *intel* offices in Baucau they were subjected to electric-shock torture. One effect is that the victim loses control of his muscles. The thumping noises we had heard were of their bodies, slumping against the door. And they endured the 'chair treatment', a crude but very painful form of torture in which the leg of a chair is placed on the victim's toe while someone sits in it.

None of the Timorese has ever blamed us for what they suffered, or accused us of being responsible for the failure of the mission. It may be that we had not been careful enough during the preparations and *intel* had been on our tail from the start. However, it was hard not to agree with Jill's suspicion that we were victims of a set-up, and betrayal from within the Timorese resistance.

Jill and Avelino, our Jakarta contact, attributed this to an article she had written after her trip to the mountains earlier in 1994 in which she alleged that large sums of money meant for Falintil had 'disappeared'. This had angered some within the resistance – and it might have been at least part of the reason for our trouble. Disunity within the resistance was the other part. Like other such movements around the world, East Timor's was beset by factionalism. Jill had been involved so long that she had become part of it.

It would take me a long time to grope my way through all the back-stabbing, petty jealousy and mutual recrimination of the vipers' nest that was the liberation struggle. I tried my best to stay aloof from all this, and to trust my own instincts about whom to deal with and whom to avoid. But I would still get bitten several times.

Even disregarding the divisions among the Timorese, it was hard to be optimistic about their chances of freedom. Despite that brief glimpse of a display of bold defiance on the way to the airport, the Indonesians seemed to have the place buttoned up. Jill's film of the Falintil fighters was, against all odds, eventually completed, shot by Dominic Rotheroe, another cameraman, who travelled on his own the following year. His pictures showed guerrilla commander David Alex leading a small platoon of enormous courage and resourcefulness, holding out in the hills and having some successes against Indonesian army patrols. But to the dispassionate observer they appeared not all that different from the ragged, ill-equipped and desperate army of Indo-nesian propaganda.

Yet Indonesia's control was not total: we had passed one road-block through simple bribery. This was a phenomenon seen across Indonesia: corruption was so endemic that it seemed at times that money could override almost any political consideration. As Goenawan Mohamad, a prominent Indonesian journalist and writer, put it at the time, 'Suharto and his clique can't do anything perfectly in this country. Everything is so corrupt that they even can't perfect repression.' Nor was corruption the only weakness of the Indo-nesian occupiers of East Timor. It seemed reasonable to guess that Johannes – at least as he presented himself to us – was typical of many in not having the heart for this venture in neo-colonialism. There was little active support for East Timor's independence movement among Indonesians either in the territory or in Indonesia itself, where there was widespread ignorance about the place's history and about what was happening there. But nor was the occupation backed by great popular enthusiasm.

The occupation was also an irritant in Indonesia's foreign relations. The UN had never recognised the annexation, although Indonesia's partners in the Association of South-East Asian Nations (ASEAN) accepted it, and its big neighbour to the south, Australia, had recognised it as early as 1979. Foreign interest waxed and waned with the level of media attention, which was curtailed partly by the lack of access, but occasionally surged, as after the Santa Cruz massacre in 1991. In 1996 the award of the Nobel Peace Prize to Bishop Carlos Ximenes Belo, the archbishop of Dili, and José Ramos Horta, in effect 'foreign minister' of the exiled resistance movement, ensured that Timor's troubles received renewed attention. But, in general, East Timor's chances of independence seemed no better than those of another sad land I had often visited: Tibet.

East Timor's best hope seemed to lie not so much in the armed resistance, nor the exiled dissidents and the faint-hearted diplomatic support they had been able to muster, nor even in the brave young people in Timor itself, ever-ready to risk their lives by taking to the streets. Rather, it lay in younger Indonesians, a generation that had grown up under nearly thirty years of the Suharto dictatorship, and had outgrown it. Only when their aspirations for change in Indonesia were realised might change also follow in East Timor.

Of course, its fate had always been bound up with that of its colonisers. It was the revolution in Portugal in 1974 that had thrown independence into East Timor's unprepared lap. And it was Portuguese indifference that brought its colony civil war and, ultimately, the Indonesian invasion.

At the time of our trip in 1994, change in Indonesia seemed a remote prospect. Even two-and-a-half years later, after the general elections in 1997, the edifice of Suharto's power seemed solid enough. His ruling party won its usual massive majority (by the usual unfair means), and it became clear that Suharto planned to secure yet another five-year term in office from the upper house of parliament, the MPR, which acted as a presidential electoral college, and was to convene in March 1998. The only uncertainty was the identity of his proposed vice-president, and hence, according to the constitution, successor, should he fail to complete his term of office. Since by this time, Suharto was already 76, the succession was the burning issue of Indonesian politics.

In early 1998, Suharto's choice became known: his minister of research and technology, Bacharuddin Jusuf Habibie. Habibie was a lifelong protégé of his, a German-trained aeronautics engineer. But he was seen as an erratic boffin – simply not credible as a president. So it seemed the nation must settle down once more to indefinite rule by Suharto, his family and cronies and the loyal military.

But by the time the MPR convened, two different, though connected, storm systems had blown Suharto's plans off course. The first was a regional financial crisis that began in Thailand in mid-1997, but was to devastate Indonesia's economy more thoroughly than any other country's. It reached its nadir in January 1998, when news that Habibie was to be the vice-president pushed the currency, the rupiah, down to below 15,000 against the dollar, from a rate a few months earlier of around 2,500. This disaster in turn fuelled the second unexpected source of turbulence: an unprecedented student-led protest movement. Students rallied against 'KKN', the Indonesian initials for Corruption, Collusion and Nepotism, which became shorthand for all that was wrong with the Suharto regime, and demanded *reformasi*, or reformation – a concept more radical than mere reform, if something less than a revolution.

This reached a climax in May 1998, when the security forces opened fire on protesting students at Trisakti University in Jakarta, killing four of them. After days of riots, arson, bloodshed and chaos, which saw more than a thousand deaths in Jakarta, Suharto stepped down and was replaced by Habibie. Suharto's son-in-law, General Prabowo Subianto, also lost power, after a short but fierce struggle with the head of the armed forces (and later defence minister) General Wiranto. This had particular resonance in East Timor: Prabowo ran the Kopassus special forces, which had such sway there.

The new Habibie government was greeted by waves of demonstrations that submerged most of the archipelago. Years of bottled-up frustration and anger spilled out from the campuses and workplaces into the streets. And the spirit of the time took hold in Dili as well. Soon after the events in Jakarta the students in Dili took advantage of the new atmosphere of relative freedom to stage 'open forum' discussions. For the first time under Indonesian rule, different groups sat around a table and discussed East Timor's future.

Meanwhile in Jakarta, in his first television interview with the BBC, Habibie said that East Timor might get 'some kind of autonomy'. He also ordered the release of a number of political prisoners, but not all of them: Xanana Gusmão had to stay behind bars, along with secessionist leaders from Indonesian provinces, the leadership of the PRD, a young left-wing party, and some old communists locked up in the 1960s.

The changes were startling. But there was still huge uncertainty about whether the process of reform was genuine and would last. That, many Indonesians recalled, was how the Suharto era had begun, more than thirty years earlier. For the time being, nobody seemed too sure about which of the old rules and laws should be enforced any more. So there was a window of opportunity to test the restrictions on visiting East Timor. I used this to return there in June 1998.

§

There was a particular reason to go at that time: to cover an unprecedented visit to East Timor undertaken by the three Jakarta-based ambassadors of Britain, Austria and the Netherlands, the European Union's current 'troika' (the incumbent, previous and next holder of its six-monthly rotating presidency), together with a representative from the EU's own mission in Jakarta.

Portugal's membership gave the EU a special interest in East Timor. Because the UN had not recognised the annexation of the territory by Indonesia as its 27th province, Portugal was still regarded as the 'administering power'. Inevitably, this was a source of tension in the EU's relations not just with Indonesia, but with the broader regional grouping, ASEAN. Indonesia's diplomats saw the ambassadors' 'fact-finding' visit, which had been scheduled before Suharto's downfall, as something of a victory for them, since they liked to present it as a tacit admission of their sovereignty.

The East Timorese, however, saw it as evidence that at long last the international community was interesting itself in their plight. Indeed, their expectations of what might come from the visit were already dangerously inflated. 'Tell your ambassador that he shouldn't come with empty hands,' the leader of the clandestine Timorese resistance in central Java had pleaded with me a few weeks earlier. 'We've had enough fact-finding missions. We want something more concrete. If they don't come with concrete plans the chances are that a lot more blood will flow for nothing.' But the EU mission, of course, had no concrete proposal. The ambassadors were there, the official statements kept repeating, 'to assist in a dialogue that would lead to a resolution that would be acceptable to all parties'.

For this second visit I took a more conventional route to East Timor, by air from Bali. I was apprehensive about being spotted by the immigration and *intel* officers at Dili airport. But that morning their little checkpoint was unmanned, and there was none of the usual inspection of visitors.

I took a taxi into the city, past a roundabout with a huge fountain surrounded by angels, which looked as if it had been abandoned as soon as it was built, on to the wide quiet streets. Dili lies wedged between the sea to the north and mountains to the south, their peaks today hidden by grey clouds. We passed the new neighbourhoods that had sprung up to house Indonesian migrants and civil servants: small identical white houses with red corrugated-iron roofs, and a little space or greenery between them. Here and there a church spire poked out between the roofs.

The town had grown during the Indonesian occupation. In the Portuguese time, it had been no more than a tiny, sleepy backwater, and although it was still quite small and remote the Indonesians had built a substantial provincial administrative quarter. Some of the wide array of government offices were housed in old colonial buildings, others in newly built concrete monstrosities.

We found the centre of town closed to traffic. The Mahkota Hotel, where the ambassadors were staying, had been cordoned off by a platoon of Brimob, the special riot police whose training had provided a soundtrack to our interrogation four years earlier. In their grey riot gear, helmets with visors, automatic weapons and large rattan shields, they seemed to have stepped out of a science-fiction film. I had no choice but to push my way through a chorus of helmets, hissing 'Hey, missis! Hey missis!'

In front of the hotel, a lively crowd of thousands of demonstrators had gathered, displaying a colourful sea of banners. They were chanting slogans calling for a referendum, and waving portraits of Xanana Gusmão and other Falintil leaders.

The ambassadors had already caused trouble – even before their arrival. Herman dos Reis Soares, a young Timorese, had been killed the night before by soldiers in Manatutu, where he and other youths had tried to stop a convoy of soldiers and Timorese supporters of integration with Indonesia from reaching Dili. The convoy had come from Los Palos, organised by its *bupati* (district administrators) an ex-soldier, who was like many *bupatis* a notorious supporter of integration. Herman's body had been carried through the streets of Dili by a large group of independence supporters, and buried at the Santa Cruz cemetery.

The next day a group of demonstrators at the airport had greeted the ambassadors with pro-integration banners. One of the demonstrators, armed with a long knife, attacked Manuel Carrascalão, a prominent East Timorese businessman and, more recently, also a human rights activist, who had been waiting in his jeep to greet the visitors.

But who were these pro-Indonesia demonstrators? Rosa Garcia, a young reporter from the local newspaper *Suara Timor Timur*, told me that she had asked a few demonstrators what it said on their banners. They had to turn them around to have a look before they could answer. Rent-a-crowds come (more or less literally) a dime a dozen in Indonesia. They had, however, clearly failed to intimidate independence supporters. I looked around the animated crowd in front of the Mahkota: their spirited, determined faces. Today they ruled the streets. Among these demonstrators might be people I remembered from my previous visit. I did not recognise any but when I walked away a bit from the crowd, a Timorese with an enormous head of black-brown curls came up to me. 'Welcome back,' he grinned and quickly pushed a folded envelope in my hand. Before I could say anything, he vanished into the crowd. Who was he? I searched my memory for clues. I wanted to ask him more but to follow him would be too dangerous. I supposed he would find *me* if he wanted to tell me more. (The envelope turned out to be a rather obscure document dating back to 1975.)

I walked slowly towards the house of Manuel Carrascalão, where the ambassadors were engaging in a 'forum' with East Timorese 'community leaders'. The beach road took me past the imposing white colonial-style palace of the former Portuguese governor, now the offices of the Indonesian-appointed governor. Everywhere I looked I noticed security forces. An armed Brimob squadron had blocked off the governor's palace, and in the shade of age-old fig trees, a group of soldiers stood smoking sweet-smelling *kreteks*, Indonesian clove cigarettes.

The forum was easy to find. Thousands of demonstrators had followed the delegation there. Inside the discussion was in full swing. Without exception, all the Timorese gathered there were in favour of an act of self-determination. They did not want Portugal and Indonesia to decide their future without consulting them. 'We have been silenced long enough,' said one of the participants emotionally. 'Now we want to have a voice too.' Another quoted Xanana: 'Anyone afraid of a referendum is afraid of the truth.'

They had put their hope in Europe, which they wanted to put pressure on Indonesia to grant a referendum. Now that Indonesia's economy was in trouble, they argued, the EU could use financial aid as a lever. To the EU diplomats, this must have sounded like a naïve fantasy. 'A referendum,' an irritable Dutch diplomat had grumbled to me a few weeks earlier, was 'the last thing we want'. He made it clear where Dutch – and by extension European – diplomatic priorities lay: 'The political situation in Indonesia is much too unstable. We have to concentrate first on Indonesia. East Timor can wait.' Such words would have been music to the ears of the Indonesian minister of foreign affairs, Ali Alatas, who during the ambassadors' visit produced a typical statement of Indonesia's position: 'A referendum is something that we think is inappropriate and is unacceptable to the majority of the East Timorese people because they feel that they have already decided [the issue] several years ago.' A referendum, he added ominously, was 'fraught with all kinds of risks'. The most Indonesia was perhaps prepared to consider was Habibie's vague offer of greater autonomy.

When the ambassadors emerged from the house, Robin Christopher, the British leader of the mission, spoke to the crowd through a megaphone. He told them that their message, along with all the other views put forward, had been heard, and appealed to them to disperse. But the demonstrators had other plans. They ran to their vehicles and escorted the delegation back to the hotel. As I followed them back, a young man jumped out of nearby bushes. 'Come at 7 o'clock tonight to the Lifau Hotel. I want to show you something,' he said mysteriously and vanished into the shrubbery again.

At the Mahkota Hotel the crowd had swollen. It now numbered more than ten thousand. Indefatigably, they kept up their impassioned speeches, and sang their beautiful, sad songs. Again, Robin Christopher took up the megaphone to appeal to them to go home. But this time, the streets in front of the hotel soon emptied.

I wandered over to the Lifau Hotel in the evening, wondering about what the young man wanted to show me. When I arrived, he was already waiting in the courtyard. From under his T-shirt he pulled a pile of pictures, and picked out one of a tall westerner and some heavily armed Timorese

1. Demonstration in Dili, June 1998.

guerrillas. 'I brought this Australian journalist to the Falintil commander,' he said, claiming to work for Falintil's 'foreign relations' department, and to be eager to arrange more trips to the fighters in the hills. He made it sound like a jolly adventure. I listened politely, made my excuses and left. This was not the time to risk deportation again through another trip to Falintil. I needed to get to know East Timor better before I set out for the hills again, and anyway I would not have entrusted my fate to a rather unhinged-seeming stranger.

On the walk back to the Mahkota, the streets were pitch-black. On a few corners groups of young men were playing guitars and singing songs that throbbed with a deep longing. They reminded me of the melancholy songs of immigrants yearning for their homeland, and the Portuguese *fado* in which some of these Timorese songs probably had their origins. The sound floated through the streets like wafts of mist, and seemed almost tangible. But it did not make Dili peaceful or pleasant. On the contrary, it seemed strangely ominous.

§

Early the next morning, I passed the University of Timor on the way to the offices of Caritas, a Catholic aid agency, to meet Antero Benedito da Silva, one of the student leaders. It was busy in the streets around Untim, as the university was known. Thousands of students mingled on the campus and outside dozens of buses and trucks were lining up.

I recognised Antero at once as the one who had translated the British ambassador's appeals to the crowd the day before. He was tall and lean, with short-cropped frizzy hair. What struck me most about his appearance were his big, long-lashed eyes. They seemed full of sorrow, as if he carried a world of worry and pain, but they also sparkled with wit and intelligence. He spoke slowly and thoughtfully, careful to find the right words to express exactly what he wanted to say.

A week earlier, his fellow students had chosen him as the leader of Dewan Solidaritas Mahasiswa Timor Timur, the East Timor Students' Solidarity Council. Antero himself had not been at the meeting. 'They only told me later,' he said quietly. 'I would rather not be a leader, but now they have chosen to give me this task, I have to do it. It's my fate, perhaps?' He smiled with a mixture of pride and self-mockery. At 30, Antero was older than most students and, in his own laid-back way, he exuded an incredible natural authority – perhaps because he is the son of a *liurai*, a local tribal king; or, just as likely, because he had been groomed to become a priest. Almost all East Timor's political leaders have sprung from the seminary. And many of the students I got to know – perhaps because it produced good English-speakers – had studied there.

Antero had gone further down the path to priesthood than most. It was not until he went to pursue his studies in the Philippines that he changed his mind about the Church, and became sharply critical of it. He started to look to the traditional religions that had survived in the mountains of Timor to satisfy his need for spirituality and moral values.

He harboured high ideals for the Student Solidarity Council. He wanted it to be an umbrella organisation for the various student groups. Ideally they would stand above politics, and become what Antero called 'a moral force'. Timorese young people, he explained, wanted to distance themselves from the historic rivalries and bitterness of the old party politics. Because exiles had taken this legacy with them overseas, it still poisoned efforts at forging unity.

The student and youth movement in East Timor was similarly politicised and, historically, split into competing factions. But for now there was a short-lived bout of student unity. The council had succeeded in bringing various groups under a single banner: the call for a referendum. This meant, said Antero, that, although everyone of course wanted independence, they also 'respected other political options'. The students had started organising weekly 'open debates' on Untim's campus, which Antero thought had been a great success. After so many years of repression the people needed to vent their frustrations and to discuss politics openly. In a few weeks he expected to take these open forums to other parts of East Timor.

Antero had a touching belief in the people's democratic instincts. He recalled how as a young boy he would see the *datos* and *lia nain*, elders, of his village sitting together discussing the issues of the day. Often this went on deep into the night, fuelled by local palm wine. Sometimes tempers flared but they would never go home before they had hugged and forgiven each other. Antero believed that colonialism had destroyed this 'democratic side' to Timorese culture, and it was time to rebuild it.

After an hour, we heard the sound of the rally coming past. Antero glanced out of the window. I wondered whether he was keen to take part. He seemed undecided. Persistent rumours that he would be arrested had caused panic among his friends and resistance groups, and over the past few days the rumours had become more threatening. He had received warnings from several quarters that his life was in danger. Falintil had sent 34 men to keep an eye on security in town. 'I even seem to have a personal bodyguard,' he said, rather embarrassed. 'But I'm afraid I might be a target for both sides.' 'Both sides?' I asked, surprised. 'Yes,' he said, 'the pro-independence movement needs a martyr.' Every night Antero would sleep in a different house. Assassinations would often take place at night, carried out by *ninjas*, death squads, masked men dressed in black.

But Antero could not suppress his curiosity about the rally. A little later a colleague and I drove with him through town. He sat wedged between us on the back seat of the taxi, using us as buffers. We caught up with the vanguard of the rally – thousands of noisy motorbikes revving their engines, their exhausts belching thick clouds of blue fumes. Out of this poisonous fog, the first trucks emerged. People were clinging to the lorries like mussels to a rock. They were hanging from the sides, balancing on the bumpers, jumping up and down on the roofs. Hundreds of big lorries, buses, pick-ups, bicycles and motorbikes had joined in the largest demonstration East Timor had ever seen. The first trucks arrived back at Untim, four hours after they started, but before the last ones had left. This was a spontaneous demonstration, not one orchestrated from Xanana's prison cell. In fact, the Timorese resistance leader had been trying to curb the exuberant impulses of Timor's young people, but today the momentum had taken over, and people had come from all over East Timor to express their feelings.

I climbed onto the bumper of one of the last group of lorries. The bonnet was covered by young people singing patriotic songs, leaving the driver only a very small gap to see the road. Everywhere people cheered the convoy on. Some onlookers had buckets and cups to give drinks to thirsty demonstrators. Others doused them with sprays of refreshing water from hoses. Everyone took part in his own way. The town was in a delirium. After 23 years of pent-up emotions and pain the population screamed it out. Even toddlers took up the refrain: 'Mate ka moris ukun rasik'an!' – 'Dead or alive, Independence!'

On one of the pick-ups stood a little girl of about ten with bright red ribbons in her curly hair. She knew a little English: 'Referendum yes! Autonomy no!' she chanted like a cheerleader, and everyone around her followed her lead.

It is hard to know how many took part in the demonstration. The students estimated a hundred thousand; Indonesian state radio reported 'a few hundred'. The students were probably closer to the truth. Counting the crowds who cheered the procession on, there could well have been more than eighty thousand demonstrators – roughly equivalent to the entire population of Dili, and more than a tenth of East Timor's. At that moment it became very clear to me that the days of Indonesian rule in East Timor were numbered. It seemed certain that if there were ever to be a referendum on its future, most of its people would choose independence.

The ambassadors missed this demonstration, and drew a different lesson from what they experienced. They had gone that day to Baucau to meet the Catholic bishop there, Dom Basilio do Nascimento. During their meeting in the town's cathedral, a crowd gathered outside. A special military intelligence unit sent to keep order panicked and opened fire, wounding seven people, including some children. One man died.

It was hard not to remember the warning I had heard from the clandestine leader in Central Java, about the bloodshed that might follow if the EU delegation came empty-handed. The ambassadors made a hasty, premature and unannounced departure early the next morning on a military aircraft. The night before this quick exit, Paul Brouwer, the Dutch ambassador, said he would like to come back without 'the glaring eyes' of the foreign press. The implication – that he believed the demonstrations and even the shooting in Baucau were caused by nothing more than East Timorese playing up to impress a handful of foreign journalists – was alarming. Foreign governments seemed not to grasp how fast pressure for change was mounting.

§

The next day a large group of students set out to attend the funeral of Orlando Marcelino da Costa, the man shot dead in Baucau. I decided to follow them and wanted to ask Antero to join me. I found him with a few other students outside the Caritas office. He wanted to come but the others looked worried. They conferred and announced that they wouldn't let him go. 'We don't want to lose him,' one explained apologetically.

So Antero stayed in Dili and I looked for other people who might be able to interpret. At Untim I found Felis and Fernãu, two students of English, talking to Bobby,[1] an American student activist who had turned up in Timor a few weeks earlier. At first I thought Felis, who spoke good English, was a journalist from Jakarta. He was very offended at being mistaken for a Javanese but flattered to be taken for a reporter. Fernãu, in contrast, had no Malay or even Asian features. His tall, well-built figure and dark skin suggested southern Africa.

The ethnic diversity in East Timor is startling. Look at the faces at the market in Dili and you might just as well be in Africa or the Caribbean as in Asia. Through the ages, Timor has been a melting pot of different tribes and races. According to recent finds by archaeologists, the first people settled in Timor around thirty thousand years ago, which suggests that Timor may have been a stepping-stone for Aboriginal tribes on their way from Asia to Australia.[2] But research is patchy and not much archaeological work has been done yet. According to one theory, waves of migrations by Melanesians, around 3000 BC, were followed 500 years later by 'Melayu' tribes from Burma and southern China. Around two millennia ago, the time of the great migrations, the Indo-Malays, who now dominate the island, came ashore. And in the fourteenth century, more newcomers arrived. A tribe called the Belum landed their boats on the north coast. They spoke Tetum, which is now the lingua franca in East Timor.[3] To this ethnic cocktail further ingredients were added when foreign traders took local women as consorts: first the Chinese and later the Portuguese and the Dutch, who arrived in the sixteenth and seventeenth centuries. The offspring of Dutch and Portuguese merchants and buccaneers, who came to be known as the '*Topasses*' or 'black Portuguese', eventually ruled large parts of the coastal areas.

Felis, Fernäu and Bobby were keen to come to Baucau. We sat squeezed in the back of a small green taxi. The last time I had travelled this road, nearly four years earlier, I had been sandwiched between military and policemen; this time I was between student activists. Bobby handed out *kopicos*, the coffee candy I had in my mouth when we were followed in 1994. I had never touched the sweets again, associating their taste with a taste of defeat. But back in Timor I thought it was time to exorcise these demons.

Felis had a loud, piercing voice, and used it non-stop. His father, he said, worked as a nurse, but for the last four years had been in jail on Atauro, a small rocky island opposite Dili, used since the Portuguese time as a penal colony. He had been active in the underground, organising medical help for Falintil. He was arrested after photos of a meeting held in his house between Xanana and a Portuguese journalist had fallen into the hands of an Indonesian spy.

Felis hated Indonesians, and the more he talked, the more vociferous he became. 'When we get power here we won't bring them to Atauro, we'll throw them into the sea, together with the collaborators and traitors,' he bragged like a schoolboy. 'After what they did to us they deserve no better.' I was a bit taken aback by his bloodthirstiness. It was hard to know how seriously he meant it all, or whether he was just trying to impress. Certainly, his father's detention had embittered him, but alongside the pro-independence firebrand was a precocious school swot, who enjoyed showing off, and accumulating knowledge, as he showed when, after a short silence, he changed the subject. 'What is another word for "breaking wind"?' he asked suddenly. 'Fart,' I said. 'Fart ... fart?' Felis pronounced the word as if he was trying to taste it in his mouth; he asked me to write it in his little notebook. Fart was apparently not one of the words they taught at the seminary.

While Felis chattered away, Fernãu hardly uttered a word. When I asked about his family, he shyly talked about his village in Ainaro, a poor area near Ramalau, Timor's highest mountain, where people scrape a living farming the land and rearing cattle. His family also worked for the resistance, he said.

We passed several checkpoints on the way to Baucau, and had to stop at one just before we reached the town. A man in plain clothes, a big gun slung over his shoulder, gestured us to get out of the car. 'ID, passport!' he demanded. I had no intention of giving him that, and asked him politely who he was and what authority he had to ask for my passport. He abruptly changed and said apologetically: 'I'm just doing my job.' He showed his ID. He was a policeman from Bali. He had enjoyed his job as a waiter in the busy beach resort of Kuta, he said, but his father pressed him to think about his career. Now he worked as a policeman. He earned less, he said, and he had to work in a place where nobody liked him. I rather pitied him. It can't be easy to feel every day that you're hated or at least not welcome. When I asked him about it he replied: 'It is like we feel all the time we have to shoot them before they shoot us.'

We arrived just in time for the procession. Six men were carrying the coffin on their shoulders over small steep paths and jagged rocks. On the main road the crowd of mourners swelled to several hundred. We reached a small, open graveyard. Around the freshly dug grave stood three priests. One was filming proceedings with a small camcorder. As the coffin was lowered into the grave, the black, red and yellow Timorese flag, banned by Indonesia, was draped over it. Orlando's young widow, holding her baby son, sobbed in long howls of grief. It was almost dark when the first clods of earth began thudding onto the coffin. Around us, people lit small candles and the graves were bathed in the unearthly glow of hundreds of tiny flames. 'They made him the martyr of the European visit,' said Felis wryly. 'We'll end up with more martyrs than university graduates.'

The priest with the camcorder came over and introduced himself as Padre Rui. He said he wanted to show me something, and took me to a lonely part of the cemetery. In the darkness, I could just make out the shape of a grave, nothing more than a heap of stones. Padre Rui explained this was another victim of the Indonesian army. 'The soldiers just dumped him here and threw a few stones on top,' he said. 'They didn't even have the decency to inform his family so he can get a funeral. And he is not the only one.' Padre Rui shone his torch around, to show me other, similar piles of stones.

CHAPTER 3

. . . .

The Past Casts its Shadow

§ THE day after the funeral I moved to the Hotel Turismo, an ugly, seventies-style, concrete building that had long since seen its best days. It is a bit out of the centre of town, facing a dirty beach. Some rooms have a sea view, and others look out over a dusty garden. As I handed in my registration form and was given the keys, I could not know that this was to become my second home for the next two years. My room was scarcely big enough to accommodate a double bed, but it did have a small terrace with some rickety chairs, from where I could see a small goldfish pond with a fountain. The hotel was notorious for crawling with cockroaches, and, worse, with *intel*. One colleague told me how, after a press conference, where he had asked the Indonesian authorities a few awkward questions, he had come back to his room to find that his notebooks had gone.

Jill had urged me to contact João Pereirra, the old waiter. She said he would make sure that the boy who cleaned my room could be trusted. I found João in the restaurant. A stooped, weary-looking figure, he was ambling slowly between the tables with their red-and-white checked cloths. When I called his name softly and told him Jill had given me his name, he pulled me close, and gave me a hug. A little later we sat at a table and talked. With his spindly frame and furrowed face, melancholy eyes, and thin, blue-veined hands spread in front of him on the table, he had the hangdog look of an animal that has been mistreated for a long time.

He had worked at the hotel from the day it opened in 1970 and knew Jill from 1975, when she stayed at the Turismo for three months – in room 18, João told me, pointing at the one I had just moved into. It's hard to believe in coincidences in a place like the Turismo. This hotel, I began to realise, was haunted by the ghosts of old memories and associations. Of the small group of journalists who stayed here in 1975, six, including the five at Balibo, had been murdered by the Indonesian army. João remembered exactly what the Australian television crews had for breakfast before they set off, never to return. And he served the last meal to Roger East, an Australian journalist who stayed behind when all the other foreign journalists left. He was executed by Indonesian soldiers on the jetty, together with hundreds of Timorese, while they had to count out loud every time a victim toppled into the sea. His remains have never been found.

João stared distractedly at a pack of ginger-and-white cats that were hissing and screeching as they fought viciously over the scraps of food left on the tables. 'They must be Indonesian cats,' he sighed. The only good memories João cherished of the hotel, which, in the seventies and eighties, had become the quarters for Indonesian army officers, dated back to the time under the Portuguese. His eyes would light up when he started to talk about the grand opening reception. A big party had been organised. The restaurant had been full of people in evening dress. The owner, João remembered, had imported a crate of sparkling wine. 'The bottles exploded when you opened them!' João still seemed excited about it. Once, he said, this place had had style, but it had gone downhill since. He wrinkled his nose and lifted his chin in the direction of the kitchen. 'They think only about money, money, money,' he grumbled. 'Style, they've completely forgotten.' In fact, João lived on a war footing with the Chinese family that ran the kitchen. Almost every day, he would have screaming rows with the woman in charge. One morning, hostilities were engaged after she proposed charging guests extra if they wanted their eggs fried rather than boiled. João was fuming, but he claimed victory: 'I phoned Mr Alex and he stopped it. Ha!'

Alex Tandjung Samara, the hotel's owner, a Chinese Catholic from West Timor, had bought the hotel from the Portuguese proprietor, who had fled the country. Alex spent most of his time elsewhere. He commuted between his family in California, Surabaya, in eastern Java, where he ran some businesses, and the Turismo. As elsewhere in Asia, virtually all business in East Timor was in Chinese hands. They had the network and the know-how. In any village with a market you could also find a Chinese shop. Traditionally, most Chinese steered clear of politics, but in East Timor neutrality was almost unattainable.

Alex, who was in his late fifties, had worked before the invasion as an agent for BAKIN, the powerful central bureau of military intelligence. After the civil war in 1975, he was responsible for putting Indonesian intelligence in touch with defeated Timorese leaders, who had fled with their army over the border to West Timor. Later he helped guide Indonesian soldiers back across that border. But there were other stories too: that in 1975 he had saved dozens of Chinese families, several lorry-loads, from an almost certain death by evacuating them to West Timor.

During the first days of the invasion it is estimated that 2,000 people were killed, many of them, like Roger East, in public executions. Eyewitnesses say about 700 of them were ethnic Chinese.[1] Outside Dili the situation was not much better. In the towns of Liquiça and Maubara, between Dili and the border with West Timor, Indonesian soldiers went on a murderous rampage, calling it a '*jihad*' against the communists. This echoed the events of 1965–66 in Indonesia, when, in the anti-communist pogrom that followed Suharto's seizure of power, perhaps as many as half a million people may have been killed.

The irony of the persecution of the Chinese was that many of them would have been among the most pragmatic of all of East Timor's people, accepting the Indonesian annexation as just another political twist, while they got on with their businesses. Alex, like other Chinese businessmen, tried to stay on good terms with both sides. This was costly. He paid protection money both to the Indonesian army and to Falintil. He also had good links with the Catholic Church, especially the Salesians, whose order he supported financially. A Salesian sister told me he had also put money into a Catholic hospital in Suay.

I asked João whether *intel* still kept an eye on the hotel. 'Oh, they are still here,' he said phlegmatically. 'They normally just sit in the entrance, smoking *kreteks*. It's always the same ones; we know them. Soon they'll be unemployed,' João sniggered, 'it's *reformasi* now.' It was probably premature to celebrate the demise of *intel*'s influence. Prabowo, so feared in East Timor, may have lost out in the power struggle and fled the country for Jordan, but not before, so the rumours had it, visiting the territory to hold a meeting with local leaders.

Over the next few days, the undercurrent of fear and apprehension I had felt since arriving on this trip seemed to intensify. Felis visited me every day with snippets of worrying information and rumour: Prabowo had flown in on a military plane; the governor had said he was ready to fight another civil war if need be; civil servants had been forced to sign declarations that they supported integration with Indonesia; and so on.

Then one day, Felis knocked on my door at seven in the morning. Breathless with excitement, he almost shrieked why he had come: to show me 'an important document' he had spent the night translating. He shoved two pages of A4 paper into my hands. They were covered in the erratic characters of the old typewriter Felis used, and were hard to decipher. But it looked like the minutes of a meeting between military and civilian authorities where a plan was outlined to expand the paramilitary forces in Timor. They would get training and weaponry with the ultimate goal of 'exterminating all opposition against Indonesia'. 'You see,' said Felis in a voice so full of vindication it sounded almost triumphant, 'they are preparing to get rid of all of us.'

§

Felis had one thing in common with the earlier generation of Timorese who had struggled for independence a quarter of a century earlier: a background as a seminarian. In 1975, East Timor, cast aside by its colonial ruler, had been left with a group of home-grown leaders with an enormous range of differing political and ideological convictions; but in most of their upbringings was the shared experience of the strict discipline of Jesuit priests, and an education at the Catholic school in Soibada followed by the seminary at Dare. This seat of Jesuit learning lay perched above Dili, like an 'eagle's nest'. It had produced many of the older generation of Timorese priests and politicians. It was here that Jesuits had taught Latin, Portuguese and philosophy to the hot-tempered young man who became Bishop Carlos Belo; and to Xanana Gusmão when he was a recalcitrant teenage rebel, studying alongside the strong and charismatic Nicolau Lobato.

It was Timor's only institute of higher education, where members of the local elite, from *liurai* families to teachers of the catechism, could send their male children. The seminary up the hill was still educating a small group of students. Most of them now went to the new seminary in Dili, built with money Bishop Belo had won with his Nobel Peace Prize. Among the young priests teaching there was Padre Jovito, whom I was keen to meet, after hearing that he had strong views about what was happening in East Timor, and about the role of the Church.

So early one afternoon that autumn I visited the imposing building. Surrounded by other Catholic middle and high schools, it looked cool and comfortable. Behind the clean, whitewashed walls and spotless windows a new generation of seminarians was blossoming. They were taught not by the old Portuguese priests from Dare, who had all been sent home soon after Bishop Belo was ordained, but mainly by Indonesian priests, who taught in Bahasa Indonesia, their national language.

The seminary in Dili gave the boys only their early theological grounding and selected those who seemed suitable for the priesthood. They had to complete their studies elsewhere, usually in Java. Many young boys felt the calling to become priests. It was a highly respected vocation, which brought many special privileges. Also, in occupied Timor, the priesthood was not only about serving God; it was about serving the people, in a way only priests could, by defying the Indonesian army. In the unlikely event that young would-be priests became too engrossed in the spiritual aspects of religion at the expense of their political consciousness, they had only to look out of the seminary's window. Just opposite the entrance lay the Indonesian army's cemetery for its soldiers lost in Timor. It was a permanent reminder that war, albeit at a low level, still went on.

I waited in the spacious, empty hall of the seminary for Padre Jovito. I had woken him from his siesta. The afternoon nap was still taken seriously in Dili, where temperatures can soar well into the forties centigrade, and hardly anyone had air-conditioning. People would get up early in the morning to enjoy the few cool hours of the day, and shops and offices closed from noon until three in the afternoon (or, in the case of many offices, until the next day).

Padre Jovito appeared, blinking against the bright white light. He was a youthful, sprightly man with twinkling eyes and a smile that seemed to reach his ears. He wore jeans, a T-shirt and flip-flops. When I explained what I wanted to talk about he ushered me through wide corridors to his office, shut the door and drew the curtains. As one of the younger generation, he had received most of his higher education from Indonesian priests in Java. Besides teaching at the seminary he was also a parish priest, and every week held a special mass in his church for young people. He was a passionate speaker, who needed little prompting to air his views, which he was clearly accustomed to expounding to an audience, and, although he became frustrated with his lack of fluency in English, he still managed the eloquence of a natural orator who loves words.

He was very gloomy about the situation in Timor, which he described as 'very very dangerous'. It might look as if reforms had come to Timor but that was misleading, since secret meetings were going on and 'the dark forces were still very alive'. There were too many competing groups hoping to do well out of the changes. The occupation had fuelled their self-interest. 'The only thing we have here is the experience of 23 years of conflict and that has not taught the leaders many lessons. People are still fighting, still killing. How can we give a referendum to these people?' he sighed. He thought East Timor needed five or ten years before it would be ready for such an exercise.

Of course he wanted a solution, and privately he saw a referendum that would lead to independence as the only acceptable one, but he was scared that if conducted carelessly, a referendum would lead to more conflict. 'I think whatever the outcome, it will lead to frustration and bloodshed.' As a priest he saw it as his task and that of the Church as a whole to prepare the people for any eventuality.

Like so many others, Padre Jovito did not think the Timorese could solve their problems by themselves. The ordinary people had become the victims, crushed between two forces. Some people who had collaborated with the Indonesians had grown very rich. They had a personal interest in maintaining the status quo. If the Indonesians left, they and their families would lose their lucrative jobs, their privileges and their power.

'They are left with no other option than to deceive and kill their own brothers,' said Padre Jovito. He had written a thesis on the role of the Church in the reconciliation process. In his view it had to be apolitical. 'The bitter experience of the 1975 civil war still lived on. Before people could move on they had to put this behind them, forgive their brothers and begin a new life.' Before the Timorese could make a decision about their future, he had concluded, they needed to be free of their past.

Talking to Padre Jovito was like consulting an oracle. It made my own sense of foreboding even worse. He was certainly right that the civil war had left a deep wound and the scars had never healed, partly because the Indonesians made sure the sores festered. The Indonesian invasion and the war that followed it had taken many more lives than the civil war. But that had all to do with an external enemy. What worried people were the enemies within: the Timorese groups that the Indonesians could turn against their own people.

§

Many of the fault-lines in Timorese society could be traced back to the brief and terrible interlude between Portuguese and Indonesian rule. The changes that were to lead to the Indonesian invasion in 1975 had begun not in Timor, but on the other side of the world. In 1974, the so-called 'carnation' revolution had put an end to decades of fascist military dictatorship. High among the priorities of the new, left-wing government was the future of Portugal's colonies. They had become an expensive embarrassment, to be jettisoned as soon as possible. This, combined with the independence movements in Portuguese Africa, stimulated Timor's own budding independence movement; Timorese students returned from Portugal brimful of new ideas and became the driving force of a new political movement.

The first political party established at the time was the UDT, the Timorese Democratic Union. The UDT became the party of the establishment: the local elite of civil servants and landowners, mainly *mestiços*, and the *liurais* of the economically important coffee-growing areas of Ermera, Maubara and the central highlands of Maubisse. The party's leadership, in short, was made up of everyone who had done well under the Portuguese.

The *liurais* used their kinship alliances to drum up support for the party. With the help of the Portuguese flag, which many Timorese invested with *lulik* – a strong, magic power – and the support of the bishop and some other Catholic priests, the UDT soon established itself as the most popular party. Its platform committed it to the development of democracy, respect for human rights, redistribution of wealth and, above all, the right for self-determination of the Timorese, rejecting integration with Indonesia. In the short term, however, the UDT wanted federation with Portugal as an interim measure until East Timor could stand on its own two feet.[2] In fact the UDT's platform was very close to that of the more moderate wing of the ASDT, the Timorese Social Democratic Union, founded just ten days later. So slight were the differences in those days that the two parties formed a coalition. ASDT also had a social-democratic platform with the stress on democracy and the right to independence. To make this latter goal more explicit, it changed its name later to Fretilin, short for the Revolutionary Front of Independent East Timor. In contrast to the UDT, Fretilin leaders were all, with one exception, the sons of *liurais* and ethnic – also sometimes called 'black' – Timorese. The only *mestiço* present at the founding meeting was José Ramos Horta. Other important Fretilin members were Francisco Xavier do Amaral and Nicolau Lobato. (Xanana Gusmão, who was the son of a teacher, joined a year later.)

Of the four other political parties, Apodeti, the Timorese Popular Democratic Association, was the most important. Its founder, José Osorio Soares, and his family aspired to autonomy within the Republic of Indonesia. It had various diffuse bases of support: the tiny Muslim community in Dili, who perhaps understandably hankered after union with their big Muslim neighbour; the Gonsalves clan of Atsabe and its kinship allies in the border area; a *liurai* in Ainaro and a small pocket of clans around Viqueque.

Another party that sought incorporation in a larger neighbour was Aditla – the Association for the Integration of East Timor and Australia. This party was shortlived, since Australia soon made it clear it was not interested in the idea. The other two tiny parties, Kota and Trabalhista, never exerted much influence, though Indonesia managed to use them as pawns in its attempts to destabilise East Timor.

Jakarta was keeping a wary eye on developments in East Timor. In public, it pledged to respect the territory's right to self-determination, and Indonesia's foreign minister, Adam Malik, said it had no interest in annexing the half-island. But behind the scenes the Indonesian military was playing a different game. A secret operation, code-named Operasi Komodo (Dragon) was already in full swing. With the help of BAKIN, Indonesia manipulated the political situation through its well-tested divide-and-rule tactics.

Its first priority was to drive a wedge between the constituent parts of the Fretilin–UDT coalition. The opportunity arose when Fretilin's fast-growing support in the countryside, and the radical ideas and communist-sounding rhetoric voiced by some of its leading members, started to alarm the UDT, as well as outside observers. The coalition fell apart, enabling Indonesia to go a step further. In the first week of August 1975, it set the UDT an ultimatum. The army's chief of staff, General Ali Murtopo, told the UDT's leaders that if they did not halt the 'communist threat', Indonesia 'would feel obliged to step in'.

§

What followed was one of the most painful periods in East Timor's political history. It all happened more than twenty years ago, but is still very much alive in the collective memory of all Timorese. To understand the period better, I wanted to talk with one of the people who had played an important and controversial role at the time: Manuel Viegas Carrascalão, the man attacked at the airport when the European ambassadors arrived, and the host of the public 'forum' they had attended.

When I reached his house, I found the iron gate closed with two large padlocks. After I had called out a few times and rattled the gate, a worried-looking guard appeared. Seeing a Western face, he visibly relaxed and led me into a large living room. It was furnished with two three-piece suites of dark imitation leather, covered with white crochet antimacassars, a large standing fan and, in the corner, an almost life-size ceramic statue of the Virgin Mary, her hands folded in devotion.

Manuel Carrascalão came in but before he sat down for the interview he turned on the television. International news in Portuguese blared through the room. The Carrascalãos, like many other well-off Timorese families in the towns, had satellite dishes so they could watch foreign channels such as CNN, BBC World and, even more importantly, the international broadcasts of RTP, Portuguese Television. Manuel's daughter, Manuela, entered with a tray of cups of coffee and orange squash. 'He always does this,' she said, shaking her head and giving her father a stern look. He shrugged his shoulders and said the television did not distract him at all. Then, somewhere in the house a telephone rang. Manuel got up to answer it, and I heard him talking in Portuguese. We would be interrupted almost every ten minutes. Manuel, it seemed, was the unofficial correspondent for Portuguese radio and television as well as a pundit for many newspapers.

He was an imposing figure in his late sixties with grey hair and a bushy grey beard. His weather-beaten face had strong Portuguese features. Like his father, also called Manuel, and his brothers, Mário and João, he was, by Timorese standards, a giant. I expected him to show some awkwardness or reticence in discussing the period leading up to the invasion and his family's role in it. Far from it: he showed no sign of hesitation, let alone embarrassment, in talking about the past.

The self-assurance was not so surprising: the Carrascalãos were important people in East Timor. This had not always been so. The father, Manuel senior, had been shipped to Timor as a *deportado*, exiled by the Salazar regime to its most distant colony for his role in anti-government demonstrations. He arrived still bearing the scars of his activist activities (he had blown off some of his fingers throwing bombs), and served his sentence on the prison island of Atauro.

Manuel senior stayed in Timor after his release, and, like other political *deportados*, such as José Ramos Horta's father, who was an anarchist, soon earned the respect of the local elite. He married a woman from a *liurai* family in Venilale and prospered as a coffee-grower – the family is still among the biggest *fazendeiros*, plantation-owners, in Timor.

At the time, East Timor was still a sleepy outpost of Portugal's colonial empire. Ruled from Goa, it was kept going mainly by Indians and a handful of Africans. Unlike in other Portuguese colonies hardly any Portuguese had settled, and after his rehabilitation, Manuel quickly rose in local society, becoming president of the town council of Dili.

The family did well. Three of his sons studied abroad and became involved in politics soon after they came home. Manuel, the eldest, was chosen as a parliamentary representative for the ANP, Portugal's ruling party. Mário, a Portuguese-educated agricultural engineer, headed the local administration's department of agriculture, and João, the youngest, studied aerial surveying in Switzerland. He and Mário were among UDT's founding members. Along with two other important UDT leaders, Domingos de Oliveira and Franscisco Lopes da Cruz, both of them customs officers, João had been part of the UDT delegation that received the Indonesian ultimatum threatening intervention.

Explaining his family's actions at the time, Manuel said he and his brothers wanted to save Timor from an Indonesian invasion. Their solution was drastic: UDT planned and mounted a coup to get rid of Fretilin, and the 'communist threat'. The coup on 11 August 1975 was a messy and bloody affair. Street fighting broke out between Timorese soldiers in the Portuguese army loyal to the UDT and those loyal to Fretilin. Fighting was not confined to Dili. More than two-thirds of the roughly 1,500 people that died lived in the mountains, especially in the area around Maubisse and Manufahi. Rival *sucos*, villages, of different political alliances, and often with other long-standing feuds, waged fierce battles. The war lasted only a few weeks, but left a deep wound in Timor's psyche, one that would cause the Timorese anguish in years to come.

After two weeks it became clear that Fretilin had won. They chased most of the UDT's soldiers and civilian backers, along with those of the other parties, across the border into the arms of the Indonesians in West Timor. Others were detained in prisons in Dili and Aileu, Fretilin's mountain head-quarters, where they were locked up, sometimes together with their children, in makeshift camps. James Dunn, the Australian consul in Dili, who visited the prisons in Dili, remarked that they were being 'reasonably well treated' and had the same rations of food as the rest of the population.[3] The UDT had sullied its name by starting the killings but Fretilin's record, too, remained far from spotless. When the Indonesians invaded, Fretilin's leadership took their prisoners to their base at Aileu, and on Christmas Day 1975, they executed 150 UDT and Apodeti supporters, dumping the bodies in mass graves. Some members of Fretilin's central committee, including Xanana, opposed the massacre at the time. But it was only at a party congress in 2000 that Fretilin formally sought forgiveness for such atrocities.

When they lost the war the Carrascalão brothers escaped across the border. Manuel had good connections in West Timor. He had married a girl from Kupang and had grown fond of the place. 'I used to think life there was much better than in East Timor,' he said. While he stayed in the West Timorese capital, his brothers were out at the border together with other UDT leaders such as Francisco Lopes da Cruz and João Tavares, a former sergeant in the Portuguese army, and Tomás Gonçalves of Apodeti.

Soon after the attempted putsch, the Portuguese administration, and its military, had fled Dili and took cover on Atauro island. So Fretilin now found itself, against its wishes, on its own – forced by circumstances to take over the day-to-day administration of East Timor while waiting for the Portuguese to return.

October and November saw a series of cross-border incursions by the UDT and Indonesian troops. The Indonesians tried to foster the idea that the fighting was all part of the UDT–Fretilin civil war. This, they thought, would later make it easier to justify an invasion. It was while trying to film one of these incursions that the Australian television crews were killed at Balibo. Their bodies were photographed dressed in Fretilin uniforms and the official explanation was they had been killed in crossfire. But several eyewitnesses have come forward over the past few years, saying that they were executed by Indonesian soldiers, under the command of Junus Yosfiah, who would later rise to the position of minister of information in Habibie's cabinet.[4] After several months of this confusion and violence, Fretilin's leaders eventually declared East Timor independent on 28 November 1975. It was a decision taken more out of desperation than conviction that it was the right course of action. The quickly organised ceremony to swear in the new government was solemn rather than triumphant, like the national anthem they sang, the beautiful 'O Foho Ramelau'. Fretilin believed Indonesia might invade any day and hoped that independence might afford East Timor more protection from the international community. In practice, even countries that had promised support, such as China, did not immediately recognise the new state.

Two days later, in a hotel on the island of Bali, leaders of the UDT and the other defeated political parties presented, as a counter to the Fretilin declaration of independence, a signed agreement to Adam Malik, which became known as 'the Balibo Declaration'. In this petition, they declared East Timor integrated with Indonesia and invited the Indonesians to 'take all necessary steps in order to protect the lives of people, who now consider themselves part of the Indonesian people'. Adam Malik replied that 'diplomacy is finished. The solution for the East Timorese problem is now the front line of the battle.'

Fretilin appealed to the world to restrain the Indonesians. Nobody was listening. For some months, Australia, Europe and the USA had pretended to be ignorant about developments in East Timor. All valued their relationship with Indonesia more than they cared about the fate of the tiny half-island and refused to heed Fretilin's cries for help.

But this was not, as it may have seemed, because East Timor is an insignificant speck on the map. On the contrary, it found itself bound up in the global insecurities of Cold War geopolitics. For the United States, Timor, or more precisely the nearby Ombai-Wetar strait, represented a security issue. It needed stability in the region so that its nuclear submarines could travel undetected through the deep channel of these waters, linking the Pacific and Indian oceans.

Just a few months after its final defeat in Vietnam, and the Khmer Rouge's assumption of power in Cambodia, Washington remained wary of perceived expansionism by the Soviet Union, its clients and other communist states. The US State Department had come to the conclusion that East Timor represented a potential 'communist threat' – 'a Cuba in Asia'. Independent observers and journalists, such as the Australian consul James Dunn, the academic Helen Hill and Jill Jolliffe, who were in Timor in 1975 and followed Fretilin closely, had all concluded that it was a far less sinister organisation than the one portrayed by analysts in Washington and Jakarta. 'It is clear that Fretilin is not a Communist Party, thought it does have a left wing,' wrote James Dunn, calling Fretilin 'more populist than Marxist'. Nor did the Soviet Union, China or Vietnam rush to extend the hand of friendship to the new state. Dili was not crawling with Russian 'advisers', as one might expect of the capital of a candidate for entry into the 'Soviet bloc'.

It was true, however, that a radical, left-wing group within Fretilin, especially some graduates who had returned from Portugal, used a lot of communist rhetoric. Their ideology later became known as 'Mauberism', from the words Maubere, a common name in the countryside. The Portuguese used it as a derogatory term to describe the backward people in the interior, and Fretilin adopted it to symbolise the common people they claimed to represent. Their activities in the countryside – they set up cooperatives and established a system of 'barefoot teachers' – were reminiscent of communist policies. But they hardly amounted to evidence that Fretilin was planning to set up a communist state.

Its use of strong Marxist language, however, was certainly a tactical mistake, providing the Indonesians with the excuse they had been looking for. They planned the invasion, code-named Operasi Seroja (Lotus) for the beginning of December but had to postpone it for a few days because of a visit to Jakarta by the American president, Gerald Ford, and his secretary of state, Henry Kissinger. It might have been embarrassing for Washington if Indonesia launched an invasion while they were there, meeting President Suharto. But by the time the visit ended, it was clear that Jakarta had Washington's blessing for what was to come. Indeed, the State Department later described the visit as 'the big wink'.[5]

Indonesia reacted swiftly. Within 24 hours, at dawn on 7 December, thousands of its paratroopers had landed in Dili.

The Carrascalão brothers now took centre stage. João Carrascalão commanded a contingent of UDT infantry that crossed the border from West Timor, while Manuel landed with the invasion force in the eastern port of Laga, not far from the city of Baucau. 'Until that day I believed that the Indonesians meant well,' Manuel continued. 'We didn't know what Indonesia was like. I thought it would be like Kupang, which I thought was governed well. I liked the people, they were well-meaning and polite.' But that very first day, Manuel heard terrible stories of killings and rape from the local people he met. They begged him to help them. And what shocked him most and opened his eyes was something he witnessed in Baucau. 'I saw soldiers killing a woman who walked on the street with a baby in her arms. The woman had done them no harm; they killed her just so they could take her necklace. She lay there in her own blood.'

The baby was still alive, and Manuel took the crying infant to the Indonesian commander and complained about the behaviour of the soldiers. 'They are behaving like barbarians, I told him.' The Indonesians had assured Manuel that they came as brothers, to help them. 'But that day I saw they came as terrorists, as murderers, as thieves.' Even Apodeti supporters, who had, like the Chinese residents, come out to greet the soldiers, had been mowed down.

The commander had listened to Manuel's complaints and the next day he lured him back to West Timor with a bogus message that someone in his family had been taken seriously ill. Soldiers escorted him back to his house in Kupang, where he came to realise that he was under house arrest.

As he recounted his story, Manuel got increasingly worked up. He talked louder and gesticulated more emphatically with his hands. But at no point did I detect remorse or loathing for his own role. I asked if, looking back, he now had any regrets for the part he had played. He looked at me, and then averted his eyes to some distant point in the room. After a short silence he spoke again. 'You have to understand that we had been thrown into the open arms of the Indonesians. We could do nothing but look for help from them and to obtain this help we had to sign papers in which we declared ourselves to be pro-integration.' Manuel spoke defensively but not apologetically. 'It was not my fault that things had gone this way. The hard-line communists within Fretilin, they had started the war; we as the UDT only wanted to stop it.'

Fretilin, he continued, was helped by communists within the Portuguese army. And, he said accusingly, it had been Fretilin that had forfeited the opportunity to join the other parties in Macau in June 1975 for a crucial decolonisation meeting with Portugal. The suspicion of Fretilin within the UDT, which had withdrawn from the coalition a few weeks before the meeting, was deepened by Fretilin's boycott. 'At the time autonomy within Indonesia seemed to me a better alternative that self-governance. I thought this [autonomy] would end the civil war and bring the people peace. Because at the end of the day that is what people want: they want to live without fear.

But that is not what we got under the Indonesians. We got more fear than ever before.'

When the Indonesians eventually allowed him to return to East Timor five years later, they soon offered him, as the Portuguese before them had done, a post in the provincial parliament. He quickly rose to become the local chairman of Golkar, in effect the Indonesian ruling party used by ex-President Suharto to bolster his hold on power. 'I tried to be a good Indonesian,' he said. But late in 1996 he fell out with Golkar and was not chosen for a fourth term in the provincial assembly.

Manuel's brother Mário became the governor of East Timor, an office he held for ten years until 1992. I asked why he and his brother had still wanted to collaborate with the Indonesians after all that had happened. He said they had thought they would be able 'to do something for the people' through official channels and the provincial parliament. 'But the fact was that we were just puppets; the Indonesians had, and still have, all the strings in their hands.' His younger brother João had left for Australia, where he became the leader of the UDT in exile.

When one of the servants called that lunch was ready Manuel invited me to join them. In a spacious, dimly lit kitchen stood a large round table with two huge steaming pans full of rice, vegetables and a plate of sardines. Around the table I saw many faces I had not seen before in the house: Manuel's third wife, an Indonesian woman; their two adopted children, who cried a lot; other assorted family members; and an old Portuguese man who, Manuel explained, had never left.

The house had the feeling of a hide-away for many. People kept wandering in and out of the kitchen. They filled their plates with rice and vegetables and disappeared again. Manuela explained that the family was looking after some 30 people, villagers from the *fazenda*, now camped out in the back yard. They had fled to Dili because they were afraid of the activities of the army and paramilitary groups.

The Carrascalão family thought they had many friends. But they also had many enemies: the family was receiving numerous anonymous death threats. Manuela did not dare to leave the house. She shivered when she talked about the threats, which were an almost daily occurrence.

But, despite these pressures, Manuel once again believed he had a vital part to play in East Timor's history, in his new role as a leading spokesman of the struggle for independence. In 1997 he had established the Movement for Reconciliation and Unity of the People of East Timor (known by the long tongue-twisting set of initials GRPRTT). The group insisted on East Timor's right to an act of self-determination, and called on the political parties to unite behind a programme of peaceful negotiation to resolve the conflict over Timor's status. It was a brave initiative considering that the Indonesians did not welcome such pressure. The movement's 30-odd board members included others similar in some ways to Manuel Carrascalão: district heads and other former government officials, who enjoyed local respect.

Initially the military commander in East Timor threatened to arrest the GRPRTT's leadership for being 'anti-Indonesian', but he decided they had too high a profile and it would be better to ignore them than to make them martyrs. The movement never grew into a very strong voice inside Timor, but it was a reminder to the Indonesians that they could not even rely on many of their old cronies within the UDT and Apodeti.

In 1998 Manuel was elected as one of the CNRT leaders inside East Timor. The CNRT, the National Council of Timorese Resistance, was the umbrella of the groups resisting the Indonesian occupation. It was the continuation of the CNRM, which changed its name in April 1998, replacing 'Maubere' with 'Timorese', as many objected to the term because of its Fretilin associations. The council became even more broad-based.

'Apart from the Bishop and the priests I'm the only one who can mediate between the different parties,' Manuel boasted. 'The extremists within Fretilin and Falintil tried to kill me. I stood on top of their "hit-list", but now we are good friends. And the Indonesian commanders, they won't communicate with anybody in the resistance but they listen to me. So it is my task to create a climate of peace.' It was, I realised, more or less what he and his brothers had tried to achieve nearly a quarter of a century earlier. It was hard to be optimistic that this time, any more than in 1975, he would get it right. It was also hard to know how to take Manuel – or indeed his brothers. How could someone so horrified by the events of 1975 have ended up so much a part of the establishment of the Indonesian occupation? Manuel was to pay a high price for trying to tread the path of accommodation and compromise.

CHAPTER 4

Requiems

§ ON the morning of 12 November 1998, a large procession filed quietly through the streets of Dili. In the front, a group of young people solemnly bore a wreath of paper flowers in the black, red and yellow colours of the Timorese flag. They were followed by thousands of other young people, marching slowly and with dignity, like a funeral cortège. The marchers had their own security guards – hundreds of boys and girls wearing white T-shirts emblazoned with a map of East Timor, a cross rising from the middle. Arm in arm, they formed a mile-long human chain. The procession had to pass the cemetery for fallen Indonesian soldiers and a number of military barracks. Everyone was feeling nervous.

I had asked Sebastião Guterres, a student from Untim's English Department, to do some interpreting for me and we had met at 6 a.m. at the Balide church for the special mass and walked up together to the cemetery of Santa Cruz. He said the fear was that the army would try to incite a confrontation, perhaps through *agents provocateurs*. 'We have seen it happen again and again,' he added wearily. But apart from a few soldiers on guard, watching the procession with hatred in their eyes, no security forces were to be seen. They had withdrawn into the commercial district and the Indonesian parts of Dili.

The worries were understandable. This was the anniversary of a day in 1991 when young people had also filled the streets of Dili. That day too had begun with a mass – a requiem service for a young man, Sebastião Gomes. He had been killed two weeks earlier by Indonesian soldiers hunting down a group of young activists.

They and others had been working for nearly a year on an elaborate programme of activities to coincide with the expected visit of a Portuguese parliamentary delegation. Indonesia had invited the Portuguese as early as 1987, after twelve years of occupation, to come and see for themselves how the East Timorese were doing. After protracted and tortuous negotiations, the visit was scheduled for the autumn of 1991.

Many East Timorese had pinned all their hopes for independence on this visit. They saw the Portuguese as the returning saviours who were at last coming to their rescue. Even at UN headquarters in New York there was some tentative optimism that the visit might bring a breakthrough in talks, which for years had failed to yield any tangible results. Xanana Gusmão himself had come down from his mountain hiding places to Dili to oversee the underground's preparations. He wanted to arrange a meeting with the delegation, and to propose that he be included as the representative of the East Timorese people in the UN-sponsored talks between Indonesia and Portugal.

Indonesia's spies soon got wind of the preparations. The army mounted a campaign of terror and intimidation to forestall any embarrassing protest. They brought in new troops and sent soldiers village to village and house to house to warn people that anyone caught organising or taking part in a demonstration against Indonesian rule would risk not only his own life but also the lives of everyone in his community. As part of their campaign, they dug deep holes – 'for mass burials' – in Aileu, Ermera and around Dili.

But the Timorese believed that protest was a risk worth taking. After all, they thought, under the eyes of the Portuguese and their entourage of UN representatives and journalists, the army would not dare to fulfil these threats. As one of the protest leaders later said: 'We didn't prepare for the worst, but for the best.'[1]

One eventuality they had not prepared for was that the Portuguese, at the very last moment, cancelled the visit. It fell through because the Indonesians refused a visa to one of the journalists in the Portuguese party – none other, in fact, than Jill Jolliffe. The news was a serious blow for the Timorese resistance. The Indonesians knew exactly who was involved in planning the protests, and almost as soon as the cancellation was announced, their crackdown began. Their first targets were young men who had taken shelter in the Motael church. The attack on the church left two Timorese dead. A man working for *intel* died of stab wounds. Sebastião Gomes was shot and killed by the military.

After this, Xanana was under great pressure to do something. Young activists wanted to take to the streets and probably would have done so even without his consent. Eventually, Xanana agreed to plans to stage a demonstration on 12 November, because that day Pieter Kooijmans, the UN's special rapporteur on torture, would be in town. This, he thought, should give some kind of guarantee that the army would show some restraint.

'So many people had taken risks, dangerous risks,' he told me in March 1999, 'and everything would be for nothing if we did not act.' This, he said, would be a special demonstration, 'a sign of unity', because not only would Fretilin be represented there, but also the other parties, notably the UDT, whose flag Xanana had arranged to be brought in from Australia. He pointed this out as most significant since it was the first joint public display in East

Timor of the two parties' cooperation in the resistance, which had started in 1986, and been formalised in 1988.

When the day came, it began with a requiem mass, a tradition to mark the first two weeks that passed after someone had died. Afterwards the mourners left the church and marched in the direction of Santa Cruz. Leading the procession were members of Sebastião Gomes's family, mainly women and little children, holding flowers in their hands, and nuns singing hymns. Of the thousand or so people who followed, perhaps only a few thought it was a purely religious procession. Bishop Belo – who had conducted the mass at Sebastião's funeral – was not told about either the requiem mass or the procession. If he had, he would have tried to stop it. Along the route, through the centre of Dili, the security forces watched the crowd but did nothing to stop them, not even when the demonstrators unfurled banners calling on Indonesia to withdraw from East Timor and shouted 'Viva Independencia!', 'Viva Timor Leste!', 'Viva Xanana Gusmão!'. Nobody knew that the young demonstrators were walking straight into a trap.

Seven years later, Sebastião Guterres recalled that morning. He was a friend of his namesake Sebastião Gomes. Like him, he turned 18 in 1991. Sebastião Guterres was studying at the Roman Catholic seminary and hoped to become a priest. He and his friends had got up early that morning to join the mass. 'The church was full,' he recalled. 'Many people were very disappointed that the Portuguese hadn't come. We had hoped that they would help us. Now we had missed a big chance and we felt very alone again.'

We reached the Santa Cruz cemetery. On the road in front a row of plastic chairs stood ready for the VIPs: political leaders of the five East Timorese political parties: Fretilin, the UDT, Trabalhista, Kota and Apodeti. They all made long speeches about their commitment to self-determination for East Timor, peace and reconciliation.

I asked the students around me who the speakers were, but apart from Fretilin's leader, Mau Hodu (José da Costa), an ex-Falintil commander, none of the politicians in the chairs was recognised. They did not feel much affinity for any of the political parties, nor for the older generation of leaders. 'The speeches go on for too long,' grumbled Sebastião. 'It looks as if they have hijacked the ceremony for political purposes.'

Sebastião and I found some shade under the cemetery's flowering frangipani trees. The blossom's sweet, melancholy fragrance hung heavy between the white and pale-blue graves. Some were marked by elaborate crypts and grave-stones, adorned with black-and-white portraits of the deceased. They stared solemnly from the stones, their eyes full of sad stories nobody will ever hear. But many of the graves were no more than piles of rubble with a simple stone or wooden cross, a name and a date. Judging from the number of tiny graves, it seemed many Timorese did not survive early childhood.

Sebastião remembered how, in 1991, the procession passed a big high school near the cemetery. 'The classes hadn't started yet, so many of these youngsters – they were not older than 14 or maybe 15 – joined us in their school uniforms. We first put flowers on Sebastião's grave and just as everyone had knelt down for prayers, I heard the first shots.' Sebastião pointed to a few big trees near the entrance to the cemetery. Dozens of boys were standing on the thicker branches. 'It looks exactly like 1991. So many people in the trees and on the walls. When I heard the shots I saw the people falling like leaves. They kept falling and falling, just like leaves.' He repeated the image as if by saying it often enough, he could take control of it, exorcise it from his mind. 'I started to run. We couldn't help people who were wounded – it was a choice: if you helped you would die yourself; if you ran you had a chance to survive. I saw them shooting the young kids, in their school uniforms, hurdling the graves. Behind the chapel I saw a friend who was shot. I panicked, and ran. We kept running until we reached the back wall. There was a girl; she tried to climb over the wall but she couldn't manage to get on it. Her eyes; I never forget the look in her eyes. I tried to help her but failed. I tried.' His voice trailed off and he looked away.

The girl, he would find out later, had survived, but in his dreams her eyes still haunted him. Sebastião was earnest, proud and a bit pompous, with the bravado of a young warrior and the sense of moral superiority of a young priest. Perhaps because he was the eldest of a large family, he had an authoritative way of treating his fellow students. He gave the impression of observing and judging everyone. That day, however, he had been confronted with his own fear, his instinct for self-preservation. He survived Santa Cruz not as a manly hero who had rescued all his friends but as a boy who had run for his life. Quite soon after the Santa Cruz massacre he had to stop his studies at the seminary. 'We think you can serve society better in another capacity,' the priests had told him, so he went to Untim. He seemed at times still hurt by the priests' judgement.

As I was talking to Sebastião, outside the gate, a group of students started a performance. From a tinny ghetto-blaster came the sound of music mingled with the crackle of gunfire. Dressed in black cloaks, the performers ran, whirled and fell over each other, and from under their cloaks silky blood-red fabric flowed. Sebastião tried to squeeze his way to the front to have a better view and returned with tears in his eyes. 'Everyone cries and now I also have to cry. I don't want to cry,' he said angrily, turned away and stared at his feet. I looked around. The men, the women, the children, were all weeping. Some howled deep and long, others cried silently, with a single tear trickling down their cheeks. They wept over their private grief; their lost loved ones. But they also seemed to be weeping collectively for a shared sorrow – not only over Santa Cruz, but also over all these long years of war and repression and fear and death. It was the first time that they could share this, openly, with others. They walked in procession to a large iron cross – the place where, in 1991, four young students were killed, and now the focal point for commemorations of Timor's martyrs – and lay down their brightly coloured bouquets of bougainvillaea, oleanders and roses. In almost every family in Dili someone had been hurt or killed, or disappeared without trace. The Timorese resistance had assembled a list of 271 names of people they knew for sure had died and another of 200 people who had disappeared.[2]

After Santa Cruz, the army also killed demonstrators on the way to hospital and even inside it. Mário Carrascalão, who was the governor at the time, saw three army trucks full of dead bodies and the wounded near Santa Cruz. But his wife, who was permitted to visit the hospital three days after the killings, found not a single patient with a gunshot wound. While she was there one of the nurses told her that they had had to put the people in the morgue, even if they were alive, and inject them with water.[3] A guilt-stricken soldier later told Bishop Belo that many of those who survived the massacre at the cemetery were taken away and killed by the Indonesian security forces 'with big stones, with iron bars and injections of a special substance'.[4] Some bodies the military disposed of in abandoned graveyards near Dili; others were never found. Mário Carrascalão said he knew the location of a mass grave in Tibar, just outside Dili, where many of the executions had taken place.

The Indonesians claimed that only 19 people died and 91 had been wounded. Mário Carrascalão said he dismissed these figures immediately as a fabrication since they were simply taken from 1991, the year of the massacre. Only after concerted international pressure did the Indonesian government admit to a higher death toll – of 54 – which was still far lower than the true figure.

Nobody's children were safe from the bullets, not even those of leaders of parties that had traditionally supported the Indonesians in East Timor. Frederico Almeida da Costa, an Apodeti leader, lost two sons. After they disappeared he stopped shaving his beard and cutting his hair. He was there too, at the anniversary procession. His long grey beard came to his belt and he had tied his hair up in a knot at the back of his head.

The Corte-Real family lost one of their two daughters. Her sister never got over this and became a nun, giving their mother the feeling she had lost both her children. Manuel Carrascalão was also present. His daughter Manuela had been one of the high school students who had joined the 1991 demonstration. Manuel rushed to the cemetery as soon as they heard about the shooting. Manuel was furious. He stood in front of the soldiers, spread out his arms, and shouted: 'Shoot *me* if you dare, just shoot *me*!'

There were other parents looking for their children, and like Manuel, they couldn't find them. When I had interviewed Manuel at his house, Manuela had herself told how she had escaped over the fence. Still wearing her school uniform, she had run into a house. She had begged the woman who lived there to lend her some clothes because she was afraid that if the military saw her in her school clothes they would shoot her.

The Carrascalãos were lucky: none of their children had been killed. But for them it was a turning-point. From that day, Manuel said, he started openly to criticise the Indonesians. Mário was similarly unable to keep his mouth shut any longer. He was soon replaced and 'promoted' to be Indonesia's ambassador to Romania. 'It changed my perception of Indonesian rule for good,' he said later. Until then he had hoped that, despite everything, annexation might still, in the long run, bring development, peace and prosperity. 'Now I no longer had the hope that we could ever trust them again.'

While people queued up to lay their flowers in front of the cross, a tiny figure appeared at the gate to the cemetery. She walked slowly up to the big iron cross, spread her arms and in a deep voice – quite remarkable in a person no taller than five feet – bellowed a command to stop whimpering, and start praying. This was Madre Margarita, of the Canossian Daughters of Charity, a Catholic order. At 84, she seemed not to have lost any of her vigour.

Madre Margarita had gained much respect for her role at Santa Cruz. As soon as she heard the shots, she rushed to the cemetery, pushed the soldiers aside, went in and prayed. She stayed there until Bishop Belo arrived. The military let him in to the cemetery, but only to give the wounded and dying his blessing. They would not allow him to do anything else. By the time the bishop and Madre Margarita returned to his residency, where she was in charge of the household, the compound had become a refugee centre for hundreds of frightened people. The bishop knew it would not be safe for them to stay so he and Madre Margarita started to move people back to their homes.

As if on cue, as soon as the ceremony ended, the sky burst and a tropical rainstorm lashed over the mourners. 'The dead are crying with us,' said Sebastião. I looked at his face but saw not a trace of irony. He looked grateful. The rain pleased the organisers too. It might deter people from lingering, and getting into trouble.

What exactly lay behind the 1991 massacre remains unclear. It may have been a show of strength and ruthlessness designed to quell such protests once and for all. Or it may have been that the army had used *agents provocateurs* to try to whip up a confrontation, but that, in dealing with it, the shooting got out of hand. But Mário Carrascalão had heard from an Indonesian commander that on 11 November a battalion that was about to leave East Timor was told 'prepare your weapons, you will have a good farewell to Timor'. Some political analysts say East Timor was used in a power struggle within the armed forces, between the hawkish faction of Benny Murdani and the more liberal generals, to whose faction belonged East Timor's commander at the time, Brigadier-

General Rudolph Warouw. The killings may have been intended to force the removal of the most senior military commanders in East Timor at the time – partly because of their alleged softness towards the resistance, but also perhaps because they, along with the governor, Mário Carrascalão, were engaged in an anti-corruption drive that threatened some high-level military and business interests. Certainly, one consequence of the massacre was a reshuffle of the army top brass, and Mário was replaced by Abilio Soares, an Apodeti supporter and a close friend of Prabowo. Soares once said in an interview that he supported a more forceful military approach, and that as far as he was concerned 'far more should have died' in the shooting at Santa Cruz.[5]

Whatever the motives behind the shooting, the massacre changed everything. In Dili, Timorese, of all political backgrounds, formed a national front against the Indonesians. Fretilin and the UDT had buried the hatchet in the agreement formalised in 1988, when they agreed to work together in the National Council of Maubere Resistance (CNRM), a non-partisan clandestine coalition of all East Timorese groups under Xanana's leadership. They were now joined by leading families in Apodeti and the other parties. Many members of Apodeti, whose followers were less suspected by the Indonesians, became useful *estafetas*.

Also, world opinion changed. They had to pay a high price for it, but the Timorese got what they had longed for – to be on the world's conscience and not to be victims of a forgotten war. No longer was it just one more strange conflict on some tiny far-flung island that seemed closer to the end of the world than almost anywhere else on earth. Video footage, smuggled out and broadcast around the world, showed young people desperately pleading for their lives; a boy with a hole in his chest, comforted by his friends; girls running for their lives pursued by Indonesian soldiers; youths beaten and dragged onto trucks. It was not the first or worst massacre in East Timor, nor would it be the last, but for the first time the Indonesians could not totally deny what had happened, the world could not close its eyes and the politicians could not avert their gaze from a simple truth: Indonesian soldiers had opened fire, without any warning, on a group of unarmed youngsters in school uniforms.

As we left the cemetery, I asked Sebastião if he had come to hate the Indonesians. He shook his head. 'I have Indonesian friends; there were four of them in my group at Santa Cruz, I don't hate the Indonesian people but I do hate the system. Do you know, it was an Indonesian soldier who saved my life? When we climbed on top of the wall I saw that the soldiers were everywhere – also in the street behind the cemetery. I didn't know what to do. Then the soldier nearest to us shouted: "Run, you bastard, why are you staring at me? Run!" We all ran. He saved our lives.' Sebastião then corrected himself. 'Well, really God saved my life of course.'

Sebastião and his friends decided to look for the soldier that saved their lives and bring him a present at Christmas. They knew his name: Panjaitan, a Muslim Batak from Sumatra. But the first year it was impossible to go anywhere at Christmas. The streets were deserted: nobody dared go out. They went a year later. He was surprised to see them. 'We understand you, we also want our freedom,' he told them. After that, they used to see him every year at Christmas and the Muslim holidays until he moved with his battalion back to East Sumatra.

§

I went back to the cemetery after dark. The unlit streets were lined with candles. Thousands and thousands of little flames formed trails of light that led from every direction to Santa Cruz. I followed one of these light trails. Small groups of people were standing quietly around. Some sat on their knees around the candles, tenderly cupping their hands to shelter the fragile flames from the moist wind. The cloudburst had long past, but the cemetery was shrouded in fine drizzle, so light that the droplets evaporated even before they touched the ground.

Some young people still mingled. They had arranged candles along the top of the walls and the gate, and, on the ground, had used them to spell out 12-11-91. Suddenly I felt a hand on my arm. Next to me stood a young woman, dressed in jeans and a white T-shirt and a head full of bouncy little curls, held back with an elastic band. 'Would you like to come with us to Herman's grave?' she asked. Herman, I remembered, was the man shot in Manatutu earlier in the year. His mother had already lost her husband and eldest son to the war. Now her last child had died too at the hands of the army. His death, like Sebastião's seven years earlier, had led to a confrontation with the army during a visit by foreign dignitaries.

In the pitch-dark the path between the graves was hardly visible. The further we got from the entrance the less space there was between the graves, until eventually the path disappeared and we had to clamber over the slippery tombs. In the far corner of the graveyard I saw the flickering of candles. We joined the people sitting around the grave to light some candles, but as soon as the first one was lit, thick drops of rain started to fall. The rain dripped in my eyes, making it even harder to find the way back. Soon the graveyard turned into a big pool of mud. On all sides, shadows struggled through the rain. We took shelter in the little chapel I remembered from the photographs of 1991 of the place where some of the wounded had crawled for safety.

'It's a happy day and a sad day at the same time,' the girl said, as if she had rehearsed a statement. 'Sad because we think of all our friends who died, happy because we could share our sorrow, for the first time. We had a commemoration without the interference by the Indonesian troops, without it becoming violent. This gives us hope for the future.'

§

I had arranged to see the girl again the next day at the Student Solidarity Council. She turned out to be 24, much older than she looked. She introduced herself as Atanasia Pires – 'my friends call me Tata' – and was a member of the student women's organisation, the East Timor Young Women's Group.

The Solidarity Council had rented a little house not far from the Santa Cruz cemetery. It was a stone structure with a covered veranda, a living room and three tiny bedrooms, which had been turned into offices. The one where the women worked was clean and neat, furnished with a few bookshelves, a table and two plastic stools. Tata and her friend Elisa busied themselves in the kitchen making cups of tea.

As in so many liberation struggles, it seemed the women did the house-work. They cleaned, cooked and swept the floor while the men held their meetings, which could go on long into the night. I had come early and many students had not arrived yet. The leader of the Students' Solidarity Council, Antero, had left Dili for Britain to follow, of all things, a course in conflict management. He was away for many months and João da Silva Sarmento had become his unofficial replacement in the office. João looked like a younger and smaller version of Antero. He also came from the eastern part of Timor and, like Antero, he had an engaging smile that spread over his face when you looked at him. But as soon as you looked away the smile evaporated and left behind a sad, tormented look.

João proudly showed me their computer room. The students had managed to buy a computer with the money from a few donations. They had an Internet connection and João was in the process of checking his e-mail. The local server was so slow that it took an hour just to download his hotmail.

João was also a product of the seminary, like Antero, Felis and Sebastião. He now studied linguistics at Untim and spoke good English. His ambition was to become a journalist or a writer, and for nights on end he would work at the computer tirelessly preparing reports, statements and newsletters. That day João and his colleagues were preparing another mission to the countryside – a 'convoy', as they called it, of a dozen lorries and buses each packed with students. It was the continuation of the idea Antero had explained to me a few months earlier: to take the 'open forum discussions' to outlying districts. The students wanted to provide some political education and inform the population about the choices they might have to make following all the changes in Jakarta. They had been to most of the district towns and now planned to head for the sub-districts. The trips had been a mixed success. In almost all districts, the local authorities, the *bupatis*, were pro-Indonesian. They tended to be *liurais*, civil servants or ex-soldiers, with strong links to the military and its business interests, and were therefore hostile to the young idealists. The population as a whole, however, greeted them as liberation heroes.

'We are not a political party and we have no political alliances. We just want to be the moral force – so we have to be neutral,' João explained repeatedly.

But in practice, the student convoys were not as apolitical as João, like Tata and Antero before him, had described them. They seemed more like campaigning than educational exercises: the students would shout pro-independence slogans, and sing 'O Foho Ramelau', the unofficial national anthem associated with Fretilin's declaration of independence, and one that carried a heavy emotional load, taking people back to the days of the civil war and the short period of Fretilin rule that followed it – days that not everybody liked to remember. The places they visited had not seen such brazen defiance for more than twenty years, and although it was an exhilarating experience for most of the population, it was also very dangerous.

While João and I were talking, a messenger came running in with a letter. He had just come from Ermera. João's face clouded over as he read it. 'Four people have been arrested and the military is threatening to kill them if we don't go there to negotiate,' he reported.

Almost everywhere the students had gone, trouble had followed. In this case, those arrested were four local organisers, who had helped the students with their forum. With Antero abroad, João and his colleagues had to handle this. João decided to set off immediately.

The next day I went back to the students' office to find out what had happened. By the time João and his colleagues got to Ermera, the four organisers had been freed. But that was not an end to it. Two were attacked in their homes at night. One escaped, but the other was killed.

The convoys were stopped. That vision of hope Tata had glimpsed at the Santa Cruz commemoration had faded fast.

CHAPTER 5

. . . .

Underground

§ WHEN he saw our little group appearing on the ridge overlooking the village, he came running, arms outstretched, to greet us with kisses on our hands. The whole village followed suit. The subservience of the gesture was rather embarrassing – a legacy of colonial times, now normally bestowed only on the clergy, not on aid workers and journalists. The villagers dragged stools out of their small straw and bamboo houses and invited us to sit down, while they remained standing. Only Bere and his eldest son took a seat.

Bere had a long white beard that age had given a yellowish tinge. His face had the wrinkles of a man who was usually in good spirits. As long as he could remember, he had lived in this tiny village in the mountains above Dili. He didn't know how old he was. But he had seen it all: the Allied forces fighting the Japanese; the Japanese occupation; the return of the Portuguese; the Indonesian invasion.

From under the layers of cloth wrapped around his waist to hold up his sarong, he pulled a little square package, like a folded handkerchief. He unwrapped it carefully and then proudly showed me two Australian silver tuppenny pieces. 'This is what the Australians paid me for working for them during the World War,' he explained. As a boy Bere worked as a guide for the Australian army in its war against the Japanese. For some time Australian soldiers were stationed in Fatabloko and Maubisse. Bere was lucky to survive. Fighting alongside 400 Australian (and Dutch) commandos, thousands of Timorese died, quite a number armed with no more than bows and arrows. When, after a year, the Australians evacuated the island, they had lost 40 of their men. But for the Timorese, of whom they took only a handful with them, mainly Portuguese and *mestiços*, the war had just begun.

The Japanese had recruited a so-called 'Black Column', a native force brought in from West Timor and the nearby islands of the Moluccas. With their help they embarked on a punitive campaign. In areas where the Australians had been active, villages were razed to the ground and whole families wiped out. People abandoned their fields and ran to the mountains. The occupiers raided food stores and requisitioned all the provisions, leaving the Timorese to starve. The arrival of the 'Black Column', combined with the typical Japanese divide-and-rule tactics of playing local rulers off against each other, revived all the horrors of wars earlier that century. Some *liurais* supported the Japanese; others kept fighting against the new foreign invaders.

When Bere returned to his village he found it occupied by the Japanese, so he worked for them too. They paid him, albeit in wartime money, a paper currency useful to many locals only as cigarette paper. But working for the Japanese gave him some security, and he and most of his family survived the war years. After the Japanese surrendered, Portugal regained sovereignty over a devastated colony: the towns had been bombarded, the villages burned, and the people traumatised. Probably more than 45,000, some 15 per cent of the population, had died. In proportional terms, East Timor was one of the worst casualties of the Second World War.

For Bere it meant that he was at risk of persecution by the Portuguese for his collaboration with the Japanese. But he was just a poor farmer who had been under a lot of pressure, so they left him alone. For years nothing much changed in his village, or any village in East Timor. Portugal lacked the money to rebuild the colony and it remained a poor and sleepy backwater, and a peaceful one, until life was shaken up again by the revolution in Portugal and the Indonesian invasion.

Bere told his story without a trace of embarrassment or shame. He had done what many others had: chosen to follow the authority, the strong side, without asking too many questions. And he survived. But what about his family? When I asked how many children he had, he looked puzzled. He didn't know exactly. The whole village, who seemed to be mainly his clan, started to count. Two wives, and a total of 24 children. His oldest son sat next to him. He was in his sixties. How old was the youngest? I asked. He called over one of the little boys. He was eight years old. The whole village doubled up in laughter when they saw our startled expressions.

§

A little further up the road from Bere's hamlet was the village of Balibar. There lived Francisco Martins, a friend of Afonso, the taxi driver who had driven me to Baucau in June. Afonso had introduced us, to help me understand what life in the villages was like and how the resistance was organised. I had visited the Martins family's small wooden house several times.

We talked about the war in the privacy of his living room, a bare but neat space, with a few Catholic prints on unpainted walls and, as furniture, only a wooden sofa and three chairs. Before the war Francisco and his wife had worked as teachers and Fretilin cadres in Ermera. When, during the civil war, the UDT's army started to kill Fretilin supporters there, the Martinses had

2. Bere with his oldest
and youngest sons.

fled to Fretilin's headquarters at Aileu. Francisco joined Falintil, and later
became the Fretilin party secretary in Aileu.

At first Francisco had been suspicious of my interpreter, Sebastião, and
relaxed only after he explained that his father was part of the resistance too.
Afonso, Francisco and Sebastião's father Filomeno were all ex-Falintil fighters.
Everyone had their story – stories they kept as well-guarded secrets, even from
each other. Bishop Belo once remarked that 'half the population of East Timor
is paid to spy on the other half',[1] and in this climate of fear, people did not
share their feelings openly. So the Indonesians did not actually need to have
every other Timorese on their payroll: the perception itself was potent enough.

Sebastião's father had fought the UDT after its ill-fated coup in Dili, and
had been close to the Fretilin leadership during the party's brief stint in power.
During the war, he became a political officer. He worked with Sa'he (Vicente
Reis), the brains behind Fretilin's ideology and Falintil's policy of setting up
an underground network among the civilian population.

I remembered what Filomeno had told me about his surrender to the

Indonesians. He had come out of the mountains to see his mother. His brothers had persuaded him not to go back. 'They won't kill you,' one had assured him. The army officer who came to the house had questioned him. 'I think we have the same ideology,' Filomeno replied, 'only you might not understand that.' After all, he said, he knew that the Indonesians had also fought a liberation struggle against their colonisers.

One Indonesian soldier who had defected and joined Falintil was called Edy. He was from Surabaya, and had become a trusted ally of the Falintil commander in the Viqueque area. And when he had been made an adjutant, Filomeno had been on the committee that awarded the promotion. Edi would accompany him as he conducted his political schooling of Falintil. 'They made me come here; I don't want to kill you,' Edy would say.

After his surrender Filomeno impressed an English-speaking officer with his stories of life in the jungle. He was brought to Dili where he was made the driver of Major Aziz, the head of the Indonesian military intelligence, perhaps the most important man in Timor. Aziz had rescued other ex-Falintil cadres and Fretilin central committee members. Filomeno trusted him as 'a good man'. He had showed him a registration book in which the army kept a record of its killings. 'Look,' he had said to Filomeno, 'I'm not stupid, I did not kill any Timorese.' Aziz wanted to wage a 'hearts and minds' campaign in Timor, but lost his position in the anti-corruption drive towards the end of Governor Mário Carrascalão's time in office.

Francisco Martins had also been lucky to survive. He was arrested a few times in 1976 and was saved by the intervention of the bishop at the time, Dom Martinho da Costa Lopes. After his release he settled in Balibar and looked for work as a teacher. But under Indonesian rule, Portuguese had been replaced by Bahasa Indonesian, a language Francisco couldn't speak at the time, and even now was not comfortable with. But in 1983 he was, despite his political background, made village head, a position he kept for ten years.

Whenever I heard stories like Francisco's and Filomeno's I wondered about the motives of the Indonesians in giving these former soldiers and resistance fighters such positions of responsibility in the occupying regime. Aziz had never asked his 'private prisoners' to become his informers. In Francisco's case it may have been simple: he was the only literate person in the village and the Indonesians had little choice. Or maybe they thought it better to incorporate people like Francisco and Filomeno into the system: in that way they could keep an eye on them. A post such as that of village chief, moreover, had interesting bonuses and opportunities for corruption. It was a way to make them accomplices and collaborators, to bind them to the hand that fed them.

Francisco's wife and his twelve children had gathered at the other end of the room and followed our conversation intently. The children, six boys and six girls, had been born consecutively, 'boy, girl, boy, girl!' Afonso had pointed out with some awe in his voice. The eldest was studying at the university and the youngest one had not entered school yet. His wife brought a tray of coffee and bananas. Francisco put the cup to his lips and took a big sip. 'I drink only coffee, never water,' he sighed contentedly. Like many Timorese, the Martins family were subsistence farmers. They were able to grow enough food to feed themselves, and from the bit of surplus that cash crops such as coffee and cacao provided they could afford clothes and shoes.[2]

While we drank our coffee Francisco talked about the resistance in the countryside. Surrendered Falintil soldiers became part of a clandestine support network for Fretilin (later the CNRT) and for Falintil, which, over time, formed into different groups. In all there were some 1,700 tiny cells spread across the country, Filomeno had told me. Each cell was allocated its own mission, and within the cells tasks and responsibilities were assigned. For security reasons, contact between cells was kept to a minimum. Filomeno's cell was responsible for the welfare of the people in the neighbourhood. Some cells even had Indonesians in them, local residents who opposed the government in Jakarta.

Afonso was one of those with responsibility for communications. As a taxi driver, he could move around with less trouble than most Timorese. People in the countryside were not allowed to leave their villages without permission. When they wanted, for example, to visit a family member in town, they had first to ask the permission of the local army commander.

The network had representatives in every village and hamlet and were known as *nureps* and *celcoms*, who acted also as links between the Falintil fighters in the hills and the civilian resistance. Francisco was a *nurep* leader. In 1992, when he was still village head, he had received a message that Xanana needed a new hiding place. Xanana had stayed near Dili for some time, building clandestine networks in the town. For two months Francisco kept him hidden in a small shed between the coffee trees. The children would bring him food, water and medicine and through Afonso and other *estafetas*, messengers would go to and from Dili.

After six weeks Francisco realised that he could not hide Xanana safely any longer. The area was frequented by Chinese coffee traders and he was afraid that they would alert the army to his presence. Xanana moved down to Dili, first to Felis's family and then to the house of a cousin. This would be his last hiding place. Soon after Xanana's arrest Francisco heard the dreaded knock on the door. 'The soldiers threatened and beat me, but I remained silent,' he said. Since they did not have enough proof to keep him for long they let him go. Not long after that a Timorese girl was sent to the family. They could not turn her away, and she moved in, as Francisco put it, 'to look for the weak spot'.

After she left, a few months later, the soldiers returned. They took Francisco blindfolded to a bridge and hung him off it. 'You don't have to tie me up. If you want to kill me do it now, I'm ready,' Francisco said. But instead they had locked him in a filthy toilet and tortured him with electric shocks. 'I told them everything: how I had hidden Xanana and how we had fed him, but they kept on torturing.' They wanted him to confess that all the villagers had been involved, but he refused to do that. After some months they released him. He lost his post as village head.

The experience seemed not to have broken the determined spirit of resistance in his family. I remembered my first visit in July. *Reformasi* had just arrived in Timor and they had bubbled with infectious optimism – an optimism that bordered on recklessness, I had thought at the time. The older children had proudly showed me a little *reformasi* office they had opened along the main road, near the barricade kept as a checkpoint by the local army. On the wall of the small white building they had written in big red letters: 'Referendum Yes!'

A couple of boys ran inside, and came back with a Timorese flag. To my dismay they started to wave it in the middle of the road. 'Take a photo! Take a photo!' they chanted. I looked around, anxiously. To wave this flag could be a sure way to die. The Indonesian army shot independence activists for flying their flags, not only in Timor but also in other restive parts of the archipelago. But the military was nowhere to be seen.

When they bade me goodbye they presented me with a *tais*, a piece of traditional hand-woven *ikat* – a sign of honour that I accepted with embarrassment. Had I aroused the wrong expectations? I knew that many Timorese thought that foreign journalists were important allies and that somehow we had lots of power. And I also knew how little this was worth.

The whole family escorted me back to the taxi, and I saw the youngest boy carry a little suitcase. Where was he going? 'He wants to go with you. He wants to go abroad,' laughed his mother and took his hand.

Now, a few months later, on my return to the Martinses' village, I noticed how the mood had changed. The '*reformasi* office' no longer existed. The slogan was painted over and the door bolted. The military exerted even greater control in the villages than in the towns. And many soldiers, who had not received their regular pay since *reformasi*, had started to steal more from the villagers.

Higher up the mountain, around Aileu, mysterious big holes had appeared in the ground. When people had asked about them the military had warned them that they could be for them. The population of the area had had traumatic experiences with mass graves, and even the suggestion could sow terror. Francisco said he had been warned several times by his friends to be careful. 'When the water is clear again they will catch the fish,' they had cautioned him. But he had not wanted to listen. 'We have waited for 23 years to express what we want. Now the time has come we should not be afraid,' he said with fire in his eyes. What do you want? I asked, knowing the answer already. 'Independencia!' shouted the family as one.

CHAPTER 6

. . . .

The Bishop on the Mountain

§ FROM the rear-view mirror, a crucifix dangled from a rosary of blue plastic beads. Every time the *bemo* lurched round one of the hairpin bends, it swayed from side to side like a frantic metronome. On the mirror itself, small pictures of the Virgin Mary and the Sacred Heart were fastened, and on the dashboard a sticker of the Holy Family. It seemed the car's only non-religious decoration was a big, multi-coloured, knitted caterpillar that lay along the windscreen. Under its head the driver kept the fares he collected from his passengers. He had even gone so far as to christen the *bemo* – 'Sagrada Familia', the Holy Family. Women, children and small animals sat inside; men and goats travelled on top.

The *bemo* stopped just outside Manatutu, at the holy spring of St Antonio, a basin built in the rocks with a little vault housing a small statue of the locally popular patron saint. The passengers got off. They blessed and splashed themselves and drank from the cool mountain water.

While everyone got back on the bus I looked for the path to the nearby village of Behada. It was easy to spot. Along the mountain path stood bamboo flowers, skilfully crafted by peeling the outer layers of bamboo sticks, and folding the fibres back to the stem to form rosettes, traditional ornaments to honour important guests. The special guest today was the Bishop of Baucau, Dom Basilio do Nascimento.

A week earlier I had travelled to the area around Manatutu with Antonino, a Timorese aid worker, from Yayasan San José, a local foundation. We had made a trip through the mountains with the village chief of Laclo. He had struck me as the region's dynamo: the engine for change. He was a tall man with a long drooping moustache who sported a floppy cowboy hat. He had boasted that *his* area was free of Indonesian military interference. The local commander had asked him if he could guarantee their security. 'I couldn't, so he would not stay longer in these hills.' He had wanted to use the opportunity to take me to one of the Falintil commanders in the area, but the trip had to be called off because the commander was away. Instead he invited me to join the village to climb a local mountain, Ili Manu, together with the bishop.

I was late; the bishop had already arrived. He was having his breakfast in one of the bamboo houses and when I entered, apologetic for my late arrival, he graciously invited me to share the feast the villagers had prepared for him and his companions, of fresh fried fish, bread rolls and little cups of strong sweet coffee. Bishop Basilio do Nascimento was a stout, jolly man in his late forties, with a round, balding head and twinkling eyes. He had a beautiful voice, deep and resonant, and an infectious laugh. He was born in Timor, but had spent most of his adult life abroad and only returned home in 1994. He was made bishop in 1998 when the bishopric of East Timor was split in two. His diocese stretched from Manatutu to Jaco, a tiny islet off the eastern tip of the island. The western part formed Bishop Belo's diocese. After studying for the priesthood, Bishop Basilio worked for more than twenty years in Portugal and France. So, like Bishop Belo, he had missed the worst years of suffering and trauma experienced by his people in East Timor. Instead, he had seen the world, spoke several languages, and had read many books; he knew about the world in a way that many of his parishioners, high in the mountains, could not begin to imagine. This, however, seemed not to have created any gulf between the bishop and the people he worked with. Rather, his good-humoured, friendly nature enabled him to put everyone immediately at ease.

Certainly, around the breakfast table, the atmosphere was informal and the air filled with laughter. The villagers, it seemed, had forgotten that they had a bishop in their midst – or at least, they had forgotten that they were supposed to be overawed. One of them later said they saw him like 'our father or our brother – he doesn't stand above us at all'.

The people of the area had invited the bishop to join them on a pilgrimage to the top of Ili Manu. They wanted him to talk to the young people of the district. Their young, they worried, were too engrossed in politics and demon-strations; they were stirring up trouble, taking too many risks, abandoning their studies. The pilgrimage would be a two-day affair with a night spent in a village near the summit. I was unaware, but would discover later, that there was another, more spiritual side to it all: a new cross was to be placed on the top of the mountain, securing another remote part of Timor for the Christian faith.

Ili Manu, with its clouded summit, Mount Curi, is the highest mountain in Manatutu. As in so many cultures, high mountains, especially if they are shrouded in clouds, peculiarly shaped or located in an auspicious place, are thought of as sacred, their summits revered as the abodes of deities and spirits. So also in mountainous Timor. The higher the mountain, the more sacred it is. Ili Manu is not as high as Mount Ramelau, East Timor's highest mountain, or as well known as the Matebian, the sacred mountain of the 'souls of the dead', where many people died during the first years of the Indonesian occupation. But it stands on an outcrop of land and rises majestically up from the sea. In traditional East Timorese belief, spirits travel to the mountaintops to unite with the Uru Watu – the supreme deity, representing both sun and moon.

Belief in *lulik* is embedded in the way of life of the mountain people. *Lulik*, a Tetum word that is hard to define, means something like 'holding spirituality' and is part of ancestor worship. *Lulik* can manifest itself in different forms: the earth, stones, trees and rivers or man-made objects such as a special carving, a piece of cloth or a flag. Hundred-year-old Portuguese flags, for example, were still kept in the *uma lulik*, sacred houses, for their strong *lulik* powers. *Uma lulik* play an important part in the organisation of traditional Timorese society.

There is something else about Ili Manu. When I had mentioned my planned trip in the student office in Dili, João had been very excited. Ili Manu is known to shelter the last 'aboriginal' *knua*, hamlets, of East Timor, he had said. No coloniser or foreign invader – Portuguese, Japanese or Indonesian – has ever set foot there. 'Life in these *knua* is still how it used to be for hundreds of years. And their inhabitants are the real Timorese.' João also told me that they possessed a very mysterious fruit, the *aidila-sabraka*. He had written the name in my notebook. 'It's the only place in Timor and perhaps in the world that it grows. Ask them to show you one,' he had urged.

The sun was already high and it was mercilessly hot when the village women saw us off on the climb with a traditional dance accompanied by much loud clanging on metal gongs. The bishop was given a big wooden walking stick to support him. This was not the first mountain he had climbed recently. Only a few weeks earlier he had led a procession to the Matebian. He had also scaled the high peak of Ramelau. But the villagers warned us that this mountain was even harder to climb, rising from just sea level to an altitude of 1,345 metres.

The bishop's entourage consisted of an East Timorese captain in the Indonesian army from Manatutu, two parish priests and a few local government officials. We set off, followed by a couple of hundred young people who, being much fitter, were soon in the vanguard. Most were carrying nothing more than a plastic carrier-bag with a towel and a toothbrush, but some were better equipped, with little backpacks, and a few had guitars slung over their shoulders.

Everything, it seemed, had to be carried up the mountain. Even a small generator was hauled up by two men carrying it hanging from a stick over their shoulders. The path was narrow and steep, taking us alongside a deep ravine. The rainy season had just started and all around us the mountain slopes were dotted with little tufts of bright fresh green grasses that had sprung up between the rocks and eucalyptus trees.

I climbed up alongside one of the parish priests, Padre Francisco Pinheiro. Walking in the mountains with so many people, he said, reminded him of the time he was forced to flee with his family from their home in Same. He was ten years old at the time. 'Many families went up Foho Ramelau. It is to the Tata Mai Lau, its highest peak, that the people of my region believe they will go *after* they die. But while I was there, I saw so many people *dying* on the mountain.' We walked in silence for a while and I saw his eyes clouding over with the memories. 'The worst time was when the bombs started to fall, they killed people, so many people. We had to leave the dead behind, and worse, sometimes even the living, the starving little babies, the sick grandparents. They were left with a candle if the family had such a thing, or with a handful of food. The people prayed that God or the ancestors, the spirits of the mountain, would take care of them. I almost died too. A bomb fell right next to where I was hiding, but the shrapnel and all debris, the stones and earth went straight up and over me. I wasn't hurt at all. It was a miracle.'

Padre Francisco worked in the parish of Laclubar in the mountain range on the far side of the Laclo river, an area where Falintil had a strong influence. He seemed to be not very keen to talk about Falintil in a direct way, but from the subtle references he made, I gathered that he and his colleague, Padre Mario, from the nearby parish of Soibada, had very close links with them. As priests they could help in many ways. Money, medicines and messages often reached Falintil through the clergy. Priests had more freedom of movement; they had cars and were unfettered in their contacts with all kinds of people – even the outside world.

After a climb of almost six hours we reached Unile'eng, a *knua* of eight simple bamboo houses with thatched roofs hidden in a protective hollow. It was inhabited by only two families, a few dogs and some chickens. Scattered over the mountain were a few more, even smaller, hamlets. This is how the Timorese used to live all over the island before the Indonesians came: in hundreds of tiny *knua* of small clans, Padre Francisco said. Even today families can be traced back through their family names to their *uma lulik* in these original clan villages. But of many of these there remained, after forced resettlement into 'strategic villages', nothing more than an abandoned grave-yard.

On the path just outside the village, a group of small girls was nervously rehearsing their welcome dance. They were dressed up like adults: their faces caked in thick layers of powder, eye-shadow and lipstick; brightly coloured *tais* around their skinny bodies; and their bouncy curls coiled tightly on top of their heads in traditional buns fastened by silver hairpins with Portuguese coins. Their faces earnest with the importance of their task, they banged on small wooden drums they held under their arms, while a little boy with feathers on his ankles whirled around. They reminded me of a flock of brilliant birds. The dance they were rehearsing was not very different from those that their ancestors once performed for local kings, or perhaps at ceremonies held before an attack on a neighbouring village.

I sat with Padre Francisco and João das Neves, the director of Laclo's high school (who turned out to be an uncle of Sebastião), on a tree trunk waiting for the bishop to arrive. 'What does Ili Manu mean?' I asked. 'Land of the birds,' João das Neves said. I looked around, but could not see any birds in the trees or in the sky. The only sound was the soft rustling of leaves as the wind ruffled the trees. Even in a metropolis like Hong Kong, with ten times as many inhabitants, where I used to live close to the centre of town, I would be woken up by birdsong in the morning. In East Timor, I had not even seen sparrows in the gardens, only the occasional pigeon, and, more rarely, a bird of prey. Their absence was eerie. Where were these birds? Had people eaten them all? Padre Francisco looked puzzled by my ignorance. 'Before the war, there were many more birds,' he said, 'but when the bombs started falling and kept falling, the birds all left the land, and they haven't returned.'

The bishop arrived, and suddenly the air was full of sound. The dancing children escorted him to the village elders, who welcomed him with ceremonial *tais*, which they draped over his shoulders. The bishop asked them about the situation in the village and one of the two village elders, the *kuku nain*, or shaman, Luciano de Oliveira, explained that five of his children had moved down to Laclo. 'They wanted to be closer to the road and the sea. But for me this is all I want. No foreigner has ever come up here and disturbed us. We are safe here.'

'Could you ask why the Indonesian soldiers never came up here?' I whispered to Padre Francisco, who translated the question. 'They are afraid,' said the *kuku nain* triumphantly. 'Not of us, but of the spirits of our mountain, they're really strong spirits.'

Then they showed us their *lulik* treasure: an ancient piece of silk cloth with a name and a date scribbled on its border. A messenger of the king of Laclo brought it to the village over a hundred years ago together with that strange fruit João had talked about, the *aidila-sabraka*, 'papaya-orange'. From the seeds of the fruit grew a tree that has borne fruit for the village ever since. They showed one to the bishop. From the outside it looked like a small papaya, but inside it was – instead of hollow with black pips – filled with a perfectly shaped small orange surrounded by white flesh that smelled and tasted like papaya. We all had a taste.

But the origin of the fruit remained a mystery. Padre Francisco told me later that he suspected the fruit had been brought to Timor by Angolan soldiers serving in the Portuguese army. Perhaps the shape of the tree that produced the fruit might have solved some of the mystery: the papaya plant is totally different from a citrus tree. The elders had been horrified by this suggestion. No stranger, they said, had ever seen the tree and they were not willing to take anybody to it. 'The villagers believe this fruit has a powerful *lulik* and strong magic,' Father Francisco laughed, 'so they are afraid that if you see the tree you might take this magic with you. They won't show it to anyone, not even the bishop. There is probably someone guarding the tree at the moment.'

I could understand their anxiety. Already, the tiny village looked under siege by the visitors from Laclo, who had set up their camp a few days ago. They had made shelters and tents by stringing blue plastic sheeting between trees and hanging it over poles. The effect was of something between a campsite full of Scouts and a refugee camp. Everywhere people were crouching around small fires, boiling water for coffee and instant noodles. Some of the young people were sitting around in circles, playing guitar and singing songs. Among the crowd I recognised the village chief of Laclo. When he saw me he bared his betel-nut-stained teeth in a wide grin and whispered something I could not understand. I thought the betel had gone to his head. His eyes were shining, but he seemed much less self-assured than when I had met him before, and appeared not to want to be seen with me for too long.

Maybe he spotted, among the people around us, *intel* spies. Even religious gatherings in Timor were sometimes turned violent by *provocateurs* paid by the army, and everyone was anxious to avoid this. Also, the Church's youth organisation, as well as the army captain, who carried a Motorola walkie-talkie, kept a sharp eye on the proceedings. They accompanied the bishop to his room in a large communal village house, a building so new and out of place that it looked as if it had been purpose-built for the occasion.

Nearby a group of women was cooking supper. They had dragged everything up the mountain – the huge woks, and all the food. In Timor, such occasions demand a certain style. So even up here, high up the mountain, the bishop was to be treated to a big feast in the Portuguese manner: steak with fried potatoes, beef stew with carrots and a salad of lettuce and tomatoes. When the bishop later invited me again to sit down with him I felt embarrassed. I would rather have sat with the village chief in the second row, a wooden bench in an outer circle around the table, where people were eating their food from plates on their laps. I tried but it was impossible to refuse the bishop's invitation, so I sat down next to Padre Francisco.

The discussion at the table was about the need for more priests. The people of Laclo had requested their own parish priest. They had everything prepared, including accommodation and a large church they had already built. The trouble was, the bishop said, that there were not enough priests. Many localities were asking for resident priests. In some remote places, priests visited only occasionally. Often they had to travel long distances, from one village to the other, to conduct Sunday mass, to hold baptisms and hear confessions. 'The demand is much higher than the supply,' he concluded with a smile.

East Timor had to import priests. Quite a number of parish priests came from Indonesia: central Java or Flores. And some of the Catholic missionary priests came from places even further afield, such as India, the Philippines, Italy or the United States.

The territory did not have its own training facilities, so theology students had to finish their studies in Indonesia. Padre Francisco, for example, had studied for seven years at the university in Malang in East Java. The bishop later grumbled to me that the training would-be priests received at such places was poor. They would come home stuffed with theological theory, but lacking spiritual insights. At the practical level, they often could not translate religious concepts into Tetum. 'Even if the people are open to spiritual schooling,' the bishop said, 'the young priests can't really enlighten them.'

The shortcomings of the local priesthood had become even more important since the Indonesian annexation. In nearly five hundred years of its history in East Timor, the Catholic Church had never been as popular as it was when the territory was ruled by invaders from a largely Muslim country. The Portuguese had not forced the population to convert to Christianity, and by the time of the Indonesian invasion only about 30 per cent were Catholic. Since 1975, however, there had been a big rush to the Church, as the Timorese converted *en masse*.

There are many legends about how the Catholic faith entered Timor. Portuguese Dominican missionaries had come, as early as 1515, to the Indonesian archipelago as the Western maritime powers vied with each other to establish footholds in the Spice Islands.[1] These priests were a rough bunch: missionaries who were at the same time enterprising traders, and, if need be, even soldiers. In one of the legends about the first encounter between these adventurous proselytisers and a Timorese tribe, the Dominicans had come ashore on the island to establish contact and stock up with provisions. The Timorese, so the story goes, had no interest in giving these strangers any assistance, let alone in exploring the new faith they promoted. Rather, their inclination was to cut off their heads and drink their blood. 'I don't care about your god, and I don't want to know about your religion,' the tribal chief is reputed to have told the missionaries. Sensing danger, the Dominicans threatened to tow the island – with everything and everybody on it – back with them to Portugal.

This did not do the trick either. But then, legend has it, a miracle happened. The locals were about to chase the Portuguese back to their ships when the island was rocked by a fierce earthquake. The Timorese were stunned by this evidence not just of the newcomers' magical powers, but even of their apparent ability to carry out their threat to dislodge their island. They soon agreed to provide the visitors with what they needed, and Catholicism gained its first Timorese converts.

The flags and sails with the Dominican cross are still kept as sacred objects in the crypts of churches around the archipelago and in the *uma lulik* of East Timor. The missionaries served more than just the religious end of saving more souls. Religion also smoothed the way for new trading alliances.

So, in legend, the Timorese adopted this alien faith for all the wrong reasons. Perhaps that was still true of the mass conversions of recent years. When I mentioned the story to the bishop, he laughed, but soon became serious. 'The people have turned to the Church not out of religious conviction,' he admitted, 'but as an affirmation of their identity.' Christianity was one more way in which East Timorese could show they were not Indonesians. 'Although the quantity of the faith is high,' the bishop said, 'the quality is still lacking.' A thin layer of Christianity sat on top of centuries of animism.

I remembered the trip I had made with Antonino, the aid worker. We stopped on a remote mountain path and he asked some local people what kind of help they needed for their community. 'A *capela*,' they had replied. He had been irritated. 'When you can produce enough to feed and dress your-selves, then use the surplus to build a *capela*,' he had told them off. Antonino was frustrated by the endless requests for churches from people so poor that they did not even have enough to eat or tools to work their land. But for the villagers, who were probably much closer to traditional animism than to the Catholic Church, a *capela* represented something else essential to their lives: a safe haven – somewhere where they might be spared harassment and per-secution by the omnipresent Indonesian military.

Another reason for the Church's popularity is the disruption that Indonesian rule brought to traditional belief. There were fewer opportunities for tradi-tional ceremonies, so people turned to the Church to compensate. For them, there was no contradiction in this: they integrated their traditional belief into Christian ritual. So attending church had become a search for protection, sanctuary, an expression of nationalism and a compensation for traditional rituals. But the spread of Christianity was also encouraged by Indonesia's own constitution. The state ideology, *Pancasila*, has as one of its five principles a 'belief in *one* God'. This obliged people to choose one of the five recognised religions: Islam, Hinduism, Buddhism, Protestantism and Catholicism. Anim-ism or atheism were both illegal, and were linked in official suspicions with communism. In East Timor, Catholicism had of course been the obvious choice.

Whatever the reason, every Sunday Timor's churches filled with people of all ages, including many teenagers and children. Even so, the bishop was apprehensive about the future of the Church. East Timor was one of the few countries in the world where the number of Christians was increasing. But he was worried Christianity might suffer the same fate as it had in parts of Eastern Europe, such as Poland, where church attendance had collapsed along with communism.

But such post-independence worries still seemed remote that evening. After sunset the camp was dark and cold. In front of the improvised *mandi* people were forming long queues, as if they were getting ready to go to sleep. I did the same. But just as I curled up under my blanket of newspaper sheets and a plastic rain poncho, I heard the sound of clapping. I got up to investigate, and found the bishop surrounded by an audience of hundreds of youths and some villagers. The generator that I had seen being carried up was powering a microphone, and there were even a couple of lightbulbs hanging from trees.

The people listened attentively as the bishop spoke of the political choice the people might have to make between three options: independence, autonomy and integration. It was a long but lively speech, laced with examples from the bible and world history, and spiced up with little jokes that had his audience roaring with laughter. When he had finished, he invited questions.

A girl in a white sweater was the first to stand up, voicing the sort of thinking that had so perturbed her elders. 'How can we ever reach independence when everyone needs to study hard all the time? We need independence first; when we have that we'll study.' Another youth got up to take issue with what the bishop had said. 'You say that as a bishop you can't lead the independence struggle. But if we, the students, lead it we'll be killed. They won't listen to us but they will listen to the bishops.'

Bishop Basilio answered calmly: independence would mean that everyone had to work extremely hard and the best way young people could contribute was by finishing their studies. As for the responsibility of the clergy, if priests started telling people what political choices to make, they would disunite the people even more.

In private, I asked him about this again. 'It's important that the Church, at this moment, should play a more political role. We have to prepare the people for the future.' Personally he supported independence but as a bishop he stayed neutral, so he could keep in contact with all the different factions. He saw his task as promoting dialogue and working on reconciliation.

He had nothing good to say about the students' attempts to organise 'open forums'. When the students came to Baucau to see him, he had refused to receive them. 'They are creating chaos and confusion in people's heads,' he said. 'They are too young and inexperienced.'

'For a while the people screamed as loud as they could, but now they just want to be left in peace. The Indonesian army has never understood this, and the students don't understand this either. They come, shouting slogans about independence and Xanana Gusmão, and talking about a referendum. But the conflict among the people is still present; and the students don't take this away with their dialogues; they make it worse.'

§

The next morning, I woke up just before sunrise, feeling bitterly cold. It was still quiet. There was no birdsong other than the raucous crowing of the cockerels, ever present where there are people. I got up and wandered around the village in the grey morning light. The families sat huddled together in little clusters, the women preparing a breakfast porridge of tapioca and corn, while the children played around in the dust. They all looked poor, sickly and malnourished. I wondered how they survived. Apart from chickens and dogs I did not see any livestock and there was only a small field with some corn, sweet potatoes and tapioca.

The first time the people remembered a Catholic priest coming to the mountain was in the early 1990s. He had come to baptise them and at the end of his stay he had planted a small wooden cross on Mount Curi. So now, in theory, they were Catholics too, living in the shadow of the cross. But that seemed hardly to have dented their traditional isolation and independence. All they really wanted, said the old village shaman, was to be left in peace. They did not long for a *capela*; no pictures of the Catholic saints hung in their houses; and when the bishop put on his robe and mitre to begin mass, the women did not even take the trouble to feign interest. They stayed at home, feeding their babies and grinding their tapioca roots.

The devotees that morning were the people from the valley. Many of them followed the mass on their knees with their hands folded piously in front of them. Nearby lay a huge iron cross, soldered together out of iron pipes, watched over by a group of about twenty men who wore brightly coloured *tais*. Over their naked shoulders they carried bows and arrows. The ten-metre-high cross had to replace the old wooden one, which they feared might rot away soon.

After mass, five of the men heaved the huge cross on their shoulders and led the procession on to the steep winding path to the mountain ridge. I was ready to follow when the village chief came running up to me: 'You can't carry anything black up the mountain,' he shouted. 'The spirits do not like that colour, and when they get angry there will be very bad weather.' I looked up to the blue sky where the sun was shining fiercely. But not wanting to offend anyone, I left behind all my black things: my camera bag, rain poncho and umbrella. I was allowed to take my camera, which was also black, thanks to a last-minute ruling by the village elders.

The landscape became wilder and wetter; huge old trees stood in high savannah grass, criss-crossed by tiny streams. Most of the trees were hollow, blackened trunks. Padre Francisco explained that a few times a year hunters set fire to the long grasses to round up wild pigs and deer so they can shoot them with their arrows. We had hardly been on our way for half an hour when a loud peal of thunder rolled across the still blue sky. I looked around, and noticed that a few people were indeed wearing black. Maybe the village elders had not spotted them. A few minutes later the sky broke open. Wishing I had been less 'culturally sensitive' and still had my rain poncho, I took shelter with a couple of other people in one of the giant hollow black trees.

When we resumed our climb the path had turned into just one of the many rivulets. As we reached the ridge leading to the summit I noticed a commotion. A group of warriors with bows and arrows, whom I had not seen before, stood around Padre Francisco discussing something, while a group of women looked on from a distance. The warriors, from the other *knua* of Ili Manu, had come to protect the sacred peak of their mountain, Padre Francisco explained. 'No woman has ever set foot on the top, let alone a foreign woman. They still have their doubts but the bishop has said that it's OK. So now reluctantly, they have agreed to let women to go on. But whatever you do don't touch the stones,' he warned me. What stones? I asked myself, somewhat alarmed. As soon as we reached the summit I saw what he meant. The warriors had already arrived. They stood guard around a few scattered flat stones, marked with bright red cloth.

While some men dug a deep hole next to the wooden cross, I saw the bishop wandering off with a few of the warriors. They lifted one of the stones up for him. Underneath was a small hole. 'A communication channel for the mountain spirits', they called it. The bishop gently touched the stone and smiled benignly.

All of a sudden the village head stood next to me. He looked less nervous and more pleased with himself. 'They are here,' he whispered. 'Who?' I asked. 'The men of the forests.' He winked conspiratorially. 'I have to tell you that they are very happy to see you here, they want to talk but it is too dangerous with all these people around.' He stole a glance towards the government and army people.

So Falintil had come too. Who were they? I looked at the mountain warriors. But the village chief was not going to reveal anything more. He had turned around to walk away when he seemed to remember something. He handed me a piece of paper carefully folded into a small square. 'I have more letters I needed to give you,' he said, 'but I left those in the village.' Why I was given this message – a list of names of UDT members in the area – was mysterious to me then, and still is.

The village head had joined the women, who had started singing. The hymns wafted through the bluish fog that had replaced the rain. Slowly the men erected the cross by pushing it up and securing it in a deep hole. Near to the cross I saw something that looked like some age-old foundations. Padre

Francisco saw me looking at it. 'Many years ago, the Portuguese built a small structure here, perhaps a kind of beacon, but the villagers don't like objects on their mountain so they destroyed it almost immediately.' When we left the mountaintop the warriors stayed behind, still guarding the stones. They looked fiercely proud, defending their religion – the sacred bond with their *rai*, the mountains and land.

Bishop Basilio laughed when I told him the story about the black objects. 'It always rains on these mountains, it has absolutely nothing to do with colours or spirits.' He thought it was funny that I had left my black rain-clothes behind, that I should have taken any notice of something he clearly regarded as a primitive superstition.

He, like other priests in Timor, preached almost every Sunday that the congregation should abandon superstition, their belief in spirits and magic. But many of these practices have remained very much alive. Reasons for many of the age-old customs have been lost in history. However, not only were these practices hard to phase out, complained the bishop, but new manifestations surfaced all the time. Young people in Baucau had started to wrap their crucifixes in small pieces of red cloth. These amulets, they believed, protected them from being killed by any weapon. The bishop found it hard to discuss these things. It is often taboo to discuss the *lulik* of something, even the meaning of the colours in the Timorese national flag. When I asked a student to explain these colours to me he got upset. It would bring un-speakable harm to him and his entire family, he said, and before I could I ask him anything else, he quickly left the room.

For years Christianity in Timor has been grappling for supremacy with other traditions of belief. And, as the bishop recognised, much of its recent resurgence has had as much to do with nationalism as with spirituality. For many, however, it has provided a very complicated form of comfort. Padre Francisco, for example, who had devoted his life to the Church, told me that only independence could really heal East Timor's wounds. When we had been climbing up the mountain, he had told me how his own decision to become a priest had been sparked by the 'miracle' of his survival of bom-bardment. 'It made me think, you know, that I had to do something to deserve this – it was thus I made a vow, that if ever the war would end, I would study to become a priest.' The memories brought sadness to his eyes. When I remarked on this he said firmly: 'It's not all bad, you know. It made me strong and prepared me for my vocation.' He had needed that strength all the more, as the people had needed the Church, when, 'after all, the war never stopped'.

CHAPTER 7

. . . .

Timor's Joan of Arc

§ FOR weeks, I had been looking for Sister Maria de Lourdes. I had been given her name in Jakarta by an Indonesian women's activist, who had worked with her researching violence against women in East Timor. She had recommended I look up Sister de Lourdes, describing her as a 'feminist nun' who had set up a training institute for girls. Maria de Lourdes, she had said, was emancipating the women of Timor. But she had proved hard to track down, and only the day before my planned departure did I meet her by coincidence.

'Sister Maria de Lourdes?' I exclaimed, surprised. 'I've been looking for you!' Apparently sensing my happiness at having found her, she put her arms around me, gave me a tight hug and kissed me on both cheeks. I was taken aback. I had lived for a long time in Asia and was not used to such physical displays of affection.

'Come and stay at my institute,' she said warmly. After talking with her for a few minutes I felt as if I had known her pleasant, open face for some time and wondered if she elicited the same feelings in everybody she met. I would have loved to visit her institute. But my flight ticket expired the next day and I had to leave.

However, the very next morning I met her again. It was six o'clock and I was just about to set out for a last sunrise stroll along the beachfront when I saw her coming into the hotel reception. She was looking for Dan Murphy, a retired American doctor, who had arrived in Timor a few weeks earlier to do volunteer work. One of her girls had fallen on her head and now felt ill. The doctor was already stirring and they left together to see the patient.

When I came back from my walk I found them having breakfast in the garden. I joined them to listen to Maria de Lourdes' story of her life. She was born in Asu Manu, a small village in the mountains of Liquiça. Her family had a *fazenda*. They were reasonably well-off and all the children, four girls and three boys, went to school. When Maria was twelve years old, the war started. Her school closed and Maria started to help an old parish priest. They travelled on foot, climbing from village to village, in the rugged mountains.

She saw how the poor people lived. 'They had no health care, no education, not enough food and clothes and the children were dying of diseases.' When the priest got too old to climb the mountain, she would go alone. The people were always very happy to see her coming. She was cheerful and energetic. 'The villagers liked to listen to me – I'm charismatic,' she said, describing the impact she made without false modesty: charisma was something she saw as bestowed on her to do her work well. Her talents were spotted by the bishop at the time, Dom Martinho. 'He told me that I was destined to be one of Timor's leaders and urged me to continue my studies.'

So in 1985 Maria de Lourdes packed her bags and went to Indonesia to study theology at the Jesuit institute in Yogyakarta on Java. Women cannot become priests in the Catholic Church, so she studied to become a catechist – a religious teacher. There she met Father Tom Jacobs, an old Dutch Jesuit priest. He became her 'guru', her mentor and close friend. On her return to Timor, four years later, she established her own religious order, which she called Maun Alin Iha Kristo, Brothers and Sisters in Christ. She recruited novices – or *aspirantes* as she calls them – from the villages, and built a training institute for young women and girls on her father's coffee plantation in Dare. She had worked hard and her institute had grown. Now, nearly a decade later, she ran, beside the training institute, two orphanages, a couple of boarding houses and a kind of guesthouse for sick people without family in Dili – her 'Sick House', she called it.

Over breakfast she decided to offer Doctor Dan, as she had started calling the doctor, a room with her family in Dili. 'He has come to work for the poor and he should not pay a lot of money for a hotel.' But her spare room was without furniture. She had used the beds to furnish the Sick House; now she had to go to buy some new things.

'Why don't you join me?' she said. 'We could find Father Tom. You can't go before you meet him.' Maria de Lourdes, I would learn, believed strongly in signs and premonitions. Perhaps she was predisposed towards me by the way we met – by coincidence in the back of a car of a mutual acquaintance, and then again in front of the hotel. It also helped, I think, that I am Dutch, like her favourite, Father Tom. She was so persuasive that I felt I could hardly refuse to join her, and before long we were cruising in a taxi looking for him. This, I was to discover, was typical of life in Maria de Lourdes' company.

We finally found Father Tom in the local branch of Gramedia, Indonesia's biggest chain of bookshops. He was selecting religious literature for the library at Maria de Lourdes' institute. He was a tall man of about seventy, with a slightly bent posture, who moved slowly and deliberately around the shop scrutinising the books carefully.

The shop boasted a large selection of popular religious books – Bible studies and comic strips about the lives of Catholic saints – but also a few books on Islam. Apart from religious books there were a tiny selection of general non-fiction, some computer books and Indonesian–English dictionaries. All the books were in Indonesian. No Tetum-language printing, not even a Tetum–Indonesian dictionary, was ever produced. Nor were Portuguese books available. Among the non-fiction books I found a booklet about Nelson Mandela – part of an Indonesian series about Nobel Peace Prize laureates. Two notable omissions from the series were East Timor's own laureates, Bishop Belo (who was actually an Indonesian citizen) and José Ramos Horta.

Father Tom had visited Maria de Lourdes every year since she returned to Timor in 1989. This time he planned to stay for three months. He would be teaching members of Maun Alin Iha Kristo, and also holding 'retreats' for other groups of Catholic nuns and priests. From a lifetime's teaching, he had acquired the habit of speaking slowly and deliberately, stressing words of importance.

During the fifty years he had been teaching at the Jesuit institute in Yogyakarta he had seen many students, but none had made such an impression on him as Maria de Lourdes, or 'Mana Lou', as he called her, using the respectful Timorese form of addressing a woman as well as a religious sister.

'It's a funny story, how I got to know her,' Father Tom grinned. All his students had to write a dissertation. He admitted he found marking these very tiresome. So, one year, he told his students he would look at their work only if they wrote it in a foreign language. 'I didn't think anyone could do this, so I would be free of this chore.' He chuckled conspiratorially. To his surprise one student put her hand up. 'I'll write it in Portuguese,' she said. That was Mana Lou. So Father Tom had to study Portuguese to read her dissertation. 'I was glad I had. She wrote a brilliant thesis.' Mana Lou had based it on South American liberation theology, as applied to the situation in East Timor.[1] On a marking scale of ten, Father Tom gave her a ten-plus, a mark he had never awarded anyone before. 'But she not only had written a brilliant thesis – what *really* impressed me was that she started to put her ideas in practice as soon as she returned to Timor.'

While listening to this story, I looked rather nervously at my watch. I only had two hours left before the plane took off, and still had to pack. Mana Lou was whizzing around the shop selecting some more books and I reluctantly said goodbye to her.

Back in my hotel room I feverishly stuffed my belongings in bags. But Mana Lou's story kept nagging at me. At that time flights with Merpati, one of Indonesia's domestic airlines, never very reliable at the best of times, had started to leave even more erratically. 'Today the flight will go – but after that we don't know,' the man behind the counter had said rather ominously when I made my reservation. If I didn't leave that day, my ticket to Bangkok would expire, but I was too intrigued by Mana Lou.

Here was someone with insights, learned at the grassroots, into Timor's twin curses: poverty and violence. By the standards development agencies use to measure the level of a place's development, East Timor was the poorest and most backward province in Indonesia. Official Indonesian statistics compiled for 1996 showed that life expectancy at birth was just 47 for men and 49 for women. Infant mortality stood at 135 out of every 1,000 live births. The main causes of early death were the diseases of poverty: tuberculosis, malaria and pneumonia. More than half of the population was illiterate.[2]

Mana Lou had put a lot of thought into how best to help improve the lot of her people, and that meant not just doing development work but asking fundamental questions about what was wrong in Timor and how to change it. And she not only aspired to change – so many people do that – she was working at it. I sensed that she might be able to give me insights into some aspects of East Timor that few others could provide. I stayed to find out.

§

Mana Lou's institute was perched on the northern slope of the hills above Dili. She had built it on her father's land in the middle of the *café laran*, the coffee 'forest' and the Reine de Cacao, tall, acacia-type trees, which provided shade for the coffee plants.

The last mile to the institute we walked. The muddy track, shrouded in a cool blue-grey beady mist, led through quiet, dripping, lush plantations with a few small huts scattered among them. When we got closer to the institute we heard soft guitar music and singing and Mana Lou whispered: 'Let's be quiet. They are Indonesian soldiers. They might ask questions if they see you.' The army post, manned by 15 soldiers, was alarmingly close to the foot of the steps that led to the institute. But the soldiers seemed too absorbed in their singing; none came out to inspect. As we climbed the big stepping-stones to the main building the drizzle stopped and the air was full of earthy smells and the chirruping of crickets. A couple of young girls, around nine years old, came running down to greet us. One carried Mana Lou's bag; the other took my hand to guide me through the dark.

'Everything here I built with my own bare hands,' Mana Lou pointed out repeatedly, and almost accusingly, as she showed me around the buildings, two simple airy structures resembling large sheds. She had built them with wood, the hard spines of palm leaves (traditionally used to make walls) and corrugated-iron roofing. 'The hardest work was to prepare the land. We had to terrace the mountain, hacking away giant rocks. At that time the Indonesian soldiers who stayed here helped me a bit. Unlike this lot now.' She nodded to somewhere below us: 'They don't do anything but hang around.'

I followed Mana Lou to the kitchen – a little bamboo shed near the main building. A group of young women was preparing supper. On wood fires stood big pots brimming with mixtures of rice, corn, beans and a mysterious green vegetable. 'Everything we eat we grow ourselves or we find in the forest.' Mana Lou showed me a few young fern shoots, the leaves still curled up. 'The people in the town find this hard to eat because it smells bad – but it is very healthy.'

Everywhere around our feet crawled puppies – so many that I had to be careful not to step on them. Mana Lou said they had tried to keep pigs, but they all died. From Sumatran soldiers, they had learned to eat dog. Now the children sometimes ate one. It was good, she said, for their protein intake, and other meat cost too much.

The dining room was a big airy space with long wooden tables and heavy wooden stools. The tables were covered with plastic cloths and the younger girls – most of them between seven and twelve years old – sat around the longest one; the *aspirantes* – nine young women in their early twenties – sat at the other ones. They spooned their rice and corn from plastic bowls. Mana Lou had her own table, a round one in the corner by the window. We had china plates and better food, I noticed: eggs and special vegetables. As if she could read my thoughts Mana Lou said: 'When I come up here, I come to gain strength and I need sleep and good food.'

The next morning, at six o'clock, I was woken up by soft noises outside my window. A group of little girls was sweeping the grounds around the building and fetching water for my *mandi*. By the time I got up they had gone into the chapel room and the cool morning air quivered with the Latin Christmas carols, which they sang in beautiful clear voices. It was the kind of sound that sends shivers down the spine. Mana Lou was not in the chapel. She was still asleep, said one of the older girls who was preparing breakfast – corn and rice porridge.

Mana Lou did not believe in forcing religion or pious behaviour on her charges. She called herself a 'secular nun' – a bit of a contradiction in terms – but she meant that she lived like the people she worked with. She did not wear a habit, something many Timorese found difficult to understand. Even her trainees were perplexed. They wanted to dress like nuns, which would give them a social standing. But Mana Lou wouldn't hear any of this and told them: 'It's all nonsense. It's the inside that counts, not the outside.'

Mana Lou had her own experience of the established religious orders. Before she went to Yogyakarta she was a novice with the Canossian Daughters of Charity, the same order as the formidable Madre Margarita. 'These orders don't make women grow up. They don't make them strong and self-sufficient,' she said. 'In their hierarchical structures, the women have to listen to a mother superior. This keeps them children.' The nuns in her class in Yogyakarta were much older, but they were still very childish in Mana Lou's eyes. 'My girls are not living in comfortable and clean convents, in which they can escape from society. They live within the community, on the same level as the people.'

Whenever Mana Lou started to talk about the Catholic Church in Timor, she became rather bitter. She had felt very alone during the first years after her return from her studies. She got hardly any support from the other nuns. 'They pray a lot but they don't have a heart. Once I went to them to ask for a bit of food because my children had nothing to eat that night. Their reply was: "O well, that's good for them, just like Saint so and so, this will cleanse them and make them ready for heaven."' She grimaced. 'Can you understand how they can do that? My poor children.'

§

One morning, Mana Lou asked me to give her girls some English lessons. After the little ones had gone off to school and the *aspirantes* had finished their tasks we sat around the table. Some understood a bit of English, others hardly any at all, or were too shy to speak. To break the ice, I decided to start with some simple questions like: How old are you? Where are you from? How many people are there in your family? And so on. When I saw their eyes I couldn't believe my own stupidity. Quite a few of the girls had ended up with Mana Lou precisely because they had no family left.

Like Rosa. Her eyes brimming with tears, she answered that her father and mother were both dead. She had gone into the forest to collect firewood and when she came back to the village she saw that it was surrounded by Indonesian soldiers. They were shooting and she saw how they shot her father and her mother. Shaking with fear she ran back into the forest and hid herself. When she went to the village the next day she found her whole family, including her grandparents and baby brother, lying in the yard in front of the house, all dead. The village with everything in it was burned, the food supplies gone. Rosa searched through the rubble and found a bit of corn and some beans. With this little supply tied in a scarf she went in search of a way to survive. She was eight years old.

It was the time of a military campaign against villages suspected of helping the Falintil guerrillas. Other children besides Rosa had been orphaned, and lived in the forest. After a few weeks Rosa met Maria, who was nine years old, and they became friends. The two little girls travelled through the hills looking for a livelihood. They found some work picking coffee and cocoa. Maria's greatest wish was to go to school, but for that she needed money. So they saved the little money they made on the plantations to pay the fees and enrolled in a primary school. In the afternoons they worked on the plantation, at night they slept in the forest, but in the morning they went to school. With her determination to study, Maria went on to middle school, where she met Mana Lou. She became one of Mana Lou's first *aspirantes*, and Rosa followed later.

3. Mana Lou rehearsing traditional dance with a group of children.

For many of the girls the details of Rosa's and Maria's stories were as new as they were to me. The girls didn't talk much about their pasts. Mana Lou had stopped them. 'We all have our sad stories,' she would say. 'It doesn't help to keep going on about them.'

In the afternoon the girls showed me the garden. On small, terraced fields, they grew tapioca and sweet potatoes. A few of the young girls were busy weeding and raking. Mana Lou's organisation didn't get any subsidies or funding from aid agencies. It survived on a few small private donations, but mainly on what she produced on her land. Near her orphanage in Viqueque, where her family also owned land, she grew rice and corn. Everyone had to work hard; even the smallest girls had their duties. But no one complained; life at home in the villages was much more demanding.

Not all of the girls were orphans: some had one or both parents, but they were too poor to take care of them and many of them would not have had the chance to go to school. Only 66 per cent of the children in Timor went to primary school and only 20 per cent to secondary school.

Higher up on the hill behind the main building grew fruit trees: banana, papaya and mango. Between the trees, on the hillock summit, Mana Lou had constructed what she called a 'meditation garden': a cluster of thatch um-brellas that sheltered tables and stools made out of tree trunks. As we climbed up there, the girls pointed out which plants Mana Lou had told them could be used in traditional medicine. As in many other places in Asia, traditional medical knowledge was handed down orally within the families of healers and shamans. But in Timor, with the total disruption of the village structures and with many families dispersed and some totally wiped out, a lot of this wisdom had been lost. Mana Lou tried to revive it. She collected books on the subject and taught the bits she knew to the girls, who could use it in the villages.

It was all part of Mana Lou's strong belief in self-sufficiency, not only for her institute but also for Timor. She thought that Timor had become too dependent on what she called 'boat rice', subsidised rice imported from Indonesia. 'It made us lazy,' she grumbled. Her idea was not so different from what Fretilin had promoted in 1975: to improve the lives of the villagers with the means available to them. She had no time for development workers, and despised 'projects', with the notion they carry that something lasting can be achieved in a set period of time. From the people who worked with her she expected total dedication: only when they committed their lives to development would change be possible.

§

Mana Lou poured another cup of herbal tea and spooned sugar into it. Through the chicken wire that spanned the glassless window frame of the dining room we could see Dili lying stretched out along the sea like a long thin lizard, basking in the sun. It was Sunday and Father Tom had arrived with boxes full of books. He had started to study Tetum three weeks ago, and was now preparing his first Tetum sermon for tonight's mass. He was impatiently waiting for the girls, due to come back from their villages for a retreat. Mana Lou and Father Tom bickered a bit about it. He was irritated about the lack of organisation and she was defending herself: 'We have no transport, no communications; it'll take the girls days to walk here.'

I had now lived with Mana Lou for a week and tried to understand how she worked. This was not easy. I could not really see what she actually *did*. Not that she was idle. She spent her days in Dare whirling around, doing whatever task came her way. Sometimes she would give the girls religious instruction, or rehearse songs and dances with the children (she had written 15 songs of her own, mainly about unity and reconciliation) or lead the evening prayers. It looked rather chaotic and unfocused. But to understand Mana Lou better, I had to understand what motivated her. When she spoke, she reverted to the same themes again and again: the need for national unity; the loss of culture; the lack of shared moral values and of a sense of good and evil. She was always eager to talk about her ideas. But, mainly because of language difficulties, I could not always follow her.

That morning I tried, with the help of Father Tom, to clear up some of my confusion. Mana Lou's inspiration, he explained, lay in liberation theology.

Liberation theology grew out of Christian communities in Latin American in the 1970s and 1980s. Its adherents, some also known as the 'Church of the Poor', encouraged people to challenge the sources of social injustice and to work together for change, to establish the Kingdom of Heaven here on earth. Influenced by the Brazilian educator Paolo Freire, they saw their pastoral task of evangelisation as 'education for liberation'. Church leaders in the Congregation for the Doctrine of the Faith, the Vatican's doctrinal watchdog, felt threatened by this seemingly 'left-wing' interpretation of the Bible, and Pope John Paul II, from anti-communist Poland, criticised it openly, castigating some of its more prominent clerical advocates, such as the Cardenal brothers, who served in the Sandinista government in Nicaragua, as too politically engaged.

Mana Lou stood above this theological debate in the Church. Her conviction, she said, had grown out of her *own* experiences. She believed Timor – as a colonised country – had lost touch with its own identity. The impression some foreign observers had, that it was already a nation and now only had to become a country, could not, in Mana Lou's eyes, be more wrong. 'People know who they are definitely not: Indonesians. But we don't really know who we are.' The roots of this identity problem, she said, went back to the Portuguese time.

On the surface the Portuguese had, at least compared with North European colonisers, lived in greater racial harmony with the indigenous population. But, however jolly and affectionate the Portuguese liked to be with a tiny minority of educated natives and those of mixed blood, the distinctions they made were profound and divisive. This made their system in practice as bad as apartheid – or even worse, according to some who lived under it.

The Portuguese had introduced a racial and cultural hierarchy. The white Portuguese, the superior race, stood at the top of the power pyramid. The *mestiços* came second, followed by the so-called *assimilados*, Timorese who could speak Portuguese and had adopted the Catholic faith and European mores. Somewhere at the bottom were the Timorese masses, the uneducated peasants, despised by the Portuguese and, often, by the *mestiços* and *assimilados* as well.

The constitutional rights of the people in Timor depended on the degree of 'assimilation'. Only the children of the ruling class of *liurais* and *datos*, who had often been integrated as *chefe de suco*, village administrators, and of some *assimilado* families were allowed to go to state schools. The Portuguese wanted to use them as local administrators and civil servants. They wanted to mould the local elite according to their own ideas of civilisation and patriotic duty. The rest could only get education at one of the few schools run by Catholic missionaries. Not surprisingly, fewer than 10 per cent of the children went to school.

Census figures from 1950 showed that there were 568 Europeans in East

Timor, 2,022 *mestiços*, 3,128 Chinese and 212 other non-indigenous people. Of the indigenous people the Portuguese had classed just 1,541 as *assimilado* or 'civilised' and the rest – 434,907 people – as 'uncivilised' and ineligible for citizenship. Adult illiteracy was estimated between 95 and 99 per cent.[3]

'A colonised nation does not develop,' said Mana Lou. This was especially true for the Timorese under Portuguese colonial rule. After ruling Timor as a colony for more than four hundred years, Portugal left it unprepared for nationhood. Not only had it failed to build paved roads and schools to educate enough people, it had also robbed the country of its culture and self-respect. The Timorese had, according to Mana Lou, lost their spiritual identity, their feeling of self-esteem. This is why they are so easily used, by all sides, as pawns to fight one another. The Portuguese walked around as a superior race. 'At school we had to learn everything about Portugal and its colonies. We thought Portugal was the world and the world was Portugal.' Mana Lou didn't know anything about Indonesia. When the soldiers came in 1975 and told her they were from Java she didn't even know where it was, let alone that it was in Indonesia. 'The Portuguese', she concluded, 'deliberately kept us ignorant.'

Education alone was not enough to give the Timorese back their identity. People need first to feel better about themselves, before they will even be able to start thinking about education. And, even then, education needs to be of the right sort. The only way to restore their spirituality, Mana Lou believed, was to live with them, on an equal level. 'Respect is too often based on fear in Timor. It's part of our colonial heritage. And that is why it is not good to come from the towns, with piles of books and loads of knowledge and tell the people in the villages what to do. My girls teach through giving them an example. The people have to become stronger and learn to work together. The schools only teach them reading and writing – no culture or morality. And the priests don't prepare the people either.'

Father Tom agreed. To have religion purely in the hands of the priests, he said, takes all initiative away from lay-people. The key was how to motivate the people by creating a group of engaged people – that, he said, was the basis of her secular institute. 'It won't come from the Church. For the Church, her ideas and institute are revolutionary. She wants to get rid of the separation between religious life and everyday existence, to integrate spirituality into daily life. She translates that in turn into social and economic development. The future of the Christian faith lies here, not in the Church. This is a historical fact.'

On her return to Timor in 1989, Mana Lou fought a hard battle with the male-dominated Catholic clergy. She was even threatened with excommunication. Father Tom remembered how he went with Mana Lou to see Bishop Belo. He saw that the bishop had no clue what Mana Lou was talking about.

'I don't think he was even listening; he clearly had no interest in what she wanted to do and, like the other clergy, he was suspicious.'

Mana Lou needed the permission of the Vatican, through its representative Bishop Belo, to set up her own order. She tried many times to submit the necessary documents, but every time she found the bishop too busy to receive her. Finally she handed them to his assistant. 'He took them from me and slapped me around the head with them and said: "We don't want women behaving like priests here." I began to cry and breathe very oddly.' Mana Lou acted out what looked like hyper-ventilation. 'I was so angry. I told him: "If you want to kill me you are going the right way about it!" He then put his arm around her and promised to read her papers. But it was only in early 1998 that the bishop recognised her religious order (on a trial basis – *ad experimentum*, in formal terms). This history still rankled with Father Tom. 'Now the bishop sees that she is getting more influence and has been successful and active in many areas, he is supporting her.'

More evidence of Mana Lou's fraught relationship with the local ecclesiastical authorities hung on the wall of the institute in the form of an innocuous-looking photograph, showing a middle-aged Australian woman meeting the Pope. Once, when Bishop Belo had been going to Rome and was to have an audience with the Pontiff, Mana Lou had given him a letter to deliver, asking for a papal blessing. When the bishop came back, so did the letter – unopened. The bishop said he had forgotten about it. So Mana Lou had tried again, through the mother of a friend, and, this time, her institute had secured the blessing.

As Mana Lou and Father Tom were talking, we were keeping an eye out for the *aspirantes*. I was looking along the muddy track. There were no cars, not even motorbikes, and only a few families had passed on foot on their way back from mass, their brightly coloured Sunday clothes sparkling between the leafy trees. Suddenly the silence was broken by the sound of a heavy engine. A flatbed truck rumbled along the road and stopped in front of the lower building. A dozen adults and a child climbed from the back. Had the girls come back, or were these visitors? Mana Lou went down and I saw her guiding the people to the dormitory building. When she came back up she had the group in tow. She introduced them as Falintil guerrillas, who had come to ask her to teach their children.

Mana Lou already had one Falintil child, Anakela. Her mother had brought her to nuns in Dili. When Mana Lou visited the sisters, Anakela, who was a headstrong two-year-old, chose not to leave her side and Mana Lou took her back to the institute. In the first few weeks Anakela ran around singing Falintil songs, making everyone nervous about the trouble this might cause with the Indonesian soldiers so close by. But this was the first time Falintil soldiers had visited the institute, and the girls were watching them with open-mouthed curiosity. For many in Timor, Falintil was almost a mystical force, often spoken about in whispers.

Their leaders seemed to be two young men, one with long curly hair and a wispy beard wearing a black T-shirt emblazoned with a skull, the other clean-shaven, with short hair and a striped T-shirt. They sat at the small round table with Mana Lou and Father Tom. The atmosphere around the table was tense. Mana Lou and the Falintil soldiers – the one in the striped T-shirt was a political officer – engaged in a lively discussion. I could see by the way she smiled that she was annoyed.

'I'm not collecting figures for human-rights organisations,' she said. 'That's their responsibility. It's easy to collect some numbers – my task is to prepare the ground for a new Timor. And I want to help the poor people.'

'So do we,' replied the man in the striped T-shirt.

'But you don't,' she said. 'You confront and confuse, and as a result the population suffers. You are only busy with politics. You'll have to work on unity.'

The man in the skull T-shirt straightened his back. 'We want to liberate our land from the Indonesians first, after that we'll think about the needs for the future,' he said.

The only thing they agreed on was that, at the moment, the CNRT was doing nothing but talk. The Falintil men craved action. They wanted to take revenge on Timorese who collaborated and worked as informants and asked Mana Lou's opinion. She bristled. 'You only think about violence and more violence. There are other ways than the way of the gun.' The men had clearly filled Mana Lou with contempt and she was not shy about showing this.

I noticed how quiet it was elsewhere in the room. Everyone was following the discussion intensely. '*Mana*, do you have any problems with the soldiers at the army post?' the skull T-shirt asked when we finished our lunch. 'If so we could attack it and burn it down.' Mana Lou recoiled. 'What about me and the children? We live here and they will take revenge on us.'

At the end of lunch Mana Lou raised herself to say grace. She prayed for peace, reconciliation and unity and I saw that her cheeks were wet with tears. Everybody stood tense and rigid, until, half-embarrassed, she busied herself with piling up the dishes in a tension-breaking clatter. After the group had left Mana Lou was still fuming. 'They came to ask my opinion, but they did not really listen.'

§

One morning, Mana Lou was in a hurry to get to a meeting in Dili, when an elderly woman walked through the door. 'Bom Dia, Tia Fernanda!' cried the girls and rushed over to kiss her hand. 'It's my mother,' explained Mana Lou, and led her to our table. Tia Fernanda was a scrawny woman somewhere in her sixties. Although she had walked for more than two hours over mountain paths to get here, she showed no signs of fatigue; on the contrary, she seemed full of beans. After a quick cup of coffee, she jumped up again to walk over to her husband's house, near to the institute. Ten minutes later she was back again. This time she was crying. 'O dear, she had a fight with my father,' sighed Mana Lou. She hugged her mother dutifully but I noticed her face clouding over wearily.

'What happened?' I asked Mana Lou later, as we walked down the muddy track to catch a *bemo* to Dili. Her brows furrowed. Her father and mother had lived apart for more than ten years, she said. Her mother lived in Viqueque, where she was in charge of the plantations, while her father managed the land here. 'I remember when our family was still united. My father and mother formed a good team. They are both strong people.' Mana Lou's father had an open mind for new ideas; he liked to invest in new technologies and was interested in new political developments. Their coffee business thrived and her home was a happy one. Then it all went wrong. Looking back she saw that politics had somehow drifted into the family, that 'what divided Timorese society also divided my family'.

Her mother came from a family rooted in strong traditions. They had alliances with the UDT and Apodeti. 'Her brothers were against my father's ideas and also jealous of his success. They tried to split him and my mother up.' Mana Lou's mother took their side and conspired with them to get her father locked up in jail. 'Only my younger brothers stayed with her. They were too small to understand what had happened. I and my older sisters and brothers chose to stay with my father.'

It was her own family's troubled history, Mana Lou said that explained her vocation. She was a driven, inspired, and, for some, a maddening figure. Doctor Murphy, who had moved into one of her family's houses in Dili, called her affectionately 'East Timor's Joan of Arc', with the difference, he added, that Mana Lou is 'not mad, but ambitious to be the best in working for the poorest of the poor'. But I also heard people compare her ambition to that of Mother Teresa. Usually, they did not mean this as a compliment.

The origins of Mana Lou's zeal, I realised, lay in her conviction – one held by so many Timorese – that the personal was political. When her parents parted, she had, like many children of divorced parents, felt that she had failed. 'I wanted so much to unite my family but I couldn't. It was then I made the vow. "God," I pledged, "if You look after my family and unite them I'll devote my life to uniting the people of East Timor."'

I noticed Mana Lou's eyes had filled with tears as she told the story. Impatiently she pulled a handkerchief out of her pocket. 'Sorry,' she said, and blew her nose. 'I cry a lot. Crying makes me feel stronger. First I cry, then I fight.'

CHAPTER 8

· ·

The Crocodile Bares its Teeth

§ ONE day in October 1998 a crocodile appeared in the sea off Areia Branca, Dili's 'White Beach'. It appeared at the far east end of the bay, just beneath the headland topped by the big statue of Christ that overlooks the sea and the capital. It was the first time in years that one had been spotted so near the capital. The crocodile did not stay between the rocks, but came to Lecidere, where an Australian journalist saw it clambering about on the polluted beach near the Turismo.

News of the sighting spread quickly. Crocodiles play an important role in Timor's folklore. In the island's creation myth a little boy saves a young crocodile from certain death. In gratitude, the crocodile promises to make sure no harm is done to the boy by other crocodiles, and the two become good friends. For many years they swim and play together in the sea, the boy often riding on the crocodile's back. Then one day the crocodile, who has grown big and strong, feels a powerful urge to eat the boy. He asks advice from other animals. They tell him it would be evil to kill the person who saved his life, and the crocodile overcomes his consuming passion. When he grows old and knows he will die soon, he wants to repay the boy for his kindness. He swims to an empty space in the sea, and upon his death, his body slowly transforms itself into a large island for the boy and his descendants to live on.[1] With a bit of imagination, the island of Timor does look like a crocodile, with its head in Kupang in the West, its body in the wider central part, where the mountain ranges resemble a spiky spine, and a tail stretching out to Lautem in the East. All over Timor the crocodile appears as a recurrent motif in art and handicrafts, in ornamental carvings over the doorways of *uma lulik*, as well as on totems and woven into *ikat* cloth.

Old people in Timor still call the crocodile their ancestor. When they cross an estuary where crocodiles live they shout: 'Crocodile, Crocodile, I'm your grandchild, do not eat me!' In some parts of Timor, people take the precaution of tying a young palm leaf around their hands, legs or head, and bring a dog as an offering, so that the crocodiles will not harm them. If someone is attacked and killed by a crocodile anyway, it is believed that this person must have committed such great evil that the ancestors placed a curse on him.

The crocodiles in Timor are sea-going and live mainly in and around the broad river estuaries on the south coast. The only one I had ever seen lived in captivity, in the backyard of the Motael church: a 7-metres-long, greyish specimen imprisoned in a cage so small that it could not turn around and, as far as I could see, it spent its time in a comatose sleep. Now that one should be seen so close to the capital was taken by many as an ominous sign and added to the general mood of uneasiness. There was a feeling that great changes were in the offing.

Oddly for an island people, Timorese in general do not venture into the sea much. They seem to have an innate fear of it, although once upon a time their ancestors must have overcome this, perhaps when compelled by even more frightful circumstances to cross the high seas in their canoes to reach Timor. Once they arrived, most settled on higher ground. Even today, the sea is not part of daily life and fishing boats and canoes are few and far between. On Sundays, when families picnic on Areia Branca, only the children play in the sea. The only Timorese I knew who went swimming every day was Sebastião, who persisted in this habit even after the crocodile had appeared.

Sebastião himself brought news that seemed to justify the sense of foreboding. One evening he bolted into the Turismo looking agitated. 'It is getting worse every day!' he blurted out. 'I would like to take a gun and shoot them all!' He seemed exasperated at his own powerlessness. Almost daily, news reached Dili of killings in the countryside. The Justice and Peace Commission, a human rights group linked to the Catholic Church, had recorded a near-doubling in human rights violations over the previous year. Reports of killings and torture had tripled. Most of the victims were young supporters of the independence movement but, in some places, those killed included Timorese soldiers who worked for the Indonesian army as spies or informants.

That evening, Sebastião had just heard about a large-scale Indonesian military operation against the population of Manufahi, a regency south of Dili. In Manufahi it seemed to have started with the killing of soldiers. He had been brooding about who might be behind the murders. No one doubted that the army was involved in the killing of independence supporters. But who was killing the soldiers and spies? It all looked a bit more murky and complex than just another story of Indonesian oppression. I had heard some of the students suggest that Indonesian intelligence officers were killing their own informants to prevent them from defecting and revealing secret information. Others spoke of reprisals carried out by the resistance against collaborators and spies. I had to think of the meeting I had witnessed at Mana Lou's institute. The Falintil group that had visited her had talked about getting rid of the worst collaborators and killers.

Bishop Basilio had told me of a worrying recent development. In the past, when people came to tell him about a father or brother who had been murdered, they often knew exactly who was responsible, down to the name of the soldier and the number of his company. But now they would say they knew who did it but were afraid to tell, for fear of being killed. 'I know then', Bishop Basilio concluded, 'that they are talking about Timorese people.'

But who were these Timorese? Even the bishop had whispered when he talked about it and had asked me not to write about it in a news story. Was Falintil involved? Or were there other groups? What were the reasons? Perhaps some of the killings had something to do with ancient family feuds. I had heard many times from Timorese that their compatriots had long memories and that feuds could be carried over from one generation to the next.

Around the time the crocodile appeared most Timorese leaders were in Dare attending a reconciliation meeting organised by Bishop Belo and Bishop Basilio. Dare was a fitting place, since so many of the leading figures had gone to school there with the Jesuits. Representatives of the different factions met each other for the first time in year. But afterwards Padre Jovito was even gloomier than he had been in July. The meeting had led to nothing, he said: 'They just made small talk, and exchanged stories about their time at school together.' The older generation of leaders had deeply disappointed him, he said. 'They have not learned the lesson of the past.' 'Our dreams', he concluded, 'fade away like dust in the wind.' He also complained that the faction leaders were setting a bad example for young people. One of the Fretilin leaders, he said, had asked a group of youths to beat up another CNRT leader.

§

The chain of events that had triggered Sebastião's outrage that night had been going on for weeks, after starting in Weberek, a village in the regency of Manufahi. Indonesian army spies had tried to infiltrate a meeting between the local resistance, Falintil and students. Of the four men, three soldiers and a civilian, one managed to escape. The others were found dead the next morning. A week later, Falintil overran an army post in Alas, just across the mountains from Weberek. They killed three soldiers and seized 36 M16 rifles and some ammunition. They took twelve soldiers with them. All of them were ethnic Timorese.

The Indonesian army immediately sealed the area and launched a massive operation to track down the guerrillas. They retaliated against Alas' population by burning 36 houses, killing a village chief and taking the rest of the villagers hostage. The local church had become a refuge for the women, children and elderly who could not, as young people did, escape to the mountains. A militia group, a rag-tag band of men in red-and-white headbands, armed with rifles and home-made guns, had taken over the village and would not allow aid to be distributed.

Together with two colleagues, I had tried to enter the area as a tourist. Although the military let us pass through its road-blocks, it still proved impossible to reach the remote village. The dirt track through the large Suharto-owned sugar plantations that sprawled along the south coast had been transformed into deep, oozing mud. Evidence of tension was everywhere. In eerie, empty villages, full of abandoned houses, we found a few terrified people, who confirmed that all the young people and well-known supporters of independence had fled the area. Many of the young people had gone up to the mountains to join Falintil. Others had taken shelter in the Catholic church at Same.

The priest there, a middle-aged Timorese who had returned from Portugal a few years earlier, had little sympathy for the young independence activists. They reminded him too much of the radical students who had returned from Portugal in 1974 and 'sown confusion and unrest'. Since the students had conducted their dialogues in Manufahi the situation had become unbearable, he said. 'The dialogues had stirred up hatred.' Shops owned by Indonesians were looted and a few had been burned down. Collaborators had received death threats and Javanese schoolteachers were beaten up by their pupils. The priest said the military had showed great restraint, but that after their own people were killed, they had been provoked into action.

On my way back to Dili I met one of the Javanese high school teachers the priest had spoken of. He was on his way to the ferry, he said, because he had become too afraid to teach. He was not the only one who left. In the autumn of 1998 Timor saw an exodus of teachers, doctors and many other Indonesians – about thirty thousand of them, crowding the ferries that would take them back home.

After the attack in Alas, terrified villagers started arriving in Dili with stories of murder. A human rights activist from Same showed me gruesome photographs of the mutilated body of a young man, half-buried in the ground. The events in Alas were fast becoming an international issue. Bishop Belo had declared that more than fifty, perhaps more than a hundred people had been killed. The tripartite talks at the UN in New York had been put on hold by the Portuguese delegation.

It was a mess. Estimates of the numbers killed and disappeared put out by local and international human rights organisations varied from day to day until, eventually, the International Committee of the Red Cross (ICRC) was given access to the area. But even before its visit, the ICRC published what was for it a rare press release. In a statement from its headquarters in Geneva, it said that only four people had died in Alas: three TNI soldiers and one local village chief. The tripartite talks resumed; the story died in the press.[2] The

ICRC press release had infuriated the armed resistance. Falintil announced that, as far as they were concerned, the ICRC was no longer welcome in Timor. The ICRC had not been able to visit Alas until *after* the controversial press release, and only a week later did it update the figures – to nine killed, and seven detained. Aniceto Guterres, the director of Yayasan Hak, an organisation of human rights lawyers in Dili, said that the young people who had been captured had been badly tortured and the women had been raped. Even so, this hardly amounted to a massacre and the world press did not reopen the issue, but kept silent.

At the time, the story remained extremely murky. Only in retrospect did it become clear that what had happened in Alas represented the first clear sign of the build-up and arming of local militias. It was also the first and only big clash between Falintil and units of the Indonesian army responsible for arming these groups.

§

These events in Alas signalled the prelude to a militia movement that would later devastate the whole of East Timor. Paramilitary groups were not new phenomena. The Indonesians, like the Portuguese before them, made use of deep-rooted local rivalries, or, if necessary, created some themselves. Timorese were forced to take up arms, or, in some instances, because of these old hatreds, had done so willingly.

According to Indonesia's Defence Act,[3] the whole population shared responsibility for defence and security. Those not active in the armed forces were organised in militias and emergency services, commonly known as Civil Defence (Forces). Hansip, Kamra and Wanra were auxiliary forces that had been set up in East Timor in 1975 by the Indonesian military. One of their nicknames in Timor was the 'three-months army', referring to the three months' training new recruits received in Java.

The civil defence force was designed according to a military model: one militia section in every village, one platoon in each sub-district. Often these auxiliary troops were made up of East Timorese, retired soldiers, serving army men, and local thugs. In the autumn of 1998 Jakarta decided to train and arm more civilians, in response to the rapidly deteriorating security situation in the archipelago. These groups were called PAM Swakarsa or 'community self-defence groups'. The idea had met with fierce opposition from Indonesian human rights organisations. They saw the obvious danger that these groups would be used against the population, as they had been in the past.

The recruitment drive coincided with a resurgence of even more shadowy militia groups. A few were still active – the Indonesian military in Timor under Prabowo had used them for the notorious *ninja* attacks in the nineties

– but others lay semi-dormant until the summer of 1998, when the Indonesians rekindled them; yet others were new creations. The build-up of these forces corresponded in detail with the scheme mentioned in the minutes Felis had been so excited about when he showed them to me a few months earlier.

East Timor would soon experience the consequences. By November 1998 at least eleven militias had become operational.[4] Three of the core groups occupied the border regencies of Kovalima and Bobonaru and the strategically important regency of Liquiça. From here they could monitor and control the movement of the population to and from West Timor. Their power bases, in these rich coffee-growing areas, would also become essential to integrationists for their plan to secede and join Indonesia.

Apart from being a transmigration area, Alas was also the easternmost point on an imaginary 'borderline' pro-Indonesian factions seemed to have drawn. Everything west of it, they would later declare, should secede and integrate with Indonesia, if East Timor opted for independence. So it was probably not a coincidence that the latest tension had broken out here, in this isolated area close to Falintil's stamping-ground.

The heads of the local authorities, the *bupatis*, were often the informal leaders of the militias, or were in cahoots with them, protecting and supporting them with money and a 'licence to kill'. Soon, all over Timor, the Indonesian army would distribute arms: automatic rifles, other guns and hand-grenades.

§

In a parallel development, the resistance, which had operated underground in Timor for years, had come above ground. It floated like an iceberg with most of its network still invisible. The tip of the iceberg was the newly opened CNRT headquarters in Dili. Its spacious white villa on Balide had no signs identifying it as CNRT headquarters and from the flagpole on the front lawn hung not the blue-white-and-green CNRT flag, but the Indonesian red-and-white. Only inside did small notes on the doors betray it as the seat of a shadow government. Behind doors labelled health, social affairs, finance and coordination were small, spartan offices, in which CNRT representatives would gather to discuss blueprints of government departments for a future, independent, East Timor. Many of them were civil servants who worked for similar departments within the Indonesian administration, an issue that would come to provoke Indonesia's anger.

These developments were mirrored in the countryside, where CNRT offices sprang up in all the districts. In some places, such as Ermera and Liquiça, almost all civil servants supported independence from Indonesia, and this was reflected in the way they interpreted the law and enforced Indonesian rule.

The Indonesians, of course, did not recognise the organisation, which was

4. Student activists Tata Pires and Elisa da Silva at a demonstration in Dili.

still illegal. But for the time being nobody seemed to threaten the office. There was not even much security at the gate, which often stood open. Only a few old guards sat in the small outhouses hidden behind the main building. Some of the students who had been in jail recognised them, to their horror, as former prison guards.

It was odd to see this supposedly clandestine organisation functioning so openly. It robbed the resistance of its mystique. But scenes inside the building did something to compensate for this, and the atmosphere in the villa was still that of twilight secrecy. Like moles blinking against the light, people shuffled through the dim corridors. Some I knew by name: Father 'Maubere' Domingos Soares, whom I found behind a desk in the coordination office, his cross discreetly concealed in his breast pocket; David Dias Ximenes, a Fretilin leader who had been freed after serving a long jail sentence in Cipinang, stalking around with an air that exuded authority; João Alves, a civil servant with the water board, who I knew had ferried journalists from Falintil 'camps' to the relative safety of Kupang airport.

The atmosphere was not exactly buzzing. In truth, it was hard to detect that much of anything was going on – let alone what that might be. At that stage, the CNRT did not pay much attention to its relations with the press. Journalists would drift in and out of the building, not knowing whom to ask what, or where to get their information. Even on the occasions when press briefings had been scheduled, the few journalists who turned up would be met by the friendly but slightly startled faces of people who had no idea what was going on. We would often wait in vain for someone to show up to give us some information.

§

One morning in December I found Elisa, Tata and other women from the student organisation on the roof of the DPR, the provincial parliament building. Tata's silhouette looked thin and fragile against the stark midday sun but her voice sounded strong and unwavering through the megaphone. 'We have to demand justice!' she shouted. 'In this time of *reformasi*, the government should be accountable for its deeds.'

This was the third time in a month that the students had occupied the building to protest, and to demand a meeting with local government officials. They saw in the killings in Alas an opportunity to test the limits of *reformasi*. Besides the call for an enquiry into the killings, and the prosecution of the soldiers responsible, they also called for the withdrawal of the Indonesian troops from East Timor. After they waited in vain for the governor to come to talk to them they took the demonstration to the governor's palace, where at one point a group of hotheads (or possibly *agents provocateurs*) had tried to take the Indonesian flag from its pole.

This was a dangerous move that could have led to a violent confrontation. Sebastião, who had just returned from negotiations with the governor, tried to cool tempers, but calm only returned after the formidable Madre Margarita, who was quickly brought over, raised her hands and made everyone kneel down in prayer.

The governor finally agreed to investigate what happened in Alas and to dispatch a joint investigation team of police and pro-independence people. But when a delegation of students and CNRT members got as far as Same, they were attacked and shot at, and had to return before they could reach Alas.

Felis had watched the protest rallies from the sidelines. It seemed that he had demonstratively turned his back on politics. He had fallen out with the Students' Solidarity Council and took no part in the demonstrations. He had found a job as a translator and with the money he earned had bought flashy clothes: a white silky shirt and trousers, a black belt and shiny black shoes. Dressed in this spotless fashion, he would watch from his perch on his glossy motorbike, wrapped, as in a protective cloak, in an air of boredom and indifference. Bobby had left him a mobile telephone that he would carry demonstratively everywhere he went. Everything about him seemed to scream: 'I don't belong here.'

His father, Matias Gouveia Duarte, had recently been released from prison. As soon as he was free he started climbing on to rooftops to make speeches. He danced in front of the microphone, loving to perform and clown around.

Like Felis, he seemed to glow when he was the centre of attention. His passionate speeches attracted a big audience, who would greet them with laughter and applause. Felis watched him with a mixture of embarrassment, pride and anger. It upset him that his father had chosen politics over the family. His public exposure could easily land him in trouble again, and Felis thought his father owed it to his family to be with them for a while. Felis had good reason to worry: his father's speeches carried a radical message. Since Timor had already declared independence in 1975, he argued, a referendum about the issue would be redundant. The only thing they needed was the restoration of the independence that, historically, was theirs already.

It was a controversial argument. Independence had been declared on 28 November 1975, in front of the governor's palace, by Fretilin. The other parties in the CNRT did not recognise that declaration of independence, nor the flag Fretilin raised that day.

From his jail cell in Jakarta, Xanana had requested people not to commemorate the anniversary of the independence declaration, since this would only stir up old divisions between Timorese themselves. But a group of students had different ideas. They supported Matias's position. The cracks in the student movement, which had been apparent for some time, widened into a formal split on 28 November, the 23rd anniversary of the declaration. The students held their ceremony in the indoor sports hall behind the governor's palace. They had made a little 'altar', decorated with pictures of the independence ceremony in 1975, and of their hero Nicolau Lobato, and they sang 'O Foho Ramelau' until they all had tears in their eyes. In front of CNRT and the other political leaders they had invited, they declared themselves as pro-independence activists.

I looked for Tata and João but they weren't there. Later, Tata would tell me she had decided to stay loyal to the apolitical ideals of her women's group. Her goal was independence; but she thought this should be reached through a referendum.

But among the students wiping their eyes with big white handkerchiefs stood Sebastião.

§

I had been looking for Sebastião. For some time I had been talking to him about a visit to Falintil, and was anxious to pin him down. He was planning to join Falintil for what sounded like a kind of 'military service' after he finished university in December. It was something he was looking forward to with mixed feelings. He saw it as a family duty: both his father and his uncle were Falintil veterans. Although Sebastião's father had surrendered in 1979, and had worked as a driver for the local *intel* chief, he had continued to work for the underground movement as the leader of a cell in his neighbourhood.

For Sebastião, serving some time with the fighters was expected of him. But he wasn't sure what his role there would be.

When I had met Sebastião a few months earlier he had hinted he had been assigned to do what you could call 'press relations' work for the resistance. 'When I see journalists I always go up to them so I make sure they get the right story.' But it seemed he not only looked after the press; he also raised funds.

Sebastião would be handed elaborate shopping lists. Often the requests were for medicines. A couple of times, when a new list had reached his family and Sebastião had helped me out with some translation work, he would tell me that he used the translation fee to buy malaria pills or other items on the list. His family did not have enough money, and if they failed to deliver there could be trouble – what kind of trouble, he did not want to go into.

When foreign journalists wanted to visit Falintil, Sebastião would receive more elaborate lists. The items could vary from video-tapes and medicines to sums of cash or a Polaroid camera. In return for their largesse, journalists would be granted a meeting with Commander Lere Anan Timor. Some journalists played along, but I took part in heated discussions about the practice. I had no objection to bringing some medicine or food, I said, but did not want to pay money for an interview. Usually, Sebastião would simply end all our debates with: 'These are the rules.'

This time he tried a change of tack: 'You will have to promise to write something positive about them, and absolutely don't ask after details like how many soldiers or weapons Falintil has.' I was not too bothered about the second part of the request – all armies are secretive about numbers – but I did object to the first condition. I told him that as a journalist it was impossible for me to make that promise. Sebastião sighed and looked at his hands. 'You don't understand,' he sighed, 'they will kill me.'

My first thought was that he exaggerated. Falintil, I had been told, had the respect of the people and, unlike many other guerrilla groups around the world, had been consistent in not killing civilians. Then a remark of Mana Lou sprang to mind: 'Respect in Timor is always based on fear, not on admiration.'

'Remember the story of my cousin?' Sebastião said when he looked up from his hands. I remembered that, months ago, he had mentioned something about a cousin who just got married and was killed at his home together with his young wife. 'You know by whom?' he said, as if it would be a bad omen to speak the name of the killers out loud. When I had heard the story for the first time I had automatically attributed the killing to the *ninjas*, the feared death squads that moved around in the night killing independence activists at their homes. 'No, no, it was Falintil,' Sebastião whispered now.

§

Two weeks later I saw the students in action again. A UN official had arrived from New York to prepare for the visit of Jamsheed Marker, the special representative of the UN secretary-general. Sebastião, João and others had been invited for a consultation.

For some time, the Timorese resistance had been asking to be included in the talks held under the auspices of the UN in New York. They felt that decisions about their future could not be taken over their heads. But these requests had been ignored. Indonesia didn't recognise the CNRT as an organisation that represented the Timorese, whom it did not want at the talks.

The students and the Timorese resistance suspected that the UN, and to a lesser extent Portugal, were leaning towards accepting an Indonesian proposal, under which Timor would get a special status within Indonesia and wide-ranging autonomy. This, Indonesia said, would represent a compromise solution between those who wanted independence and those who insisted that East Timor should remain integrated with Indonesia. Up to now the UN had maintained that there could be no solution without a consultation of the Timorese, but many in East Timor were suspicious about their real intentions.

There had been many rumours. Falintil, went one, had plans to kidnap the UN envoys. The Indonesians were very nervous and didn't want the UN delegation to stay in the Turismo Hotel. In this charged atmosphere the UN envoy met one evening with the students and Forsarepetil, in the garden of the Turismo hotel. There were no women among them. It was after 9 p.m., too late for them to leave their homes.

The pro-independence groups were convinced things were moving their way, and some had made it clear to the envoy that they did not see why there was a need to look for a political solution. 'Just give us independence now,' they had argued. Autonomy was not something they even wanted to contemplate. Since the Indonesian occupation was illegal anyway, what was the point of a referendum?

But the majority view was the one the CNRM had spelled out as early as 1989 and I had heard articulated by Padre Jovito: they needed time. In five or ten years of special autonomy within Indonesia, and after the withdrawal of the Indonesian army, they thought they could sort themselves out. After this period they would be ready for a referendum in which they could make a well-informed choice about their future status.

This request was labelled by the UN as unrealistic. The Indonesians would not continue to subsidise East Timor if there was a risk that they would, eventually, choose independence. As the meetings drew to a close, I heard a young representative from the Indonesian foreign office, who accompanied the UN negotiator and pretended to work for him, haughtily accuse the Timorese of violating human rights. After all, he said, those who died in Alas were Indonesian soldiers. Then he pointed around the dimly lit garden. 'If

Indonesia left, you would not have electricity,' he told a member of Forsare-petil, who replied laconically: 'We lived hundreds of years without you and we survived, we'll survive without you again.'

Sebastião was at least satisfied that the students had been able to make their point. But the UN representative would later note that he had found the meeting frightening. His meeting with the resistance groups ran counter to Ali Alatas's advice and he found the students and CNRT members he talked to aggressive, arrogant and impatient. It seemed to him that the newly re-cruited members, who used to be pro-integration and had openly switched sides, such as Manuel Carrascalão, felt the need to prove themselves, and so were even more outspoken, radical and critical.

From the other side – government officials and pro-integration leaders such as Abilio Soares and Armindo Mariano – the UN heard that they had become victims of intimidation and attacks. Similar complaints came from some people in the villages, and from ethnic Chinese residents, about the CNRT's and Falintil's involvement in protection rackets. People were asked to contribute towards the CNRT but, in some places, saw that its leaders put the money in their own pockets.

All of this did not bode well for the UN. On 20 December, during the visit by Jamsheed Marker himself, I stopped on my way to the airport to say goodbye to the students. They had again occupied the provincial parliament building and I found Tata in the midst of a long convoy of vehicles preparing for another rally, a very large one. She looked worried. The frustration with the UN had come to a head, because Jamsheed Marker had not held a public dialogue, and now the students wanted to force him to speak to them.

Marker, who only a few months earlier would have been welcomed as a liberator and East Timor's brightest hope, was now despised. The students had felt betrayed when he had, a few months earlier, avoided Dili and had flown to Baucau for meetings. In that way, he avoided a big demonstration that had been planned for Dili. The students felt he had robbed them of the 'momentum for change' that they had been trying to generate for many months. Their frustration at this lost momentum still lingered.

Another reason many in the resistance mistrusted him was rooted in his background. They suspected him of being too close to the Indonesians, especially to Ali Alatas, since both had been ambassadors to the UN in New York and they were friends. And they wrongly assumed him to be a Muslim – in fact he is a Parsee.

Youth groups and Falintil accused him of not standing up for Timor. Falintil, some rumours went, even wanted to kill him and even Xanana, apparently uncertain of his own authority, had mentioned this to Marker. So he had been forewarned about this change in sentiment and had, in what the students saw as evidence of 'cowardice', opted not to check into the Mahkota hotel, where foreign dignitaries usually stayed, but instead took up residence with Colonel Tono Suratman, the Indonesian commander in East Timor.

On my way to the airport to catch Merpati's flight to Bali I caught up with the vanguard of a long convoy of trucks and buses filled with students. They had blocked the main road to prevent Marker from leaving without addressing them. But the military had taken him along a back road to the airport's VIP lounge, which had been sealed off by a Brimob battalion.

Infuriated by this second deception, some of the young people broke through the Brimob cordon lines and ran onto the tarmac, waving the Timorese flag and shaking their fists. The pilot of the incoming Merpati plane must have seen the commotion on the tarmac, because he aborted the landing at the last moment. Without touching the ground the aeroplane took off again, as Jamsheed Marker, flanked by Indonesian soldiers, ran as fast as he could to an army helicopter. That was how the personal representative of the secretary-general of the United Nations made his narrow escape. It was a foretaste of other, more severe, trials in the UN's relationship with Timor.

Tata and her friends had come to the airport in a small blue *bemo* and pleaded with the crowd through a megaphone for people to disperse in an orderly way. A group of nuns, who happened to be at the airport to see off their colleagues, also tried to defuse the tension by standing between Brimob and the Timorese and calling on the young people to join them in a prayer, and to shake hands with the riot police. Many dutifully did so.

Tata squeezed my hand hard. 'This will be the last big demonstration. From now on things will change. It will be very bad.' I saw the tears welling in her eyes as she continued. 'Note my words,' she said. 'When you come back we'll be in hiding again. Some of us may even have died.'

CHAPTER 9

. . . .

The Dam Breaks

§ ONE rainy afternoon in early 1999, Antero knocked on the door of my house in London.

The Students' Solidarity Council had won the 'International Student Peace Prize', a student alternative to the Nobel Prize, awarded in Norway. That spring Antero and Tata travelled to Trondheim for the awards ceremony and Antero stopped off to visit England on his way back, and spent some time talking to experts on 'conflict resolution'.

In my living room, Antero looked out of place, a large tropical plant in too cold a setting. Having spent part of the winter in northern Europe, he had lost some of his colour, and his languid tropical movements made him look rather drowsy and dreamy. He did not complain about the cold but I turned the heating up anyway. With him around, memories of Dili's sweltering heat made my place feel even more chilly. In London, East Timor was always in my head; with Antero's visit it wandered into my living room.

While he was watching a football match on television, I was busy trying to juggle various tasks: packing my bags for a trip to Jakarta, brewing some tea and baking an apple crumble. When the football match had finished he said suddenly and quite formally: 'Irena, I have to ask you something.' He sounded so serious that I came in from the kitchen and sat down. 'What do you think the future of East Timor will be?' He looked at me hopefully.

It was such a big question that I couldn't help but laugh. 'What do you think yourself?' I asked.

Things had suddenly moved very fast. In January 1999 Indonesia's president B. J. Habibie had astonished the world by decreeing that if the option of greater autonomy within Indonesia was not acceptable to the Timorese they could 'separate from Indonesia in a dignified and good manner'. Among those taken by surprise was his own foreign minister, Ali Alatas, who had over the years been a fervent defender of Indonesia's annexation of Timor.

Habibie's announcement brought the curtain down on the long first act of negotiations over Timor's future. They had lasted for over a decade and had been fruitless. Now the curtain would rise for the second act of a drama, under the command of a director who was familiar with neither the stage nor the actors. Habibie knew very little about East Timor, or about the role his military played there. He had come under increasing pressure internationally, notably from Australia and Europe, to grant the East Timorese a referendum. In every high-level international meeting Habibie attended this would be brought up again and again. He found it unbearably embarrassing, keen as he was to impress the West with his commitment to democracy and human rights. The East Timor issue was a persistent irritant that would not go away – in Ali Alatas's famous phrase, 'a pebble in the shoe'.

The final straw for Habibie appeared to have been a letter he received from the Australian Prime Minister, John Howard, which spelled out Canberra's support for 'an act of self-determination'.[1] Australia had been quick to give official recognition to the annexation of East Timor, as early as 1979. Now, at a time when Jakarta needed all the friends it could get, it could ill afford to alienate Canberra. It was clear that an offer limited to a special autonomous status for East Timor would not be enough either for the Timorese, or for international opinion.

Momentum for a once and for all solution was also building domestically. Habibie's advisers, many of whom were members of the influential organisation of Islamic intellectuals, ICMI, which he used to chair, argued that at a time of national crisis, it made no sense to keep spending precious money on a half island full of recalcitrant Catholics – a territory that would probably split off anyway, sooner or later.

That rainy afternoon in London, Antero took a sip of tea and said that he, like other Timorese leaders, had no doubt that if the UN organised a referendum in which every Timorese could vote freely, they would turn down Indonesia's proposal for autonomy and choose independence instead. But then what?

For Antero the referendum was a formality. He was thinking beyond it. What, for example, would the UN do after the people had voted for independence? Would they leave East Timor to sort itself out? We talked for a bit about what had happened in Cambodia and the way the UN deals with similar situations: a referendum, followed by national elections. Then, when a democratic national government was formed, the UN would leave.

He pondered for a bit. The conclusion he had drawn from the talks he had had on conflict resolution was that conflict could be averted when different political ideas and forces could be represented in different political parties, who would then agree to set their differences to one side. As Antero saw it, a referendum would immediately be followed by elections, leading to the formation of a 'national council of unity', in which each party would be represented according to the number of votes it won. It was too early for people to come to terms with the idea of a 'loyal opposition'. It would have to be an election that everybody won.

Habibie's change of heart had triggered a flurry of activity at the UN in New York. The shift in the Indonesian position had opened an unexpected window of opportunity, and even Alatas was now singing from a different hymn sheet. 'If they want to have their freedom, they are welcome,' he had said, but added the worrying caveat that it would have to be decided by the MPR, Indonesia's highest legislative body.

A UN official told me that, the day after Habibie's bombshell, the Indonesian delegation in New York seemed 'confused and disorganised'. The presidential decree had not been translated into a new policy or even a concrete plan of action. 'They had no clue what to do.'

Indonesia and Portugal agreed to leave it up to UN Secretary-General Kofi Annan to come with ideas on how to conduct the 'consultation'. The UN started work on it immediately. The Timorese, who had complained for so long that they had been left out, needed to be consulted. Otherwise, as Kofi Annan put it, it would be like 'Hamlet without the prince'.[2] After a long discussion with Xanana in Jakarta and a visit by a UN mission in February to East Timor, where many, according to the UN, still harboured unrealistic ideas, three options were presented.

The first was that the UN would 'assess the mood'. This undemocratic approach would leave the decision entirely in the hands of Kofi Annan. The second was a traditional one-person-one-vote ballot on the options. The third was to hold elections for a council of representatives, which would then vote on behalf of the population.

The Indonesians preferred a version of the first option: to leave it to the UN to play the role of arbitrator. A special UN mission could make a series of visits in which it would make an assessment of the mood of the population, and this would be combined with a restricted ballot in which a selected group of community leaders would vote.

Xanana and the UN, however, anticipating that the Indonesians would not accept the second option, had seen advantages in the third one – a universal ballot for a council of representatives. This would avoid the risk a referendum posed and create a democratically chosen council that could serve as an interim assembly under either outcome.[3]

All these options were vulnerable to manipulation by the Indonesians. In the first option the local authorities would try to influence the UN mission's view by forcing people to demonstrate in favour of autonomy. A vote restricted to community leaders also carried depressing echoes of an earlier, shameful chapter in the history of the UN's involvement in decolonisation – one that, for the Indonesians, was a happy precedent. In 1969 the UN had conducted a 'consultation' exercise in West Papua, to determine the future of the territory, which the Netherlands had held on to at the time of Indonesia's foundation, but which it had, under American pressure, eventually to relinquish. The consultation was heavily manipulated by the Indonesians and the vote, held exclusively among community leaders and tribal chieftains, was in favour of integration with Indonesia. The UN at least, had learnt its lesson since this disgraceful sham, and preferred for East Timor a 'one-person-one-vote' ballot.

In March, during a meeting at Kofi Annan's home, Ali Alatas, under enormous pressure, had blurted out his acceptance of the 'one-person-one-vote' option. This could have paved the way for an agreement on the staging of a referendum. But the Portuguese made the agreement public, laying Alatas open to a counter-attack from Indonesian hard-liners, who forced him to backtrack. The idea of a referendum went back on ice for a month.

In the meantime, in East Timor Habibie's announcement had opened a Pandora's box. The pro-Indonesian faction reacted furiously. They felt betrayed by Habibie. The security situation in East Timor worsened. Pro-integration militia groups, armed and trained with the help of the Indonesian armed forces – like the one that had caused the trouble in Alas – started to show themselves more openly.

They opposed any extension of autonomy, and simply wanted a continuation of the present *de facto* total integration. At the beginning of February a group of integration leaders and pro-Indonesia civil servants established the FPDK, the Forum for Unity, Democracy and Justice, the political wing of the pro-Indonesia groups. During its inauguration ceremony at a hotel in Jakarta, retired military officers assured them that when the referendum and subsequent independence reached the MPR, they would never be allowed to proceed.

The resistance received the forthcoming referendum with mixed feelings. Of course a referendum was what they had demanded all along. But any item of news coming out of Jakarta was regarded with suspicion, and people tried to read between the lines of the latest offer. The resistance, which had argued that East Timor would need time to prepare the population for a referendum to prevent unnecessary bloodshed, found itself overtaken by the pace of events.

Habibie was clear enough about his own timetable. 'We don't want to be bothered by East Timor's problem anymore by 1 January 2000,' he said. 'We will fully concentrate on the interests of our remaining 26 provinces.'

'As a friend,' he said, 'we let them decide by themselves ... If someone asks me about East Timor, my suggestion is, give them freedom. It is just fair.'[4] But few Timorese could see the Indonesian government in general and Habibie in particular as a 'friend'. Many were wary about the president's power – or lack of it. In his short time in office, Habibie had already become notorious for erratic and unilateral decision-making. It could not be assumed that he had the backing of the army for this decision. And, people worried, what would it mean if the military did not agree with it?

Antero had enough to worry about. After he had checked his e-mail he had come down from the study looking despondent. 'Again two students killed in Dili and one killed in Baucau,' he said with a weary, haunting laugh. Stories of intimidation, terror and killing of pro-independence supporters had become daily news. The pro-Indonesia militia groups were gathering strength. With the help and encouragement of the Indonesian army, they had started to attack and kill pro-independence students and activists. In one e-mail Antero had received, João da Silva of the Student Solidarity Council had written that 'Timor is a pool of tears'.

'It's the young that are dying. With every dead young person another three die, because when Timor loses them it loses part of its next generation.' Antero was quiet for a while. 'We could have killed them all, you know. It would have been an easy solution for the problem. There are not many of them,' he mumbled. I was taken aback by this. Perhaps the strain of the depressing news and his own inability to turn the tide on the militia violence had taken a toll.

But even if it was a remark born of frustration and anguish, it still raised a disturbing question: had it really crossed his mind that killing all the opponents of independence might be some sort of solution? Did he think they could root out ideas by killing some of the people who held them? And, if an intellectual, sensitive ex-seminarian could make a remark like this, what hope was there for Timor?

It reminded me of what Bishop Basilio had said: 'The quantity of faith is high but the quality low.' I knew that when Antero had turned away from his priestly vocation he had also turned his back a bit on the Catholic Church, but still he startled me by bristling. 'What does he mean by "quality"?' he demanded. 'It's not really wrong to kill if it is necessary, for example in a war. After Peter cut off someone's ear Jesus said: "Put your sword back in its sheath," he didn't say "Throw it away."' Antero seemed to think his stored-up Bible knowledge won the argument. But I kept pressing: 'Would you have defended a decision to kill them?' Antero shuddered. 'Anyway, we have decided not to kill them.'

§

From the outset the most difficult issue in the UN negotiations had been that of security: who would ensure order during the 'consultation'? An international security force was out of the question from Indonesia's point of view, and, according to one of the UN negotiators, remained a 'taboo' at the Security Council. Suggestions that the Indonesian army, the TNI, might withdraw some of its forces from Timor, or have them stay in cantonment sites in

Dili, met with fierce opposition from the TNI itself. The army did not want to give up control before the referendum in August. It was a difficult dilemma for the UN negotiators. The situation was far from ideal but they felt they had to grab this opportunity, as it might only come once. And they had to do it at once. 'It was either this', said one of the negotiators, 'or nothing.' Even among Timorese leaders, like Xanana, who realised they had no other choice, the consensus was to seize this opportunity and go ahead with the referendum despite the foreshortened timeframe and worries about the TNI's role.

So it was agreed that the Indonesian police would have responsibility for security, before, during and after the referendum. The police had been, at least on paper, separated from the army. They enjoyed a slightly less sullied reputation than the army. Colonel Timbul Silaen, East Timor's police chief, told UN negotiators that if the TNI was in charge of the democratic process, there wouldn't be one. The police, by contrast, he assured them, could handle the disarmament of the militias. 'If there is the will we can do it.'

The number of police officers in East Timor at that time was 2,800. They needed to be supplemented by Indonesian civilian police who, it was optimistically expected, would provide a breath of fresh air. But when the Ministry of Foreign Affairs read in the press about the promises the police chief had made, it reacted furiously. It told the UN that any requests on issues such as the training of police or the disarmament of the militias had to be handled by its international relations section in Jakarta. In charge of that office was Dino Patti Djalal (one of Ali Alatas's 'golden boys', and the son of another famous Indonesian diplomat), a strong supporter of Timor's integration with Indonesia.[5]

Because of opposition from the Ministry of Foreign Affairs, and because of tactical differences within the UN's own negotiating team, no Indonesian concessions on security were won. The police were to be responsible for ensuring 'a secure environment devoid of violence', but there was no guarantee of the disarmament of the militias. The victory the UN could claim – that the negotiators in New York had won one-person-one-vote consultation for East Timor – was soured by this defeat, which was to have grave consequences. But as one of the UN team later wondered aloud, it may have been that not even a written guarantee could have prevented the catastrophe that was to come.

. . . .

CHAPTER 10

Big Brother Xanana

§ A FEW weeks later, on Easter Sunday, I was waiting in front of Xanana Gusmão's prison house when I felt a hand on my shoulder. 'Passport please!' said a deep voice behind me. Startled, I turned around and looked into the grinning face of Antero. He had just arrived in Jakarta and, like me, had come for a meeting with the leader of the Timorese resistance.

We were not the only ones. A group of more than twenty people were waiting eagerly to be let in. Most of them were young Timorese, but there were also a few elderly Indonesians. 'We used to see him in Cipinang prison every Sunday,' said an old Javanese from a church group that visited prisoners. 'It has become very difficult to see him. He never has time any more. We see less of him now he is more free and we really miss his company,' he complained.

This was where Xanana had been moved, when Habibie, partly at Kofi Annan's urging, had agreed to grant him more freedom to allow him to play a more active role in the consultation process. The house faced the high whitewashed wall and watchtowers of Salemba prison, of which it was officially an 'extension'. (Indonesian law did not make provision for an official house arrest. But Jamsheed Marker pointed out that the British colonial administration got around the same problem by detaining Mahatma Gandhi in a private residence and declaring it officially a prison.)[1] The neighbours, seeing a business opportunity, had opened a little coffee shop in the small alley to cater for the waiting crowds. Every time I went back they had stocked up on a larger variety of snacks and drinks and provided a few more chairs to sit on.

Visitors to Xanana's compound had to show their identification through a little pigeonhole in the high iron fence around the house. Before they opened the gate, the prison guards would check their list to see whether the Ministry of Justice had granted permission. As a foreigner I had to go through the Office of International Relations section of the Ministry of Foreign Affairs to get to the Ministry of Justice. It took days, and eventually Djino Jalal flatly refused to give permission. 'I can't see how your visit would be beneficial towards an acceptable solution,' he told me and added meanly: 'You can see him when he is free and that will be soon.' 'Soon?' He smiled haughtily. 'Probably in four to six weeks. You just wait.'

But, as with everything in Indonesia, there are always other ways to get where you want to go. I had seen Xanana several times now.

The house, a small white bungalow, the type normally occupied by middle-ranking Indonesian civil servants, had three rooms. There was a small living room furnished with a cheap three-piece suite and a dinner table with six chairs. One of the bedrooms doubled as Xanana's study, and in the other slept his lawyer, Antonino Gonçalves. Antonino and his wife Pauline ran the household. Pauline did the cooking and cleaning and Antonino acted as a point of contact with the outside world.

In the parking space, the prison guards had set up their post. They spent most of the time around the table, all four of them, playing dominoes. Two tall, muscular young Timorese from Los Palos – Xanana's bodyguards – hung around in the courtyard. 'Every day Xanana gets death threats,' they said, 'so we have to be extra careful, especially with other Timorese.' They knew better who was who than did the prison guards.

Despite the death threats the atmosphere seemed quite relaxed and amicable. The prison guards appeared to be on good terms with Xanana. They were enjoying the change from their usual prison environment. They marvelled at all the different people they had seen coming through the gate. Some had been polite, others angry. And some were world-famous, such as Madeleine Albright, the US secretary of state.

From my place on a bench behind the guards, I could hear Xanana talking in Tetum to the group Antero was part of. He was holding court. In a long monologue he briefed the young Timorese about the latest developments and his take on them. He expressed his worries about the splits in the student movement and urged them to unite and cooperate. 'Socialism, *mauberism*, and all other -isms and ideologies needed to be put to one side for a while. It is the time to be united,' he said, 'time to overcome our differences and work closer together.'

'Happy Easter,' I greeted Xanana when it was my turn to go in. He laughed: 'Easter? Who cares?!' On the wall behind him hung two large pictures of the Virgin Mary and Jesus, both with bleeding hearts, smiling benignly. I don't know who had hung them there but Xanana, like Antero and some of the other Timorese leaders, made no secret of not being a practising Catholic.

Kay Rala Xanana Gusmão, or Maun Boot Xanana, Big Brother Xanana, as the Timorese respectfully and affectionately call him, had so much of everything that makes a legendary rebel leader that talking to him was almost like interviewing a cliché. Regardless of his personality, his history had coated him in the charisma of armed resistance: ten years of fighting and surviving as a guerrilla leader in the mountains, followed by six years of hiding in and

5. Xanana Gusmão in 1998 in Cipinang makes a fist salute.

around Dili and other urban areas setting up the underground network. He had come to personify the Timorese fight for freedom, and years of confinement in an Indonesian prison had served only to heighten his mystique.

In Timor the most incredible myths had sprung up around him. People believed he had a strong *lulik*. Even Javanese soldiers, who on their home island are familiar with such 'hidden forces', had come to believe that it was thanks to his superhuman powers that he could hide from them for so long. His sister Armandina had told me a story about how soldiers had once burst into her house and threatened to kill the small white dog she was cradling. They believed, she said, that Xanana had the power to change himself into the shape of animals.

Xanana had qualities shared by many populist leaders all over the world: a handsome, open face, a sharp wit and easily tickled sense of humour, a love of talking, and, above all, the ability to appear genuine. He behaved not like a politician but like someone who sincerely meant what he said. And he had that rare gift, of being able to make anyone who met him feel special. To complete the picture of the perfect late-twentieth-century hero, Xanana the rebel-poet had been befriended by Nelson Mandela. After meeting him in Jakarta in 1997, President Mandela was reported to have said that Xanana was one of the most impressive people he had ever met.

No one in Timor so enjoyed the respect and trust of all the different parties. He was indispensable to the political process leading to the referendum and to independence. The international community had pinned their hopes on him. Without such a leader, Timor would have probably been less successful than it had in winning the support of the UN, national governments and international solidarity groups. Who, after all, needs yet another tiny and impoverished country? Xanana was one of the things that made Timor a special case.

His prison house was now the nerve-centre of planning for Timor's future. UN envoys, who appreciated his reasonable, conciliatory approach, consulted him before they went to Timor; diplomats and Indonesian opposition leaders became regular visitors; foreign government ministers on visits to Jakarta would pop in; perhaps most remarkably, Timorese leaders from across the political spectrum would hold long meetings in his living room. The Timorese resistance took almost no decisions without his personal consent. All of this gave him a lot of power.

I was curious about the man whose image the Timorese wore on their T-shirts and in their hearts. The person they had put their hopes in. Did they really know the hero they idolised? Or had they fallen for a myth? Half of Xanana's life he had lived in isolation and confinement – first 16 years as a guerrilla leader and later seven years in prison. How had this shaped his character and formed his ideas?

My first encounter with Xanana had been brief. In the chaotic days after Suharto's fall, President Habibie had released a handful of high-profile political prisoners; and somehow the prison door had been left open to allow in government representatives, diplomats and a few fortunate journalists.

Jill had used the confusion of that time to sneak back into Indonesia and had set her mind on doing the first interview with Xanana for Portuguese television. Once again, I would be her camera-operator. By chance we arrived at the same time as a visiting American congressman who promised to try to arrange a press conference in the prison after his private meeting.

My first impression when I saw Xanana among the other prominent political prisoners in Cipinang's meeting room was how relaxed and young he looked for his 52 years. His eyes shone with an optimism that had never been extinguished. When Jill asked him whether he hoped he would now be released soon he replied: 'It's not about my freedom, it's the freedom of my people I'm concerned about.' At the door I turned around to see him leave the meeting room. He had turned around too, grinned and gave the Fretilin salute, his hand clenched in a fist above his head.

During the last years in Cipinang, Xanana had enjoyed remarkable privileges. With money provided by the overseas resistance a huge number of prison guards had been induced to allow him all sorts of perks. He even had a mobile telephone hidden in his cell. In his prison house these privileges had been extended and he could receive calls (monitored by the prison warders) and write and receive letters. Faxes, e-mails and press releases were handled by a personal office in a house round the corner. Apart from a few Timorese aides, all men, his personal assistants and secretaries were young Western women. They controlled reporters' and activists' access to Xanana.

Xanana had the raw charisma of a person untainted by 'real world' politics. He could set his mind on pursuing higher goals. And the power he enjoyed because of his authority over the Timorese resistance had not affected him – yet.

The first evening I spent in his house a small cat came wandering in, clearly at home. 'Is this your cat?' I inquired, curious. 'Oh no,' he said, waving dismissively at the tabby, 'I don't like cats.' It belonged to Jacob Rumbiak, the leader of the Free Papua Movement, OPM, which was fighting for Irian Jaya's independence. He was still in Cipinang and thought Xanana could give it a better home. He had been close to Rumbiak and other political prisoners, with whom he use to play football and work tending vegetable plots in the prison garden. 'When we get our freedom I will help the OPM to free their country,' he said. 'We have a lot of experience in fighting the Indonesian military.'

Had Indonesia's generals overheard that remark (as they probably had, as it was likely that the house was bugged), it would have confirmed Indonesia's worst nightmare: that an independent East Timor could lead to more unrest elsewhere and eventually to the disintegration of Indonesia. Tug on this thread too hard, they would have argued, and the whole archipelagic tapestry might unravel. For that reason, it is not something that Xanana would have said in public. Later on he would probably not have said it at all. But at that peculiar time, he was still adjusting to his new role, learning to conform to the constraints of 'realpolitik', and to give up some of the relative ideological luxury of being a rebel leader.

Xanana had agreed to give me the opportunity to spend more than a week observing his life and talking to him whenever he had some spare time. Maybe, as a writer himself, he sympathised with my needs. He had been released from Cipinang for only a couple of weeks and he was getting a taste of what the 'real world' would demand of him. When I asked how he felt at being out of Cipinang at last he blurted: 'Every day I wish to be back there again. There they would give me a pencil and two sheets of paper a day. I could think, I could write. Here there are always people who need attention and there is so much work to think about.' He complained that the stress of the sudden change made his head spin. He couldn't think clearly and hardly slept, a syndrome common with prisoners who had been released from a life in solitary confinement.

But Xanana loved to talk, and he seemed to forget the time as we talked several times late into the night, drinking coffee and chain-smoking red Marlboro cigarettes. He was not used to speaking English. He spoke no faster than I could write, taking his time, carefully looking for the right expression, and leaving long pauses. When he couldn't find the right word he would get frustrated and use some Portuguese instead, asking me to guess at an English equivalent, so he would know if I understood correctly.

He was an artist at heart, had become a warrior out of necessity and was, it seemed obvious even then, a future president. But when I asked him about his role in an independent East Timor, he was wearily emphatic: 'Everybody asks me this. I don't want to be the president!'

This was not just a diplomatic posture, although it is true that in Asian, and especially Indonesian, political cultures it is not done openly to avow ambitions for the top office. But Xanana had also sworn to his comrades that he would never take up the presidency. One such promise was in a letter to José Ramos Horta in 1990.

> I will never accept, however, a comparison with, or appointment to, statesman. My only ambition, which I continue fulfilling with all my strength, is to contribute to the liberation of the Homeland. After that, and if I live until then, I only wish that I will have the time to walk the trail again trying to recognise the footprints left by Falintil in the forests of East Timor, remembering everything they have done and all their sacrifices. Any pretension to a personal career would be an affront to the suffering of my men and I shall not be so vile as to commit such an act!

He had read the history of former Portuguese colonies in Africa and had concluded that 'Good resistance leaders don't become good presidents.' I reminded him of Nelson Mandela and Vaclav Havel, but he was adamant. 'People have the tendency to look for symbols, to make comparisons, but Timor is not South Africa or the Czech Republic; I'm simply not the right person.'

He had fulfilled his role in the liberation struggle and besides his principled objections to becoming a political leader, he seemed genuinely tired. He also wanted to be 'something more valuable than a political player'. 'I know myself,' he said, 'I won't be a good president but I will be good in building a strong civil society.' If he had to he would take Timor through the transition period to work on unity. After that, others could take over.

But the more reluctant Xanana was to be the leader, the more the people seemed to want him to lead. This was a theme that had repeated itself during his life. He had never dreamed of becoming a soldier, nor a guerrilla leader, let alone a president. 'I had so many dreams,' he said, sweeping his hair back from his forehead with his hand in a weary gesture, as if acknowledging that, even at the time, he knew his dreams would never be realised.

His current dream was to return to Timor and retreat to the small, uninhabited island of Jaco, which hangs like a drop from an icicle off the eastern tip of the island. There, he thought, he would find time to write poetry, paint and at the same time help to strengthen civil society on Timor.

His sister Armandina had told me a story of a very old man Xanana had met on one of his marches. The ancient mountain-dweller had approached him, grasped his hand and looked at him intensely. 'My son, you are destined to become the leader of our people,' he had told Xanana. The old man was called Kay Rala, a name Xanana liked and added to his name. He now signed himself Kay Rala Xanana Gusmão. When Armandina told this story to her mother, she was amazed: Kay Rala turned out to be the name of her grandfather. Surely, omens like this must have left him with some feeling of destiny. He laughed. 'My sister believes that it's all written down, I like to think you make your own destiny.'

Xanana was born on 21 June 1946 as José Alexandre Gusmão, the eldest son in a family of seven children. His father was the only child of landless peasants from one of Timor's poorest places, the village of Laleia, in the barren coastal land of Manatutu. Exceptionally for a poor ethnic Timorese, his father had become a teacher. The family moved around Timor and most of Xanana's happiest childhood memories were of life in the mountain village of Ossu, where his father taught at the Catholic school.

He had not, he said, had an easy youth. He had to fight every step of the way. After his primary education his father sent him to the seminary in Dare, the only place where indigenous Timorese who were not the sons and daughters of *liurais* could obtain further education. The Jesuits' strict and often harsh rule made Xanana experience his school years as an imprisonment. He wanted to escape out of this 'antechamber for saints', as he called it in his autobiography.[2] Too much of a rebel to become a priest, he dropped out of school at the age of 16, much to his parents' distress. Back home with his family, who had moved back to Manatutu, he worked as a draughtsman and as a teacher to support his sisters' schooling.

With the help of a little money saved by his mother, Xanana returned to Dili to enrol in evening classes at the Liceu, the state-funded high school. He had to work his way through school and it took him years of misfortunes, run-ins with the colonial administration and a multitude of odd jobs before he finally managed to finish junior high school.

Whenever I asked a Timorese what Xanana's profession had been before the war I would get a different answer. This puzzled me and made me think that nobody knew. Now I understood: everyone had been right. Xanana had been all of them: construction worker, fisherman, fishmonger, teacher, telephonist, typist, electrician, journalist, and so on.

Jobs were very hard to come by in Dili, and the only good ones were with the Portuguese colonial administration. With his high-school diploma in his pocket he again made the rounds of government offices. But again he experienced humiliation and discrimination. 'They threw me out of their offices, hurling insults. Such an arrogant lot,' he sighed. 'For *mestiços* it was easy to become a civil servant, for the Timorese very difficult.' Eventually, one of the departments gave him a job as a messenger boy. When they saw he worked hard and had initiative he was quickly promoted.

In the late sixties Xanana married Emilia, a teacher. They held their ceremony in the registry office, not in church, because he had managed to insult the priests. They had two children, Nito and Zeni. He did not baptise them because he said he 'wanted them to make that choice themselves'.

Besides acknowledging the important role it played in the liberation struggle, he did not have many good words for the Roman Catholic Church, nor for Christianity in general. The people had run to the Church to hide. But after liberation, he hoped, the people would 'feel free to retain their indigenous traditions and spirituality'. This had put him at loggerheads with some of the conservative clergy in the past, but had not lost him popularity in Timor.

§

Timor's swinging seventies arrived: years of budding rebellion against the Portuguese, of careless Marxist rhetoric and talk of free love, brought back from the Motherland by homecoming students. Change hung in the air. Xanana could feel it but did not know how or where it was likely to come from. As I had heard so many times from other Timorese educated during Portuguese times, Xanana said he had been largely ignorant about the outside world. The Portuguese had taught them everything about the Motherland and their colonies and nothing about anywhere else. 'Portugal was the world and the world was Portugal.' Indonesia remained abstract. The colonial regime censored the newspapers and magazines. The radio station – television had not yet arrived – broadcast only news about Portugal, a little about Europe, and not much else. So he did not know that Indonesia was a huge and powerful country and was unaware of the slaughter of hundreds of thousands of alleged communists that took place there in 1965–66. For Xanana, as for Manuel Carrascalão, Indonesia was Kupang and Kupang Indonesia.

The only other place outside the Portuguese empire Xanana knew a bit about was Australia. He was so disillusioned with the colonial system that, in the early 1970s, he travelled to Darwin to prepare to emigrate there. When he returned to Timor to arrange for his family to join him, his friends talked him out of it, and persuaded him to become politically active. He resisted the pressure for some time, preferring to move between the parties, and not to commit himself to any of their slogans. Both the UDT and Fretilin tried to win him over, but he declined party membership. 'I always wanted to be independent and write for a newspaper. I wanted to be an observer,' he told me.

He started to send poems and articles to local newspapers. There were two popular newspapers at that time, *Voz Timor* and *Seara*. In the late sixties and early seventies, *Seara*, a Catholic paper, became a forum for critics of Portuguese colonialism. As a Church publication, it escaped the normal censorship and its columns soon filled with contributions from many of the young Timorese elite, who would rise to power in 1975: Nicolau Lobato, José Ramos Horta, Francisco Xavier do Amaral, Manuel Carrascalão, Mari Alkatiri. (Seara was closed by the PIDE – the Portuguese secret police – in 1974.)

Xanana's aspiration to become a writer and poet led him to look for a pen-name. He grinned. 'It is a funny story how I got my name. I had written a poem and an article for one of the papers and I needed a pseudonym. There was this popular song at the time that went: "Sha na na na na, I love you."' He started to hum. 'I liked the song and decided to publish my writings under Shanànà. But my name didn't remain a secret for long. Perhaps my style betrayed me because one day I was walking in the street when someone called, "He Shanànà!" and I turned around.' From that day the name stuck, though the spelling was changed to Xanana because in Tetum the 'Sh' sound is written with an 'X'.

From the money he earned he bought books. 'Lots of books, all kinds of books.' Among those he most cherished was a book about Buddhism, a philosophy, he said, that spoke more strongly to him than did Catholicism. In the evening he would discuss what he had read with friends, such as the poets Francisco Borja da Costa and Justino Mota.

Xanana loved debating about almost any subject, any time and anywhere. He bluffed himself into the circles of the educated elite, and would gatecrash their social gatherings. He would raise topics with them such as philosophy, economics and politics and provoke them into discussing them with him. 'Some looked a bit surprised at first – after all, I was the youngest there – and when they noticed I knew more than they did they looked even more taken aback. I didn't care, I was never too shy to speak to people who stood above me. I impressed these members of the old guard with their stifling ideas with my knowledge. They would say, "Ah yes, yes we never thought of that."'

It would take Xanana until May 1975 – a year after the party's founding – to join Fretilin. He had been moved by the support it enjoyed among the people in the mountains. He identified with them and with their life close to nature and Timorese tradition. He became editor of the Fretilin publication *Timor Leste: Journal do Povo Maubere*. Only when he had to publish a list of names of the Central Committee of Fretilin did he notice, to his dismay, that his name was among them. Reluctantly he accepted that it would be impossible to avoid the responsibility: a decision that would change his life.

Xanana saw himself as a poet and a writer. He dreamed a lot, but never about becoming a politician or a fighter. He dreaded being drafted into the Portuguese army, and managed to avoid it for three years, until he was threatened with being conscripted to serve double time. That could amount to eight years, spent in Angola or Mozambique. 'So I had no choice,' said Xanana. 'I had to go.'

CHAPTER II

. . . .

A Difficult Time Never to be Forgotten

> Bitterness of fate
> Which ended a march
> In the struggle
> The long march of
> The best years of life ...
> A destiny ...
> The turning of a yellow page
> Of a difficult time
> Never to be forgotten.
> (Xanana Gusmão, November 1995)

§ XANANA may not have wanted to be a soldier, but by the time of the Indonesian invasion he had volunteered to fight for the army of an independent East Timor. On the day of the invasion itself, Xanana's army unit was stationed on the Loes river, to the west of Dili. The Indonesians had already occupied the nearby village of Atabae. On 7 December he woke up before dawn to the droning of aeroplane engines and recalled that he felt that 'something very bad was happening'.

When the news that Dili had been invaded reached the front, Xanana was sent to Balibar, a village near Dare. From there, he watched the attack on Dili: the frigates shelling from the sea; the aerial bombardments; the fires and big columns of smoke snaking up all around town. Helpless, he watched as Indonesian soldiers looted warehouses and depots. Most townspeople were already on the move, heading for Fretilin-controlled areas in the mountains.

For the first two years, the war did not go too badly for Falintil. They had 20,000 men and newly acquired NATO weaponry, left behind by the Portuguese. They held on to most of their positions, which they said accounted for as much as 80 per cent of the countryside. Only the coastal areas, some strategic roads and most of the border were under Indonesian control. Food was not a big problem either in those early years. They had enough rice, and the villagers had their cattle and cornfields.

Fretilin had time to define its political direction. One of its visionaries was Vicente Reis, code-named Sa'he, who was responsible for the party cadres' political education. From those meetings, Xanana understood that it would be a long struggle. The only way they could survive, they concluded, was with the help of the population.

Xanana had no idea about the '-isms' of the party ideologists. Only when, at the end of 1976, he got hold of a copy of *The Thoughts of Chairman Mao* could he make some more sense of what he had heard in the political education meetings. The book became the only personal belonging he travelled with. Mao Zedong's thoughts were also popular with Sa'he, the ideologist. Mao's dictum about guerrilla warfare – 'The people are the sea, the army the fish' – was followed by Sa'he, preparing the ground for the development and long survival of the armed resistance in Timor.

Sa'he aspired to set up a revolutionary, Maoist, party as part of Timor's liberation struggle. Xanana himself said he, too, 'could not conceive of liberating the homeland without liberating the people'. But when Sa'he asked him whether he would join the new party, Xanana declined. He still didn't know exactly where he stood, politically.

Xanana was made vice-secretary of the East Viqueque area, which included the villages of Uatolari and Uatu Carabau. Travelling around the region, he made his debut as a politician by giving speeches to the soldiers and the villagers. Antero's father was a *liurai* in Uatu Carabau, and Antero remembered going with him to one of the meetings Xanana held in his village.

At that time the radical Marxist group within Fretilin had gained the upper hand and started to purge the party's own ranks. Some of the *liurais*, who had supported Fretilin but fiercely opposed Communism, and 'could not clench their left fist in a Marxist greeting', were declared reactionaries. Some of the men had come to Xanana, crying at his feet, begging not to be handed over to party headquarters.[1] To Xanana's horror, a number of commanders, notably Alarico Fernandes, Fretilin's minister for internal affairs and security, had started to use torture to extract confessions. One common practice was to put burning coal on the stomach or other parts of the body. That some people died because of this is without doubt, but exactly how many is hard to know.

One of the people singled out in the purge was Francisco Xavier do Amaral, Fretilin leader and president of the Democratic Republic of Timor Leste (RDTL). His idea had been not to escape to the mountains, but to negotiate with the Indonesian commanders. On the day of the invasion he had stopped the car in which he and other leaders were fleeing, meaning to return to Dili. Only when one of the commanders put a gun to his head did he continue to Aileu. During their stay in the mountains he had urged his colleagues again and again to let the civilians among them go back to their villages so they could start an underground support network. In 1977 the radical Marxists accused him of being a traitor and took him prisoner, after capturing most of his followers. At the end of that year he surrendered, during a battle, to the Indonesians. He later claimed that Fretilin killed 50,000 people, and was responsible indirectly for the death from hunger and Indonesian bombing of the many others it did not allow to go back home.[2]

With its internal opposition out of the way, Fretilin's central committee officially adopted Marxism as its ideology. That same year Indonesia changed its strategy. The army was frustrated and embarrassed by the continuing resistance and its slow progress. When planning the invasion, its strategists had boasted of having 'breakfast in Dili, lunch in Baucau, and dinner in Los Palos', as they swiftly and smoothly subdued the whole territory. But, two years after the invasion, the army still controlled less than a third of the population.

It was at this time that the Indonesians received more military aid from the United States than ever before. The Carter administration even increased the original request for $25m in military sales to more than $100m.[3] With the new specialised weapons it obtained, the army now started its push to root out the Timorese resistance.

Falintil and the population in their areas were driven higher and higher up the mountains. One of their most important strongholds and hiding places was the Matebian, the sacred mountain in the east. There, surrounded by the souls of their ancestors, and the smell of peppermint and marigolds that covers the hillsides, the people would hide inside the huge boulders that littered the higher slopes. The rocks had corroded and split, leaving openings in which whole families could shelter from the bitterly cold winds – and from air-raids.

Every day the planes came. During the first years they were small and slow and Falintil shot at them. But later the Broncos came. Xanana called them 'black scorpions', because of their upturned tails.[4] And sometimes the air was pierced by high-flying jets.[5] Whatever the size, they rained bombs. In the dry season the clear blue skies over the Matebian betrayed the people hiding in its recesses. The big stones became graves for entire families, and sometimes a single bomb would wipe out a whole *knua* or clan.

But there were other days, too. Days when Xanana felt that *rain-fila*, a trick the land plays on intruders to make them lose their way, protected them from air-raids, or from Indonesian soldiers in hot pursuit. Thick shrouds of mist would swirl up out of nowhere, and veil them from their enemies' view. Sometimes they would be so close that they could smell them: Indonesians smelled of soap and detergent, and of their pungent *kreteks*.

In the beginning the people had grown corn and potatoes on little plots of land. Later, as they were pushed higher up the mountains by the advancing Indonesian army, they were cut off from food and water and Xanana saw many people die of starvation. 'On the Matebian, the mountain of the dead, we lived with the dead. We saw dying people and dead bodies every day.

Higher up the mountain there was no water, so people made lines to get the water up. I saw a whole line being wiped out in one of the attacks.' He took a sharp breath. 'It was indescribable.'

He remembered thinking at the time: 'If only we had a camera and could show the world pictures, or a foreign journalist, who could tell our story. Later, when I saw pictures of starving people and children in Africa, I thought that is what we looked like, but no one knew about our suffering.'

Indeed, one of the many tragedies of this war was that there were no foreign witnesses, no journalists, no photographers, no television crews, nobody who could tell the outside world what was happening in East Timor.

Xanana, the survivor, asked the question all survivors do: 'Why me?' And he felt that he had 'survived perhaps to bear witness to that time'. But he wasn't eager to talk about what he had witnessed. To talk about that time was to bring back memories he had long tried to suppress just to be able to sleep.

However, some images he had been unable to erase: 'I stayed in a hiding place on the Matebian. Below me I could see a large group of people, women, children, hundreds of them. I was on my way to the other side of the ridge when the jets came, four of them. I hid inside a rock. I remember thinking that the pilots were so skilful that they must be Americans. They dive-bombed for 45 minutes.' Falintil was powerless. They couldn't shoot them down. They had no heavy artillery – only guns, a few M16s they had captured from the Indonesians. The large columns of smoke and dust that followed the big explosions obscured the valley from his view. But after each bomb he heard people screaming. 'I cried,' he said. 'It was so awful to see all this destruction. When the dust settled I only saw an enormous hole. Nothing remained of the hundreds of people I had seen there. I only saw a strange yellowish ash and charred rocks. Then the air filled with the unearthly sound of the wailing and moaning of a few people who were still alive.' He never knew for sure what they were bombing them with. 'I think they used napalm. I saw bodies burning, and during the next rainy season it was very difficult to grow anything in the areas where the bombs had fallen.'[6]

Xanana took another cigarette from the pack he kept close at hand and inhaled deeply a few times. 'There is another incident I remember,' he continued. Taking my notebook, he made a rough sketch of a tree. 'A group of men were sitting here under a big tree. I had been with them but left to fetch water from a stream not so far away' – he scribbled a rough picture of a stream. 'Then the planes came and when I returned I saw the ripped-up pieces of human bodies hanging from the branches of the old tree.'

He was quiet for a while. 'Some people said it was our fate. There was not much we could do. They were resigned to it, but for me, it made me more determined to fight on, to continue the struggle. I couldn't accept it as fate.'

By 1978 Xanana realised that Falintil had come close to defeat. They could not defend their Matebian bases any longer. He urged the population to make use of an amnesty the Indonesians had announced, to go home to their villages. Some Falintil commanders, however, prevented people from leaving. A student had told me how his father had to kill a Falintil soldier to be able to take his family down to the valley, a deed that had haunted the family ever since.

The Matebian, Falintil's last base, fell in November 1978. The Indonesian army had brought the retreating population to 'strategic hamlets'. The people were in bad shape. The army would not let them go to their fields because they suspected them of maintaining contact with Falintil and of providing the guerrillas with food. So hunger and disease worsened. International aid agencies sent food supplies but often these were kept by the army, who sold them on the market or used them as bait to lure people into collaboration and denunciation of Falintil.

With the main Falintil base conquered, the Indonesians concentrated their forces on capturing Nicolau Lobato, Fretilin's president and Falintil's commander-in-chief. He was killed a month later in a battle with a unit supposedly led by the young Lieutenant Prabowo. Xavier do Amaral, who was at the time held as a prisoner by the Indonesians, was brought over to the airport to identify Lobato's corpse. The Indonesians, he said, had proudly displayed Lobato's embalmed body and boasted of having killed a further 20 Fretilin leaders with him.[7] Dispirited and exhausted, a number of Falintil platoons surrendered. Despite Suharto's 'amnesty' many were executed or tortured to death, and their families imprisoned on Atauro island.

A few were spared, such as Sebastião's father, who was employed as the driver of the Indonesian *intel* chief in Timor, and Xavier do Amaral, who was taken by Brigadier-General Dading Kalbuadi to Bali, where his status was not much better than that of a servant – a calculated insult, designed to humiliate Fretilin's president.

By March 1979 the Indonesians thought they had eliminated Falintil and abandoned their special operation. They have never made public the number of casualties they suffered, but Falintil claimed that 16,000 Indonesian soldiers died on the slopes of the Matebian and more than 20,000 in Timor. This very high number is hard to substantiate. The only evidence is anecdotal. Priests in Yogyakarta saw planes with body-bags arriving almost daily until the early 1980s. Resistance leader José Ramos Horta later heard from generals in Jakarta that in total 27,000 soldiers had been killed.[8]

Nor is it clear how many Timorese died in the war. A number that has gained currency internationally – 200,000 – was extrapolated from a demographic calculation of how big the population would have been in peaceful circumstances.[9] The Catholic Church in Timor and many Timorese believe that 300,000 died. Whatever the number of casualties, however, it remains true that the Indonesian invasion unleashed on the Timorese people one of most dreadful humanitarian catastrophes that any nation has ever suffered. Even Pol Pot did not succeed in killing, proportionally, as many Cambodians, according to journalist John Pilger.[10]

In the middle of 1979 Xanana set out with a small group of his soldiers in search of surviving members of Fretilin's Central Committee. The communication lines had broken down and he did not know whether the leadership was still alive. He travelled from east to west and back again, but of the original group of 50 he found only two still alive and fighting: Ma'Huno Bulerek and Txay. On his travels he spoke to the people in the resettlement villages, which he called 'concentration camps'. The people were sick and starving, but the old men had hugged him and begged him to carry on the fight.[11] With his best friends killed or captured, Xanana had to take a lonely, painful decision. Later he wrote in his autobiography: 'I assumed without hesitation the command of the resistance, without the slightest feeling of vainglory, but bathed by my own tears.' He knew he had no choice. The task ahead could crush him, but to forgo the responsibility would be to betray his own ideals.

Xanana's first move was to get all the commanders together to reorganise the resistance. The meeting took place in March 1981 in Bibileo on the southeast coast. They adopted a new strategy. East Timor would be divided into four regions, each with its own commander and sub-commanders, and they would continue to fight in small guerrilla units. They also appointed Xanana commander-in-chief of Falintil and president of Fretilin. Xanana had become the *comandante*. Friends started to salute him. They gave him special privileges and better food. He did not want this treatment, and it made him weep again.

It had taken many months to organise the meeting and the Indonesian military had got wind of it. So when they were ready to leave, they found themselves surrounded. They had gathered at the time a new campaign was launched by the Indonesian army: Operasi Keamanan or Special Operation, also known by the more sinister name: Operasi Kikis, Elimination. It was a massive campaign of encirclement and annihilation. The army had forcibly recruited 80,000 people, including boys as young as ten and men up to 50, to form a human chain.[12] This tactic, known in Indonesia as *pagar betis*, fence of legs, was also used by the Indonesians in other islands, and by armies in other parts of the world such as Burma. They used the population partly as a human shield but also as extra 'legs' to 'comb' the jungles. The plan was to draw the circle closer and closer, like fishermen dragging in their nets, and ultimately close the 'net' in Manatutu.

As the guerrillas dispersed after the meeting in Bibilieu, Xanana faced a horrible dilemma. To break through the 'human fence' they would have to fight their way out, risking hurting and even killing fellow Timorese. But to stay put meant certain death. Xanana decided to break through the 'fence of legs' in small groups. The people in the 'fence' tried to protect them, shouting directions of escape routes. Others tried to hide the guerrillas among them, but almost all of the fighters came from the eastern part of East Timor and couldn't understand the local dialect. When they regrouped at the agreed rendezvous points they had lost three companies, some 250 people. Only a small number of the guerrillas had managed to escape. 'Again I cried and cried. So many of us had died.'

With a lot of difficulty they reached their regions and started attacking Indonesian army units like angry wasps, just to make clear they were not defeated.

§

Xanana's appointment as the new commander became known to the outside world only when, in 1983, Falintil had, as they themselves put it, 'conquered a right to dialogue' with the Indonesians. Two meetings were held in March 1983 with Mário Carrascalão, the governor at that time, and Pruwanto, the commander of the Indonesian armed forces in Timor. They led to the signing of a ceasefire agreement. In a letter to Suharto, Xanana outlined his proposal: unconditional withdrawal of the Indonesian troops; entry of a UN peace-keeping force; holding of free consultations with the people of East Timor; and maintaining Falintil troops in the mountains in order to keep the people free of intimidation. A few months of peace followed. Xanana and his men could take a rest, see their families and find medical treatment for their wounds. The ceasefire also meant that people could move more freely, leave their resettlement villages and work on the fields to plant some crops.

Until the ceasefire a naval blockade and total news black-out had been in place. Now that they had a bit more freedom, priests and nuns managed to smuggle out stories of the horror of the war. It is hard even now to imagine the true extent of this, and for some time the Indonesian propaganda machine tried to play it down. Some stories were met with disbelief, and many governments preferred to be left in blissful ignorance of the Indonesian atrocities.

As soon as the outcome of the ceasefire negotiations became public, hard-liners in the Indonesian military leadership – notably the newly appointed commander-in-chief of the armed forces, General Benny Murdani, a Catholic from Java and former head of military intelligence – moved quickly to discredit it.

According to Mário Carrascalão, it was Prabowo, a close associate of Murdani, who thwarted a peaceful solution. Prabowo went to Timor without the permission of Pruwanto, the commander in Dili, and travelled to Viqueque. While the preparations for national day celebrations (17 August) were in full swing, the wife of a local member of Hansip was raped. Carrascalão accuses

Prabowo of having provoked the incident. The raped woman's husband had been a contact person between the Indonesian army and Falintil. He now escaped to the jungle and asked Falintil for help. As revenge for the rape Falintil killed 16 Indonesian soldiers. The population of the area had fled to the mountains but Prabowo, who at the time, according to Carrascalão, was actually liked and trusted, persuaded them to come down. When they did, his troops took 30 men and executed them.

Then they proceeded to Kraras, a resettlement village near Bilileo. There they massacred all the males, including infants. More than 260 people were killed in Kraras, now known in Timor as 'the village of the widows'.[13] One Indonesian soldier reportedly said to a Timorese after the killings: 'When you clean your field, don't you kill all the snakes, the small and large alike?'[14] General Benny Murdani promptly sacked Pruwanto, the commander who had brokered the peace deal, and warned Xanana to 'cooperate or be destroyed'. Peace had lasted only five months.

The failure of the peace agreement was a big blow. Benny Murdani was keen to finish Falintil off once and for all. The Indonesian army started a new campaign: Operasi Sapu Bersih, or Operation Clean Sweep. Since the invasion they had recruited hundreds of East Timorese into the infantry. Others had been organised into civil defence units. Above them stood the special forces, Kostrad and Kopassus, which ran East Timor more or less as their institutional fiefdoms. Xanana had cultivated contacts with all these groups and with the village heads, who had been installed by the Indonesians.

After the attack on Kraras, large groups of Timorese in the Indonesian forces defected to Falintil with their guns and ammunition. Their commander, Falur Rate Laek ('Dove without a Grave') *nom de guerre* for Domingos Raul, later said he had had enough of the senseless killings of civilians. He became the commander of Region 3 for Falintil. In other areas as well, Hansip and Timorese army soldiers defected. This boosted Falintil's faltering morale and its ability to attack Indonesian forces.

Operasi Sapu Bersih concentrated on Ponte Leste, the easternmost part of Timor, where Falintil had its strongest bases. The Indonesians used anti-personnel cluster bombs and heavy artillery. But by the time the operation ended, in 1985, the Indonesian army had to admit that all their strategies to wipe out the resistance had failed.

They could not root out the guerrillas with military force, because the small band of armed men in the jungle had the support of almost the entire rural population. A network of villages supplied them with food and medicines, clothes, money and new recruits. To eliminate it they would have had to slaughter almost the entire population. So the Indonesian army, belatedly, embarked on a new approach, to co-opt the population by 'winning their hearts and minds'.

For Falintil, too, it was time for a strategic rethink. During his first years as commander-in-chief, Xanana remained loyal to Marxist ideology, partly, he said, 'out of respect for his fallen comrades'. But he soon realised that, globally, Marxism was on its way out and Timor could not expect any help from communist countries. He gave up the rhetoric of class struggle and revolution in favour of that of a struggle for national independence. Liberation of his homeland and independence had to come first: the liberation of the people would have to wait. This, José Ramos Horta would say later, was the time of 'East Timor's *perestroika*'.

In a bitter message on the twelfth anniversary of the Indonesian invasion, 6 December 1987, Xanana criticised Fretilin's 'political infantilism', which, he said:

> tried to defy the world, obsessed with our non-existent capacities ... From the very beginning we presumed ourselves to be heroes of a bloody revolution ... This political infantilism has since 1974 allowed no margin of disagreement, but rather has exhibited all the political extremism which would be, from that time on, our very death sentence. We have committed crimes against our own brothers and, during this difficult war, we have spent more time in arresting and assassinating compatriots than in thinking effectively about capable defence of the homeland.

This, he concluded, had nearly resulted in total defeat in 1978.

He continued to denounce Marxism and laid out the reasons for the reorganisation of the resistance. Xanana understood that the front should not only be with Falintil in the jungles, but should incorporate the cities, and spread overseas to involve activists in Indonesia as well as internationally. He started to work on the reorganisation of the resistance and liaise with student groups in Timor and Indonesia.

His next move was to de-couple Falintil from Fretilin and in 1988, he formally stepped down from Fretilin's presidency, so opening the way for a coalition of all the resistance groups in Timor under his leadership. He launched the umbrella organisation, the CNRM. (This coalition changed its name in 1998 to CNRT and survived under Xanana's leadership until just before the democratic elections in 2001.)

§

When he started to talk about his time with the people in the mountains and forests, Xanana's face would light up and his eyes become bright with memories. Many of the pictures he painted in jail feature the giant *ai bubur*, eucalyptus trees, which cover the higher slopes of the mountains, or vistas of rolling green mountains rimmed by a deep turquoise sea.

He felt very close to the mountain people. He had found his spiritual roots among them and their *lulik rai*: the old people, with their strong reverence for the land they lived on and lived off; the traditions of warriors and spiritual healers; the traditional beliefs that bestowed a divine importance on sacred ancestral land. All of this touched something deep inside him. 'I believe that what links the people with the land, the elements of earth and stone of water and air, is the reason they could fight on, the reason that they could offer their lives for their country.'

In answer to a question raised by a journalist, he once wrote: 'Would I say my country is beautiful? Perhaps yes and perhaps no. The thing which enchants me is the primitive harmony of the relationship that exists between human beings and the natural world. And how beautiful it is to feel an instinctive fondness for the cool mountains which are not blue, no, they're not blue. It's the fragrance which hangs in the air, close to the earth, which is blue.'[15]

The longer he lived in the forest the more he became part of it. His instincts sharpened. He could read the stillness of the wind. From the way the birds acted, he could tell whether there were strangers in the forest. He and his men would move in harmony with the forest sounds, hardly speaking, reading the pattern of the leaves and the shape of the savannah grasses.

With great tenderness and awe he spoke of the time two village girls had guided his platoon for more than a week through an unknown area. The girls had been young, but they had led the forty soldiers unperturbed with a confidence that Xanana felt stemmed from their closeness to the land. They knew where to look for water and where the best places to shelter were. 'They sort of commanded us. "Maun," they would say, "you stay here while we will scout out the village to make contacts." Or when we would suggest a place to sleep they would know a better one.' These were Xanana's people: the ones in whose strength he would never lose confidence. Their strength became his inner strength when he stubbornly refused to give up believing in 'his people'.

'I admire the courage of the women and the children,' he told me. He said that women make up 60 per cent of the clandestine movement, but that Falintil had not wanted them to carry weapons, telling them: 'If we all die, you can, but for now, let us.' But he said that many women, although unarmed, were braver than men carrying weapons.

'Small children', he said, 'already understood who are "our people" and who are the ones they have to suspect. Sometimes the children would come running to us. "Uncle, you have to hide, close the door and the windows." Then they would go around singing, although still out of breath, to lead the people they suspected away from the house where we were hiding.'

In the middle of his discourse about Timor's mountains and their people, Xanana suddenly put his hand on my knee. 'You have to go there and spend some time with Falintil; you'll enjoy it.' He grabbed my mobile phone from the coffee table and made a call. My units had run out by the time he had finished. 'So that's arranged,' he said. But he left me in the dark about what was arranged exactly and with whom. I would be called, he simply said.

§

Thousands of soldiers hunted him relentlessly for years, but it took them until 1992 to capture Xanana. He had been staying in Dili for some time to organise the urban underground resistance. Sometimes he moved to the hills around the capital.

Xanana had two main hiding places in Dili. One of the houses was in Lahane, and belonged to Abílio Araújo's mother and his sister Alianca.[16] He knew that the Indonesian army was hot on his heels. Two weeks before his arrest he had received a letter that one his *estafetas* had been captured and badly tortured – so badly that he coughed up blood. According to Xanana, the messenger had not been able to bear it any longer and had betrayed his hiding place. One of the rumours about the circumstances of his betrayal that circulated years later in Dili gave a different reason: Xanana had supposedly had an affair with the wife of his cousin, and the enraged husband had gone to the military.

When the Indonesian military stormed the house, Xanana sat hidden in a special underground cell, whose entrance was concealed under a cupboard. Within days the Indonesians rounded up his family members and other people associated with him, subjecting them to torture and rape. Victims included Xanana's sister Armandina and her husband.

Soon after his capture he appeared on national television. Looking worn out and subdued, he described himself as an Indonesian citizen appealing for his followers to lay down their arms. This came as a shock for the Timorese. Many, including Bishop Belo, thought he must have been badly tortured or brainwashed. Xanana had, however, been surprisingly clear-headed and knew that cooperation would give him a chance to stand trial, whereas if he was difficult, he might as well have signed his own death warrant.

Xanana's trial would last more than three months. He had been allowed to present his own plea in defence. He had managed to write a 27-page document and had even somehow been able to copy it on to little scraps of paper he had collected. Even more remarkably, he had managed to slip these into the pocket of a visiting UN representative.

After the court heard the first minutes of the statement, in which Xanana withdrew everything he had said after his arrest, he was quickly cut off and the document was confiscated. But by that time the resistance got hold of the copy and it got into the newspapers all around the world.

Xanana was sentenced to life imprisonment, a sentence that later would be commuted to 20 years by President Suharto, who had come under intense international pressure. With its leader in prison many thought this would be a death blow to the resistance. But, as Nelson Mandela and others had proved, imprisonment need not close all political doors.

Xanana experienced the first year of his imprisonment, spent in Semarang in Central Java, as the most difficult. Here he was locked up in solitary confinement for long periods of time. Later, when he was transferred to Cipinang, he got more freedom. In his cell, in a small bungalow, measuring three by four metres, he could read books, write, paint and learn English. After the second year he could even keep in regular contact with the jungle, and for six years he commanded Falintil from his prison cell.

In the early years, when his jailers punished him, he would be put back in solitary confinement. 'This builds character,' he mused. 'I began to know myself better. Every day and every hour I thought about Timor, about the war, about the sacred mountains, about people I had met, about spirituality. One day I would like to put it all into writing, in an epic poem in the style of Camoes.'

§

One morning I arrived at Xanana's house just as a photographer from a newly launched Indonesian women's magazine (*Pro-TV*) was conducting a photo-shoot. Peering through the shutters, I saw Xanana standing in his combat fatigues: a camouflage overall, with Falintil's flag sewn on his shoulder, and a red beret. He was sweating under the big studio lights.

'Cross your arms, please, and look sternly over your shoulder! No, no, don't smile!' the art director commanded. Xanana complied, but when he spotted me at the window he rolled his eyes up and pulled a face, making the photographer growl with frustration. 'What will you do with the photos?' I asked the journalist outside. 'Back page pin-up,' he said. 'Xanana is a very attractive man.'

It was a typically busy day for the prison house, with constant comings-and-goings of journalists and photographers, of East Timorese, Indonesian and foreign activists, of foreign dignitaries and Indonesian politicians. Xanana was rapidly becoming one of the most popular men in Jakarta, and the darling of the press. 'He is the coolest man in town,' said a female American journalist. 'He is so nice, he held my hand when I interviewed him,' sighed an Indonesian journalist after she finished her interview. 'If only we had a leader like him, then we would know who to vote for,' another Indonesian reporter told me while he was waiting patiently for his turn to meet Xanana.

After the photo-shoot Xanana called me in for lunch. The heat of the photo lights still lingered and he had taken the top half of his camouflage overalls off, so the sleeves hung abandoned on his lap, exposing a crisp white

T-shirt. We talked about his popularity. When I told him about the pin-up poster, he just laughed. 'Yes, I think they might get a lot of money for these photographs, but never mind, whatever, I just let them.' He picked distractedly at his plate of rice, fish and vegetables. 'Xanana hardly takes time to eat,' grumbled Antonino, his lawyer. 'I've been used for years to only one meal a day. Now I suddenly get three, and not enough exercise,' Xanana replied.

Xanana was a keen football player. Before the war he had been goalkeeper for a football club in Dili and he had been the captain of Cipinang's prisoners' football team, which, thanks to a donation from the mayor of Lisbon, played in the colours of Timor's national flag – not that this dawned on the prison guards. In Xanana's new situation, however, he could play only once a week in the grounds of the neighbouring prison.

'The first thing I would do when released?' He frowned and stared at the table for a while. Then he turned his face up and laughed boyishly. 'Kiss the ground. See my friends. And organise a veterans' football competition.' He started naming the famous football players he would invite: 'Cruyff, Maradona, Gullit, Pele, Van Basten.'

His optimism and light-heartedness were infectious. When he told me his idea I did not even think it was terribly far-fetched. I could imagine him fulfilling his dreams, even the one in which he played football with the world's greatest stars on the sandy turf of the Dili stadium. But in the light of the events that would follow, it all sounds so naïve and carefree.

Xanana could often look as if, any moment, he would play some naughty schoolboy trick. At other times however, he was the *comandante*, authoritative and in charge. He did his best to suppress his impatience and short temper. He told his life story with a deep sadness but with a surprising lack of bitterness. He had had a long time to think when he was in jail, he said.

He couldn't, however, entirely suppress his passionate temperament. Under the surface of jesting grins, powerful emotions ran like a strong undertow. Sometimes I would see them stir. Other times they took me by surprise. Once, in the middle of a sentence, he got up, straightened his back and summoned someone called Pedro in a loud, commanding tone of voice. Pedro came running: 'Yes, Comandante?' I do not recall what it was that Xanana demanded, but it was done immediately.

My last evening, before my return to East Timor, we had another long talk. I had promised to teach a small group of Timorese to make programmes for a new clandestine FM radio station, for which the transmitters had been provided by Bobby, the American activist throwback. Bobby's experience the previous year had made him cautious. He had tried to help the Students' Solidarity Council but had ended up caught between rival groups, who had fought over the money he had been distributing. He had to be saved by Antero from a severe beating.

The phone kept ringing that night. Xanana talked for a long time and every time he returned he looked more worried. The situation in the countryside was worsening by the day, he said. 'They keep crying war war war!' He gestured around in desperation. 'I feel the temptation to kill them all, to get rid of the problem, but we can't! We have to respect human rights so we can't do that.' There it was again: the same sentiments Antero and Sebastião had uttered when they felt desperate. For Xanana to say something like this, his patience must have been tested to the limit.

The next day Xanana lost it completely. After he received a message that a massacre had taken place in Maubara, near Liquiça, he fell into a rage and smashed the furniture against the walls in sheer frustration. He screamed and yelled. Then he sat down to write a fierce letter to the foreign missions in Jakarta and to the international community, in which he outlined the situation in East Timor. The TNI was arming Timorese militia. He said he knew that the people would suffer another bloodbath and that they were prepared to make all the sacrifices needed to free their homeland. But he had concluded that the situation had reached 'an intolerable limit'. 'I am compelled', he went on, 'to authorise the Falintil guerrillas to undertake all necessary action in defence of the population of East Timor.' For years he had been urging restraint, telling the population to follow a painful policy of passive resistance. Now, he seemed to have given up: 'In response to the numerous appeals from the people of East Timor, I also authorise the population to undertake a general popular insurrection against the armed militia groups, who have been killing the population with impunity under the indifferent eye of the international community.' His signature was preceded by the words: 'Homeland or death! To resist is to win! The struggle continues without respite!'

The next day, on the plane from Bali to Dili, I saw a smirking Basilio Araújo, the spokesman of the FPDK, with a few other members of the pro-Indonesia faction. He had reason to smile. They had Xanana exactly where they wanted him. He had stepped with both feet into their trap. 'Civil war' is how the Indonesians wanted to depict the situation in Timor. Any fighting they blamed immediately on Falintil and the pro-integration groups. They interpreted Xanana's appeal as a war cry, justifying their next steps.

CHAPTER 12

. . . .

No Sanctuary

§ AS the aeroplane prepared to land at Dili's Comoro airport, I looked out of the window, half expecting to see the glow of burning houses, or perhaps a column of smoke, near Liquiça. But nothing disturbed the clear blue sky above the small town; nothing betrayed the massacre that must, even then, have been going on.

The political climate had deteriorated since my last visit. Even at the airport the changes were tangible. A Timorese dwarf with a misshapen arm came up to me and thrust his cold limp hand into mine. It felt like a dead octopus. 'Welcome back,' he hissed. His grin made the hair on the nape of my neck stand up. I had seen him before in the luggage-retrieval hall and guessed that he was there to point out suspected journalists to the *intel*. A foreign nun living in Timor, who knew the dwarf and had been followed by him, would later explained that 'the disabled, like children, are often used since they are perceived as being beyond suspicion'.

Despite the encounter with the dwarf I again managed to sneak through the checkpoints without registering. There had been other journalists on the flight but only one, an Indonesian cameraman working for APTV, who had good contacts in the Indonesian security forces, had rushed off to Maubara to shoot some pictures of what we thought had been an attack the day before. He came back with a story of some badly wounded people in the house of the *bupati* in Liquiça, but had not realised that another, much bigger massacre had taken place that very morning, 6 April. He spoke of it all in a blasé way; he had seen so much blood and had filmed so many dead people over the past year in Indonesia that he had not thought much of it. So it was not until midnight that we heard about the slaughter at the church in Liquiça, the worst massacre since Santa Cruz.

At least twenty-five people were reported dead, and no one knew how many were wounded. It took more than a day for the first ones to arrive in Dili. I went to the main hospital in Toku Baru. Two armed policemen stood guard outside the building with the casualties from Liquiça. In the ward I found three wounded men. One, a civil servant from Maubara, took my hand and gave me quickly the distinctive, thumb-clasping handshake used by the resistance. Most of the wounds I saw – deep gashes in the neck, severed ears, gunshot punctures in hands and legs – looked red, swollen and infected. These, however, were the lucky ones, the survivors. One of the men told me that he had worked for the Indonesian police for more than twenty years and never had expected to be shot by them. Another was a civil servant in the department of foreign affairs. But with the nurses in earshot they were too scared to say much.

Some were so afraid of staying in the hospital that they asked their families to take them to the Motael parish clinic, which was run by Carmelite sisters. It was a nice new building but it had no facilities to deal with badly wounded people. However, it was the only place the Timorese trusted. They were scared to go with gunshot wounds to state-run hospitals. They knew what had happened to people after Santa Cruz, when the military came into the hospitals to drag the wounded away with them, never to be seen again.

In the ward of the Motael clinic, I found a young mother feeding her three-month-old baby boy. As she began to tell her story a young Timorese man at the other side of the ward started to scream: 'I want all journalists to leave now! What we need here are peacekeepers! We have enough of telling our stories. It changes nothing!'

The woman, who was called Pauline de Jesus, took no notice of the commotion and continued her story. Early in the morning she had taken her baby to her mother-in-law's house in Dato, a village near Liquiça. They were making paper flowers for the funeral of a family member, when suddenly a group of armed militiamen arrived and started to attack them. 'I ran clutching my baby in my arms. But the men had surrounded the house. They came after me. One of them grabbed me and hit my head and cut my face. I fell to the ground trying to protect my baby. He stabbed me again and again in my shoulder and back. Than the man left me lying there. There was blood everywhere. Probably he thought I was dead already and left.' She lifted the hospital sheet to show me the wounds in her back, her shoulder and the side of her head. Her swollen eyes were still blank with the horror of the attack; her bandages soaked with blood. 'I don't know why they attacked me, I had done nothing.'

§

The image of Pauline and her little baby preyed on my mind for days. What could make people so angry that they would attack a young mother and her infant? I was still thinking of her when I was on my way to Liquiça early in the morning of the first Sunday after the massacre. First I had to pick up Tata and Elisa from their homes in the poor, Timorese part of town. It was too early and too dark for them to go out on their own. They had offered to help with translations. I had some reservations about their joining me, but they had insisted. 'We have to bear witness,' they had said. Although I was worried, I also thought I should not smother their initiatives with my fear.

The day had started badly. We had missed a convoy in which the bishop was travelling and had to go on our own. The taxi driver had been grumbling ever since he had found out that we were going to attend a mass led by Bishop Belo. He wanted to change out of his T-shirt and cap and wear something respectable. But I pressed on: we had little time to lose.

The road to Liquiça closely follows the shoreline, and just outside Dili the sun rose over a smooth silvery mirror of a sea framed by jet-black rocks. For a few seconds the tranquillity of the scene gave me a feeling of peace. Then reality came crashing in. From every house in every village flew red-and-white Indonesian flags. Beneath them stood men in red-and-white T-shirts. Some had knotted the Indonesian flag around their necks like a cape, and wore matching red-and-white bands around their arms and heads. In their hands they held *katanas*, long samurai-style swords, and sticks. 'Besi Merah Putih,' whispered Tata, clearly shaken. The Besi Merah Putih, Red-and-White Iron, was the local militia group blamed for the massacre in the church.

Our taxi had blackened windows and Elisa, who was sitting in the front, wound her window down, smiled and waved. She was wearing a photographer's vest. 'This way they think a I'm reporter from Jakarta, that's safer,' she said with a wink when I commented on her outfit. The men waved and we proceeded without being stopped and searched.

Elisa's and Tata's first encounter with the Besi Merah Putih was still fresh in their minds. They had talked to them earlier that year in their headquarters in Maubara in a reconciliation exercise, to tell them that Timorese should not kill other Timorese. It was one of Antero's efforts to get young women involved in conflict management, his area of expertise. The men had listened to them non-committally. They had grievances of their own. They complained that the CNRT had started to collect 'taxes' from the coffee farmers and the more corrupt of its leaders had bought expensive cars. Manuel Carrascalão's name also came up as the big *fazendeiro* in the area, whose father had, just after the war, been granted many hectares of coffee-growing land by the Portuguese. The Carrascalãos did not have to pay for the plantation, if they could run it profitably. This, combined with their arrogant behaviour and use of an army of 'private thugs', had angered the local people. They did not trust the Carrascalãos. They saw them as 'double traitors'. First they had supported the Indonesians, now independence.

When we arrived in Liquiça it was just after six. A lonely church bell was chiming through the deathly quiet of the streets. It seemed an attractive little town with some nice old colonial architecture, adorned with an abundance of purple and orange bougainvillaea. Its large church was set in a sprawling courtyard dotted with big leafy trees and flowering shrubs that starkly contrasted with the backdrop of the turquoise sea.

Bishop Belo had already arrived, and his purple silhouette stood in the narrow opening of the back door of the church. He had to wait for almost an hour before the first little clusters of women and children trickled through the gate. As soon as they greeted him with a kiss on his hand the tears started to run down their cheeks. He would later remark that it was the first time he had ever arrived at an empty church.

The church bell kept chiming every ten minutes and slowly the pews filled up. Among the women and children sat a few older men. Young men and boys were conspicuously, and ominously, absent. Every single person appeared to be in shock. Many wore black, and all were weeping silently. Madre Margarita walked grim-faced along the aisles, leading the congregation in a solemn prayer. It was in this church that, less than a week ago, a large group of people had taken sanctuary.

Liquiça had been a stronghold of independence supporters. Quite a few had positions within the local government. The pro-Indonesia group was small in comparison, but had the support of the *bupati* and the Indonesian security forces. Months of hostilities came to a climax on 4 April, when the Besi Merah Putih, trying to extend its influence, attacked the house of a pro-independence village chief. The villagers fought back, chasing away their attackers, who then fled for protection to the military headquarters in Liquiça. Padre Rafael dos Santos, the old parish priest of Liquiça, brokered a reconciliation meeting, scheduled for noon the next day. But early the next morning the militia returned to Dato village and killed four people, wounding many, such as Pauline de Jesus. It had been this attack that had triggered Xanana's emotional outburst.

The frightened villagers fled into the mountains, or sought refuge in the church in Liquiça. According to the International Committee of the Red Cross (ICRC), which came to check on the refugees, about two thousand people, many of them women and children, had taken shelter in the church. In the afternoon the ICRC representatives had to go back to Dili. When they tried to return the next morning, they found the road blocked. By then, militiamen, armed with home-made guns and *katanas*, had surrounded the church; behind them stood armed Brimob police and soldiers. They demanded that armed members of the resistance come out and give themselves up. When nobody surrendered, the militia, led by Eurico Guterres, stormed the compound, hacking and shooting adults and children to death.

Padre Rafael was standing on the doorstep of the rectory into which many people had fled. In his white flowing robe and long grey beard, cradling a little girl in his arms, he called out: 'We surrender! We surrender!' But the shooting continued. As Padre Rafael recalled later: 'A militiaman tried to kill me with a home-made gun but the gun failed to go off. Then he tried it with a knife, but I ducked and managed to avoid it. Finally he tried to hit me with a stone but missed again.' Policemen intervened and took the priest to the military headquarters before the final assault.

José Seriau, the civil servant from Maubara, whom I had found in the hospital with a severed ear, was one of the few survivors. He had told me that at least a hundred people were inside the rectory. They had hidden everywhere: under the beds, in the bathroom, in the attic. José Seriau ran outside with his hands up in a gesture of surrender, while his four-year-old son clung to his chest. A militiaman hit him from behind with a sword while another tried to grab his son. Bleeding profusely from his head, he lay on the ground, desperately holding on to his child. 'I was left there lying in a puddle of blood.' Like Pauline and others who survived, he thought they had left him because he looked dead.

The videotape shot by the APTV cameraman, not long after the massacre, showed blood running through the street. There was so much blood and people were so seriously wounded that some newsroom staff at the BBC were physically sick when they saw it, and the pictures were judged too horrible to be shown on the television news.

The military maintained that the reason for the attack on the priest's house was that it had contained weapons. Padre Rafael said that apart from two knives, there were no weapons. That day a military officer told Bishop Belo that 25 people had died. But a day later the military retracted this figure and said there were only five dead, 'all armed resistance fighters'.

The army moved quickly to get rid of the evidence. They rounded up survivors, herded them onto two army trucks and drove them towards Maubara. A few people managed to escape and reported that soldiers dumped many bodies in a large swamp along the way. Yayasan Hak, a human rights organisation in Dili, compiled a list of 57 killed and 35 wounded. While the military cleaned up the bloodstained house, they withheld permission to travel to Liquiça from both the ICRC and Komnas Ham, the Indonesian Human Rights Commission, which sent a team from Jakarta to investigate the massacre. When Komnas Ham was eventually allowed to investigate they had to conclude that they could not find proof that a massacre had taken place.

It was not until months later, after the Indonesians had left, that a forensic team would find more than thirty decomposed bodies in the swamp.

§

On that Sunday, as people slowly trickled into the churchyard, I walked over to the rectory, a spacious white bungalow a stone's throw from the church. The house had been freshly painted, the ceiling boards replaced, new panels fixed in the doors, glass put in the windows, the floor-tiles cleaned of blood-stains, and the paving stones scrubbed meticulously. The only bits of evidence left were a couple of bloodstained ceiling boards, pierced with bullet holes, which stood forgotten against the back wall of the house. It could have been my imagination, but I felt that the thick smell of paint and cleaning bleach had not purged the place of an unmistakable sense of tragedy that somehow lingered in the air.

When I returned to the church, mass had begun. Hundreds of people stood under the trees and in the small triangle of shade alongside the church. They sang hymns that quivered desolately with their tears. They listened intently to the sermon. Nobody whispered or spoke; many wept quietly behind their handkerchiefs. Bishop Belo sounded weary when he spoke about the massacre. 'I see Liquiça is in crisis,' he said. 'The town is in shock and it'll need time to rest. But one day we shall love again and build the town again. In a few days I'll come back again to look after you, to be with you. Now let's continue our mass.'

I found Tata and Elisa each holding a thin old lady in their arms. The women looked so fragile that I was afraid they might collapse at any moment. They sobbed uncontrollably through the whole sermon and Tata and Elisa cried silently with them. 'Tia Angelina told me her brothers and her sons have all disappeared,' said Tata, her voice choked with tears. 'She thinks they're all dead. Now she is all alone, she has no one left.' When the sobbing group went up to Bishop Belo, who was giving holy communion, he urged them sternly to dry their tears: 'Stop crying, Tia, you can't accept the body of Christ when you are crying.' And he waited impatiently while they wiped away their tears.

After mass no one lingered in the courtyard. It was too dangerous to talk. Outside the church compound the militia were lurking on motorbikes. They glared at the people angrily. The bishop had gone for an after-mass coffee with the nuns, who lived not far from the church. I waited outside with Tata and Elisa, sitting on the pavement, as a militiaman came roaring by on his bike waving an big *katana*, and making a sign with an all too obvious meaning: 'I'll cut your throat.' 'Did you see what he did?' I asked an Indonesian police-man who stood near us. 'Go back to your car!' he retorted. But I was too annoyed and kept pressing him. 'This is criminal behaviour, what will you do to stop it?' He shrugged and looked away.

One of the bishop's assistants urged us not to go back in the taxi but to find room in one of the four-wheel-drives. We squeezed into the small luggage compartment of a colleague's Kijang, our legs crammed on top of the spare tyre. On the outskirts of Liquiça the convoy stopped. The bishop wanted to pay a quick courtesy call on the police headquarters. Within minutes a band of militiamen swarmed around our car, brandishing home-made weapons. Some looked no older than 13 or 14.

They came closer and closer, pressing their noses against the darkened glass of the windows to see who was inside. Their faces were contorted with rage, their eyes bulging, bloodshot and deranged, as if they were under the influence of alcohol or drugs or both. I looked at them, unwavering, not wanting to show how anxious their wild insane eyes made me feel. I had not been very afraid before, but their eyes convinced me that they would be capable of anything.

Shortly afterwards our convoy moved on. Around a bend we drove straight into an ambush. A tree trunk blocked the road. More militiamen thronged around the cars, banging their weapons against the windows like angry wasps. Tata and Elisa, shaking with fear, hid their heads on my knees, whimpering over and over: 'They are going to kill us.'

When we moved again, the stones came. Two big ones hit our car. Glass flew everywhere. The next missile was a long iron bar decorated with a red-and-white piece of cloth. It went over the head of a British colleague, who had luckily already ducked when he saw a big stone smashing the windscreen of the taxi in front of us, the one we had come in. We had been lucky; the improvised lance had landed in the back of the car without wounding anyone.

Pursued by a horde of militiamen on motorbikes, our convoy raced back to Dili. The armed police, who had escorted the bishop from Dili, lost their nerve. They drove like crazy, gesticulating frantically that we had to hurry up and get in front of the bishop's entourage. Their automatic weapons pointed at us instead of at our pursuers. It was hard to know whether this was just a piece of theatre – helping foster the fantasy of a militia force that was growing out of control – or whether they were genuinely scared of the thugs.

All over Indonesia the police were known for their cowardice and inactivity when it came to protecting the local population. They would rather stand watching with their hands in their pockets than get involved. So it may be that the uniformed police were not part of a conspiracy. But it did also seem clear that the people in charge of the ambush had a greater scheme in mind, one into which the notion of a militia force that was running amok would fit rather snugly.

Back in Dili I saw that the taxi I had hired had its whole front and rear windows smashed. The big stones still lay in the car. The taxi driver seemed to take it all philosophically; he even smiled. But my relief evaporated when I saw blood trickling down the side of his face. He took his baseball cap off and exposed a bleeding head wound. The message of the attack was clear. The militia were ready to inflict serious harm – serious enough to scare journalists and other foreign observers away from Liquiça and the border areas.

The timing of the Liquiça massacre suggested that the military thought they could derail the imminent agreement between Portugal and Indonesia on the referendum and render a peaceful solution impossible. It also sent a clear signal to the people of East Timor: the Church was not going to be a safe haven. The priests and the nuns, even the bishop, would not be able to provide protection. They were no longer untouchable; they too could be killed.

Padre Rafael had left Liquiça, and it was unlikely that he could go back as long as the militia remained in control. And today the foreigners were fleeing town as they would time and again in the coming months, confirming what the people of Liquiça already knew: that they were at the mercy of brutal thugs, and no one would come to help them.

§

I did not want the militia to think they had scared me. 'They feed on fear, it makes them more powerful,' I thought, as I walked towards the headquarters of Aitarak, 'Thorn', a Dili-based militia group. The best way to beat fear, at least for me, is to confront it. I wanted to show them, and myself, that they had not managed to intimidate me. By turning up in the evening twilight at their headquarters I thought I was doing just that.

Their headquarters was the Motel Tropical, a dilapidated and seedy three-storey guesthouse, near the government palace. Groups of young men and a few women surrounded by a handful of undernourished, dirty-looking children watched silently when I walked towards the back of the courtyard. Behind the hotel stood a big, factory-style building and I peeped around the corner of the open door. In the dimly lit hall I noticed a few men sleeping on a big stage under posters and banners proclaiming loyalty to Indonesia. Near them lay a pile of orange T-shirts with the Garda Paksi emblem. It was Prabowo who had founded this force, and he had put Eurico Guterres, one of his protégés, in charge. Recently Eurico had changed the name Garda Paksi to Aitarak.[1]

On my way out I asked the men, who looked more taken aback than threatening, where I could find Eurico. '*Pak* Eurico,' they said, using the polite Indonesian form of address for a superior, had gone to the bishop's residence. He had heard about the mass in Liquiça and wanted the bishop to conduct a mass for them too. We chatted a bit and they told me they came from West Timor and the nearby island of Alor. It was only a small group I had talked to, but they had confirmed my impression that many of the militiamen active in Timor came from outside. I soon realised that without their big boss around, no one was going to volunteer more information. I needed to talk to Eurico.

From the Motel Tropical I walked towards the bishop's residence, which took me past the house of Manuel Carrascalão. Manuel, I remembered, had told me when I had seen him in December that he was the one who was able to talk to all sides. I found Chris, one of Manuel's daughters, in a state of high nervous tension. She was in her early twenties and had a lot to deal with. As on my first visit, the house was full of refugees who been terrorised by militias in Maubara. Recently a number had returned to their villages, but 130 men, women and children were still camping in the backyard. Many of the refugees were families who worked on the Carrascalãos' big coffee plantations in the mountains above Maubara. They had a long history with the family and Chris felt it was her duty to make sure they were safe and had enough to eat.

The telephone rang constantly. Chris ran up and down to answer it. She looked worn out but also determined. 'Every day we receive death threats.' She shuddered. 'They become a part of our life. What can we do? We can't leave because we have a responsibility to the refugees. Where else can they go?' She was quiet for a bit and then said: 'I saw the list of names of people killed and disappeared in Maubara and Liquiça – many of the names I recognised – they were people who stayed here. After they left they got killed.'

'Can you protect them here, do you think?'

'I don't know. We have no weapons to defend ourselves, just some stones.' She pointed at a small pile of stones in the corner of the living room.

'I guess the only thing we can do is wait and pray.'

While Chris was on the phone Vicente Soares arrived with his five-year-old son. I recognised him as one of the members of Forsarepetil, the pro-independence group of intellectuals. He looked distressed. From a high-placed Timorese in the police department, he had heard that he and his family were in grave danger. A 'clean sweep' operation was imminent. Death lists had been circulating for some time and his informant had said his name was high on the list.

Vicente had looked for help. He had first gone to Bishop Belo, who had told him he could not give him protection. 'They have no respect for me and I'm even not safe myself.' He had proceeded to the ICRC, next door to the bishop's residence. An ICRC worker had replied: 'We can't help. This is no safe place, the militia are intimidating us too.' Finally, Madre Margarita's Canossian convent had taken the family in but Vincente was close to despair. 'What am I supposed to do? I think we had better send our wives and children somewhere safe outside Timor – perhaps the Portuguese could take them – and I can go with the men up into the mountains again. We'll have to take up arms and continue our struggle from there.'

Manuel Carrascalão came home despondent and angry. Like everyone else in Dili, he had received an order to put an Indonesian flag in front of his house before the end of the week. He fumed, but felt he had no choice but, grudgingly, to comply. 'We had a lot of hope, you know. But now I and the other pro-independence leaders, like Vicente here, who stuck their necks out, have become targets.' While he was talking he got more agitated. 'We need United Nations intervention now but the international community stays deaf.'

He and Vicente agreed. 'The UN is responsible, by doing nothing it is co-operating with the Indonesian army to kill the people of East Timor. The people cry and cry but nobody hears them.'

§

In retrospect, the assault on the church in Liquiça seemed to have marked the start of an all-out attack on the CNRT. In the same week reports reached Dili that militias, aided by the TNI, had attacked CNRT supporters in the Ermera, Ambeno and Bobonaro districts. A well-planned campaign was under way. The strategy was to destroy the CNRT and to drive its members underground, recruit all males over 17 as part of a territory-wide militia force and establish political organisations backing autonomy and integration with Indonesia. 'The militia is building up in Dili. They are brought in by military helicopters and are everywhere,' Manuel Carrascalão had said. Dili, it seemed clear, would be the next target.

The sense that the militia could launch an attack any moment was not confined to the Carrascalãos and other leaders of the independence movement. When I returned to the Turismo, I found the gates already closed and Bobby, the American activist, walking around with empty bottles, with ribbons of torn-up sheets hanging out of their necks. He begged for some petrol from one of the drivers, who refused to give him any. 'I don't understand why they don't see we need to do something,' he said in exasperation. Bobby had been annoyed with what he called the 'pacifism' of the Timorese students. He had called the Timorese resistance in the United States to check on bomb recipes, and I had overheard him discussing different types of petrol bombs, and how to use them, with an Irish activist in the dining room of the hotel.

Bobby had boasted of experience in Eritrea and Central America, two other parts of the world where 'hidden wars' simmered. There the resistance had been more militarised, and he thought something similar would be needed in Timor to safeguard the population from attacks. 'They know how to fight in the jungle here,' he conceded, 'but they don't know enough about urban guerrilla warfare. When the militia come they can't just let them kill everyone, they have to defend themselves.' A little later I saw him again, this time with two female hotel staff, each carrying a Molotov cocktail.

CHAPTER 13

. . . .

'Fear is the Parent of Cruelty'[1]

It's not power that corrupts but fear. Fear of losing power corrupts those who wield it and fear of the scourge of power corrupts those who are subjected to it. (Aung San Suu Kyi, *Freedom from Fear*)

§ THE student office looked deserted. The front door and all the windows were closed but the back door was open and I found João Sarmento busy at the computer with a skinny little puppy at his feet. The students had baptised the sickly-looking black thing 'Tavares', after one of the most notorious militia leaders. 'When Tavares comes here and hears the dog is named after him he will first kill the dog and that will give us time to·escape,' João joked wryly, but with an undertone of genuine apprehension.

I had gone to see the students because I was curious about what they thought of the statement Xanana had made about the people's right to self-defence. João said he was pleased. 'In the end, the thing that'll kill us all will be our patience. If we wait much longer we all could be slaughtered like animals.'

He told me the story of a man who had lost five sons to the Indonesians. He went mad and could talk only about politics, and would roam the streets spouting a political message that nobody understood. 'Do we all have to become like that?' João would wonder when he couldn't sleep.

João was upset. Eight students had been jailed for carrying knives while armed militiamen were still walking free. 'It is not only that there is no justice, but justice is against us,' he said, frowning. I looked over his shoulder at the computer screen. João was working on a list of militia groups and their leaders. He showed it to me. Fifteen groups had sprung up across the country. 'Look,' he said, 'they've really chosen their names to scare people.' I copied some of them in my notebook: in Suai the militia was called Laksaur, Monstrous Bird; Viqueque had Darah Merah, Red Blood; Ainaro's was Mahidi, Dead or Alive for Integration; and in Atabae, near the West Timor border, there was Halilintar, Thunderbolt/Lightning.

'Some of these are worse than others.' João pointed at the names of the militias in Baucau: Tim (Team) Saka and Sera. 'A number of them are ex-Falintil soldiers.' João explained that they were captured in 1996 and working for the Indonesians might have been the only way to save their lives. One of their leaders, Joanico Belo, had a house next door to the student office, and that was, according to João, the reason the students had not been attacked yet.

I remember that Xanana had said he knew them from the jungle as ruthless killers, but he also seemed not too worried about them. Like João, he was optimistic that 'they, and for that matter most of the Timorese within the armed forces and the police, were either opportunists or actually on the side of the resistance'. But this seemed wishful thinking; the militia in Baucau appeared more an exception than a rule. In most other districts the Indonesian military had an iron grip on their Timorese allies.

In almost all East Timor's districts existing paramilitary organisations had by now fused into militia groups and had become an important tool in the political game Indonesia was playing. I had to think about what Padre Jovito had said, when he told me that East Timor was not ready for a referendum: 'The dark forces are still alive.' At the time I had been hopeful that he was wrong. But just as he had feared, the legacy of the civil war had come back to haunt Timor. The oldest of the paramilitary groups to re-emerge was Halilintar, which had existed since 1973, but had not been heard of since 1976. It was closely associated with the TNI. Its front man was João da Silva Tavares, a former soldier in the Portuguese army, who had fled in 1975 with the UDT to West Timor and, with the military backing of the Indonesians, had led incursions across the border.[2] The three most active – and cruel – of the militia groups were Halilintar, Mahidi and Besi Merah Putih. Between them they exerted almost total sway over the western, more prosperous districts. They controlled the roads, the movement of the population and the lucrative coffee trade. These western districts were also important in the scheme the integration groups held up their sleeve: the secession of these regions in an 'Anschluss' with Indonesia.

João was wondering whether the students could still influence the situation. When the students had attended the reconciliation meeting in Dare in September 1998 they had, like Padre Jovito, returned disappointed about the lack of any concrete results. Worse, from the students' point of view, the meeting had jeopardised the role they wanted to play as mediators. Bishop Belo had included them in the pro-independence camp. In their eyes this ruined their chance of playing the part of a moral force rising above the old political divisions that still haunted their parents' and grandparents' generations.

§

Fear hung heavy in the air: if it had a scent, the whole town would have smelled of it. As soon as the sun set at six o'clock people rushed back to their houses and the streets became deserted as if there was a curfew. Night-time was the most dangerous time. Apart from patrols by militiamen on motor-bikes looking for activists it was eerily quiet.

One evening Edu, a Falintil contact who was dealing with the FM trans-mitters, had called Bobby and me over to the house where he was staying. In the weeks after the massacre in Liquiça it had become impossible to find taxis after dark and we had no choice but to walk. Luckily we did not have to go very far.

Although we tried to stay out of the streetlights and in the dimness of the shadows of the walls, I felt countless invisible eyes following my every move. I could hear soft voices hissing: 'Hé mister, Hé missis mississss!' I couldn't see anyone, but knew that people huddled next to their unlit houses. In the darkness they could see better what happened around them. Many neighbour-hoods had organised watch rotas with alarm codes so they could warn their neighbours if they saw any danger. When we reached Edu's house, I found the gates closed. I didn't dare make a noise and I called his mobile and whispered where I was.

Edu had remembered me from my first visit to East Timor in 1994. He was one of the young men involved in getting us to Falintil. I had met him again a few days earlier, when he, Bobby and some of the other people Xanana had contacted had come to pick me up to test the FM radio trans-mitters that Bobby had brought from America. They were very excited. The resistance had not had a radio transmitter for years. They had lost the only one they ever had when Alarico Fernandes, Fretilin's information minister, surrendered to the Indonesians, taking the radio with him. We found the new transmitters in the seminary hidden in boxes under Padre Jovito's bed. Bobby was walking up and down impatiently. He grumbled that he had already been trying to get the transmitters to work for two weeks. But Padre Jovito objected to testing them in his room, which would involve climbing on the roof with a big antenna and might put the whole seminary in danger.

The radio equipment had since been assembled, and now lay spread out on the coffee table in Edu's spartan living room. It needed some fine-tuning, Bobby decided, and he tried out a few frequencies, until suddenly the radio sprang into life. Edu took the microphone and made his radio debut: 'This is Radio Maubere!' he said excitedly. 'We will be on air every day.' Then he stopped. He did not know what else to say and Bobby switched the transmitter off again. Now the question was where to set up the antennae.

While Bobby and Edu discussed the options I tried to recollect my earlier encounter with Edu, but I couldn't find a vivid picture of him in my memory. He tended to blend into the background, muddled up with many other faces. Like other Timorese who had spent time in the jungle, Edu was soft-spoken;

and like others who had spent time in jail he tended to be guarded. He had been arrested nine times, and jailed eight times. His last stint in prison was in January 1995.

Immediately after our abortive attempt to reach Falintil in 1994 he had fled to an agricultural training institute run by Father Locatelli, a Salesian priest who had worked in Timor since the 1970s. It was there that he was arrested. But Edu somehow managed to escape from prison and ran to the mountains, where he joined the guerrilla group led by David Alex, one of Falintil's most legendary commanders. He stayed with that group till David Alex was captured and reportedly died in 1997. His death remained shrouded in mystery. Many Timorese refused to believe he had died. Even Bishop Basilio, who had been shown a photograph by the Indonesian military commander, had told me he had his doubts.

Since then Edu had joined David Alex's successor, Commander Taur Matan Ruak. Edu wanted to call him to talk about the transmitter. I lent him my mobile. Edu was my hope of keeping in touch with Falintil. I still wanted to complete my 1994 journey. On our way back we chose our route carefully, avoiding army posts. We walked in silence.

I was thinking of what the nuns had told me recently: 'Dili is starting to look like 1975, a town with almost only women and children.' To escape from the stress of life in Dili I would sometimes go to the Salesian convent for a breath of sanity. The nuns would pamper me with cups of espresso and bowls of fruit salad. Like everyone else in town they had become more nervous. 'People are more afraid than in 1975,' they had said. 'The situation is worse. Back then, the Indonesian soldiers respected the priests and nuns. This time, if no peacekeeping force comes, they'll kill us all. They want the land, but without the people.' I had heard the same from Tata and her family. Every morning before eight o'clock she would call me to tell me she was safe but also to plead with me. 'Please, please help us, they'll kill us all. Please do something!' Sometimes her father would come on the phone too. He worked as a civil servant. Before the war he wrote poetry, published in the same newspaper as Xanana's; now he kept a low profile, but still feared he might be a target. 'Please tell our story to the world. Nobody will listen to us. You're a journalist – it's your responsibility to do this,' he urged me again and again.

I felt a growing despondency. The militia had threatened to attack Dili and journalists did not have the power to change anything. All I could do was to do my work and tell the story as many times as anyone would listen and hope that through international pressure Indonesia would put a halt to the onslaught. Perhaps in other times East Timor would have made more headlines, but now it was difficult. One editor at a magazine I worked for once joked that he could make room for only 'one small war' a week. With a NATO bombing campaign in full swing, the world's attention was directed at Kosovo and there was not much room on the front pages for this little war in faraway East Timor.

§

The seventeenth of April, a day the militias had been advertising as the date of an attack, started with a parade in front of the governor's palace. On the large square stood squads of wild-looking, poorly dressed and fiercely armed men. Under the cloudless blue morning sky it resembled a film set, vaguely reminiscent of the Woody Allen movie, *Bananas*, about a demented dictator in some fantasy banana republic. It all looked so absurd, almost comical, that I had to remind myself it was very real and very disturbing.

Hordes of militiamen had been bused – or even flown – from all over Timor by the TNI. Some platoons wore clean, identical red-and-white head-bands and held wooden sticks that looked brand-new, probably handed out that morning. I took a close look at them. Some men and a few women had eyes that looked more scared than menacing. But there were others, too. They looked ferocious, armed to the teeth and with eyes that flamed with hatred. Their weaponry was crude: bamboo bows and arrows, spears, *katanas*, enormous medieval-looking blunderbusses and pistols made of iron pipes welded together. Only a few carried more modern, factory-made rifles. Later, when they had to sing the Indonesian national anthem, I noticed that they moved their lips but no sound came out. None of them seemed to know the words.

The supreme commander of the militia, João Tavares, made his entrance in an open blue army jeep that drove slowly past the lined-up platoons of riff-raff. He wore an old-fashioned, dark-blue suit that was too tight for him. His hair was dyed black to hide his age – almost 70. The most disconcerting aspect of his appearance was his face: it seemed to be made of wax; not a muscle moved when he saluted his 'troops'.

João Tavares was a stereotype of a stooge. He had long been a willing tool in the hands of Indonesia. The rewards for collaboration were high, and his clan had done well. Tavares lived in a large house, more a fortress, that perched on a rock overlooking Maliana, the district centre of Bobonaro near the border with West Timor, of which he had once been the *bupati*. Some credited him with having protected the East Timorese from the worst excesses of the TNI during that time, but lucrative business deals with Indonesian commanders had brought his family power and riches. Such privileges depended on his loyalty to the Indonesian army. He was heavily in the army's debt, in many ways.

From under the colonnades of the government palace, the entire Dili government watched the spectacle with satisfied smiles on their faces. The police chief, the governor and representatives of the local government mingled amiably with militia leaders, laughing, hugging and kissing.

Everyone seemed to be extremely jolly, but there was an undercurrent of deep anxiety. They felt betrayed by President Habibie, who had forced the idea of a referendum upon them. If the Indonesians withdrew, Tavares and the other collaborators would lose all their power and privileges. Underneath all the bravado, I felt, they were scared, like vicious cats trapped in a corner.

After the Indonesian national anthem, João Tavares took the microphone for a brief speech in slow, heavily accented Indonesian. He seemed not to enjoy the limelight much and as soon as he had announced the inauguration of the pro-integration forces, known as the PPI, he disappeared into the shadows of the colonnade. His newly appointed vice-commander in the western region was Eurico Guterres, the leader of Aitarak. Eurico obviously thrived on attention. He walked around with a growing air of self-importance, like one of the fighting cocks so prized in Timor, which had just had a blade attached to its claw.

When it was his turn to speak, he took his time. Standing on a central platform, he gave the impression that this was his long-awaited hour of fame. In an inflammatory speech he declared 'war against the Carrascalão family', he screamed: 'They destroyed the social fabric of our society and sell the East Timor issue for their own benefit.' The attack on the Carrascalãos seemed to be a warning to supporters of integration not to switch sides as the Carrascalãos had done. They would be seen as traitors and treated with no mercy.

Eurico also called for a clean-up among the ranks of the civil servants, of those he called the 'defilers of integration', who bit the hand that fed them. 'Whether or not the governor agrees we'll conduct Operasi Sapu Jagad against civil servants who are against the government. Starting from today we will enter their houses and offices and confiscate all facilities. Arrest them, and kill them if necessary.' Some in the crowd responded enthusiastically, chanting: 'Kill them, kill them, kill them!'

While I was watching this scene, Basilio Araujo joined me. He looked even smugger than he had on the flight from Bali. 'What you see today is a consolidation of forces,' he explained. 'You have to understand that we were provoked by Xanana's call for war. When Xanana shows force we'll show force.' The Carrascalãos, he explained, were seen as opportunist *mestiços* who first had been instrumental in inviting the Indonesians, and now had turned against them. Pro-independence civil servants were an ungrateful lot that used their privileges, jobs, houses, cars against their employer: the Indonesian state. 'We have got lists,' he said. (He worked in the office of Governor Abilio Soares, in the Department of Foreign Investment.) 'And we know exactly who they are,' he added ominously, 'because after *reformasi* they came out of the woodwork.'

Basilio spoke good English. He had been the first East Timorese student to receive a grant to study at a British university, so he couldn't be as stupid as the things he was saying suggested. I looked at his face but nothing betrayed the slightest embarrassment when he continued, 'The idea of a referendum is against our culture, we want to come to a consensus. What our groups really want is total integration with Indonesia; autonomy is already a concession. So we expect the other side to make a concession too.' The international community, he said, was about to make a big mistake, a mistake that could lead to more bloodletting in Timor.

The ceremony's grand finale involved the Besi Merah Putih showing off the workings of their blunderbusses, which were stuffed with match-heads, nails, bolts and screws. They lit their fuses with cigarettes and fired with great eagerness, while their commander screamed at them to keep the guns directed in the air. Some of the weapons didn't work but most went off with loud bangs and a lot of smoke. Shots echoed back from the other side of the square, where another group had responded spontaneously with some rounds of gunfire of their own. This triggered a couple of panic-stricken Indonesian plain-clothes officers to come running out from under the trees where they had been monitoring proceedings. 'Only shoot on command!' they yelled. They couldn't have it made it any clearer who was in charge.

I followed the militia to their trucks in front of Eurico Guterres's headquarters. They made preparations to go around town in a convoy of motorbikes, trucks and buses, as I had seen independence supporters do. I chose a truck that had only a small group of women in the back. The driver invited me into the cabin and as soon as we moved off, he whispered that he was a supporter of independence. 'They forced me to take part in this, you know,' he said adding that the women in the back only joined because they were promised 200,000 rupiahs, more than a month's salary for most Timorese.

We were towards the back of the convoy of about fifty trucks and two hundred motorbikes. Now and then the convoy stopped and I could see smoke billowing up in the distance, and some minutes later we passed burning houses and the smouldering skeletons of cars and motorbikes. We drove through Lahane and Becora, where the military and police cheered the convoy on and provided snacks and drinking water.

Seeing the destruction, the women on the back of the truck started to look mortified. Like most people in the convoy, they did not take part in the burning and looting. The hard-core militia in the vanguard burned at least a dozen houses – including, curiously, the houses of Eurico's sister and aunt. He apparently had personal scores to settle with some of his family who supported independence.

The bus depot and market in Becora, a target of several previous attacks, went up in flames again. But even after more than two hours of destruction, the militia were still not satisfied. Their next target was Manuel Carrascalão's house. The police had blocked some roads but the road to this house, which was almost next door to Aitarak's HQ, had been left open. When the militia arrived there they were met by Manuelito, Manuel Carrascalão's 17-year-old son. Manuel and his daughter Chris had gone to Colonel Tono Suratman, the commander of the armed forces in Timor, to ask for military protection. Colonel Suratman was at the time in a meeting with David Andrews, the Irish foreign minister. Mr Andrews later recalled that Colonel Suratman flatly refused to send his soldiers. 'The military must remain neutral, you'll have to take care of the situation yourself,' he had told the Carrascalãos.

The military and the police, in the meantime, had gone to the house of the Carrascalãos and joined the militia, who were killing the people hiding there. Journalists who had come too near had been beaten up and chased to the Makhota hotel, where most of them were staying. Next to the hotel, the offices of the newspaper *Suara Timor Timur* went up in flames. The editor was a supporter of Indonesian rule, but the newspaper's brave journalists had reported with surprising objectivity about the militia activities.

A few hours later the Irish minister and his entourage saw Manuel Carrascalão again. He barged into a meeting between them and Bishop Belo. Terrified and shaking, he cried: 'My son is dead!' The Irish minister cut his visit short. He and his entourage were anxious to get back to their aeroplane, which was still waiting on the tarmac.

§

The Motael clinic looked like an army medical unit. Most of the people in the wards had been shot or badly cut with machetes in the attack on the church in Liquiça. Now they were joined by the wounded from the attack on the Carrascalãos' house. One of the Carmelite sisters who ran the clinic was securing the doors and windows. The temperature in the un-airconditioned ward had risen to unbearable levels, and the patients were bathed in sweat.

The sisters had received several warnings that the militia were planning an attack on the clinic. Just after the massacre in Liquiça, Eurico Guterres had turned up to demand to know why the sisters took care of the wounded 'criminals' from Liquiça.

The sisters had not slept for days, and looked exhausted. 'Everyone is telling us not to take care of these patients,' one of them said. 'Even Bishop Belo asked us to be careful and not to treat victims of shootings.' She shook her head in disbelief and gestured with her finger to her head. 'I don't think he is really thinking before he speaks.' She threw her hands up in the air. 'Where else can they go?'

When I walked into the main ward I heard somebody softly calling my name. It was too dark to recognise anyone and only when I came closer I saw that it was Antonio Moniz, a teacher I had met on Ili Manu with Bishop

6. From left to right: Manuel Carrascalão, João Tavares, Bishop Basilio, General Wiranto and Bishop Belo after the signing ceremony.

Basilio. He showed me his leg. The wound looked red and swollen. He had been playing football with some of his students when a soldier had walked by, aimed his gun, and shot him in the leg.

In the bed next to him lay one of Manuelito Carrascalão's friends. Both his arms and his hands had deep slash wounds and were wrapped thickly in white bandages, stained with big dark spots of blood. He was still in shock. Trying to fend off the blows of a samurai sword, his hand was cut to pieces and the fingers on his left hand were almost entirely cut off. The extreme cruelty of the violence he had witnessed had left him numb, and he did not tell his story till some days later.

He told how he saw people butchered, cut up like animals. Babies were taken from their crying mothers and smashed against the wall. When he saw one of the militiamen cut the breast of a girl, he pretended to be dead. Lying motionless in a pool of his own blood near the kitchen door he heard the soldiers and police talking to the militia. 'They told them they should hide the bodies immediately, otherwise journalists would find out what happened.'

When the violence subsided, he managed to escape through the back. He remembered thinking: 'If I die, my body will be taken by my parents to be buried as a small person who knows nothing of the world of politics.' And he hoped that at least someone would survive to bear witness. He did not get far. A Brimob policeman shot him in the back of his knee. An ambulance arrived. He was thrown in with the rest of the bodies, some dead, others still alive. He ended up in the military hospital where doctors operated on him without anaesthetic. Eventually, his family took him to the Motael clinic.

The clinic did not have the resources to take care of serious injuries. Bullet wounds were a problem when they needed to be operated on. There was only one surgeon in the whole of East Timor, and he worked in the military hospital. But a French team – a surgeon and an anaesthetist – from Médecins du Monde had arrived, by lucky coincidence, a day after the Liquiça massacre. The French had come, like Doctor Dan, without a work permit and had smuggled their scalpels and a few other instruments in with a cover story. The Indonesians did not allow foreign doctors to work in Timor's hospitals. President Habibie's policy was to reduce, not to increase, assistance to Timor. And anything that exposed what was going on in Timor's hospitals was perceived as a threat by the military.

Doctor Dan had been quick to recruit the team for the clinic, and they had started work immediately. They had not expected to be dealing with war wounded, just caesareans and appendicitis. They needed to improvise. The clinic had a room reserved for operations but lacked the most essential equipment such as sterilising kits, or even pins to hang a broken leg in a hoist. They had to go to the market to find a big nail, which they had sterilised.

I would visit the clinic often, still troubled by the question that kept preying on my mind: What could make people so angry that they kill mothers, babies and children? 'Drugs' was an answer I had often heard. Or the murder would be blamed on a combination of common thugs, contract killers and Muslims from other islands. The further away, people seemed to say, the more cruel and the less compassionate. But what about the Timorese whom I had seen, taking part in the orgy of violence in Dili?

One important factor was probably fear. It can take many forms, and the fear of losing and the fear of dying provide fertile ground for cruelty. If people anywhere have a choice between their own life and that of others, including even women and children, most will choose to save their own skin and perhaps those of their families.

§

Antero, like most of the Timorese leadership, had been attending a conference on the development of East Timor in Melbourne when the Liquiça massacre had taken place. He was one of the first to return. He arrived on the day of the attack on Dili. I met him the following day among the hundreds of people who had defied their fears and flocked to Sunday-morning mass in the compound of Bishop Belo. Immediately after mass, people fanned out in utter silence. The deathly hush of the streets reminded him of the time after the Santa Cruz massacre, Antero said as we walked in the direction of Manuel

Carrascalão's house and Motel Tropical. He wanted to speak to Eurico Guterres. He seemed keen to use his newly acquired conflict-resolution skills.

Antero knew Eurico, who was 27, three years younger than he was. They had both been involved in the 'St Anthony Movement', a clandestine youth group that had been active around the time of the visit by President Suharto in 1988. Eurico had been one of the young leaders of the movement and was involved in plans to blow up Suharto's aeroplane 'with the use of black magic'.

Eurico was arrested in Viqueque in 1990 and put in jail in Venilale. At that time Prabowo was in command of the Kopassus in Timor, and one of his homes was in Venilale. Edu, who had been locked up in the same prison, told me that Prabowo had visited regularly and tortured at least five prisoners he knew, and 'all of them died'.

No doubt Prabowo had come across Eurico. Perhaps he recognised some potential in the teenager. After all, he collected young Timorese protégés. Some he had taken to Jakarta where they all lived in one of his houses. In general these children came from Apodeti families, but he also fostered at least one son of a resistance leader. Others, like Eurico, he took under his wing in East Timor.

A typical military intelligence tactic was to torture the prisoners and threaten their families while at the same time offering them a way out with promises of big money or other bribes, such as a motorbike, if they would agree to work for them. This tactic was a double-edged sword. Prisoners who were released early were routinely suspected of having sold out to the Indonesians.

Antero thought that something similar had happened to Eurico. He said Eurico had become 'Prabowo's good son'. After his release, he was ostracised by his old friends in the clandestine movement. This, according to Antero, wounded him deeply and might have driven him even closer to Indonesian intelligence. Eurico refuses to talk about this period in his life. In interviews he denies ever having worked in the independence movement. But Mana Lou, whose sister married one of Eurico's brothers, had confirmed Antero's version and added that she knew him as 'bossy, ruthless, ambitious and lazy'.

When we came to the top of the street leading to Motel Tropical and the house of Manuel Carrascalão we saw that the police had set up road-blocks. We walked on but an anxious policeman stopped us. 'Don't go in, they'll shoot you,' he warned, pointing at the mob that stood in front of the Tropical. 'We have no control over them,' he added, shaking his head as if in disgust. Again I wondered whether he was truly afraid or if it was all a clever charade.

Out of nowhere a blue taxi appeared and we decided to take another look at the burned-out Becora market. Becora was a predominantly Timorese neighbourhood and had turned into a notorious trouble spot over the years. It looked like a large village. A maze of muddy paths and small bamboo houses, surrounded by leafy banana trees and high coconut palms. Among its population lived a number of Falintil family members. The neighbourhood was known for its outspoken support of the resistance, but the military also had a large presence. More than half of the Indonesian garrisons present in Dili were quartered there.

Two army trucks with soldiers in full combat gear passed us on the way. When we came near the market we could see and hear that a battle was going on. There were long bursts of automatic gunfire; men armed with bows and arrows were running from behind trees and disappearing between the houses; trucks loaded with armed militiamen were driving in circles shooting at anything that moved.

A few people from nearby houses watched the scene anxiously. One of the women told us that three people had been killed, right where we were standing: in front of the police station. Early in the morning the military had arrived and taken up positions on the hill overlooking the market. The woman pointed them out to us. This was a familiar pattern, and the neighbourhood people knew that an attack by the militia was imminent. They had gathered at the market prepared to defend themselves with sticks, knives, bows and arrows. Within an hour some ten trucks with Aitarak militiamen had arrived and fighting had broken out.

While we stood there watching the distant shooting an ambulance arrived. The driver said they had been called to pick up someone who had been seriously injured. We followed the paramedics to a small army post, a mere hut. The soldiers appeared on full alert. They sat crouched behind trees and sandbags, their rifles pointing in the direction of the main road. On the ground between them lay a man with a chest wound. He gasped for breath and his face looked greenish-white, drained of all blood.

Suddenly a radio started to squeak inside the hut. This seemed to be the signal for the soldiers to relax their vigilance. They stretched their legs and lit cigarettes. They explained that the wounded man had arrived on a motorbike and collapsed next to the army post. He was stabbed by pro-independence supporters, they said. But as the paramedics lifted him up, I noticed a big wound in his back that looked more like a bullet-hole than the result of a stabbing. (Later I would learn that he was in fact an independence supporter who had been shot, and that he died on the way to hospital.)

The soldiers had been on alert the whole morning because they had intelligence from Aileu that Falintil had planned an attack. Antero started to question them conversationally. Why did they not protect the neighbourhood from the militia? he inquired in a friendly way. 'We can only tell people to stay in their houses,' said their commander. 'We can't protect them from the militia.' When we walked back to the road, one of the men armed with bows and arrows warned us that the militia were on their way back. They had burned down one of their houses the day before and they might try to destroy some more.

At the army post the soldiers refused us shelter, so we crouched behind an oil drum and waited. The first seven vehicles passed without incident but then two trucks, which looked liked army trucks, stopped. Loud salvoes of automatic gunfire echoed through the neighbourhood. I could hear the bullets whizz and saw some hit a tree nearby. 'I don't like this,' I heard myself whimpering, my voice sounding strangely high-pitched. I shivered with fear, but Antero stayed calm.

During the attack the military crowded around their post. They didn't take any action to prevent the militia from coming into the neighbourhood. Nor did they protect the population. It was obvious to me, as to everybody in Timor, that if the Indonesians got their way in New York, and security for the referendum was left in the hands of the police and the TNI, it would be a disaster. At best they would watch while the militias wreaked havoc. At worst they would be leading the rampage.

§

A few days later I saw Antero again at the student office. A Catholic organisation in Britain had arranged for a group of high-profile student activists to go to Bali for safety. Antero was undecided about what to do and wanted to discuss his options with his friends. But when I asked him a day later what the outcome was, he said he would leave. 'Sometimes', he said, 'you just have to make a decision yourself.' Again the daily burden of running the student movement fell on the slender shoulders of João, who had not even contemplated leaving.

Antero left on 20 April, the day General Wiranto arrived. The attack on Dili in full view of the Irish minister, the first Western government minister to visit East Timor since the occupation, had caused an international outcry. President Habibie dispatched his minister of defence (who also was the supreme commander of the armed forces) to find a quick solution. Wiranto had meetings with militia leaders and tabled a peace agreement. The next day a signing ceremony was held in the garden of Bishop Belo's residence. The entire militia leadership turned up, looking a little less smug than they had at the inauguration. Eurico Guterres spent the whole ceremony scowling at his hands.

Wiranto made a long speech (one he would cite six months later as proof of his innocence in the total destruction of East Timor). He urged the armed forces and the police not to 'take sides in the conflict' and the Timorese factions to 'abide by the law'. But he did not mention the disarmament of the militias, nor did he acknowledge or take responsibility for the part the armed forces had played in the massacres. Something else he did not mention was that on the night of the attack on Dili a military aeroplane had landed in Dili. From it had stepped General Zacky Anwar Makarim and Major-General Kiki Shyanakri, the head of the Bali regional military command.

General Zacky, a former head of intelligence on Timor, had stayed closely connected to the territory and was believed to be behind the strategy of pitting the Timorese against each other. Operasi Sapu Jagad, an operation reminiscent of other 'clean-sweep operations' conducted by the Indonesians since 1975, was said to have been his brainchild.

The effort to destabilise Timor had worked from the point of view of Indonesia's generals, though perhaps a little too well. They seem not to have expected such a strong international reaction. But they had come close to making a referendum impossible. The UN, after all, was not going to step into what looked like a civil war. In New York, Jamsheed Marker had said: 'Clearly it's not possible to hold these consultations in an atmosphere charged with fighting.'

Even the peace agreement served to propagate one of the army's favoured myths: the idea, which the Indonesians liked to impress upon the international community, that the problem lay with the Timorese; they were fighting each other. The agreement was silent on the role the Indonesian army played. The Indonesian line got picked up by some influential international media, such as CNN and sometimes by the BBC, which kept reporting 'clashes between the pro-integration and pro-independence factions'. When I raised this with the CNN Jakarta correspondent she defended this stance by saying she had to balance the story. A good principle, but in Timor the truth was that the pro-independence group had been remarkably restrained. Falintil had, apart from a few isolated incidents, hardly fought back at all.

The peace agreement was greeted with relief and a large dose of scepticism. People welcomed a pause in the most blatant forms of violence, but they also knew that in the long run it was not worth the paper it was written on.

In Jakarta, Xanana had signed a faxed copy of the agreement. He had no choice. After his earlier angry statement that had been interpreted as 'a call for war', he had painted himself into a corner and needed to show his willingness to cooperate. He also knew that the agreement was a precondition for further UN involvement. And anyway, in his eyes, anything was better than more bloodshed. In Dili, the only representatives of the resistance present, Leandro Isaak and Manuel Carrascalão, who were at the time living under protection at the main police station, signed on the CNRT's behalf. João Tavares and Domingos Soares, representing the military and the political factions of the pro-integration groups, added their signatures. The only ones at the ceremony who refused to sign were the bishops. Bishop Belo had intended to, but Bishop Basilio thought it was a bad agreement, and after a discussion they had decided to word their refusal diplomatically, as: 'We need permission from the Vatican.'

The signatories hugged and João Tavares whispered something in Carrascalão's ear. I later asked Carrascalão what he had said. 'I didn't do it,' he murmured.

Afterwards, in the bishop's garden, I heard Basilio Araujo explaining to some journalists from Jakarta that the attack on the Carrascalãos had been spontaneous. 'When the militia saw that their family members were held in Manuel Carrascalão's house they lost their tempers and got so emotional that they couldn't restrain themselves.'

Earlier that morning I had heard him on BBC radio saying: 'We have to kill for peace.' I asked him to explain this bewildering statement. 'We need the Indonesians, as we needed the Portuguese. The people trust in a third force rather than in the Timorese. When we are left on our own we'll fight each other.'

It was often excruciating to listen to Basilio Araujo. He had become the pro-integration 'spin doctor'. He used what George Orwell called the language of politics: 'defending the indefensible'. And what I found most disturbing was that he seemed unaware of it, or perhaps believed his own fabrications.

What had happened to Basilio Araujo and Eurico Guterres, who, in their youth, like 99 per cent of young Timorese, had been supporters of independence? What had made them turn into such fanatics for integration with Indonesia? Torture had probably played a part in Eurico's case. But then again, countless others had suffered terrible torments at the hands of the Indonesian army and yet had not lost their belief in independence. And what about Basilio?

When I had asked Xanana this question he had replied: 'Money is what happened. When you want to kill a Timorese with a weapon you'll fail, but with money it's easy.'

CHAPTER 14

Blood Rites

§ JUST how bad the situation had become in the areas under militia control could only be guessed. The students did not travel any more; it was too dangerous. After the massacre in Liquiça and the killings in the Carrascalãos' house, it also became very difficult for journalists to get out of the capital. Many taxi drivers had left town, and the ones who stayed were too afraid to drive into the countryside. Travelling in the western part of East Timor had become virtually impossible. Militia groups had set up road-blocks and searched all vehicles. Foreigners, especially Australians and journalists, had become targets. The few foreigners who had travelled in the border area, among them an ignorant French back-packer who had not read a newspaper for months, came back with stories of being pulled off buses and questioned for hours. Their interrogators, they said, had been keen to find out whether they worked as reporters.

One of the few places west of Dili that, surprisingly, could still be reached was Ermera, the coffee-trade centre. It was one of the two districts where the militia had not yet been fully established. Ermera's *bupati* had not been keen on a new militia force. He argued that Ermera already had a paramilitary force, the Kamra, and did not need more than this for its security.

Ermera was also the town of Tomás Gonçalves, an uncle of Antonino Gonçalves, the lawyer I had met in Xanana's prison house. 'Go and talk to my uncle,' Antonino had urged me, 'he collaborates with the Indonesians and he knows a lot.' Tomás Gonçalves came from a powerful *liurai* clan that had supported Indonesia since before the invasion. Antonino had added that his uncle had been with the Indonesian armed forces in Balibo when they had killed the five journalists in 1975.

We set out early – so early that the militia on guard at the road-blocks were too sleepy to come out of their shelters. Along the road the green coffee bushes hung heavy with clusters of shiny red coffee berries. But no one was there to pick them. The first people I saw in the plantations were Indonesian soldiers in full combat gear who were clambering down a dry riverbed. They had been hunting for 'rebels', they said.

Tension in Ermera had been high for some months. Although a militia had not been established this did not mean there had been no killings. In the first months of the year the Indonesian police reported that eleven people, apparently Aitarak militiamen, had been killed, although not much evidence was produced to back up that claim.

In the second week of April, soon after the massacre in Liquiça, the army and paramilitary groups in Ermera started to kill pro-independence supporters,[1] including Antonio Lima, who was a brother of Oscar Lima, an influential pro-independence businessman. The Indonesians had picked Antonio Lima as a member of parliament, to go to Jakarta to support integration. He refused. An eyewitness told me he saw a military commander and three uniformed Kamra members stop his car, order him out and shoot him on the spot.

As in Liquiça, the local government in Ermera was dominated by CNRT members. As soon as the reforms had set in, they had established offices in the old town of Ermera, in Glenoo, the administrative centre, and in the sub-districts. They had been so well organised that they formed more or less a shadow government.

I found neither Tomás Gonçalves nor the *bupati* at home, only their servants, who said they had just left for Jakarta with their families. Tomás Gonçalves would later that month surface in Macao. He had defected. The plans put forward by the military to the local authorities had been so gruesome that he could not comply. They had told him they would kill priests and nuns, which was going too far for him. (A more cynical explanation of his defection might be that he saw the writing on the wall for the pro-integration crowd.)

Whether by design or otherwise, the *bupati* had got out of town just in time to miss the first big rally and public appearance there by the militia. The next day Eurico Guterres and members of the FPDK drove in a long convoy to Ermera. On board their fleet of Kijangs and minibuses was almost the entire national and international press corps from Dili. Without an escort, they said, it would be too dangerous to travel anywhere. Many journalists saw it as their only chance to get out of town.

Money for these rallies was flowing in from the central government in Jakarta. The governor had already allocated 6 billion rupiah (roughly $500,000 at that time, or $38,000 for each of the 13 districts, which would go quite a long way in Timor). And there was more to come. After approving the autonomy package, the Indonesian government would earmark for Timor money from its poverty-alleviation budget (which was supported by World Bank money). These funds, 3 billion rupiah per district, were allocated to the *bupatis*. Since most were pro-Indonesia, the money went directly to pro-integration activities. The Ministries of the Interior, Foreign Affairs and Defence also received Habibie's blessing to allocate funds to the pro-integration factions, and to turn a blind eye to the methods they intended to use to 'socialise' the autonomy package – that is, to sell it to the East Timorese.

The event in Ermera was part of what was called Apel Akbar Sosialisasi Otonomi – 'public rally for socialising autonomy'. To drum up attendance, people had been trucked in from all over the district. They assembled in the sports ground in the centre of Glenoo. Each group held a board bearing the name of the locality they came from. I saw *datos*, *kuku nains*, elders and tribal chiefs in full traditional dress, hand-woven *tais* around their waists, bunches of colourful cockerel feathers adorning their heads and ankles, and big silver discs hanging heavily on their bare chests. They carried knives and spears. While all the photographers concentrated on these exotic-looking chieftains, I spotted two groups of armed men, herded on to the field by sturdy, well-fed and well-groomed men who looked Javanese. They sported T-shirts and jeans and tell-tale crew-cuts. As soon as I pointed my camera at them they shielded their faces with their hands and gestured at me angrily. They started back in the direction of one of the nearby government buildings. I pursued them, inquiring who they were. They looked like Kopassus commandos. For weeks people in the western part of East Timor had complained about new groups of Indonesians who had arrived – faces, they said, they had never seen before.

One of the armed groups on the field was a Kamra unit. They wore neat olive-green uniforms and had polished rifles in their hands. The other was a ragtag band of malnourished bare-footed men who waved long knives, bows and spears. Beside the Kamra, the thirty or so militiamen looked even more scruffy.

'These are the new militias, the Darah Merah, Red Blood,' explained Mário Florencio Vieira, one of the FPDK's advisers, who had studied in the United States. 'Do you want to ask them some questions?' I felt reluctant at first. What would they be able to say? On an occasion like this they were hardly likely to tell me the truth about how they had been forced to take part in this charade. If they did it could cause them serious trouble. But I was too curious about what had motivated them to join the militia. A man in the centre of the group replied: 'The CNRT promised us that people from the international community would come here to protect us; but they lied, they lied, no one has come.' So this was what the military had told the people. I could understand their confusion and fear. When I suggested that the UN had been delayed but was planning to come in a few weeks' time the group remained quiet for a while. They looked perplexed. Then one of them shouted: 'We want integration anyway!' Some others, sounding hesitant and bewildered, echoed his call.

They did not seem to be very fanatical, and it was hard to see how this group of thirty ill-looking emaciated men could form a real threat. In Los Palos, another district where the build-up of militia groups had lagged behind, a local priest told me that the militia, called Tim Alfa, had fewer than ten members, but, he added, although that didn't sound many, it was enough to create real havoc. After all, the military needed only a small group, as a kind of decoy, the pawns they could move around to disguise who was really behind the violence. With military backing the powers of these sorry-looking little groups were almost unlimited.

In Ermera, the first task of the pro-integration forces was to wrest power from the CNRT. This had not been too difficult. Of its four principal leaders two had fled into the hills and the others had been taken into custody in the police station. 'They were not really in detention, they volunteered', as Mário put it, 'for their own protection.'

These 'protected' CNRT leaders were now led on to the centre of the field. In front of the crowds they had to renounce their CNRT membership and sign a paper that stated that the CNRT no longer existed in Ermera. The pro-integration leaders realised that this was after all just a piece of paper. So they had organised tribal elders to perform a 'sacred' rite that was used in the Timorese tradition, to mark important agreements – for example, to ratify an alliance with another clan.

Two imposing elders called out to their spirit ancestors. The cockerel feathers of their head-dresses fluttered backwards and forwards as they swayed their heads and, with long resounding howls, called up the spirits to bear witness. Then they sacrificed a cockerel, slit its throat and caught the blood in a cup. They mixed the blood with *tua sabu*, a strong, fermented local palm wine, and under the eyes of the assembled crowd the two CNRT men had to drink the concoction.

Almost every day, somewhere in Timor, pro-integration leaders organised one of these 'blood-oath ceremonies', which were believed to create commitments that were hard to break. Local chiefs, and in some cases the whole population of a district, would have to drink these potions. Sometimes the blood used was human. The rites were especially common in Aileu, which was ruled by an Indonesian *bupati* who had gone native – a bit like Kurtz in Conrad's *Heart of Darkness*. He spoke Tetum, which was unusual for an Indonesian official. And even more unusual, he had crowned himself *liurai*, in front of a gathering of traditional leaders and villagers. He said he loved East Timor as his home and considered the Timorese his brothers. He toured the district tirelessly drumming up support for autonomy with such ceremonies.

In Ermera it was Eurico Guterres, relishing his now official role as vice-commander, who took the lead. He warned the crowd that independence would mean famine and civil war. 'Do you want to eat stones? When you have independence you'll have to eat stones!' He asked the crowd if they wanted him to replace some local officials. Mário Vieira was translating the crowd's answers for me. 'Some say they want them to resign or to be replaced. But some of them say just kill them,' he said, laughing unpleasantly.

After he finished his speech I saw my chance to talk to Eurico. When I approached him he was being interviewed by an Indonesian journalist who had asked him about his hairstyle. He wore his hair short on top, often covered by a baseball cap, and long at the back. She wondered how, as a military commander, he could have such long hair. The way she put the question to him had something flirtatious in it, but this seemed to be lost on Eurico, who answered everything in the same crude humourless manner.

When Eurico noticed I had started to film him he looked hard into the camera. 'The whole world wants the ABRI (the Indonesian armed forces) out. That's fine, it doesn't matter. But I and my soldiers are prepared to die for integration,' he said. 'If Xanana returns and does not stay neutral one of us is going to die. Timor is too small for both of us and I'll have no choice other than to kill him.

'If you want to be gentle and fair,' he said, 'let the pro-integration army and Falintil fight, but never use innocent people.'

I looked around. For three hours the people had been standing in the burning sun. The ones who stood in front made a credible performance of their support of integration. They shouted the slogans, sang the Indonesian songs and clapped when they were supposed to clap. But in the back row, hidden from view, I found a few old ladies. Softly I asked one of them how she felt. She clutched her arms tightly around her chest. Quivering like a scrawny, scared bird, she whispered: 'Tauk', 'I'm afraid'.

§

As the negotiations in New York dragged on towards their conclusion in early May, the militias' grip on the countryside tightened. All over the country people went and cheered the pro-integration rallies, or took part in blood-drinking ceremonies.

This created an illusion. The pro-integration faction lived in a world of mirrors that reflected what it wanted to see. It saw that people joined the militias, put their names on lists and went to blood-drinking ceremonies. But they kept their real feelings to themselves. People were clever enough to know that it was better to show them you were with them – then they might leave you alone – than to resist them.

There was nothing noble about it. It was a matter of survival: to stick with your convictions was equivalent to suicide. The result, though, was that the pro-integration groups believed that, as long as they could keep up the pressure, they would win a referendum, or that at least it would be a close call.

§

At the time of the massacres in Liquiça and in the Carrascalãos' house, Mana Lou had been in Java. As soon as she came back and heard about the situation in Liquiça, she loaded a bag of rice into the pick-up she had recently acquired as a donation from some priests from Holland, and was on her way. I saw her in her house in Dili just after she returned. She was full of what she had seen and what she was trying to do.

Liquiça was still surrounded by road-blocks manned by the Besi Merah Putih. Since the attack on the church, they had held the town in an iron grip. They didn't allow aid agencies, or even the Church, to bring food or medicine. Mana Lou managed to get through the checkpoints by pretending she wanted to visit her family. Apart from members of the militia, she found no one in the street. People had become too afraid to leave their houses. While she was with one family, militiamen banged on the windows and gestured to her to get out.

The food situation in the little town was getting worse by the day. People were surviving on the dried food they had in store, but this was fast running out, and the first child had already died of starvation.

Mana Lou was still working desperately at fostering Timorese unity, which seemed a rather hopeless endeavour at the time. She was up against the force of the Indonesian army, which did not want unity: it wanted strife. After what I had seen happening in the past weeks, I had not much hope that she could prevent worse things from happening. I argued with her that the Indonesian army was behind it all. Even if the Timorese wanted to bury their differences, the army would find a way to force them to fight.

She angrily rejected this. 'They are also Timorese. I will talk to them and I will persuade them, at least, not to kill the civilian population.' After this outburst, she remained quiet for a bit and I saw that her eyes were moist. 'You see, if we were united, something like this could not have happened.' As soon as she returned to this, her familiar theme, her tears started to flow. 'Sorry, sorry,' she mumbled, blowing her nose. I had got used to her frequent tears, but I had not seen her so despondent before.

After a few minutes she took a deep breath and said: 'Some time ago I saw a film about Gandhi. It made me so upset that I had to leave the cinema. I couldn't carry on watching it. I kept thinking why can't we be as united as the Indian people? Why can't we mount such a powerful peaceful resistance? We make so many mistakes, we will destroy our own country.' Even in the face of their common enemy the Timorese had not united, she said. Unity was Mana Lou's mantra, and she explained everything that happened in the light of post-colonial behaviour, and the division of the Timorese by the Portuguese.

But that fragmentation, seen also in other former Portuguese colonies, could only partially explain Timor's troubles. Other explanations – for example, that greed, the lust for power, revenge and envy are part of the human condition – were perhaps too cynical for Mana Lou, who believed, or at least tried with the help of her prayers to believe, in the good and not in the evil side of people. We sometimes talked about this. Mana Lou was simply convinced that she could change people. But she would never put it that way, she would talk of what, through her, Jesus could do.

In the weeks that followed she doggedly built up a relationship with the militias in Liquiça. She believed that as long as she could show them, in her words, 'compassion and not hatred', she could change them. She started by delivering small quantities of rice. This way she could pretend she had brought it for her family, and ran less of a risk that militiamen would confiscate it. She would go on her own, taking only the driver. On one of her first trips her driver almost got killed. Reversing the car, he had backed over one of the many Indonesian flags. The militia were furious and accused him of sacrilege. With a lot of effort she managed to convince them that the driver had simply failed to see the flag because it was already dark, and they returned safely to Dili.

When I asked her something about the militias she briskly interrupted me: 'Don't call them militias. Most of them are just poor people who are used. They don't want to take part in it, but if they don't kill, they will be killed.' She tried to build up trust. When distributing food, she made sure she gave equally to the families of the militias. 'They are victims of the system too,' she argued. 'Their families don't have health care or much to eat either.'

She became a regular guest of Liquiça's *bupati*, Leoneto Martins – a pompous Timorese with a big belly and rather rude, arrogant manners – and she held what she called 'prayer-groups' at his house. She saw him changing for the better, she said. He had told her: 'Mana, when you speak you touch our heart, the sisters and priests don't touch our heart, it is important that you stay here. You have to work for the people.' 'He likes my singing, too,' she added proudly. And she had asked him if she could sing for the militia groups. But he had answered, 'No, be careful, Mana, your songs sound much too political, they sound as if you are pro-independence.'

Although the *bupati* and Manuel de Sousa, the commander of the Besi Merah Putih, seemed to listen patiently to Mana Lou, it was not clear whether they could, even if they wanted to, back out of the army's plans for them. They had all been all corrupted, either through power or money, or both, and were tightly controlled by the Indonesian military, especially the powerful Kopassus. The only way out would be to escape, like Ermera's Tomás Gonçalves.

Mana Lou felt very alone. From the Church in East Timor she received only a little support. A couple of Timorese NGOs and Church groups had given her food, second-hand clothes and a few million rupiah. None of them, including the Catholic relief organisations, could get aid to the town. And the relief organisations were too bogged down by their own bureaucracy, according to Mana Lou, to give her the rice they had in store to distribute in Liquiça.

She was also disappointed with the leaders of the Church. Bishop Belo had not, despite the promise he made during the commemoration mass a month ago, yet returned to Liquiça. He would not do so, in fact, for many months, until after the Indonesians had left. As for Padre Rafael, the parish priest, the militia had threatened to kill him if he ever set foot again in Liquiça. As if to make the point, they had killed one of his cousins, a policeman in a nearby village. No priest had replaced him, so the only Church people left in town were a small group of nuns. But they, according to Mana Lou, stayed clear of the militia. 'Why did the Church not show enough initiative and courage?' she wondered. 'And who is going to mediate?' she asked rhetorically. 'Who will talk to the people, pray with the people?'

One day on her way back from Liquiça to Dili, Mana Lou stopped in Tibar, a village spread out around a strategically located T-junction, where the road forks off to Ermera. The road around Tibar had many checkpoints and a large Indonesian army base. Usually the road-blocks consisted of one or two oil drums, sometimes with a wooden cross-bar between them. A group of men with red-and-white headbands hung around nearby, in the shade of a bamboo shelter. Often they were too engrossed in a game of dominoes or cards, or too sleepy, to get up and stop cars. Mana Lou had asked them why they spent their days sitting there at the roadside. 'We are told to sit here,' they answered. 'Don't you have to work on the land? How can you look after your wife and children? Do you get paid?' Mana Lou had bombarded them with questions, and then went into her organising mode. 'There are more than ten men here now,' she said. 'How many do you need to have to hang out here? Five? Why do you sit here with ten then?' They got a bit embarrassed and said they had been promised money, but admitted they had not received it yet. 'If only five need to be here you can sit here in turns and have time to work on the land,' she said. 'Don't let them use you!'

Later she went back to pray with them. The men wept. They told her that a few days earlier a local military commander had conducted a 'blood-oath ceremony' and forced the entire village to drink from a cocktail of human blood and *tua sabu*. Telling the story she became angry again. 'I told them not to drink the blood or the alcohol they get offered. Just pretend to swallow it and later spit it out!' she said. 'I told them you'll be drugged and won't know what you're doing, you could kill your own mother or son.'

When we parted, Mana Lou said that when she moved to Liquiça she would take a group of her women with her. 'What better training could her *aspirantes* get', she argued in her unanswerable way, 'than to work in Liquiça?' 'Please don't come to see me,' she implored while I was on the doorstep, adding, 'If you see me on the street in Liquiça don't stop and talk to me, this could make my work more difficult. I'll send you a message when you can come.'

. . . .

CHAPTER 15

Asking the Fox to Guard the Chickens

§ 'THESE are our forces!' chanted a group of children. They jumped and danced around, waving at a white UN helicopter that circled low over their neighbourhood. From behind a barbed-wire fence an old man stared open-mouthed at the blue UN flag that had fluttered since 4 June above the school compound where the UN had made its headquarters. He had walked for four days through the mountains to see the UN with his own eyes.

For many years Timorese had rallied, lobbied, fought, demonstrated, pleaded and prayed – especially prayed – for the UN to come to Timor. Its arrival had brought tears of relief. 'We hoped and prayed and finally it has happened, the world has come to Timor,' Padre Jovito beamed when I asked him how he felt. 'The people have dreamed about this day for 23 years. To see them, finally, gives a sense of security and hope that this struggle will have an end.'

The UN had chosen a teachers' training college in Dili as its headquarters. The Indonesian army was unhappy about the location: too close to the hills (and Falintil), and too close to the centre of town. They objected that they could not guarantee the UN's security there. They had in mind to base the UN near the airport in Comoro, preferably inside or next door to one of the many military compounds. They tried to put pressure on the person in charge of the teachers' compound, who happened to be one of Xanana's sisters, into making up some excuse to turn the UN down. She stood her ground.

Slowly, Dili changed. With every passing day more UN personnel arrived and more white Toyota four-wheel drives with 'UN' in big black letters on their sides plied the streets. People started to feel safer. The suffocating atmosphere of fear began to dissipate, yielding to a joyous, but cautious, optimism. Shops and restaurants reopened, taxis came back from wherever they had been hiding and people ventured out of their houses again. Every night a few more people would dare to walk the streets. Very, very gradually life returned to what passed for 'normal' – in so far as the word had any meaning while there were still army posts in every neighbourhood and bands of PAM Swakarsa, 'community self-defence groups', as the militias were now formally known, on strategic corners, spying on every move people made.

Though mindful of the dangers, many people still had faith in the international community. They believed that now the UN had arrived at last, the militias would lose their stranglehold. Pro-independence activists grew bolder again: the students established branches of their Solidarity Council in the countryside; CNRT leaders came out of hiding to reopen their offices.

Unamet – the acronym by which the United Nations Mission in East Timor was known – had to work fast. It had less than two months to prepare East Timor for the referendum. Compared with other such missions, it stood out for the smallness of its scale, and its extremely short time-frame. It required a fast deployment – the fastest ever, it was said. Not an easy task for an organisation notoriously swamped by bureaucracy. Heading the mission was Ian Martin, a former secretary-general of Amnesty International. He had a working budget of around $57m, and had to scramble to get Unamet up and running. There would be just over a thousand UN international personnel (more than half of them UN volunteers), assisted by roughly the same number of local staff, although their ranks would swell to four thousand by the time of the ballot. Human resources, like everything else in East Timor, were very limited, and the UN could not find enough local interpreters. How to get UN workers to many of the more remote parts of the island was also problematic.

§

The logistic challenges of the mission were, however, the least of its worries. The UN had also to ensure that there was fair play between two sides, one of which had no interest in the rulebook. The agreement, signed in New York on 5 May between Kofi Annan, Ali Alatas and Jaime Gama, Portugal's foreign minister, provided for the UN to arrange a 'popular consultation' to be held in East Timor on 8 August. The Indonesians had objected to the word 'referendum', because of its implications for the legitimacy of their occupation, and for the right they asserted the MPR retained to ratify the result of any vote. This was a factor in the timing. The MPR would be convened at the end of August, after parliamentary elections in June.

Despite the semantic niceties, a referendum is what it was. The Timorese would be asked to accept or reject Indonesia's proposal of a 'special status' with enhanced autonomy for the region, under Indonesian sovereignty. This was to be carried out in 'a fair and peaceful way in an atmosphere free of intimidation, violence or interference from any side'. Even before the registration of voters for the referendum could start, Kofi Annan had to make a determination that 'the necessary security situation exists for the peaceful implementation of the consultation process'.

But, from the outset, both 'fair' and 'peaceful' looked almost unattainable targets. Even the choice on the ballot paper, which looked straightforward enough, could be seen as unfair. The wording was carefully vetted by Indonesia to reflect its perception of its sovereignty. So the word 'independence' did not appear. To vote for change and freedom, Timorese – nearly half of whom, after all, were illiterate – had to reject the proposal.

The choices were: 'Do you accept the proposed special autonomy for East Timor within the Unitary State of the Republic of Indonesia?'; and 'Do you reject the proposed special autonomy for East Timor, leading to East Timor's separation from Indonesia?' Rejection would mean that East Timor could split off from Indonesia, and authority would pass to the UN, to complete the transition to independence so rudely interrupted by the Indonesian invasion in 1975.

The contents of the autonomy proposal had, in fact, been watered down over the months, in response to the old worries in Jakarta: that the precedent set by any such proposal – let alone independence – for East Timor might inspire other provinces to seek a similar deal. At the time there were concerns not just about traditional trouble spots with separatist movements, such as Aceh, but even about some other, relatively peaceful areas. As Indonesia's economy had come close to meltdown, some commodity-rich provinces began to wonder if the costs of belonging to Indonesia did not outweigh the benefits.

In the end, East Timor was offered, on paper, less freedom than, for example, Hong Kong and Macau get as Special Administrative Regions of China. Indonesia would retain control not just over matters of defence and foreign affairs, but also over policy on currency and finance, including, controversially, national taxation. The Timorese would have their own administration, police force and judiciary, but they could not directly elect their local government representatives. And the Indonesian flag would still fly over East Timor. The UN members, especially Australia, the USA and Portugal, had agreed that, if the Indonesian proposal was approved, it would initiate the procedures necessary for the international recognition of Indonesian sovereignty. But the Indonesian autonomy proposal was one most Timorese would not even make the effort to read. Whatever Jakarta had come up with at this stage would not have been trusted in Timor anyway.

As for the requisite 'peaceful environment', the reports the Security Council were getting from Unamet were not very positive: 'a climate of violence, fear and intimidation pervades much of daily life', especially outside Dili, according to one such litany of terror.[1] People who in the past used to go with their testimonies of harassment, torture, rape, abductions and killings to human rights organisations in Dili were now also knocking on the door of the UN. Dutifully, the political officers would note down the complaints and pass them on to the Indonesian police. They were, after all, in charge of upholding law and order. But nothing would happen.

Already, the price the UN would pay for not having forced Indonesia to accept an international security force was beginning to become apparent. Of course, a UN peacekeeping mission was always out of the question. The UN's members, especially the United States and Indonesia's friends in Asia, did not want it, and, above all, Indonesia would not allow it. But without it Unamet's mission would always be impossible (indeed, some people started calling it, for this reason, 'Unamiet'). It might be able to set up the technical part of the consultation, but the validity of the exercise would entirely depend on how much courage the Timorese could muster.

Unamet knew the conditions were not at all optimal, and were not improving much either. But there was not much its officials could do about it, beyond flying regularly to Jakarta for talks and returning with reassurances from Indonesian officials that things would get better. To enhance security, more Brimob and police were dispatched.

UN officials seemed ready to believe what Indonesian officials said, or at least to give them the benefit of the doubt. But many Timorese found it hard to understand why the Indonesian reassurances were taken so seriously. Few observers doubted that there was a majority in favour of independence. But how could a fair ballot be held while the Indonesian army was still around and the Indonesian police were responsible for security? 'It is like asking the fox to look after the chickens,' said Doctor Dan Murphy when I looked him up in the Motael clinic, where Antonio Moniz, living testimony to the security forces' standards of behaviour, was still lying with his leg in a hoist.

My student friends could not understand why the UN abided by conditions set by Indonesia. The UN had never recognised the annexation of East Timor; yet now it seemed to be recognising Indonesia's *de facto* rule. But from the UN's point of view, Indonesia had made an enormous concession – that a vote would be held at all – and Unamet now seemed ready to bend over backwards not to offend it.

So, in public, UN officials would keep patting the leaders in Jakarta on their backs, as if harsh words would make things worse. What did they have to lose? Why not play a tougher game? What good were carrots, if there was no stick?

An obvious stick could have been economic. Postponement of funds needed so very badly by Indonesia to build up its shattered economy might have changed its conduct. But many countries, including Australia and those in the EU, did not want to rock the boat. Indonesia, they argued, was in the throes of a very delicate democratic transition. If it was not handled with care there could be a backlash.

After a while, embarrassment was used as a tactic to shame the Indonesians into better behaviour: an old schoolmaster's trick. One day in June, for example, the UN stumbled across the Indonesian army in the middle of one of its operations in the villages, exactly as Mana Lou and others had described them. They saw a group of thugs armed with knives and sticks, followed by a platoon of soldiers, in the process of burning down houses and beating up an old man. But the only response Indonesia could come up with when the UN made complaints about such outrages was to shake an accusing finger at the Timorese resistance and the pro-integration militias, and conclude that they would have to send in more police units.

As for the UN, 'the Security Council just doesn't want to hear bad news', according to an official in New York. With bad news a taboo, Unamet's reports of serious unrest and the UNHCR's estimate of 100,000 internally displaced people – that is, one in eight of East Timor's population – were not even discussed in the Security Council.

§

In June I travelled to Liquiça for the first time since the attack on the bishop's convoy. Liquiça was a place where the shortcomings of the UN strategy were all already obvious. A low-intensity war was raging in the countryside. Tens of thousands of people had fled from the towns to the mountain villages.

I travelled again with Tata. This time we sat in a UN car with two Unamet officials – a political officer and a Unamet spokesman. Like many English-speaking students, including Elisa, Sebastião and Sicco, Tata was employed as an interpreter by Unamet. Sebastião was working in the information department, as the assistant of the UN spokesman. Falintil could be proud of one of their informal 'external information officers'.

The students worked six days a week in their new UN jobs. During the first weeks they were exhausted and complained that they had never had to work so hard in their lives. Deprived of their daily siestas, they lost weight. But they liked their work. Tata said it gave her the feeling that she was working for her country, and when she got used to the hard work it actually gave her more energy.

I watched her in the front of the car, in her blue UN baseball cap, staring out of the window. We had the same thoughts. It was less than three months since we had been chased down this same road by Liquiça's militias. Tata remembered it as the time she had been more afraid than ever before in her life. But now the UN had arrived, she felt the worst was over.

We were going to Liquiça 'to wave the flag, and let our presence be felt', in the words of the UN spokesman in our car, who had just arrived in Timor, to find that nothing that he had heard in New York had prepared him for the situation on the ground. By the middle of June, Unamet had opened offices in most of Timor's regencies, but had no presence in Liquiça. Even the political officer, who had to cover Liquiça from Dili, had not been able to establish a foothold, because Liquiça's *bupati*, Leoneto Martins, the man Mana Lou had

7. Rice for the children.

sung her songs for, objected to any kind of UN presence. He had turned back
two UN cars a few days ago and was threatening to kill any UN staff who
came to Liquiça.

So we were part of a new attempt to establish contact. This time the
presence of an Indonesian police escort, a group of human rights workers
and some journalists was meant to intimidate the authorities into talking to
the UN.

Our first stop was a village where the UN had heard that the village chief
held eight women as sex slaves for the militias. This was part of a pattern of
the rape and abuse of women that had intensified during the spring of 1999.
In areas where the militias had their strongholds, rape and the threat of rape
had become one of the most common forms of torture and intimidation.
Mana Lou's brother, Elvis, had heard of 67 rape cases in Bazar Tete, a remote
village in Liquiça district. Since most men had disappeared into the mountains,
the women were unprotected at home. I had heard from Mana Lou that
almost every night the militias held dance parties and went from door to door
looking for dance partners. They would keep the women and girls the whole
night, and often the party would culminate in gang rape. She had been very
scared for her girls and did not dare to leave them alone at night.

When we found the village chief, he told us that the women had gone
home – coincidentally, that very morning. Where to, he couldn't say. He had
probably had time to clear away any evidence, since it had taken a long time

to organise our police escort, long enough for local authorities to be fore-warned of our travel plans.

I saw that Tata had wandered away from the UN delegation and was talking to one of the women in the village chief's household. She talked softly and calmly, was a good listener and had a gentle and warm way of dealing with people. The work suited her. She didn't antagonise anyone. And soon she had found out that at least two of the women had been taken to a nearby village.

Among the members of our convoy was a rape victim from Liquiça, brought along on this trip by a women's rights organisation. She guided the convoy to its next destination, the house of her rapists. Eventually, we set off again, and so the journey continued, stopping everywhere Unamet had received complaints about ill-treatment and intimidation.

On our way back we stood for a while in front of a house that I recognised as the place where we had been attacked a couple of months earlier. A few men, smoking *kreteks*, lazed around under a bamboo shelter. They noticed us but didn't get up, just glared. 'Take a photo of them,' urged the UN spokesman. 'That might in come handy for their future trial.' I wandered around the main house. On the veranda hung a series of family portraits. One of these showed Prabowo surrounded by a smiling family. When I glanced from the photograph to where the men were sitting I recognised one of them from the photograph. He was the owner of the house, and no doubt an ex-service man. As my eyes met his, I saw cold hatred. Just you wait and see, his eyes seemed to say, we are not finished yet, we are just beginning.

§

A week later Unamet opened an office in Liquiça, and Mana Lou sent me a message that I could come to visit her. She was easy to find. The *bupati* had given her the use of a large abandoned guesthouse in the centre of town. I found her in the kitchen poking around in huge pots of simmering rice and vegetable congée. Mana Lou had set up a feeding programme. She had more than twenty young women helping her cook and distribute the food. But with the 500 kilos of rice she had collected in Dili to hand out every day, she could feed only the children and sick old people.

She had also opened a small pharmacy. Her sister, who had started to study medicine a few months before, distributed the pills and powders. She asked me to help her with the translations of some labels on the jars and wanted to know what dose of malaria medicine a baby should be given. Her questions horrified me and made me wonder how much good was done by this barefoot doctoring – or cowboy quackery. But what was the alternative? No doctors had been able to come to Liquiça yet. The hospital had as good as closed, having neither medicine nor medical staff. And children were dying.

Later that day I found out just how bad things were. Walking through a place such as Liquiça was unnerving. The women I met would turn their heads and cross the street as soon as they saw me coming in their direction. They averted their eyes so they could later not be accused by the militia of even having made eye contact with a foreigner. All the men roaming the streets seemed to be militia members; they gave me scowls and nasty looks.

In one of the side streets I found a family sitting in stunned grief around the body of their nine-year-old son. He had died of dysentery, a death that could easily have been prevented. In the same street I found another family. They had, like thousands of others, been chased from their village in the mountains by the army and had taken shelter in the burned-out shell of a house. The father sat in a corner with his ill son lying limply in his lap. He looked at me with panic in his eyes. He was too sick to lift his son up, he said. 'We all have fever and I don't know what to do. We have no food.'

When I returned I found Mana Lou still busy in the pharmacy. I told her about the people I had seen. She reacted angrily. 'Why do they not come to me? I could have taken him to the Sick House in Dili and Doctor Dan could have looked after him.'

I knew Mana Lou's Sick House. It was already full of people from Liquiça, more than twenty of them: mainly old people who had lost their families and could not take care of themselves. They almost all suffered from tuberculosis, an illness endemic in Timor. The medication they needed could not reach Liquiça any more. To be able to accommodate them all she had improvised some more space by taking doors out of their frames and turning them into beds.

While she arranged newly arrived medicines on the shelves of the small pharmacy, Mana Lou told me she had had a meeting with the UN political-affairs office in Dili and had briefed them on the militia forces in Liquiça. She had told them her solution to the problem: to establish a safe haven, a neutral area where the militiamen could escape to. If the UN could establish something like that, then she was convinced that more than 90 per cent of the men would leave the militia groups. The UN officer had listened and made notes. The UN had no mandate to set up safe havens.

The arrival of the UN in Timor had not changed the situation in the countryside. Mana Lou had travelled to her home village, Asu Manu, where hundreds of people had taken shelter. There was enough food and shelter, but the people didn't feel safe. The militias and the army had surrounded the area.

'Every night they enter the villages and when they see men or boys they try to kidnap them,' Mana Lou said. The captured men were locked up in training camps, hidden from the main road. One man, who had escaped from a camp in Bazar Tete, had told her that he had been forced to go into villages and kill the first living being on the way, either animal or human. The military would follow close behind. He was told that if he didn't comply, they would shoot him. This kind of thing was happening not only in Liquiça, Mana Lou said, but in many places in Timor.

Three young male volunteers who used to work for her in the orphanage in Viqueque had fled to Dare. They had been working in one of Mana Lou's paddy-fields when a group of ten armed Timorese soldiers from the Indonesian army assaulted them. The soldiers had screamed at them: 'You Church people, you are no good, you make us suffer,' and had pressed their guns against their chests. They told them that if they did not abandon their religious work and join the militia group, they would kill them. 'But if you support autonomy, then we will save you and take you to West Timor, while we will go back to destroy the land.' Then they had beaten them with their guns and sticks.

Mana Lou had heard many rumours of an impending civil war. Many Besi Merah Putih men had sent their families for safety to Atapupu, just across the border in West Timor, and Mana Lou had sent a group of her women along to continue working with them. When I called them 'militia families' she again snapped fiercely: 'Not all of them are for integration with Indonesia. They are just poor people.' She told me what an old man in Atapupu had told her: 'I suffered in World War Two. I suffered in 1975. Now I want to see Timor independent. They can me force me to flee, but in my heart I stay true.'

In some respects, her policy of feeding everyone needy equally had paid off. She was often the only person who could do anything for the people in militia-controlled areas. She had expanded westwards and set up a small house in Lois, between Liquiça and the border. But the militias did not show her the same respect everywhere. She had got very angry when a group of them had stopped her from taking food to Sare, a village in Ermera controlled by Falintil. Thousands of women and children, many of them from CNRT families, had fled there for protection. 'Why are you stopping me?' she had demanded. 'When I bring food to your families you let me go, now I want to bring food to the people here, you stop me?' 'They are pro-independence supporters, we don't care if they die,' they had answered.

Furious and with tears of frustration in her eyes, she had smacked one of them in the face. A Timorese woman who was with her told me later that Mana Lou was in such a blind fury and had shouted at them for so long in all the languages she knew that, eventually, her friend had to put an arm around her and point out to her that the men had jumped in their Kijang and were long gone.

Remembering the incident she became indignant with the pro-integration camp. She had told the *bupati*, 'If you must kill people, do at least bury them properly.' In Maubara she had found hands and feet of bodies still sticking out of the sand, and dogs walking around with human body parts in their jaws.

The people in the area had also given up eating fish, since many bodies were thrown into the sea and the fish ate the bodies. One man had found a golden wedding ring in his fish dinner.

Even though Unamet had opened an office, Liquiça was still without a priest. The *bupati* had housed the UN staff in the rectory, and I would later hear from one of the UN's administrative staff that he had trouble sleeping because he heard screaming every night. The local people could have explained to him why, had he asked them. They would have told him he heard the ghosts of those killed in the massacre.

Mana Lou had taken over the church, where she ran a spiritual feeding programme. 'Food distribution alone is not enough,' she had said. 'People do not exist only on food, they need spiritual guidance too.'

Every day the church in Liquiça filled up with people. They sat there quietly waiting for Mana Lou to arrive. She chose a different subject for her talk each day. Today's subject was the meaning of 'liberation'. I watched her from one of the pews. She walked with the characteristic energetic spring in her step, up and down the aisles. The people drank in her words. She spoke for at least an hour, then she gave them a pause to reflect quietly for themselves.

She told me that when she had started three weeks ago she would talk for an hour and the people had only cried. She wanted to make them stronger so they would go back to their villages, where they could take care of feeding themselves. Here they had nothing. They had asked her to stay with them longer. 'Food is not so important, more important for us is that you are with us, sing with us and pray with us.'

I recognised some of the faces I had seen in April. Tia Angela still looked fragile, but she held her head higher and her shoulders were less bent. The others, too, seemed less in shock. Some even managed a tiny smile. Although their eyes were still filled with sadness, the terror had gone. Mana Lou was healing.

§

On 4 July, not long after I visited Mana Lou, a group of 30 militiamen attacked an aid convoy passing through Liquiça. The aid workers, Doctor Dan Murphy among them, had brought food and medicine to the refugees in the mountains and were kicked and shot at. The driver of a UN car was shot in his eye. And when a UN helicopter arrived to rescue Unamet's staff, the militia pelted it with stones. During the attack, said Doctor Dan, the police stood by, in their usual fashion, and did nothing.

This attack almost brought the mission to an end. The UN office in Liquiça was closed again, and Ian Martin flew to Jakarta to complain. In response Wiranto announced that he would again send additional police. It would take a month for another aid convoy to reach the refugees.

. . . .

CHAPTER 16

Dancing with Falintil

§ AFTER all my efforts to meet Falintil, it was more through coincidence than anything else that I eventually encountered a group of them in the mountains of Aileu. I had travelled there with two colleagues after we had heard rumours from a Timorese friend about 'liberated villages' in the area. He had been elated. With a sparkle in his eye he had added proudly that his home village was one of them.

The seven villages of Lequidoe are strung like fortresses along a long, curving mountain ridge. Their locations in themselves seemed to refute claims that, before the Portuguese arrived, the Timorese lived in peace with each other. It could hardly have been simply for the beauty of the panoramic views that the villager's ancestors had chosen these positions.

We stopped in Namoleso, the main village, which boasted two churches, a school, a clinic, a small coffee house and, of course, an Indonesian army base, buried like a marmot's hole in the top of a little mound. Life seemed to be carrying on much as usual. Women carried water up from the wells in the valleys; little girls climbed the steep mountain paths balancing huge bundles of firewood on their heads; farmers sorted and washed their coffee beans. Like pied pipers, we trailed in our wake hordes of scantily dressed children with snotty noses following our every movement, their eyes wide with excitement. And, as anywhere else in Timor, the red-and-white Indonesian flag flew from every building.

The school had been without a teacher for a while, but a young Indonesian doctor from Sulawesi still worked in the clinic. Doctor Rina had not fled Timor as her colleagues had, because, she said, the poor needed her. I asked to use her bathroom, so I could talk to her away from the prying ears of the *intel*, who had been watching us suspiciously ever since our car had stopped in the village. Carefully avoiding mentioning the guerrillas, I tried to find out if anything unusual or surprising had happened in the area recently. She hinted at a recent change in the most remote of the villages, Berelui. 'I'll take you in that direction,' she said, and briskly jumped into her jeep. We followed. Fifteen minutes later, when we reached a crossroads, she stopped and pointed in the direction where the tarmac road made way for a dirt track. Then she turned back.

Soon, the houses no longer flew Indonesian flags, and people we passed did not automatically turn their faces away when they saw us. Fear, it seemed, had less of a grip. At a bend in the road a man appeared, looked into the car and grinned broadly. Perhaps because of a signal from him, within moments the bushes came to life and a large group of men jumped out. They waved their arms wildly. One wore a brown overcoat that flapped in the wind and made him look like a giant bird, trying to take off.

'Falintil,' whispered our driver with shining eyes. One of the men climbed into the car to guide the driver to a bamboo hut. A wiry man wearing camouflage fatigues, introducing himself as Commander Railakan (Lightning), gestured us to sit on a bench, while he continued a conversation on his walkie-talkie. He matched exactly my image of the older generation of Falintil: an emaciated, weather-beaten face, fiery eyes and waist-length hair streaming in long curls from a green beret.

Falintil commanders used their walkie-talkies almost continuously. They would communicate not only among themselves but sometimes also with Indonesian soldiers. They monitored their radio traffic and they would tease and joke with them: 'Hello there, it's us: you know, the ones you're looking for!' And, especially during the first months of *reformasi*, when Indonesian troops had been dispirited – after all, they had not been paid – they would exchange information on the political developments in Jakarta. After Railakan finished his long conversation he told us we would be taken to the other side of the valley, where the commander was ready for us.

The road ended in a small dusty square, enlivened by the splashing colours of flowering bougainvillaea. To my surprise, a big welcoming ceremony had been prepared. In front of the communal village house, a row of tables had been laid with white lace tablecloths and blue china coffee cups. The villagers watched in silence.

Suddenly everyone turned to look. At the top of the hill a man appeared on horseback; a scout no doubt, since moments later a large group of armed men followed. They wore army fatigues and carried heavy machine-guns. Leading them was a slightly built figure who, when he saw us, stuck his arm up and shouted: 'Viva Timor Lorosae! Viva Povo Maubere! Viva Xanana Gusmão!!!' The villagers dutifully repeated the slogans.

He approached us with a small escort of soldiers. One of them filmed him draping *tais* around our necks and another recorded every word he uttered in a large logbook. 'You are facing Falintil now. Falintil welcomes you with a warm heart,' he intoned theatrically. He introduced himself as L-Foho Rai Boot, also known by the code-name L7, which he pronounced in Portuguese:

'Elli-setti'. 'Foho Rai Boot' means both 'Big Python', and 'Big Mountains and Land'.

Here, clearly, was a man who believed in building an image. He had long frizzy hair, which stuck out from his head like a clown's wig, and a thin goatee. Across his camouflage uniform he wore a red sash decorated with a whole pantheon of saints: St Anthony, Dom Bosco and the Virgin Mary (the Holy Spirit, too, apparently, I would later be told; but that one was invisible to the human eye). His hands were hidden in red gloves – the colour of blood, he explained, because of the blood spilled in the war. Only after independence would he change to white, and, like others, he had vowed not to cut his hair during the war.

With a wooden expression, he proceeded to lecture us on Timor's history: the years of fighting; the suffering; the international solidarity. It was all covered, over and over again, in a long speech that seemed to go around in circles.

The note-taker, unperturbed, kept writing everything in his large book, but when I glanced at the interpreter, a young student called Ivo, I saw an exasperated look gliding over his face. He caught my eye, sighed and whispered: 'He just goes on and on and on.'

L7 was one of the sub-commanders of what Falintil called Region 2. This was an area that encompassed Manatutu, Manufahi, Aileu and Dili. The sector commander was Falur Rate Laek, who did not hold a lot of sway over L7. While he rambled on his head often tipped slightly backwards. He would tug his beard and his bloodshot eyes would roll upwards to the heavens as if he expected some divine inspiration. He probably did. L7, I would soon learn, headed a group called Sagrada Familia, set up in 1989 and succeeding the 'St Anthony group', Timor's largest youth organisation in the late 1980s. He aspired to the role of Falintil's spiritual leader.

'We have not been so strong in years,' he said proudly, and went on to explain the reason for the popularity of his Sagrada Familia. It was, or so he claimed, Timor's largest underground organisation, counting many young people among its members. The basis of his Familia's appeal, he said, was its motto: 'To die with a smile on the face.' L7 had a weak spot for the theatrical (as well as, I would soon discover, for the bottle).

He continued his rambling and repetitive story, pausing every couple of sentences to allow his interpreter to translate every word. 'It is the first time Falintil has met journalists out in the open,' he said. 'We never received journalists because of the oppression by the Indonesian army. If they found out, they would attack us.'

I looked around. The Indonesian army must know that Falintil had 'occupied' the village. I could see the hillock of Lequidoe's army post in the distance and anyone with binoculars could follow exactly what was going on. When I pointed this out he waved my concerns away. Now that 'NATO' – as he called the UN – had arrived, it had become easier and they had come to an 'understanding' with the army.

Such 'understandings' were not uncommon. Sometimes, during the first years of the war, Falintil and the Indonesian army had made arrangements to pretend to fight, shoot for a while and report back that they had fought a battle. Nothing new in times of war – no soldier, after all, wants to die. And most of the Indonesian soldiers in Timor would rather avoid a direct confrontation if they could.

As soon as L7 had finished his speech a larger group of Falintil soldiers appeared. Most were young. They looked anxious and ill at ease. This group did not carry weapons but were brandishing two flags: Timor's (red, black and yellow) national flag and Falintil's blue, white and green. These they planted in the middle of the clearing.

These were L7's new recruits. His group had grown quickly. Especially since the attack on Alas at the end of 1998, many young men and some women had fled to the mountains and joined Falintil. Commander Falur had told him to send them back home. Their safety was too big a responsibility, he had argued. But L7 had decided to keep them with him, and now he felt even more powerful.

Ivo, L7's interpreter, had ended up with the guerrilla group in this way. He was a student at the technical school in Hera, just east of Dili. In 1999, Hera had become the main base for the Aitarak militia. In May they had besieged the school, demanding that the student leaders surrender to them. When this did not happen they launched a big assault, with the support of the military and police. They killed four student leaders. The rest managed to escape through a hole they cut in the fence. Not knowing where to go, Ivo wandered through the mountains for days trying to find the Sagrada Familia.

During his first weeks with L7, Ivo had received some basic military training. But he had felt very uncomfortable carrying a gun and wearing a uniform. He told L7 he did not want to be a fighter. So he was allowed to carry a pen instead, and was given work at the secretariat as a translator.

The villagers, who had been observing the proceedings from a safe distance, now started to join the party. A group of women with traditional instruments filled the air with the rhythmic thud of drums punctuated by the metallic clanging of gongs. It was the dance I had seen on Ili Manu mountain. The women made intricate little movements, and swayed slightly. They had serious-looking, even sombre faces, but a few flashed betel-stained smiles when three soldiers grabbed some of the instruments and danced and jumped about, holding their guns in tight embraces.

L7 took the video camera in one hand; in the other he held a Walkman with a speaker, from which droned Chinese instrumental music, while he gave a running commentary on the celebration. The party grew wilder. A group started to dance the *tebe tebe*, a traditional circle dance, while others played guitars and sang ballads about Xanana Gusmão and patriotic songs about the years of struggle. More people arrived in a pick-up truck loaded with supplies brought in from Dili, including a television and a set of big speakers.

I suddenly felt trapped. Were we still guests? It was all very amicable; but I was no longer sure whether we had any say in our next move. We had planned to return to Dili that evening and I was worried about our driver. But L7 made it clear that we could not leave before we had dinner and the driver seemed quite excited about it all. In any event, it is a sound principle not to argue with men with guns. We followed L7 into the village hall where a table was laden with food – brought in from Dili. Joining us around the table were the cadres of this group: L7's niece, Rosa da Camera, known as Bisoi, whom he introduced as a representative of the OMT, the women's organisation of the resistance, Antonio, the secretary of the Sagrada Familia; and Ivo, the interpreter.

The commander stood at the head of the table, took off his beret and gloves and folded his hands in prayer. I noticed that most of the fingers of his left hand were missing. The prayer was like his other monologues, a long-winded affair, punctuated by the names of saints. When we started to eat, he offered profuse apologies for the inadequacy of the cutlery. 'During the Portuguese time we ate with a knife and fork,' he said, holding up a crooked spoon, 'now we only have this.' He seemed obsessed with table manners. After independence, he said, he would like to make eating with a knife and fork a legal requirement. After all, 'We are a civilised nation.' He picked distractedly at his food and spent more time twirling his moustache and fiddling with his beard than eating. And the flow of stories was unstoppable.

L7 was born in Laga in 1945 as Cornelio Gama. Because of the martial reputation of his grandfather, a local *liurai*, it was only natural that he should want to become a fighter too. He had received his training as a soldier in the Portuguese army, but had served with Falintil since the day it was established by Fretilin, on 20 August 1975. He bragged about the number of soldiers he had killed, the arms he had captured from the Indonesians and the discipline demanded by Falintil. 'Democracy is something for civilians, what we need here is a dictatorship,' he said repeatedly.

L7 was the commander who had attacked Alas in November 1998. His men had killed the three soldiers and taken twelve hostage. They had not realised that the army outpost holding the guns they hoped to capture was guarded, but L7 did not regret the killings. 'They were very bad men, who had many murders to their name. They deserved to be killed.' The secretary agreed. He had worked for the local government in Alas and had run to

Falintil after the Indonesian army took its revenge on the population in the area. After two days of 'political education', two of the soldiers they had taken hostage chose to defect from the Indonesian army and stay with Falintil. They were based in Region 2, but were not with us that evening.

At one point L7 asked a rather baffling and alarming question: 'Who will come to look for you if something happens to you out here?' What could he mean? No one knew where I was. When he saw our puzzled faces he was quick to reassure us that they would not kidnap us, as the resistance in West Papua had a group of Westerners earlier that year. 'Your government must be very proud of you,' he smiled at the three of us. 'You are the first ones to have found us; and you're all women!'

L7 had been pleasantly surprised to hear we were from the Netherlands. His brother Mauk Moruk (Paulino Gama) lived in exile there, he said, and he asked us to take him some photographs. His brother, however, was, to say the least, controversial. Many thought he was 'turned'. He was close to Abilio Araújo, the ousted left-wing leader of Fretilin, who had close business links to Tutut, one of Suharto's daughters.

Outside, the soldiers were making preparations for a night-long *festa*. The television was switched on and we all had to watch footage of L7's group marching triumphantly into a village, followed by our own reception. After this bizarre show L7 stood up to give instructions on the etiquette for the rest of the evening. At the prospect of a party, the crowd was growing audibly more excited. The words 'Dansa, dansa' buzzed around me.

'Do not dance too long with the same partner; and do not dance too close,' warned L7, adding that men had to escort their dance partners politely back to their seat. Every dance would begin with a shout of either 'Buibere zan' or 'Maubere zan', meaning that men and women could take turns to ask partners to dance, a tradition that had its roots in Fretilin's revolutionary days.

At night a biting cold descended on the mountain. The villagers huddled in their thin cotton sarongs, which they pulled over their heads. A few had towels or woolly hats; even fewer had blankets. I heard the children sniffing and coughing. I decided that to keep warm it was better to join the dancing. I had long forgotten my few dancing lessons of 20 years ago, but luckily the Portuguese dance music permitted only some slow fox-trots and timid polkas.

Shy at first, a few guerrillas plucked up the courage to ask us to dance. They taught me the simple steps and with the better dancers I managed not to look too clumsy, I thought. But every time I returned to my seat, Ivo told me that my steps were still too big. He urged me to move my feet hardly at all. I thought of Xanana's remark about the good and bad times in the forest: 'We did dance and sing a lot too.' Was this what L7 had meant about dying with a smile on your face: a lot of drinking and late-night dancing?

Apart from a few of the girls, the villagers watched the party from the

8. Commander L7 and Bisoi in front of the Timorese flag.

sidelines. 'They're not afraid,' L7 had assured me. But to me the people looked slightly bewildered. I asked an old man with a long yellow beard what he thought of it all. 'Of course we like having them here,' he said. 'We feel safe with them. But what will happen to us after they leave?'

The old man had reason to worry. As in any conflict between a guerrilla group and an established army, it is often the civilian population that suffers most. Falintil earned a reputation as a disciplined force that did not victimise civilians. But even so it could not prevent people from being killed because of retaliation by the Indonesian army, as had happened in Alas.

L7 kept up an impressively steady consumption of alcohol through the afternoon and night, and went to sleep while the party was still in full swing. At about 3 a.m., a fight broke out between three armed guerrillas. They rolled around in the dust like wild cats. Ivo nervously urged us to go to sleep.

I shared a bed with Bisoi, the OMT woman. Like everyone else, we had only a sheet to cover us, and as the night dragged on, the sharp cold meant I hardly slept. In the room next to us the commander snored loudly. I didn't know what to make of him. He was clearly wildly eccentric. But was he actually mad? Or was this what happened to you after 23 years of living in the jungle like a hunted animal, starved of food and without medicine? And was he typical of other commanders? He boasted that he had been Xanana's bodyguard, but when I mentioned his name to Xanana in Jakarta a week later, he sighed in a rather irritated way: 'Oh, him.' He refused to elaborate.

The next morning everyone apart from L7 seemed to have a hangover. He looked in good form. He started his day with a glass of sweet red wine, left over from the previous night. 'I never drink coffee or tea,' he bragged, 'I drink only *tua.*' He told us he had devised code-names for us so we could send him messages. Like a sort of passport, this would make it easier for us to return. And when we did, he added, could we perhaps bring some medicine for his eyes, his rheumatism and his stomach, as well as copies of the articles we wrote about this trip.

One of my colleagues he named Bo'ek, meaning shrimp, which came with an explanation of an animal that travelled long distances over the bottom of the sea overcoming many obstacles. Mine was less poetic: 'Irma', which stood in this case for 'Sister of Falintil'.

Again we had to postpone our departure. L7 insisted we had to witness how he punished his soldiers for last night's fight. He ordered the three to lie on their bellies in the dust and made them crawl up the hill until they reached a big tree. There they would have to stay for the rest of the day, said L7. It did not look too bad an option after a night-long party and a hangover. I saw one culprit lift his head in defiance and wink at us mischievously. As if L7 could read my thoughts, he said, without a trace of irony: 'We have human rights here.'

§

After this display of revolutionary justice, we were allowed to drive back down to Dili. When we returned to the hotel, a receptionist I trusted signalled to me not to pick up my room key. I went to the garden and waited. A little later she came over and whispered that three new *intel* officers, two men and a woman, were looking for me. They were now lurking in reception, waiting for us to come back. Luckily they seemed to have no idea what we looked like. I wondered why they were after me. Had they caught up with us already because of the visit to Falintil? Or was it because of what had happened a week earlier, when I filmed a raid led by Unamet officers on a house in Maubara?

That raid had turned into a big incident. The Indonesian Foreign Ministry had accused Unamet of ransacking the house, destroying a Catholic shrine and beating up an old lady. They took it up with the UN in New York to discredit Unamet. They even showed a videotape of a hysterical old woman, in a totally destroyed house. It was sheer fabrication. The house had in fact been wrecked by TNI soldiers, and then filmed by Indonesian television.[1] The UN told them they knew of the existence of another video, showing the actual raid. I had shot that one. I left East Timor the next day to let things cool down.

§

When I returned, a month later, I travelled straight back to Falintil. By then much had changed. To show they were eager to cooperate with the United Nations, Falintil were in the process of withdrawing into four 'cantonment' sites. The largest of these was in Uaimori, where all Falintil detachments from Regions 2 and 3 had gone. It was the largest gathering of Falintil guerrillas since 1987.

Edu, whom I had last seen trying to use the FM radio transmitter, had resurfaced in Dili after Unamet arrived. He had sent a message that we could visit Taur Matan Ruak, Falintil's vice-commander-in-chief – second-in-line to Xanana himself.

I remembered Taur from *Blockade*, Jill Jolliffe's film, as an extravagant character with big mounds of frizzy hair around which he wore as a bandanna a colourful *tais*. A thick black beard hid most of his face, revealing only deep-set, very dark, and haunting eyes. We would be the first journalists to meet him for more than a year.

Edu picked us up early one morning in an old jeep. We travelled with Jonathan Head, the BBC's Jakarta correspondent, and his cameraman. I shared my seat with a resistance fighter, who had just been released after spending seven years in Cipinang, and his seven-year-old son, a child with long curly hair and the face of an angel. It was their first trip together and the child was painfully uncomfortable with his father.

It took us five hours to reach Liaruca, a village at the foot of Mundo Perdido, the Lost World, a mountain of sheer, black rock that rises up from a plateau landscape of green rolling hills. The Portuguese had chosen the name well; it felt like entering some enchanted fairyland.

Like every other village in Timor, Liaruca had a TNI army base, but I did not see any Indonesian soldiers. Falintil had threatened to disarm them if they harmed the local population. Outnumbered, they had disappeared from the village and the only soldiers I saw were armed guerrillas. They led us to a house where a woman served us coffee. After a while one of the soldiers came to inform us that he had spoken to the commanders but that they were too busy to receive us, and we should come back the next day. It did not matter how much Jonathan argued with them, they simply did not want to let us go on. Only when I asked them to make radio contact just one more time and use my code-name, Irma, did they, to my surprise, get the green light.

Uaimori lies hidden in a remote river valley, and the only way to reach it is by foot. We marched over the hills in single file. Sometimes we stopped when the Falintil soldiers with us wanted to smoke, or to point something out, such as the wreck of an Indonesian army helicopter. One of the soldiers explained that he had studied at the famous technical college in Bandung on Java, where he got hold of a helicopter manual. 'You know you have to shoot the tail rotor,' he said, showing off his helicopter know-how. 'And that's exactly how we shot this one down!'

The helicopter had come down with the entire top brass of the Indonesian army's regional command, just after Suharto's fall from power in 1998. At the time Falintil had claimed responsibility for the crash but the Indonesians had said it was an accident caused by bad weather. I was sceptical about Falintil's claim at the time, and even now was not entirely convinced. I was sure they were capable of bringing a helicopter down – they had done it before. But my instincts and the timing of the crash made me doubt so convenient a story.

When we arrived in Uaimori at the end of the afternoon Edu ushered us to a small bamboo shelter. The commanders, he told us, were still in an important meeting. 'Put your bags here and take a rest,' he said. 'Don't walk around on your own before the commanders have met you.'

I looked around. Small cooking fires lit up clusters of simple raised bamboo huts and shelters. A few women were cleaning vegetables and stirring steaming pots of rice. Of the fighters, some were cleaning their guns, while others were strumming guitars or sitting around playing cards. Uaimori was a familiar haunt for many of them. They used to visit regularly, to recuperate and rest. The river runs all year, providing fresh water. They hunted deer in the forest and nearby villages supplied corn and rice. It was also strategically well-positioned: protected by deep river gorges on both sides, yet having enough escape routes to allow Falintil to melt into the forest if attacked.

I would hardly have recognised Taur Matan Ruak, who had shaved off his beard since being filmed for *Blockade*, had it not been for his penetrating – and haunting – eyes. They darted around, seeming never to rest. He looked like an ageing rock star – his long frizzy hair in a ponytail and his faded jeans topped by a Portuguese army camouflage jacket. He apparently preferred this to the Indonesian camouflage fatigues the rest of his troops were wearing. He greeted me with a jovial hug, and said with a big, mischievous smile: 'So you made it at last – after five years!' Taur remembered that he had been waiting for us in 1994 in the mountains – by coincidence, not far from where we were now.

Behind him I noticed other familiar faces: Mau Hodu and Ma'Huno Bulerek, both former Falintil commanders, and some CNRT leaders, including Leandro Isaak and Hendrique Corte Real. It was their first chance to sit all together around a table. They had discussed their approach to disarmament and voter registration, and that evening had decided to invite Unamet to come to the cantonment site.

Among the UN's proposed preconditions for the consultation process were that the militia would be disarmed, the size of the Indonesian military presence reduced and soldiers confined to barracks. A month before the vote, Falintil, too, was expected to undergo cantonment in a designated area, where it could wait for demobilisation and reintegration into civil society. These proposals had not been accepted by Indonesia as part of the 5 May agreement. But Xanana, eager to show that he and his forces were willing to be helpful, decided unilaterally to accept the cantonment of Falintil.[2]

We slept in our sleeping bags on a bamboo platform, under a palm-leaf roof. Two fighting cocks dozed beneath us, every so often waking me up with a deafening crow.

At daybreak I could see that the camp stretched much further along the river than I had noticed the night before. The fighters lived in little groups around their regional command posts on the edges of an open field the size of a football pitch. Besides housing more than 250 fighters and their families, the area was also home to a few hundred refugees, who had built huts on the surrounding hills.

I found L7's quarters on the far west side of the camp. His group was still busy building their huts. They had been the last to arrive. L7 had received a message from Commander Taur setting a deadline. If they failed to meet it, they would be disarmed; that was the last thing L7 wanted to happen. He hadn't had enough time to walk to Uaimori so they had rented seven trucks, and transported the whole group, with all their weapons, right through the centre of Dili. 'Were you not afraid?' I asked him. He looked at me in amazement: 'Why should we be afraid? We had weapons!' I tried to explain that that was precisely why I was worried on their behalf: they could have been in trouble because of the weapons. But he still looked nonplussed.

On the big field a group of guerrillas were chopping down bushes and long savannah grass with machetes. They were preparing a landing strip for the UN's helicopter. Others marked the landing area neatly with a circle of small stones.

At the edge of the field, soldiers formed a guard of honour, and their commanders inspected berets and uniforms. 'This is a historic moment for Falintil,' said Taur proudly. 'We have survived to live for this day. We never surrendered, because the belief that this day would come kept us going.' His grin reached almost to his ears. 'For the first time we will meet the international community face to face.'

He wanted to make a good impression. He carefully inspected his troops; he tucked a strand of hair under a beret here, pulled a collar into shape there, or readjusted the angle of a beret. All eyes were gazing eagerly on the cloudless sky. When a small speck eventually appeared and grew bigger and bigger, an expectant hum buzzed through the crowd that had formed around the fringes of the field. A white helicopter with black UN markings landed in a cloud of grass cuttings and dust. The Falintil soldiers saluted, and the crowd clapped enthusiastically. Falintil had invited Ian Martin, the head of Unamet, but the UN had sent instead its chief military liaison officer: Rezaqul Haider, a Bangladeshi brigadier.

The group also included Djoko Soegianto, a member of Komnas Ham and a representative of the Peace and Stability Council, KPS. This body had been established to oversee the implementation of the peace agreement brokered by Wiranto on 21 April. From the outset it had been clear that the KPS was totally controlled by the Indonesian authorities. The CNRT had one representative, Leandro Isaak, Falintil none at all, and Unamet was kept as much as possible out of it. But it was worse than merely useless: it made it difficult for the UN to set up a new, more independent, body. As with so much else in the 'consultation' process, the idea the UN and Xanana had had, to establish some sort of peace commission, had been hijacked and corrupted by the Indonesian army. This had contributed to the stalemate over disarmament. Under pressure from the UN, the KPS had eventually arranged a meeting in Jakarta with Xanana, Leandro Isaac and two pro-integration leaders, João Tavares and Domingos Soares. On 18 June they had signed an agreement to refrain from all violence and to lay down their weapons. But Xanana made it clear that it all depended on who would oversee the disarmament, and that before the agreement could be implemented the TNI should close its village posts and confine its soldiers to barracks.[3] Disarmament in East Timor never escaped this impasse. The militias were still flaunting their weapons openly. The Indonesians kept insisting that the existence of these groups was a direct reaction to the activities of Falintil and that they would disarm only if Falintil did so as well. But Falintil refused to see itself equated in this way with the militias. They were Timor's armed forces and if there had to be an equivalent it was the Indonesian army.

General Wiranto had pushed hard for the disarmament of Falintil and had told the UN that if Falintil were ready to surrender its weapons to the Indonesian police, he could guarantee that the militias would be disarmed within two days.[4] The Indonesian standpoint was widely reported and Falintil had read about it with mounting concern. They wanted to clear things up with the UN.

Taur explained the cantonment idea and he asked Unamet to monitor the whole process of assembling Falintil's soldiers, 'so that Falintil won't be accused of being the guilty party for all the disorder and trouble in the villages and towns'. Cantonment, however, was only part of the story. The most pressing and emotional issue was disarmament. Xanana had already said that he did not want Falintil to hand over their weapons to the Indonesian police, but he did agree to disarm to a neutral international body. Even that was very controversial with many of the Falintil guerrillas.

Commander Taur demanded clarification. His forces, he said, were being forced to hand over weapons to the aggressor. 'How can we hand over our guns to the invader we have been fighting for 23 years? Why is this happening?' he asked passionately. I could see the muscles around his mouth tremble. 'Is the UN in a position to change our situation?'

The brigadier tried to calm his emotions. 'We are not forcing Falintil, neither have we asked Falintil to give their arms to anybody.' And when he offered Taur a gift of a statue of a tiger and added, 'I'm from Bangladesh, and we also fought a liberation war,' loud applause rang through the tent.

How did Commander Taur feel about seeing all these people, including the Indonesians, I wanted to know after the UN helicopter had left. 'I'm very happy,' he said. 'For many many years I felt sad not just with the Indonesian government, but with the whole world, which has been hypocritical about our situation, the struggle of our people, the suffering, the misery and death. I was thinking no one would come to solve our problems, but now at last they have come and I'm confident that they will try their best. We stay and wait, the responsibility rests now in their hands.'

That night there was a party at L7's quarters. He had been told that he could not dance every night, there had to be discipline. 'Only on Sundays,' Taur had ruled. But tonight was special.

I watched them waltzing in the moonlight. The UN's arrival heralded the end of Falintil's era of guerrilla warfare, but I did not think many on the dance floor were yet aware of that. When I asked L7 how long he would stay in Uaimori, he had answered automatically: 'Falintil never stays anywhere for more than three or four days. We'll move on.'

And when I had asked Bilesse, one of the Falintil women fighters, who had just given birth to a baby boy, about her hopes for the future and the conditions in which her son would grow up, she said she expected Falintil to take care of his upbringing – 'So if he grows up a responsible man, he can be a fighter too.' Even now, Bilesse was far from alone in refusing to acknowledge that the war might be coming to an end. And even among those who did, Falintil had come to embody an almost sacred mission far bigger than that of just an army. As Xanana himself put it: 'There will be Falintil until the last member of Falintil dies.'

CHAPTER 17

. . . .

Life in Uaimori

§ I HAD to go down to Dili from Uaimori to send my radio stories to Europe but travelled back with Edu as soon as I could, in early August. This time we took another route, along the Lalei'a river valley. In the village of Cairui a truck with more than fifty young men and women had joined us, and we continued along the rocky riverbed until the valley narrowed and the water became too deep and the stones too big.

The truck had to be unloaded. Out came boxes of beer and noodles, bags of rice and even a television and a collapsible *parabolo*, satellite dish. Everything went on top of somebody's head, even the television, although this proved too much even for these experienced heads, and I later saw it hanging from a shoulder-pole.

I realised I had become part of the 'unarmed army', the supply lines that had for so many years carried food and medicine to Falintil. It was with the help of people like these that Falintil survived as long as it did (not, of course, that television sets and *parabolos* were part of a typical provisioning run).

Our procession set out cheerfully. Soon after night fell, our guides lost their way and we ended up following the wrong branch of the river. We must have been wading through the river for a couple of hours by moonlight when the dark cliff face suddenly stirred with movement. From its shadows, a figure emerged. He was wearing a black balaclava, and pointing a big rifle at me. A second figure shone a torch into my eyes. I stood rigid, like a rabbit caught in headlights. To enter a Falintil area as a foreigner you needed a letter signed by one of the CNRT leaders, but I did not have one, only an open oral invitation from Taur, and my code-name. I looked for Edu and was about to speak when the gunman peeled off his balaclava to reveal a big grin. 'Welcome back,' he said. I felt the tension leaving my body. It was Susar, one of my Falintil dance partners.

The camp was another hour up along the river. The worst of our hike was over. By two in the morning we made our final river crossing. It was too late for the commander to be awake; we had to spend the night on the riverbank.

As soon as the camp stirred to life I went to look for L7. I found him in his headquarters, a bamboo hut that functioned both as his living quarters and as the secretariat of the Sagrada Familia. L7 wanted to celebrate my arrival with some cans of Guinness, but I opted for the coffee that stood steaming in large buckets behind the mess tent. We had a breakfast of instant noodles, rice and chillies. And while L7 enjoyed his Guinness, I noticed his wife, who had recently joined him in Uaimori, pulling faces and gesturing with one hand that he drank far too much and with her other that he had a screw loose.

L7 had surrounded himself with relatives and people from his hometown of Laga. His wife had brought two of their children with her, and they ran around with uncombed hair and snotty noses. Another new face for me was Nina, a young trainee nurse, who aspired to study to become a doctor. She had come from Dili to spend her summer holidays helping out at the small camp clinic.

Soon after breakfast, at eight o'clock, hundreds of guerrillas poured on to the parade ground for the daily flag-raising ceremony. Their berets, which came in a Smartie-box variety of colours, were, like their uniforms, often war trophies seized from Indonesian soldiers. I noticed the red of Kopassus, the special forces, the green of Kostrad, the strategic reserve, airforce blue and marine maroon. And there were even pink and yellow ones. Almost all wore Indonesian uniforms, often still bearing the names of their former, probably now dead, owners. Some wore Brimob shirts and jackets, and a few even sported pro-autonomy T-shirts. They looked out of place, like football fans who find themselves stranded among supporters of the wrong team.

A group of older men with gleaming polished trumpets and a tin drum set the pace of the march. They had defected from the Indonesian army and had taken their instruments with them.

L7 led the parade. He shouted 'Umbro ... errrmmm' and the two hundred or so soldiers presented arms. It would all have seemed a bit pathetic, were it not for the fierce pride of the men.

Slowly the blue-and-green flag with Falintil's coat of arms rose up the mast. Carefully avoiding the flag, I made my way to headquarters to notify the commander of my arrival. Rules in the camp were strict. One forbade walking through the shadow of the flag, even when it was cloudy and there was no shadow. Safest not to go near it at all. This rule must have been an inheritance from colonial times, when Timorese who dared to walk over the shadow of the Portuguese *bandeira* could expect a thrashing.

Two soldiers, one of them unusually large and tough-looking, stood guard. The large one wore two cartridge bandoliers that crossed over his chest, and a heavy machine-gun. His nickname was the 'bullet-eater' because his body, other soldiers told me, had swallowed countless bullets without their killing him. He was gifted, they said, with especially strong *lulik* protection.

This *lulik* talisman was their secret, not to be shown to anyone. It could be anything: a twig, a picture, a piece of special cloth such as a flag, some wood from one of an *uma lulik*, even a bit of earth, often wrapped up in a piece of red fabric and tucked under the waist belt or sown into their clothes. It was the sort of practice of which people such as Bishop Basilio so much disapproved.

The tent I had seen on my first visits had been replaced by a windowless shed covered with plastic sheeting. Taur came out to greet me. Through the open door I noticed the screensaver on his laptop: a portrait of himself looking like the archetype of the bearded guerrilla leader. His command post, which was strictly off-limits, functioned as his communications centre. He loved electronic gadgets, especially the ones that seemed invented for guerrilla armies, and besides two laptops he had a couple of satellite telephones and a few digital video cameras. Taur gave me permission to stay in Bisoi's room in L7's quarters, but I had to promise him to join him at mealtimes. He was eager to practise his English.

When I walked back to L7's area I came across a big Australian with black dyed hair and beard. Falintil called him Niki Mutin, White Bat. He was a shadowy figure who gave the impression that he was hiding from something.

There were more children around the camp. The school holidays had started and the nuns had sent the children back to their parents. The boy with the angel face – who was now nicknamed Timor Leste – ran around as the leader of a band of little boys. They played war games and posed with machine-guns for photographs.

I had found his father sitting under a tree, looking forlorn. He couldn't sleep, he said. The previous night he had dreamed his wife had been raped and he felt he had to return to Dili immediately. His son clearly wanted to stay. Later, at lunch-time, he sat next to Taur. His father was nowhere to be seen.

Mealtimes had something of a family atmosphere. Taur's relations had come to visit him. He had not seen them for 23 years. His parents had died: his mother in the mountains in 1979, his father more recently, in 1997, after he was beaten by Indonesian soldiers. The families of Falintil commanders were often closely watched, and were singled out when the Indonesian security forces conducted their operations. Taur's cousin, who had escaped from jail, sat with us at the table; the women hovered in the background with plates of meat and chicken. There was plenty of food and even some Australian red wine friends had sent him. But Taur hardly drank and did not smoke. He remained intense, even when he relaxed.

Taur Matan Ruak, his *nom de guerre*, was, as he translated it, fitting: 'He who with eagle eyes watches over the country'. But Taur was born José Maria Vasconcelos in Baguia, a remote village high up the slopes of the Matebian, the heartland of the Makasai tribe, which has a proud warrior tradition. But he had managed to escape that environment. He had gone to school and

9. Bilesse with her baby son.

studied Portuguese and English and found a job in the Resende hotel in Baucau. Timor's second city was, back then, a tourist destination of a kind. Its international airport received flights from Lisbon and Darwin, bringing in a small but steady stream of tourists – mainly Australian backpackers, looking for a cheap beach. The very first publication of the now ubiquitous back-packers' bible, *Lonely Planet*, was a guide to East Timor.

Taur, like Xanana, had never fostered ambitions of becoming a soldier, let alone a commander. 'I dreamed of travelling the world, but instead, I have only seen the forests of Timor,' he said with regret. He spoke softly, as if he still needed to whisper, as they had to when they moved through the forest. When the war broke out he had just turned 20. From 1983 to 1993 he had been responsible for commando operations, first in the east, then in the west and finally in all districts. He became assistant chief of staff in 1986. After Commander Konis Santana died in March 1998, he took up the position of deputy commander (a decision not ratified by Xanana at the time).

What had he missed most in all those years? 'Peace,' he said simply. A predictable answer perhaps, but somehow, from his mouth, it rang true. Taur gave the impression that he could not wait to take off his uniform. He and his men were tired, very tired, he said. They all looked forward to spending time with their families. Unlike other commanders Taur had never married. First the struggle had to be won, he said, before he could make time for a family.

Like Xanana, he wanted to work, after the war was over, in civil society, in his case setting up a charity to take care of Falintil's war victims, the widows and orphans and disabled. The years of death and destruction had left their marks on his face and a shadow of sadness in those restless 'eagle' eyes. The same shadow could be detected in the eyes of many in the camp. Indeed, I learned to tell from the eyes if they had been in the forest for a long time. If they had, they acquired the darting, alert but edgy look of hunted animals; their eyes, like Taur's, never seemed to rest. The younger ones, the new recruits, looked different. In their eyes I saw more excitement than sadness, more fear than pain.

At times when he was recalling his memories of the war he seemed to become mesmerized by visions that percolated from the depths of his mind: memories he alone could see but not put into words. Unlike Xanana, he was still too close to it all to be able to reduce the war to a series of anecdotes. How to pack all the horror into an hour-long interview? How to explain it to somebody who had grown up in a peaceful country, and had slept between clean sheets without fear of being killed in the night?

He simply said he was surprised to be still alive. He had survived the internal purges. He had survived detention by the Indonesians. He had even, amazingly, survived being hit by a grenade. That, he said, was his most difficult time. And the reason that he always wore sunglasses: bright light hurt his eyes.

'So many very good commanders, good fighters died. It is almost too much to comprehend,' he said. To see Falintil's forces depleted from a strength of 20,000 to just a small group had been his most painful experience. I did not ask how many had survived, but, he added, ever the cautious military commander: 'Let's just say what the Indonesians have always said: 50 old men.' These old men I had seen every day on the parade ground. They had names such as Sabica, Terra Mau Bulak, Mau Timor, Mau Lesa, Mau Wairai, Coco Rui. None of them used his Portuguese Catholic name.

Each sector had now its own satellite dish. They could receive CNN, BBC World and the Portuguese international channel. Sometimes in the evening, when they sat in front of the generator-powered televisions, watching an interview with Xanana or a special report on East Timor that mentioned the suffering during the war, the many people killed, I would notice them taking big white handkerchiefs to blow their noses and wipe away the tears that had welled up in their eyes. I tried not to stare, not wanting to embarrass them, but I was glad, in a way, that they could at least still weep. The trauma was not so deep that it had dried up their tears and turned them into emotional zombies. In that way, they were better off than some of the people I had met in the towns and villages, whose tears had dried up deep inside them years ago.

§

I was still in Uaimori when Falintil officially completed its cantonment in all the regions. They had reported to Unamet that they had 670 soldiers spread over five cantonment sites.[1] In the east they had no problems but in Region 4, in the west, the cantonment sites had turned into refugee camps and there were constant threats of attacks from powerful local militias and the army.

That night all the commanders joined Taur for dinner in his mess tent. They had just finished discussing a proposal made by Xanana and the UN that Falintil should hold a series of dialogues with the Indonesian army and militia commanders. The meeting with the Indonesian generals was on everyone's mind. 'I have agreed they can come here, so I'll receive them,' said Taur, rather sourly.

At the end of July, the TNI's regional commander, Adam Damiri, had promised that if Falintil submitted to cantonment, the TNI would leave their village posts and stay in their barracks, keeping their weapons under strict guard. The militias made a big show of handing in their homemade weapons for safekeeping in a central arsenal. But neither they nor the TNI had made any effort to pull back into restricted areas or barracks. Around the same time, on 13 August, a new commander, Colonel Mohamed Noer Muis, arrived to take the place of Colonel Tono Suratman. Officially this was a routine rotation, but privately the TNI admitted to the UN that they had made the change in response to international pressure to do something about the dire security situation.[2]

I had noticed before that Taur had a nervous twitch around his mouth. It seemed more pronounced when he talked about the Indonesian army. 'First they want our heads, now they want our guns,' he said grimly. 'Falintil has survived them all. They never managed to completely wipe us out. That is their frustration – they with all their might and we with no outside support. I think sometimes, I'll tell them I'm the real general here.'

At this point, as if a thunderbolt burst in a clear sky, his face exploded in laughter. He, after all, had seen off countless Indonesian commanders, and did not believe that Colonel Muis would be any better than his predecessors. There was a Portuguese phrase Taur liked: 'The shit changes, but the flies remain the same.' When he laughed, he threw his head back and his face became all teeth. He was often solemn but he liked to tell stories – especially about how he had outwitted the Indonesian army.

Despite his sometimes bitter jokes Taur was, like Xanana, surprisingly conciliatory: perhaps the clemency of a man who knows he will win in the end. But he also knew that the end was not yet in sight. Over lunch one day, he told me and an Australian journalist that if, as in 1975, all foreigners had to evacuate we should not leave but join him in Uaimori. He still regretted not taking journalists in 1975, and he did not want history to repeat itself.

When I got back to my sector of the camp, I found that the generator had broken and everyone was sitting around little candles. Hundreds of insects danced in the flames. There was still music, as they had batteries: melancholy songs were being played. A cold wind was whistling through the valley, and I looked for shelter behind a plastic sheet. It had started to rain softly. Black phantoms with guns passed silently in the darkness.

§

It was still dark when I heard a single gunshot echoing in the river gorge. Immediately Bisoi sat straight up. 'Indonesian soldiers,' she said, and groped nervously around for a candle. She swung her legs from the small platform that served as our bed and pulled aside my rain poncho, which separated our room from the rest of the hut. I could see L7 pacing around with his machine-gun in his hand looking for his bullets.

His bare scrawny torso was covered with tattoos, and the muscles stood out rigidly. Hastily he put on his jacket, strapped the bullets around his waist and snatched his knife from his bed. Bisoi had grabbed her pistol and ran swiftly after him. An Indonesian attack? Now? I didn't think so, but then again you never know. Perhaps an Indonesian patrol had strayed, and stumbled by accident on Falintil's sentries along the river.

In the pre-dawn darkness the guerrillas ran around like ants in a disturbed ant hill, guns at the ready. One of the soldiers screamed through a walkie-talkie and then, as suddenly as it had started, the frenzy subsided. 'False alarm,' said Bisoi. A Falintil sentry had fired his gun by mistake. 'He has been disciplined already,' she said sternly, although I couldn't make out from her face whether she was glad or not.

Bisoi was a robust, feisty woman who wore a faint smile on her lips, behind which, I felt, she hid her secrets, as well as her feelings. A Mona Lisa in fatigues. The war had clearly hardened her. She had been twelve when the Indonesian army had attacked her village in Viqueque and killed her mother. She had run into the forest and ended up in the care of her uncle, L7.

She told her story in her typically detached way. But one evening she showed me a picture of her little daughter, Domingas Santiana, whom she called Lekas Susar, a pet name meaning 'quite a handful'. Her features softened when she looked at the girl with wiry curls sitting in a meadow with flowers. The father was Commander Falur; he was married already and she was his so-called 'second wife'. To give her daughter the chance of an education, Bisoi had sent her to live with the Carmelite sisters.

At night I heard Bisoi's teeth chatter. Her sarong did not offer much protection against the cold that crept up through the thin bamboo floor. But her chattering was sometimes accompanied by soft whimpering and I could hear others, in nearby huts, also cry in their sleep. These nightly sounds of distress chilled me more than the cold did.

One day, Bisoi took me to meet two young women who had fled from

Alas. One had been raped, and the other had lost her whole family in the retaliation from the Indonesian army that had followed the Falintil attack. The rape victim spoke; her friend just stared quietly to a point somewhere behind me and hardly said a word. 'Girls who are raped cry a lot,' Bisoi remarked. 'We let them weep for a bit. Then we talk to them and we tell them that we all suffer; this is part of being Timorese: "We are born crying." I tell them: "You can destroy flowers but not destroy spring. We are like leaves; when the hot season comes the leaves fall down, but after the rain the leaves will come back again." For example, before Xanana was captured we fought, but after his capture we fought even harder.'

Bisoi was a revolutionary *nom de guerre*. Like other Falintil and Fretilin women with names such as Bilu, Bilesse, Bivali, Birally, Biberani, she had chosen to use the prefix Bi-, from Buibere, the female equivalent of Maubere, in front of her name.

Many, like Bisoi, had been in their early teens when they started to work with Falintil as barefoot teachers in literacy programmes run by student brigades. They had travelled in large groups, protected by Falintil, and taught villagers to read and write. Only a handful of these women remained in the jungle. Many had died, others had gone back to their towns and villages and formed the core of Fretilin's women's organisation, the OPMT.

Of the women, Bisoi was the only one I saw active in political work. The others worked in the clinic, a small bamboo building in the centre of the camp. Apart from a few bottles of paracetamol and some disinfectant, I could not see any medicines. In the treatment room, Nina and three other women, Bivali, Aurea and Veronica, were taking care of one of the refugees, who had a deep cut in her leg. They treated the wound with iodine and a traditional concoction made from mango leaves, a remedy Bivali had developed over the years. Like Bisoi, she had started out as a teacher but later worked as a medic, mixing medicines from leaves. Sometimes, she said, she would 'suddenly get an inspiration about some leaves' and she would try them out as medicine. Banana and mango leaves, for example, were good as dressings for wounds; papaya leaves were useful as a treatment for malaria.

She always wore black, 'out of respect', she said, 'for the many many people who had died in the mountains'. Four of her five siblings had died in Matebian, and in 1979 both her parents had been killed. She had married a Falintil soldier, but he had also died and she had sent her only son to the Salesian brothers in Venilale.

Nina and Aurea had been working for Falintil as *estafetas* since they were eight years old. Children were often the only ones who could do this kind of work, since all adults were automatically suspected by the Indonesians of maintaining contact with Falintil.

Nina came from L7's home village near Laga and as a child she used to bring him food and clothes, until a massacre in 1984 in which Indonesian soldiers killed 14 men in the village. The women were tortured to reveal L7's whereabouts, but said they couldn't find him. Fearing more torture, Nina's mother and aunts fled to Dili, leaving her in the care of her grandparents. Deprived of his support base, L7 moved to Los Palos. When he returned to Laga in 1990, he contacted Nina again and she would bring him cooked food every day, since it was too dangerous for him to make a fire.

Aurea's father had been killed when she was a baby. She was an only child, and had never even told her mother of her involvement with Falintil. When she grew older and acquired a motorbike she was asked to buy bullets from Indonesian soldiers for $2 a piece, and she would ferry Taur and other commanders to meetings in Baucau. Hearing her talk about it now, I could sense how exciting she had found it all.

The fourth woman in the clinic was Veronica. I had seen her in L7's camp with her little son Apai. She had a tired, pained look in her eyes. That day in the clinic she gave me the same kind of answers about wanting to help the Falintil and work in the clinic, but much later I would hear that she had an another important reason for joining Falintil.

She had fled her home in 1998 because her husband had tried to kill her, when he discovered that she worked for L7. She had promised to stop helping the guerrillas but she was terrified that if she stopped L7 would get suspicious, bringing even worse trouble for her whole family. Either choice was dangerous. So she kept doing her clandestine work, until her husband found out again. This time, he beat her so badly that she was taken to the hospital in Baucau, more dead than alive. It took her three months to recover. Her husband's brothers, who were in the pro-Indonesia camp, tried to poison her in the hospital. So when she was well enough, she fled with her youngest son to the mountains and joined L7, the commander she had risked her life for since she was a child. She left her baby girl with her sister and her older children with her husband.

'Women and men are equal within Falintil,' L7 would repeat *ad nauseam* in every speech. But female emancipation was not really evident in daily life in Uaimori. Some women wore army uniforms and Bisoi even carried a pistol, but most spent their days in the clinic, or cooking and mending uniforms. When I asked Aurea and Bivali about this, they said they did not mind the household chores: Falintil was their 'family'.

§

One morning I joined Taur and a small group of soldiers on an expedition down the river. Taur walked in front, with his dog Black at his heels. We followed a narrow path between man-high savannah grass. The soldiers fast disappeared between the reeds and it took some effort to keep up with them.

'The forest is our home,' Taur had told me. It had been exactly that for many years, but more recently Taur and his men had often stayed with the civilian population, only regrouping when, for example, they planned to launch an attack. They operated in small units, of not more than ten or twelve men, the same number as our little group today. They did not have a headquarters or a safe area as such. While they were moving around the forest, they had to be extremely careful. Dom Rotheroe, the film-maker who eventually finished the camera-work for Jill Jolliffe's documentary, told me that the idea Jill had given us, that Falintil had some safe area or base somewhere, could not be further from reality. When he lived with them in the forest they slept on beds of leaves, tying up the bushes so as not to break the twigs, carefully burying any rubbish, and, before moving on, scattering the stones and leaves they had collected. Sometimes, they had told him, it rained so much that they had to sleep standing up.

Now Falintil was engaged on a different sort of mission, the preparation of their 24th anniversary, a party for which it had invited the entire population to join them. 'It will be a huge party, our biggest ever! We will have seven *karau!*'[3] Taur's black eyes had sparkled.

Taur wanted to check the progress of a road they were building to make access easier. Somehow they had got hold of a bulldozer from Baucau. The yellow beast uprooted shrubs and bushes, pushing earth and stones aside to create a wide dusty track. Grinning broadly, Taur hoisted himself into the cabin. His soldiers hung whooping from the sides with their guns sticking in the air, making it look like some monstrous killing machine on its way to war.

Edu followed Taur, carrying a video camera and a black briefcase. Throughout the outing he ran up and down the track to record everything, like a professional film-maker. Only when we were ready to return did I find out what the intriguing briefcase held: a satellite telephone. Edu – more for show than for any serious purpose, I think – opened it up and talked to headquarters.

By the time I returned to Dili a few days later, the Falintil car that came to pick me up was able to come as far as halfway up the river. When we reached the asphalt road it was night-time and the dark road was deserted till we reached Hera, where Aitarak men were hanging round campfires. They had set up a road-block – two oil drums with a piece of wood over the top. 'They know this car,' the driver said. He put his foot down. The beam of wood banged against the windscreen and I ducked – head on my knees, heart in my throat. I didn't dare to look up until we reached the top of the steep pass that led to the lights and relative safety of Dili.

CHAPTER 18

. . . .

Party in the Jungle

§ A CLEAR blue sky; a little white church perched on a rock; a colourful crowd of people; from a distance, it looked almost idyllic. Coming nearer, I could see that many of the people looked thin and tired, and were dressed in rags. But they were chatting happily and smiling. They had walked for more than six hours from their hiding place in the mountains to reach the little chapel that Unamet had turned into a voter-registration office. Many in the long, winding queue were timid, fragile old men and women from Cailaco, one of the most violent places in Timor.

It had taken Unamet two weeks of intense negotiation with the local authorities, army and militias to ensure safe passage for Falintil guerrillas and some 400 refugees to come down from their camp. The determination of the people to register had been awe-inspiring. Despite everything – the violence, the burning of villages, the shootings and killings, the tens of thousands displaced and driven from their homes – despite it all, the Timorese had turned out in their hundreds of thousands.

On the very first day of the process, 16 July, long queues formed in front of the registration centres; by the fifth day more than 100,000 people, or more than a quarter of the estimated number of eligible voters, had registered. By the end of registration 451,792 voters, a third more than the UN had expected, had come forward.

The Timorese showed that they were prepared to take huge risks for the right to decide their own future. It was a display of enthusiasm and courage that made it hard for the UN to call the referendum off, even if it wanted to do so because of the poor security environment. The UN had already postponed the ballot twice, not only because security was so bad and it wanted to give the Indonesians time to create a 'level playing-field', but also for purely logistic and organisational reasons – to allow Unamet to conduct the registration process successfully.

To postpone the vote any longer would mean allowing it to slip into the period of the MPR's general session, running the risk that Indonesia might delay it further. The Western Sahara, whose history in many ways mirrored East Timor's, loomed as an ominous precedent. There, a UN-sponsored referendum had been postponed indefinitely.

By now, one of Unamet's greatest headaches was that caused by the 'internally displaced people' or IDPs, as the UN calls refugees who do not leave their own country. The UN's High Commissioner for Refugees estimated that by the time the registration started, about 100,000 people had been displaced from their homes and villages. Many had lost all they owned, often including their birth certificates and ID cards. According to one UN official, the Security Council in New York simply did not want to know about the issue. It complicated matters too much, and so was not even discussed.

During Unamet's visit to Uaimori, Commander Taur had asked for special arrangements to allow the refugees to register in the cantonment sites. The registration offices were many hours' walk away, and Falintil worried about their security. Unamet, however, had neither the money nor the people to open new ones. Instead, it tried – and failed – to secure a formal undertaking from the Indonesians that Falintil soldiers would not be arrested if they registered.

But here, in a small village near Maliana, Falintil soldiers had come down from their cantonment site. They waited patiently in makeshift tents opposite the church. They wore civilian clothes but it was no secret that most of them were fighters.

According to the 5 May agreement, eligible voters must either have been born in Timor, have one parent who had been born there, or have married an East Timorese. They had to show two ID cards, but many had lost all their papers and the UN agreed that affidavits would be acceptable. Here, it took a long time. Almost everybody needed an affidavit from the local priest, who sat behind a table in the chapel. When the people emerged they proudly clutched their voters' cards to their chests. Before the day was over they all had to climb back up to their hiding places. They would not return until ballot day.

This turned out to be the only place where Falintil registered *en masse* to vote. Taur and the other commanders had not left any doubt as to their intentions about taking part in the ballot. They would boycott it. 'Asking us to vote in a referendum on autonomy is an insult,' Taur had said. 'For us this is not a question. We have fought against the Indonesian invaders for almost twenty-four years. We didn't fight for autonomy, we fought for independence.' He would later say that these Falintil soldiers near Maliana who took part in the process had been misled.

§

I had travelled to Maliana with Antero. Xanana had urged all independence supporters not to organise rallies and other political events during the campaign that might fuel tension and lead to more bloodshed. The students' idea was to return to their home villages, to inform people about the referendum in small meetings, or by going door to door. Antero was going around to see how they were doing.

The Students' Solidarity Council's office was a simple structure, a bit up the hill from the fortress-like residence of João Tavares and Maliana's church. When we arrived we found at least a hundred people sitting on the floor in the sparsely furnished room. They were waiting for Antero. I looked around. In the dim light I could make out people of all ages. An old lady in a faded brown sarong stood up and in a loud crackling voice thanked us for risking our lives by coming to her town. She soon ran out of words and sat down giggling contentedly. Her welcoming speech was taken over by one of the organisers, who very formally introduced Antero listing all his achievements and prizes. Sitting next to me, Antero shifted rather uneasily. 'It's like a God coming down to the town,' he whispered shyly.

One by one, people reported intimidation and terror, house-to-house searches and ways of preventing people from registering. A student said that after the UN had urged the militia leaders to stop harassing the general population, they had now shifted their attention to the students. A woman told how a whole village had been prevented from going to register.

Maliana, and the whole district of Bobonaro, of which it was the administrative centre, had been among the worst trouble spots. The *bupati*, Guilherme dos Santos, worked closely with the local army commander, Lieutenant-Colonel Burhanuddin Siagian, and with João Tavares, the commander-in-chief of the Pro-Integration Forces. The feared local militia, Halilintar, was Tavares's personal force. Its core of 121 men had a close working relationship with Kopassus's intelligence unit, and some of Kopassus's own commandos had slipped across the border to join the militias.

In the run-up to Unamet's arrival the militias had successfully silenced the CNRT, and forced many of its leaders to flee. The generous funding they received through the central government meant that they could offer handsome pay-offs to the local authorities; the police chief, the *bupati*, the district judge, and so on.[1]

But by the time I arrived with Antero in Maliana, the UN reported optimistically that many of the thousands of people who had fled to the mountains had come back down to register as voters. And although the people at the meeting were complaining about continuing security trouble, the militia stranglehold, they said, appeared to be weakening, a little. Newly recruited militia members had defected *en masse* and pro-independence supporters were becoming more assertive.[2]

I noticed that some of the local students even sported T-shirts with pictures of Xanana and pro-independence slogans. 'Is this safe? Aren't you afraid?' I worried. They laughed my concerns away. This was their time, they said. And anyway the UN was now in Timor.

On 19 August a group of armed militia besieged the UN compound and attacked the student office, killing at least two students.

§

Antero returned tired but unharmed from his travels around the country to Dili. He moved into the building next to the Student Council, connected to it by a hole in the wall. The 'Social Institute', it said on a wooden board above the door. The institute was part of Antero's dream of setting up civic education projects in the countryside. There was nothing he talked about with more zest. He had an entire plan worked out. When I listened to him, straining to follow his train of thought, I could not rid myself of the feeling that this stubborn concentration on the future was a kind of shield against the present, and the urgent things he had to deal with.

In Viqueque, the opening of a student office had ended in a shooting and two young men were killed. Antero himself was lucky still to be alive, but when I asked him about it he reacted in his usual laconic, understated way and just said that it was as bad as the shooting in Becora we had witnessed together.

In July, the *Dobonsolo*, a ferryboat plying the Jakarta–Denpasar–Dili route, brought large numbers of Timorese students back. Thousands of Timorese studied in Indonesia, thanks to Mário Carrascalão, who in his time as governor negotiated Indonesian grants for study at universities in mainly Java and Bali. They had come back not only to register and vote in Timor but also to take part in promoting the referendum. The Student Solidarity Council tried to coordinate these efforts. In the beginning I had seen both the groups sitting on the floor in the office discussing their strategy. But it soon became clear that the students who had returned did not want to work under the Solidarity Council's umbrella. Instead they had opened their own offices and made their own, rival, plans.

Representing the students who studied at Indonesian universities were two organisations, Impettu and Renetil (National Resistance of East Timorese Students). Renetil was originally set up in 1988 by a group of East Timorese students in Bali. It had soon become part of the CNRM (and later the CNRT) and an important vehicle for the struggle for independence. They had better access to communications and were able to make contacts with human rights activists, unlike their colleagues in East Timor. At the same time the Indonesian army had set up Impettu, East Timor's Students' Association, with branches in every town where Timorese studied. All Renetil students were therefore part of Impettu as well. It did not take long for the likes of Prabowo to realise that Impettu was out of Indonesia's control and that, instead of nurturing young

10. Falintil soldiers dancing *tebe tebe*.

pro-Indonesia intellectuals, it had turned into a pro-independence organisation. Impettu remained active. It looked like an innocuous students' union that organised football tournaments and dance performances. In truth, it bred independence activists.

The groups were competitors not just for local support but for foreign funds – not that Antero was too bothered about raising money. One day around this time when I was visiting him, he had just launched into another long discourse on community education when an Australian activist entered the courtyard. He handed him a cheque from an Australian support group. Antero glanced briefly at the cheque and put it back into its envelope.

'I can't accept it, it's far too much,' he said to the surprised activist, who tried to persuade Antero to change his mind. But Antero was adamant: too much money would bring all kinds of complications. Eventually the bemused activist put his cheque away. Antero was a study in contradiction: a clear-headed activist; and the most maddeningly vague of dreamers.

§

A few days later I was on the road with Antero again: back to Uaimori. The track I had seen being bulldozed was ready. Antero and the women from the Solidarity Council had organised a *bemo*, and we sat squashed between bags of rice in the back.

Tata and Elisa had been very envious. They desperately wanted to come to the party too but they, like Sebastião, were now Unamet staff and had at least to appear neutral. João stayed behind too. He did not agree with the idea of a party just a week before 30 August, the day of the ballot. He thought it would only distract the students from more important things. 'We would do better to spend our last days preparing the people in the villages,' he had grumbled.

The women in the back of the *bemo* chattered excitedly. None of them had visited Falintil before, and most had never laid eyes on a guerrilla soldier. Only one of them, Teresa, had a brother who had joined the Falintil earlier that year.

Antero had mixed feelings about the visit. I had heard that after the attack on the student office in Viqueque the Solidarity Council had some problems with Falintil, which accused it of stirring up trouble with its activities in the districts. Antero would have to explain himself.

§

'Bem Vindo a cidade das Falinti'. 'Welcome to Falintil town', someone had scrawled on a piece of cardboard nailed to a tree near the final river crossing. 'Here we can think and say what we want,' Antero grinned, but not without a trace of irony. But for most of the students and the thousands of people who poured into the cantonment site it was a little like entering a liberated area: a taste of freedom, some respite from the relentless pressures the militias and Indonesian army exerted. Falintil, through the very fact of its existence, embodied their hopes of liberation.

Many had taken great risks to come, but come they did: on trucks and buses, on motorbikes and on foot, thousands and thousands of them. They cut down trees along the river and with each passing day the military base looked more like a refugee camp. The atmosphere resembled something between Woodstock and a political protest camp, like Britain's 1980s women's campaign against the deployment of Cruise missiles at Greenham Common.

Nowhere in Timor could the CNRT openly campaign, or even display their posters and flags. But here, images of Xanana, looking like a politician in a grey business suit and tie, adorned every big tree. It was also a time of great reunions – an emotional sea of hugs and kisses, as many people found long-lost family members and friends, and of tears shed by those disappointed in their hopes of finding their missing family with Falintil.

When I saw L7, he was practising his parading skills again. Up and down he marched in front of his headquarters, his knees high and his hands, in his bright red gloves, swinging rigidly beside his body in time with his marching feet. He tried to make the perfect 90-degree turn. On the big day, he said, he was to lead the flag-raising ceremony. He seemed in his element, enjoying the growing attention, but he was also even more wound up. As far as I could see, he had stopped eating altogether and his only intake of calories came from the wine and beer he drank (in abundance). Most visitors did not come empty-handed, and a handsome stockpile of boxes of beer and bottles of wine and spirits was building in L7's HQ. Soon it all became too much for him. On the morning before the great day he collapsed on the parade ground and was brought back on a stretcher.

The Sagrada Familia was also getting ready for the big event. From six in the morning until late at night I heard the rattling keys and jangling bell of the big typewriter. Antonio, the secretary, was tirelessly producing long lists of members and their financial contributions. When I asked him about his diligence he looked at me but his fingers did not leave the keys. 'It's my duty. This is public property, we need records for the future.' Next to the typewriter lay a huge stack of Sagrada Familia ID cards. 'Look,' L7 said, pointing proudly at the pile, 'we have more than sixty thousand members.' I thought he was exaggerating, but Antero confirmed the figure.

Every day L7 addressed large crowds that gathered on the benches in front of his headquarters. His speeches sounded almost identical to the rant I had heard in Lequidoe, spiced up with some news stories Taur had picked from the Internet and got his interpreter Ivo to translate.

With the help of Ivo I had mastered some Tetum. He was a good teacher and encouraged me to speak, and to my surprise I soon managed to make myself understood, and, even better, to understand simple conversations. One evening I was working on my laptop in the little office when I was jolted by the sound of sustained automatic gunfire that seemed to come from all directions. It turned out to be a tape in the karaoke machine, amplified to the speakers surrounding the dance area. It lasted for at least twenty minutes, and it took me a while to realise what was going on. L7, it transpired, was tormenting an Indonesian driver who had been captured. He had been hired by a group of Timorese to bring them to the party. They, Ivo said, had already been 'disciplined' for this breach of security. As for the driver, the poor devil sat speechless on a bench, looking absolutely terrified. 'Military tactics,' Ivo said. 'Security reasons, I guess.' When he talked about military issues his face would take on an ironic expression, or he would laugh coyly. The tape, he explained, was recorded during attacks on Alas. Sometimes, between the shooting, I could hear L7's voice, yelling 'Don't be afraid, don't run away!'

L7 had returned with more beer, and gave the driver a can too. Perhaps he was trying to take the sting out of this psychological torture. L7 reassured him that nothing would happen to him, but he was ordered to remain where he was to watch the entire evening programme of drama, songs, sketches and dancing. Before being sent away, he had after all to be convinced of Falintil's superiority and its hospitality. I remember him sitting immobile, the expression on his fat face unchanging all evening.

In the days before the anniversary L7 was authorised to organise as many *festas* as he liked. Every night they danced into the small hours. He did, however, remain watchful that dancers did not stray too close to a little chapel he had built. It was a simple bamboo building with a roof of palm leaves. The walls were festooned with flags and banners: the national flag, a Falintil banner and one of the Sagrada Familia, a map of Timor splashed with red paint representing blood. A few weeks previously an elderly bishop from Melbourne, Bishop Hilton Deakin, a staunch campaigner for East Timor, had made the exhausting walk along the river. 'It took a lot of walking on water to get here,' he had joked when he arrived, to great excitement. He was the first bishop ever to have visited a Falintil camp. He did not stay long but before he left he blessed the new chapel, naming it 'The Freedom Chapel of the Holy Family'. Somehow L7 had acquired an electric organ, and on Sundays he stood in front of the chapel and conducted prayer services like a catechist.

'God fights on our side,' L7 told me once. But it was not his preaching of the Catholic doctrine that attracted his followers. The people came for something else. Over the years many myths had sprung up around him and 'the men in the forest'. Wild stories circulated about their *lulik* and magical powers, and they had become part of Falintil's mythology. I had heard many claim that commanders such as Nino Konis Santana, David Alex and even Nicolau Lobato were not dead. Such powerful fighters simply could not die.

For many Timorese the physical and metaphysical worlds were one. For them the biblical scriptures could easily go hand in hand with their spirits. When I joined a pilgrimage to the top of the Matebian I had asked the local people how they felt about the statue of Christ on top of the mountain of the souls of the death. They had answered that Jesus was the leader of these spirits.

From the few other journalists who had spent time with Falintil, such as Dom Rotheroe, I had heard about the rituals Falintil performed before and after they launched an attack. A shaman would cut open roosters and read their entrails, looking for auspicious signs, while *tua sabu* would be passed around like communion wine, and ancestors and Catholic saints invoked for their blessings.

L7 behaved like one of these 'Catholic shamans'. His aspiration to be Falintil's spiritual leader dated from the time he had been visited in a dream by a powerful spirit, one of those that dwell in the land and on the mountain-tops, in places such as the holes under the stones wrapped in red cloth on Ili Manu. His followers believed that he possessed magical powers. His talisman was said to have extraordinarily strong *lulik* powers to protect him. He could make himself invisible to the Indonesian army, and his skin impenetrable by bullets; he could move like a whisper of the wind, or change himself, at will, into a tree. Understandably, people were in awe of him, not to mention afraid.

Magic ran in L7's family. His grandfather, Leki Naha, as well as being a legendary warrior, had been a shaman possessing phenomenal gifts. In battles against the invaders of his time, the Japanese, he was decapitated seven times but by using his *lulik* power his head every time magically re-attached itself. Although he sometimes offered different biblical explanations, it was probably to honour the auspicious legacy of Leki Naha that his grandson had added his initial and the number of his decapitations to his code-name, L7.

I tried my best, but it was hard to find out exactly what the Sagrada Familia was. Its doctrines seemed a potent blend of the Timorese notion of the sacred *rai*, and Christian belief and ritual. Whenever I asked for an explanation of the animistic side of the sect, I met a brick wall. As I had found on Ili Manu, many words have magical meanings and cannot be spoken aloud, or at least not to a foreigner.

Timor's mountains had bred many such sects and cults. The cult around Saint Anthony, for example, especially strong in Baucau and Manatutu, where he is, according to one of nuns there, 'more important than Jesus'. People pray to him every day for help with planting and harvests – but for good measure, they also sacrifice a dog.

The stories of *lulik* and magic had their effect on the Indonesian soldiers, too. Many of them came from communities where witchcraft played an important role, and the special abilities the Timorese seemed to possess terrified them.

§

The grand day started with a long mass. Among the four priests helping conduct the service I saw a grinning Father Jovito. For mass, the guerrillas took off their berets, but their rifles did not leave their shoulders. Then it was L7's turn, his big day in the spotlight of the television cameras. As he led the flag-raising ceremony, there was a rousing chorus of Falintil's anthem. He looked more proud than ever.

Xanana was going to make a speech by satellite telephone to the people in all four cantonment sites simultaneously. This elaborate technical feat was to be the finest hour for Taur's fascination with telecommunications. But he had trouble with the satellite link-up. It took endless failed calls. The crowd grew restless. By the time the connection finally worked, the line was bad and not helped by the quality of the sound system. Xanana broke down in tears when he recalled his comrades that had died during the struggle. Not many people could hear what he said, but just the voice of their leader, roaring among them around the dusty field, was auspicious enough.

The rest of the day people strolled around, enjoying the company of their long-lost relatives or just relishing the unknown sense of freedom. Not seven, as Taur had been so thrilled to boast, but no fewer than sixteen *karau* were slaughtered that day. The ground under the 'slaughter tree' was coloured red with their blood. The meat was cooked over hundreds of fires, from which smoke swirled up to mingle with the dusty wind. A large cake, painstakingly decorated with a map of Timor and the CNRT flag, stood melting in the sun.

The thousands of feet that had invaded the cantonment site had killed off the last bits of grass. The camp couldn't cope with the influx, and the normal routine that had become part of life there was totally disrupted. There were precise rules. It was forbidden to bathe upstream in the river. The women had a few hours in the morning and men in the afternoon when they could wash themselves, a rule strictly enforced by sentries along the river. Especially in the afternoon, the Uaimori river looked like a small replica of the Ganges. The little wells in the riverbed that were used to collect drinking water had become muddy and polluted. Empty bags of detergent and toothpaste boxes drifted in the once pristine water.

The next day, as the party was winding down, a sudden frenzy engulfed the crowds. A group of men were hustled on to the podium, some of them bleeding. 'Spies, spies!' yelled the furious crowd around me, with the little boys shouting loudest. A cordon of Falintil soldiers had to restrain people from storming the podium to lynch the men. Some hurled insults; others made threatening gestures with their fists.

One of the men had started to weep. I saw his lips move. 'I'm innocent, I'm not a spy,' he cried. Commander Falur took the stage and calmed the crowd down. He led the trembling man through the still-fuming onlookers to Taur's headquarters, where he was received warmly. The crowd fell still. 'He is one of us,' Taur explained calmly, but I could see from his mouth that he was upset. 'He worked as a double agent. The information he gathered he brought to us.' To leave no room for any misunderstanding he put his arm around the still shaking man and told the now embarrassed-looking crowd: 'He is my friend.'

This sour note did not spoil what was otherwise a happy interlude for most of those at the party. It was as if they had taken an advance on the victory celebrations that should have followed a vote for independence. In retrospect, it was as close as they would come to being able to celebrate it.

CHAPTER 19

Kings of Cassa

§ I LEFT Uaimori in a long convoy of trucks. The militias had threatened to attack the revellers on the way back, so Taur had suggested that we all go at the same time – a strategy of safety in numbers. Unamet police officers and military observers had been alerted to the threat, and stood at strategic points along the route to monitor what happened. But the militias kept a low profile, and we arrived back in Dili without incident. The people along the road hailed us as victors. These were the last days of campaigning before the referendum, and the trucks, full of windswept but happy people, were seen as part of this.

João had followed the celebrations on television. It was the talk of the town. 'I wish I could have seen the faces of the Indonesian commanders when they saw all our fighters. They must have been shocked,' he sniggered, relishing the idea that the sight of hundreds of armed Falintil soldiers might have embarrassed the Indonesian generals, who had always dismissed Falintil as a small group of sick old men. The pro-independence lobby, he concluded, could not have wished for better propaganda.

During the campaign the streets had been dominated by the pro-integration groups. Indonesia had provided them with money and resources. So half the population walked around in red-and-white T-shirts emblazoned 'Otonomi Yes', and matching baseball caps. Some wore these clothes for protection – dressed like this, they were less likely to be suspected of supporting independence – others simply because a crisp new T-shirt was a luxury not to be spurned.

To prevent clashes, the two camps were not allowed to campaign on the same day. On the first day of its campaign, the CNRT had opened its new office and had, for the first time in Timor, hoisted its blue, white and green flag, a flag that looked almost identical to Falintil's. It was an emotional moment, accompanied by tears and exuberant *tebe tebe* dances.

For the rest of the campaign period, the CNRT heeded Xanana's advice and kept a low profile. But on the penultimate day, independence supporters took to the streets on trucks and motorbikes, for the first time since the large demonstrations in 1998. The rally was remarkably peaceful, and the only casualty was a campaigner who fell to his death off an overcrowded truck.

§

Antero had prepared another excursion. He wanted to go to the mountains south of Dili – to Aileu, Same and Ainaro – to see how the students there were doing. Mana Lou, too, had gone in that direction, to see her *aspirantes*. 'To give them courage' was how she put it. I would have liked to travel with her, but she said it was too dangerous for her to take me. Antero, however, seemed to be more than happy for me and a colleague to accompany him.

We left in the morning of the last day of the campaign, 27 August. Our driver carefully manoeuvred our pick-up truck through a vast convoy of red and white. It was the autonomy camp's last chance to upstage the CNRT rally of the previous day. Everywhere I looked I saw people dressed in the colours of the Indonesian flag. Many of them looked no older than twelve, and would probably have waved any flag for money and something to eat.

The pro-integration factions had united in June under the name UNIF (United Front for East Timor Autonomy), and Basilio Araujo had become the group's official spokesman. I had heard from him and others in his group that the Timorese in the countryside did not want to be bothered by a referendum, that they had no concept of politics, and so on.

But people in Timor were not as politically inexperienced as Basilio tried to make us believe. Even the smallest village was politicised. People knew what to expect of life under Indonesian rule. It was a bit like living under a restraining order: whenever the villagers wanted to leave the village, they needed permission from their local military commander first.

Xanana, asked why the CNRT did not campaign, joked that, over the years, the Indonesian army had conducted the most effective of political campaigns. It had managed to convince people of what they wanted: definitely not more of the same. Few people knew at that time what exactly they were voting for, but they certainly knew what they were voting against.

The students were worried, however, about whether people would understand the ballot paper. Many could not read, so the symbols on the paper were important, and had been subject to tortuous negotiations. Both sides had chosen the symbol of a map with flags projecting from it. The autonomy group had a small Indonesian flag and traditional *uma lulik*; the CNRT had their flag. Still, however, the question on the ballot referred only to 'special autonomy'; nowhere was the word 'independence' mentioned. Further confusing matters, some government officials told voters that if they punched a hole through the CNRT flag, this meant that they rejected that option. Another rumour was that the Indonesians had a powerful satellite that enabled them to look into the polling booths and see how people voted.

It had been Unamet's task to prepare the people for the vote. Voter-education teams had roamed the countryside explaining the technicalities. The most important message was that people's votes were secret. The television spot produced by Unamet about voters' education had become an instant hit. A sprightly, feisty old lady, of the type you can find everywhere in Timor, sits on her veranda surrounded by a crowd of grandchildren. 'Otonomi,' she shrieks while she turns her head to spit betel-nut juice on the ground. 'Independencia,' she yells, and turns to the other side to unload some more scarlet spittle. Then, with defiance in her eyes, she looks straight at the camera. 'It's my secret.' And then she breaks into a loud cackling laugh.

This message had even reached the countryside. But there, people had to do some play-acting of their own. In a tiny hamlet along the road, an old man approached us. 'We are all for autonomy here,' he declared loudly even before I had asked him anything. In his hand I saw he had one of the sample ballot papers the UN used for voter education. He opened it and pointed at the option with the CNRT flag. With a wide grin on his face, he quickly folded the paper again.

From students coming back from the countryside I had heard that many people had put their names on lists declaring that they supported autonomy. It was better to sign up, they argued, since that would mean relative peace for their village; at least for as long as the militias and the Indonesian army continued to believe they would win.

Everywhere we stopped, we found people making preparations for the time immediately after the ballot. CNRT families would leave for the hills as soon as they had cast their votes. They had been told for months that if autonomy were rejected, all hell would break loose, and they had no reason to doubt this. They knew very well what the Indonesian army and its Timorese allies were capable of.

The only people who remained fairly unconcerned and upbeat were the international staff working for Unamet. We found a group of them sitting around a table in a little restaurant in Same. I entered the restaurant in a dark mood. I was still thinking about what one of the students, whom I knew was not easily scared, had whispered anxiously when he had met us furtively at the town's graveyard: 'We have to prepare for the worst.'

'Everything in Same was just fine,' one of the UN staff had answered when I asked how things were. They actually seemed a bit surprised when we explained our qualms. One of the UN volunteers from Suai said that perhaps in other places there might be trouble, but in Suai everything was very peaceful. When my colleague asked if she or the others actually had time to talk to people, she chipped in that she had talked to her cook and that he was, like her, 'optimistic and unconcerned'.

In Ainaro things were not much better. Just a few days before we arrived,

Mahidi militiamen had attacked the small office of the Students' Solidarity Council. The building had probably never looked grand, but now all the windows and doors had been smashed, and it looked even more of a shack. We had better not spend the night with them, they said, because that might provoke another attack.

Other options, however, were limited in Ainaro. There was a *wisma*, a government-run guesthouse, a gloomy, musty place that was empty but still open. We decided to walk on to see if we could find something to eat before settling there for the night. The streets were dark and empty, but we found a little kiosk that sold dusty prawn crackers and peanuts. Nibbling on the stale crackers I noticed that from the nearby rectory light was shining through the shutters. Inside we were met by Padre Mattheus, a tall, aristocratic-looking man who greeted us distantly. He looked like his brother, Francisco Lopes da Cruz, one of Indonesia's most loyal supporters. He used the same rhetoric as his brother and, like him, seemed to think that autonomy was best for the people. How much he knew and how close he was to his brother's organisation, UNIF, I didn't know, but at the end of our meeting he said: 'Make sure you're not in Dili after the referendum. All the militia groups will come through Dili. It'll be the worst place. Here you can flee to the mountains, but there you'll be trapped.'

With that warning on my mind I walked across an open field opposite the rectory to the convent of the Canossian sisters. The nuns were sitting with their backs to the door, watching satellite television news. I called out in Tetum but they did not hear. When I gingerly pulled aside the curtain in front of the door I stood face to face with a terrified-looking sister. When she recovered, she quickly invited us in and continued to watch television. 'Oh my God! Oh my God! More people have died,' she wailed. After the autonomy-supporters' rally there had been shooting near Maliana and in Dili. Among the dead was a Timorese journalist, Rosa Garcia's best friend, shot point-blank by a Brimob policeman.

'Our mother superior invites you to sleep with us tonight,' said the sister who had welcomed us in. She was called Sister Elsa and was, I would find out later, one of Tata's aunts.

The convent's mother superior was a tall, formidable woman in her forties, with handsome features. 'She is the sister of governor Abilio Soares,' sister Elsa whispered when she took us to a side room for some leftover supper. She watched us eat and mothered us, urging us to have more of the rice, beef and soup. 'You have to eat well,' she fretted, 'you have to be strong. You have to be there for the people, you have to go everywhere.' She spoke rapidly as if every minute counted.

The Indonesian security forces had distributed arms among the young men, she said. She had seen them walking with police knives. 'Do you want to kill people?' she had asked them. 'Kill me, I have had a good life, seen many beautiful places. I have many good friends, I have enjoyed life. But if you kill now then you'll be killed yourself soon.' Then she had taken away the knives from the boys.

After supper she showed us our room, an austere cell with two iron-framed beds and blankets that smelled of camphor balls. I am normally not terribly fond of this smell, but now it was strangely comforting. I fell asleep that night feeling wrapped in a safe cocoon amid all the insecurity and danger.

§

Early in the morning we walked back to the student house to pick up Antero. He wanted to go to Cassa, or 'the mouth of the tiger', as he called it. Cassa was the headquarters of the Mahidi militia, one of the most notorious and brutal of the many groups. Its leaders, the Carvalho brothers Cancio and Nemesio, were known as 'the kings of Cassa'.

As the road wound down from the mountains the landscape was lusher. I could see Mount Ramelau towering over Cassa's rice fields in the distance. Although the two places are close, they are inhabited by different tribes. The residents of Ainaro, and of most villages in that district, are Mambai. Cassa, which lies lower and has fertile rice fields, is dominated by Kemak, who speak a completely different language.

I had to think about a story that I had heard from Benjamin Corte-Real, an Untim lecturer, who was born in Ainaro. One day, many generations ago – no one knows how many but everyone in Ainaro knows the story – the king of Cassa, the Nai Cassa, killed a prince of an important *liurai* family in Ainaro. The king killed the prince in his sleep and sneaked away under cover of darkness, taking his skull back to Cassa, where his craftsmen covered it in gold and made it into a drinking cup.

No one in Ainaro knew what had happened. Some years later a son of the prince married one of the Nai Cassa's daughters. Every time the couple travelled down to see her family in Cassa, the prince would be offered wine in a golden bowl. After this had happened a few times the princess felt so sorry for her husband that she urged him to refuse the wine. But he did not understand her concern until, on the way back to Ainaro, she explained that the cup he had been drinking out of was made out of his father's skull.

The prince, furious at this treachery, secretly took revenge on the people of Cassa. He made a point of killing every shepherd he came across. After a while people started to suspect him. A man hiding in a tree watched him murder one of his victims, and ran to tell the king of Cassa. From that day on, open war raged between the two kingdoms and, according to oral history, would continue 'as long as coconut trees grow'. Benjamin, who told me the story, was the son of a famous Ainaro *liurai* family – the Corte-Reals – whose grandfather's picture featured on the old Portuguese colonial banknotes. 'We will always see the people of Cassa', he added, 'as a source of treachery.'

The people of Ainaro were confirmed in this belief again in 1975, when the king of Cassa, Mateus de Carvalho, became a central figure in the Apodeti party and one of the signatories to the Balibo declaration. The strong affiliation the Cassa *liurai* family felt to Indonesia and integration was perhaps not surprising: the Kemak tribe is a small minority in East Timor, but has strong ties with a larger group of Kemak across the border in West Timor.

Mateus's grandsons, the Carvalho brothers, the new 'kings of Cassa', were in a sense part of a local tradition. Their pro-integration leanings were obvious as we entered Cassa village. On both sides of the road and in front of each wooden house fluttered at least two Indonesian flags. In the centre of the village, on the other side of the football field, stood the house of the 'kings', a solitary stone building among the wood-and-mud huts. The only other stone house, on the outskirts of the village, belonged to the family of Felis's friend Fernãu, whose father had moved there from Ainaro and now owned some large paddy fields.

We found Cancio on the veranda, in conclave with two UN military observers. All of them wore similarly coloured blue baseball caps, and from a distance even Cancio could be mistaken for a UN worker. That the autonomy camp had chosen the same colour could not be a coincidence, I thought, and made a joke about this to Cancio, who replied: 'Yes, that's what I am: a peacekeeper.' I looked at his face for at least a hint of self-mockery or irony, but found him in bitter earnest.

Cancio sat wide-legged, dressed in a white T-shirt decorated with the ballot-paper's autonomy symbol. He looked about the same age as his colleague Eurico Guterres, in his late twenties. He called for a few more plastic chairs and more coffee.

Cancio had just been telling the UN observers that he embraced democracy and had told his people that they had to vote for the best option. 'I myself also want independence,' he said, 'but that would mean that we have no peace. That's why I support autonomy.' Antero had also been offered a chair and had pushed it as far as he could away from where Cancio sat, hiding half behind us. He was too curious to miss the opportunity to listen, but did not want to translate and kept his mouth tightly shut so the Indonesian police interpreter felt obliged to help us out.

In the meantime Cancio's brother Nemesio had arrived. A slender man with a small black beard, he made a strong contrast to his smaller, rounder sibling. He was the brother with the brains. He had studied political science at a university in Jakarta. 'To be a good leader is to fight for what is the best for the people,' Cancio continued. 'Independence means more war, so autonomy is best. If one day independence wins, than we'll have to continue our

11. Antero da Silva at the CNRT campaign rally.

fight.' It was the same 'we kill for peace' argument I had heard from Basilio Araujo. I glanced sideways at Nemesio. Did he notice the doublespeak, the sheer nonsense in what his brother had said?

But Nemesio looked unperturbed. 'What we need is the third way,' he said, an argument I had now heard many times. 'To prevent a civil war the sides who have been fighting should compromise. No one wants to lose. Autonomy is the middle way, good for everyone, so we'll have no winners and no losers.'

Cancio went on: 'We have people power, we have the people on our side.' 'People power,' echoed Nemesio, from behind me, taking his cue from his brother. 'East Timor's future is democracy and in a democracy, people power is very important. Like in America. Mahidi has people power, so it is democratic.'

I asked Cancio how big an army he had to fight for his version of 'people power'. This got him really going. 'Eight thousand plus our family makes 8,013.' The more he boasted the louder and faster he spoke. When I took out my microphone to record the interview he raised his voice even more. He was a platform speaker who never got down from the platform. 'Now we are still sleeping, we're not showing our force. If someone bothers us, and wakes us up, it will be dangerous, very dangerous,' he warned.

Two weeks earlier Mahidi had made a big show of locking their weapons inside their headquarters. 'Any time we are attacked by Falintil we can take them out again,' said Cancio. 'When we launch our big attacks Falintil will be finished.' He laughed triumphantly. 'Believe it or not; wait and see.'

I was growing a bit weary of this disturbing nonsense. Cancio's loud vainglorious language sounded like the boasting of someone who had to shout loudly to hear himself over the noise of his own insecurity. I had the feeling that he and his brother knew that they were about to lose. He had already thought of his future. They would not leave Timor, he said, but 'with our people's power we can go to the mountains and fight a guerrilla war'.

Cancio was shouting now, and I was feeling more and more uncomfortable and worried, especially about Antero. What if Cancio recognised Antero and did something to him? We could not expect much help from the two unarmed UN military liaison officers, who were listening impassively to this diatribe.

Cancio could, I knew, be very unpredictable, and had a history of mental health problems. A young Timorese nun had told me that, as a teenager, he had sometimes stayed with the nuns so they could look after him when he had 'one of his breakdowns'. She had first-hand experience of what these were like from the time when she was studying at Untim. Early in 1999 a large group of graduate students had gone to Suai to do community service for a couple of months. One day Cancio and his men had attacked the building where they were staying. To protect their male colleagues from being shot, the girls had hugged them. The militia had dragged one student out and stabbed him to death. Another, called Bernardino, they tried to shoot five times. According to the young nun, shots made five holes in his T-shirt but he was unharmed. His *lulik* talisman had, she believed, protected him. She had tried to intervene. Cancio had hugged her, staining her white habit with blood. 'Sister, I love you,' he had said, 'but if have to I will kill you too.'

In another incident Cancio had killed an eight-months pregnant woman. 'I ordered them to fire,' he said referring to his militiamen. He showed how he had pointed his gun. 'She was torn apart.' He added that she was 'the wife of a Falintil commander'.[1]

By the time we were ready to leave, the football field had become a sea of red and white. Cancio stood on the steps of his veranda looking with satisfaction at this assembly of his followers. Mahidi was going to have a big party, he said, and he invited us to stay. We declined the offer, got into our car and drove slowly through the red-and-white crowd.

Antero, who had quietly listened to Cancio's rant, had formed his own theory about the conflict between Ainaro and Cassa. In his slightly otherworldly way, he listed its many facets: tribal, historical, political, social. A rich soil in which outsiders could sow unrest. But it was too late to do anything to stop it now, he concluded.

As soon as we arrived back at the Student Council office in Dili, I noticed that something was wrong. It was too quiet. The little wooden kiosk in front of the building, where an old woman used to sell water and peanuts, was closed. Even the children and dogs had disappeared. We had just unloaded our luggage when a student appeared from the back of the house. He told Antero something in rapid Tetum. I saw Antero's eyes widen, but he didn't move.

'The student council was attacked 30 minutes ago and everybody has run away,' he said slowly. He did not know what to do next. The militiamen were still around the corner. They were burying one of their men at Santa Cruz cemetery. By this time only the militias still used the cemeteries: most other people were too afraid and buried their dead in their own backyards.

§

As the referendum approached, such intimidation and violence intensified. Antero and the other students had given up on reconciliation for the moment. They focused on the day of the ballot. They wanted to survive to vote, and after that ... well, after that, nobody knew what would happen.

Unamet still believed it could turn the tide, although at the time nobody was confident that the day of the referendum would be peaceful. Every effort to reconcile the Timorese factions – whether by the students, Mana Lou, the bishops, or Unamet itself – had failed. The latest attempt, in late June, had been led by the bishops. Known as Dare II, it was a continuation of the reconciliation meeting in Dare in 1998. It was actually held in Jakarta, so that Xanana and even José Ramos Horta were able to attend. Ramos Horta had been formally banned since 1975 from entering Indonesia, and it was the first time since the invasion that he and Xanana had been able to meet.

The talks had been quite amicable, but deep divisions remained. The participants did not get beyond agreeing in principle to respect the 18 June agreement on the disarmament of the militias and Falintil and to honour the outcome of the 30 August ballot. When, on the final day, the facilitators tried to reach a consensus on the way to carry the talks forward, the pro-autonomy faction would not commit itself to the idea of a joint commission that would secure the interests of both parties, before and after the ballot.[2] It had come close, according to a Canadian conflict-resolution expert who attended the talks, but every time an agreement was almost reached, the pro-integration faction (UNIF) had to ask for a break to make phone calls. He assumed they called their masters in the Indonesian military and foreign-affairs department; when they returned to the conference table they were unable to accept any proposals that came up in the meeting.

Bishop Basilio, who had spent months preparing the meeting, was bitterly disappointed. He had pressed for 'real substance' and knew this had been Timor's last chance before the referendum for meaningful reconciliation. Now it was up to Unamet to get the two sides to cooperate. Its first step was to work on the establishment of a transitional council of 25 Timorese, who could be appointed by Kofi Annan as the representative body the UN could work with, until the Indonesian parliament officially endorsed the outcome of the ballot.

This was an idea that appealed to Xanana, Antero and many others, who had said all along that the referendum was not an opportunity for one side to claim victory, but a chance for the people to express their aspirations. They had talked about a council of national unity with, in Xanana's words, 'no winners and no losers, no heroes and no traitors'. This council, however, now renamed the 'East Timorese Consultative Commission', never really got off the ground before or after the vote.

§

Another last-ditch UN initiative was to persuade the militias, the Indonesian army and Falintil to work out an agreement on disarmament. These were the meetings Taur and his commanders had been joking about in Falintil's camp. The UN had been very excited. The information officer had whispered for days that something big was about to happen, and had called all journalists for an early Sunday-morning press briefing in the largest of the meeting halls in the UN compound.

There, in front of the cameras of the world's big television networks, Falintil's Commander Falur and Eurico Guterres of the PPI declared that they would order their forces not to carry weapons outside their 'cantonment sites', and then they hugged each other. It was a far cry from the disarmament of the militias the UN had required as a basic condition, but it was hailed as a historic agreement.[3] And it was indeed, in one sense, an extraordinary moment: less than twenty-four hours before the referendum would start, the UN had pulled off an amazing public relations coup.

Among the smiling officials I saw Timbul Silaen, the Indonesian police chief, and the TNI commander, Colonel Muis, who vowed to ensure that the ballot went ahead peacefully and to enforce the disarmament. Eurico Guterres looked full of himself. And Commander Falur? He kept his Raybans on. In the middle sat Ian Martin, the head of Unamet, looking smug. No one pointed out that the same kind of promises had been heard many times over the past months, and had done nothing to stem the violence; nor that Eurico Guterres, after all, was in no position to sign any papers. He did not pull the strings – he was a puppet.

The whole episode of the 'disarmament' agreement made me cringe. Did the UN, after all the broken promises, believe this latest one? Or was it meant to be purely symbolic: to send a signal to voters that there was at least a little hope that the referendum might after all be peaceful? Certainly, as public relations, it was effective. Radio and television stations had broadcast it all over Timor and the world. But the idea that this agreement was worth as much as the paper it was written on sounded, even then, naïve and over-optimistic. Yet Unamet, according to one high-placed UN official, actually believed its own propaganda.

That day Ian Martin reminded me of Pontius Pilate, safely washing his hands. 'Look,' his body language said, 'we have done our best.'

'It was the most Unamet could achieve,' he would later write. 'It was not enough.'[4]

§

Four hours after he promised to lay down his arms, Eurico Guterres was seen walking around Dili with an M16 in one hand and a pistol in the other. His militiamen zoomed around the city for hours. One of his men provocatively rode his motorbike through Becora, where he was pulled off his bike by a group of independence supporters. I knew the little group. Some were from the family I had seen in April running around with bows and arrows, when I had sheltered with Antero from a militia attack. They had set up a self-defence force, a vocal little group that had vowed to stand up to the militia threats. One of them brandished a crude axe, others carried butchers' knives, sling-shots, bows and arrows and nail-studded clubs. They took courage both from what they saw as their right to protect themselves – nobody else would do it, after all – and from the *tua sabu* they drank from huge plastic jerry-cans.

They kicked and stabbed the militiaman and sent him in a taxi to the hospital. He died. This incident had put the newborn agreement under so much strain that prominent CNRT and Falintil leaders accompanied UN officers to Becora to negotiate the hand-over of João da Silva, the man responsible for the murder. I recognised him as the brother of a former national champion bodybuilder, who was one of the 50 victims of the Santa Cruz massacre the army had acknowledged. His brother had never got over the loss. Now the family tragedy had come full circle and turned him into a killer, too.

CHAPTER 20

· · · · · · · · · · · · · · · ·

The Price of Freedom

To attain all this, however, rivers of blood must yet flow, and years of desolation pass over; yet the object is worth rivers of blood, and years of desolation.
(Thomas Jefferson to John Adams, 1823)

§ IN the pre-dawn light the queues in front of the polling station looked like
a silent wake. People stood quietly in the half-light, edgily clutching their
identification papers. But as soon as the sun coloured the sky and nothing
threatening had happened, their anxiety faded somewhat, and they seemed to
relax a bit and chatted softly.

Everybody had come dressed in their Sunday best: women had put on neat
suits or colourful sarongs with shiny silk long-sleeved blouses; children had
been bathed and groomed and the men wore clean, crisply ironed shirts and
pressed trousers. On their faces, they all wore nervous smiles – smiles that, at
the same time, were full of expectation. After all, this was their day, their
turning point. Afterwards, life would never be the same again.

In some places, the entire population of a village had set off on foot in the
middle of the night to be sure of reaching the polling station in good time.
When the UN staff arrived at 4.30 in the morning, they found large crowds
already waiting. Even the old, the disabled, the sick and the pregnant had
made long, arduous journeys. They carried bags with food and clothes, and
sometimes bedding too. After they cast their votes, many would not go back
home, but head up into the hills. For the CNRT leaders and their families,
and others who felt vulnerable, the most popular destinations were the coffee
plantations in Dare.

The day before the ballot I had climbed up a dry riverbed east of the city
to gauge the mood among the refugees who lived hidden in the foothills. Some
had built small huts and cultivated tiny plots of land. In one of these huts I
found a frail old man sitting on the floor. His family had fled from Viqueque,
he said. His dark eyes were coated with a bluish film that betrayed cataracts.

Like other ancient men I had met in Timor, he did not know his exact age
– he just knew he was very, very old. He started to count on his fingers; he

had seen the Portuguese, the Japanese, and Portuguese again, then the Indonesians and now, he thought, it was time for the Timorese. He was determined to climb down the steep hill and vote, even if it was the last thing he did.

I had to think of Xanana's experience with the old villagers who had urged him 'Never give up.' Their determination had found a voice in their country's youth, and now had finally brought them the chance to decide its future.

The next day, I watched one of these old men as he emerged from a polling booth, looking a bit disorientated. A member of the UN staff guided him to the ballot box and the old man pushed his carefully folded ballot paper gingerly though the small opening. When he re-emerged he blinked against the glaring sunlight. Then he suddenly stuck his arms up in the air in a gesture of triumph and victory. Baring his blood-red betel-stained teeth, he shouted: 'I did it! I voted!' In his excitement he almost jumped around and started to kiss all the foreign faces he saw. 'If you hadn't come they would have killed us all, killed us all,' he shouted. His kiss left smelly, crusty bits of dried betel-juice on my cheek. And a lump in my throat.

The old man, still smiling to himself, slowly sauntered off in the direction of a tree where his family was waiting for him. 'I voted for independence,' he said softly, looking around anxiously. In the shade of a nearby tree I saw, to my surprise, some familiar faces. There was the tall figure of my dance partner, Susar, accompanied by two other Falintil soldiers from L7's group. They had come down from Uaimori in plain clothes, and were quietly observing the queues in front of the polling station. 'We're here for security,' Susar whispered. 'We will vote, but only when everyone else has finished.'

Everywhere in Dili and elsewhere in the country the pattern had been the same: huge crowds patiently lining up in front of the polling stations. Some people had had to wait for more than three hours in the blazing sun, but nobody complained. One young man, who had been shot by the Indonesian police, had even insisted on being carried on a stretcher from the Motael clinic to a polling station. In a queue in front of the polling centre near the Santa Cruz cemetery I saw Padre Jovito, who had come with the priests from the seminary. His eyes glimmered with anticipation. 'It's our great, great day,' he beamed. I was scouring the queues for Antero, but he had not turned up yet. I did find João, however, just emerging from the polling booth. He managed a little grin and in his earnest, formal way he said: 'Whatever happens to us now, at least I was able to do this for my country.'

Despite the worries about security, the day of the referendum itself was actually surprisingly peaceful. By noon, the UN reported that four out of five registered voters had cast their ballots, and when the polling booths closed at 4 p.m., the figure had risen to over 98 per cent.[1] Many refugees had come down from the hills to vote. Maliana, for example, had turned into a ghost town in the days before the ballot; people came down to vote and by nightfall the town was deserted again. In several places the polling centres had to close for some time because angry militiamen had threatened the staff, accusing them of bias and of forcing people to vote for independence. In Cassa, two armed Mahidi men had marched into the polling station loudly protesting about the local UN staff's lack of 'impartiality'.

The worst incidents happened in Ermera district, where the polling station in Glenoo came under fire and was attacked with stones. During the attack, the UN staff saw the police handing weapons to the militia.[2] The polling station had to close for several hours, till the UN police chief arrived with his Indonesian counterpart. Even after that visit, there was another attack in the same district. After the polls closed, TNI soldiers and militiamen assaulted the UN's Timorese staff, stabbing one to death in front of the UN and Indonesian police guards. Two others went missing and were later found to have been killed as well.

But in general it had been much more peaceful than the UN – or anyone else for that matter – had expected, and certainly more peaceful than any day during the preparation for the ballot. Unamet's spokesman was triumphant: 'The massive voter turnout is absolute proof that the campaign of intimidation, violence and threats that attempted to destabilise the popular consultation was a complete failure. It could not work, it did not work and it will not work.' It seemed to vindicate the hope – shared by many foreign diplomats – that the Indonesian government cared enough about its international reputation not to let things get completely out of hand in East Timor, and that the Indonesian security forces, together with the militia leaders, could, if they wished, keep a lid on the violence.

Weeks before the ballot Jamsheed Marker had already made it clear that he did not think there would be a need for a UN peacekeeping force, either before or after the ballot. 'The situation is not serious enough.' And this statement was repeated: 'Up to now the assessment is that a peacekeeping force is not necessary, this is proven by the events.'[3] But not everyone was prepared to give the UN the credit for the relative calm. Yayasan Hak, the Timorese human rights advocates, accused Unamet of failing to create a conducive atmosphere for the poll itself and of failing to persuade the Indonesian police to provide protection. 'It is only due to the courage and determination of the Timorese people that they came to vote,' they said in a statement. 'Many were ready to die for the future of their country.'

Many had also been successful in a tactical ruse: duping the autonomy camp into thinking they would win more votes than they did. This had the effect of fooling far more people than just the members of the militias. As their local Indonesian sponsors filed reports to their superiors, who in turn reported to Jakarta, at every link in the chain, the prospects of the pro-autonomy campaign were boosted a little bit more. So by the time they landed on the desks of the top army commanders and of Ali Alatas, they presented the rosiest possible outlook. The higher your position, the more people under you tell you what you want to hear.[4]

§

That night I broke down on the phone to my friend in London. I did not understand why I felt so sad on what had been, in many respects, such a special day. In part, no doubt, it was because it was a climactic moment, when I could release all the stress built up over the previous weeks. But it was also that I had been very moved by the dignity, decency and sheer courage of ordinary Timorese, braving all the threats and dangers. I did not believe that their oppressors would simply walk away. Nor did I have confidence in the will of the international community to afford them the protection they now deserved.

And then there was a sense of *déjà-vu*. I had seen similar scenes in Cambodia, in 1993. The people dressed in their best clothes, hope written on their faces. Hope that the future would be theirs and that democracy would bring peace. They withstood intimidation from both the Khmer Rouge and the incumbent regime in Phnom Penh that replaced them, and voted for change. They were denied it. The same people I had seen in 1993 I saw again in 1997, after a coup, thrusting their babies in my arms saying that they did not believe that peace would ever be possible in their lives, so could I please take their children to a safe place.

In Timor, I was worried about the more immediate future: the days ahead of us when the country would be exposed to the wrath of the Indonesian army and their militia stooges. But, I asked myself, even if they survived this, would all the Timorese, like the Cambodians, see their aspirations betrayed by a weak and incompetent UN administration, by venal, cruel and power-hungry local politicians, and by a bunch of greedy and corrupt business people?

Friends would tell me this was a patronising, post-colonial mindset: that Timorese were entitled to their own mistakes, their own pollution, and their own economic mess. Well, perhaps, but when they had to hold their hands up for foreign aid, and meet World Bank conditions, would they really be able to make their own decisions, even about who governed them? The outside world is always, in the end, more interested in stability than in fairness.

That referendum night the students celebrated cautiously, with a glass of beer. The enormous turnout had made them optimistic that the outcome might after all be independence.

§

The next morning bellicose militiamen roamed the streets of Dili again. The previous day's calm proved to be just an interlude. It gave way to a mood of anxiety and violence, and the universal certainty that a pro-independence referendum result would be followed by dreadful retribution from the militias. The terror started even before the votes were counted.

Townspeople who had not left yet hoarded instant noodles and batteries. Shops, no doubt, would close as they had in April, so I too joined the queues to buy some emergency supplies, at least enough to last me a few days. Soon after dark the streets became deserted. The only place that was still bustling with life was the harbour. By the orange light of the streetlamps, pick-up trucks, handcarts and taxis, loaded with the contents of houses – fridges, sofas, beds, mattresses – were driving up the wharf to the waiting ferries.

A big part of the Indonesian population had already left. They had emptied and, if they could find a buyer, sold their houses. They had sailed back with their belongings to their homes in Sulawesi, Bali and Java. Tens of thousands had already left that way, but the days around the referendum saw a new scramble. The business people, shop- and restaurant-owners, who had stayed to profit from the influx of Unamet staff, international observers and journalists, now jostled their way up the gang-planks. Among them I also noticed some Timorese families.

'Get out of town now, while you still can. Go to Falintil!' a Jakarta-based journalist urged me over breakfast in the hotel dining room. She whispered that her boyfriend, a photographer, whose father was something high up in the military hierarchy in Jakarta, had had a visit from an *intel* officer the night before. The officer had told him to leave town as soon as he could because 'This place will be hell on earth.' Indonesian journalists who had reported truthfully about the violence were at particular risk. Two had already been wounded. Some had censored their own reports.

When she left with her boyfriend a day later, on a special military plane, which took out virtually the entire Indonesian press corps, they left their food – a box full – and a flak jacket in my room. I knew I would not wear the flak jacket, but it did give me an odd feeling of security: like having an extra lock on the door, even though you know burglars can get in through the window.

The army's intentions now seemed horribly clear. They wanted every journalist and foreign observer out of town, so that they could go ahead undisturbed with whatever they had planned for Timor, much as they had in 1975. Some of the military leaders may also have had another motivation this time: to prevent journalists or other foreigners being killed. Foreign deaths would have much longer-term repercussions than killing Timorese. Having them safely out of the way would at least remove that risk.

The plan worked famously. International observer missions, which had sent hundreds of people to Timor, started to pull their people out and some major news networks left even before the announcement of the result of the referendum. The BBC was the first of the large news organisations to go. Their journalists had been caught up in a terrifying battle between a large

12. Queuing up to vote.

group of Aitarak militiamen and plain-clothes soldiers and a handful of
Timorese who had tried to defend their neighbourhood. Right in front of the
Unamet compound (and in front of the cameras) one of the defenders was
hacked to death by six Aitarak men. Then they turned on the press.

The BBC's Jonathan Head was badly beaten with a machete – luckily for
him with the blunt side. An *intel* officer who was overseeing the carnage
intervened and Jonathan escaped with a fractured arm. I saw him just after
the attack. He was walking – still in shock, I think – with his broken arm
around his attacker. Being the true journalist he is, he was interviewing the
man for the radio. The same evening the BBC chartered an aeroplane and
journalists scrambled to get on the list, thinking this might be their last chance.
For the BBC the story was not considered important enough to risk equipment
and lives. It could, they argued, also be covered from Bali.

Unamet started to pull its people out from the districts, initially mainly the
UN volunteers who had organised the elections. They were scheduled to
leave at about the same time as the ballot boxes. Some police and military
liaison officers would stay behind, and an extra 50 military observers were
scheduled to arrive. But soon the departures looked less like scheduled with-
drawals than a panicked scramble to get out.

One after another, Unamet's district offices all around East Timor had
come under attack. In Maliana, on 2 September, two local UN staff – drivers
– had been shot at their homes by a TNI sergeant, who was also a local

militia commander. Of all the UN staff, the Timorese were the most vulnerable. They had received countless death threats from the local military commander, Colonel Siagian. The town was surrounded, and only a few had been able to get to the mountains safely and join the many pro-independence supporters who were already there. Others had tried to flee to the Unamet compound in Maliana, but the Indonesian policemen at the gate did not let them through. Everyone knew from the several attacks on the Unamet office in Maliana that the UN would not be able to provide protection anyway. The only place they could go was the police station. Unusually, the police here had, according to Unamet, the reputation of being independent of the army and militia and at one point they had even been attacked for that reason.

Unamet evacuated Maliana on 3 September, leaving the town in flames. They took a few Timorese staff with them, but had to leave many behind. As they left the town, they could hear the forlorn sound of voices singing in the police station.

Ermera was also attacked. The helicopter that had tried to pick up the ballot boxes was stoned, and shots were fired in the air. UN staff managed to shift the boxes to a dry riverbed where the helicopter collected them later. Unable to get their hands on the ballot boxes, the militiamen changed tactics and prevented a convoy of 17 UN cars from leaving town. The militiamen demanded that the UN hand over the 50 Timorese staff they had with them. It took eight hours and a visit from TNI General Kiki Syahnakri, to negotiate a safe passage out.[5] In Liquiça the remaining UN staff had to escape from the back of their office, and as they ran to the helicopters an American policeman was shot in the stomach by an Indonesian policeman. 'We couldn't have stayed a minute longer,' said one of the military observers later.

The pattern was the same everywhere: the militias, backed by the army, forced the UN to evacuate the towns. By the third day after the referendum virtually all UN district offices had been abandoned. The only people surprised by the onslaught seemed to be Unamet staff. When I asked Ian Martin during a large press conference on 2 September whether the UN was surprised about the violence, he had snapped that 'Nobody in this room could have predicted it.' And even after all that had happened, the UN still seemed oblivious to how much worse things could get.

For weeks I had been asking myself why Unamet seemed not to take the numerous threats of violence after the ballot at all seriously. They had received several leaked documents, in which scenarios of mass deportation, destruction and killings were spelled out. Some of these they had judged fake, others they had interpreted as less threatening than they seemed.

That was the case with the so-called Garnadi report. H. R. Garnadi was a retired major-general working as an adviser to Habibie's coordinating minister for political and security affairs, Feisal Tanjung (who was also a retired general). After his visit to Timor in June he had reported that the situation was not as favourable as the Indonesian government believed, and that urgent plans had to be made for the eventuality that the Timorese did not opt for autonomy. He outlined a contingency plan that included the evacuation of all civil servants and Timorese security-force personnel. 'Evacuation routes must be planned and secured, possibly by destroying facilities and other key assets.'[6] A few weeks later, the ICRC informed Unamet that refugee camps with the capacity to house the alarming number of 250,000 had been built in West Timor. Initially these plans were viewed by Unamet as a positive development. It showed, they felt, that Indonesia believed its own propaganda – that there were large numbers of autonomy voters – but was at last prepared to accept defeat and one possible consequence of it, their taking refuge across the border. But they had not. By that time the evacuation plan had in fact switched to a deportation plan.[7]

The worst-case scenario, Ian Martin and his advisers had concluded, was that serious violence would break out during or after the ballot, and that the army would be unwilling or unable to contain it. Indonesia might then throw the problem into the lap of the international community and withdraw its security forces, leaving their arms for the militias, which could continue to create instability. Even more likely, he thought, was that 'despite constructive intentions, the Indonesian authorities would be unable to prevent a flight of personnel and loss of morale leading to inaction by their security forces'. Either way, his worry seemed to be, incredibly, about Unamet itself: that it would 'be sucked into security and administrative functions', and be unable to plan for an orderly transition.[8]

So the UN was not at all prepared for the 'worst-case scenario' many Timorese expected: extreme violence from both the Indonesian army and the militias it sponsored. The UN said they had seen and heard many threats, most of which had been never fulfilled. Nor was Unamet prepared for the influx of UN evacuees from other parts of the country, let alone the Timorese who had sought refuge with them.[9]

§

On 3 September, the eve of the announcement of the results, my friend and colleague Minka Nijhuis turned up at the Turismo. The landlord of the house she rented had been so afraid that he had asked her to move out. 'I've got a bad feeling about Antero,' she said, adding that we had to go to the student office now to get him out. After the attack on the student office, Antero had been staying in her house for a few nights. But journalists' homes were not particularly safe places, and now she had been forced to leave, she wanted to make sure Antero was safe. Many other students had already left town but Antero, out of stubbornness or fatalism, had stayed put. It was impossible to get a taxi after dark and we had to persuade a colleague to lend us his car and driver. When we arrived at the student office I saw a shadowy figure lurking behind a tree. It turned out to be Rui, one of the students who had stayed with Antero. He was on the look-out. At the same time a blue pick-up truck stopped some 20 metres down the road. The seven men in the back wore dark clothes and didn't look like people from the neighbourhood. There was no time to lose.

Antero sat quietly in his brightly lit room reading a book on conflict resolution. He grinned shyly when asked whether he had made any plan. 'Come on Antero, you can't stay here, the army is already in the neighbourhood,' Minka said. 'Get your stuff together, quickly.' He and Rui packed their laptops and a few personal belongings. Antero was still hovering, seemingly reluctant to go. I couldn't believe it. What was he waiting for? When we rushed to the car and pushed both the students in, we saw that the men had come from the truck and were approaching. The driver observed them from his rear mirror and accelerated fast. Speeding through the unlit streets, I wondered what to do with the two of them now.

Even if Antero wanted to leave the country – which he was adamant he would not do – it would have been extremely difficult. Eurico Guterres had announced that he would not tolerate it if the 'political elite escaped again'. This was a reference to 1975, when a number of influential Timorese had left the island for Australia. To prevent their doing the same this time, he had set up checkpoints on the way to the airport and bands of armed militias patrolled the departure hall. Many families, desperate to get out, had been turned back by the militias.

The Turismo Hotel was not a safe place, but I could not think of anywhere else we could take them. Antero seemed to be in shock, unable to make suggestions or decisions. So we smuggled him and Rui into my room to contemplate our next move. The hotel staff could not be trusted. Any knock on the door sent shivers through the room. We waited till late that night and shepherded the students out to sleep in the room of a male colleague whose bathroom looked out over the ICRC compound. With a borrowed screwdriver, we had unscrewed the metal bars of the bathroom window so the students could jump into the Red Cross compound if the hotel was raided. We knew this would happen: it was just a matter of time.

§

Early in the morning of 4 September, as Unamet released the result, Sebastião's family huddled around a television set. The small living room did not have enough chairs, and the family stood in silence when the result appeared on the screen: the people of East Timor had rejected Indonesia's autonomy proposal with 78.8 per cent of the vote. This was what the family had dreamed of all these years. Now it had finally come true, they could not make a sound; they dared not, in case it attracted attention from the omnipresent militiamen and soldiers. Silent tears streamed down their faces. All of them, even the smallest of the children, cried, sensing that something incredible was happening. Sebastião's father, Filomeno, already had his bags packed to flee to Dare. The young men and boys had left earlier for the mountains and Sebastião was sleeping in the UN compound. Sebastião's mother, aunts and his sisters would stay in Dili. 'They wouldn't kill them, not the women and the children,' Filomeno had said.[10]

Within minutes of the announcement the streets had virtually emptied and an unearthly silence fell over the town, like the eerie stillness before a storm. Silent groups of people, mainly women and children, carrying large bags, hurried along the empty roads to the churches, convents and other religious institutions. They joined the many families who had already taken shelter there.

The results had become public a couple of days earlier than Unamet had initially told the population. The UN had been afraid of leaks, and worried that the counting centre and the television and radio stations might come under attack before the results could be announced. It had mobilised all its personnel to work around the clock in shifts to count the ballot papers. Many Timorese had been taken by surprise by the early announcement. They had thought they had a bit more time to arrange their escape from Dili.

A Reuters television crew, sent out by their editors to look for people celebrating in the streets, had come across a group of men ready to defend their neighbourhood in Becora, and asked them to dance. They shot some pictures and soon I got phone calls from several radio stations about the 'street parties' in Dili. Nothing, I told them, could be further from the truth.

In the Balide church, near the house where Sebastião's family had watched the results, hundreds of people, mainly women and children and the elderly, had gathered. Many of the women knelt down praying under their breath, tears running down their cheeks, dripping on their folded hands. The atmosphere was one of loss rather than jubilation. An hour or so after the count was announced, the familiar sound of gunfire returned to the air. With every volley, more babies started to cry. And their mothers prayed more frantically. 'They are shooting in the air to make us afraid,' said one of the students who was in the church. 'They have stolen everything from us, and now they have stolen our celebration. We have to keep our celebrations locked up in our hearts,' she said as I was leaving.

Back in the hotel I went to check on the students. Rui had gone into the hills, but Antero was still in the room, doggedly typing a project proposal for civic education. He had heard the result too and was elated; the absolute majority was more than he had ever dreamed of.

§

13. Journalists being brought to the airport on police trucks.

Soon after the announcement the remaining television crews and news agencies left Timor as well. The company that arranged the satellite uplink had decided to leave, so there would be no way for them to transmit their pictures, they argued, and it had become increasingly dangerous to go out to film and report.

The Hotel Mahkota, where many of the press had taken refuge, had been shot at by a militiaman. The bullet had left a hole in the front-door window. No one had been wounded, but the journalists had been panicked by the attitude of the military and police: they had stood by, doing absolutely nothing to prevent the attack. For many this was the last straw, and more were climbing on to the trucks the police had provided to bring them to the airport.

This, it was reported at the time, was the first occasion in history when the news agencies left somewhere before the UN did. Of more than four hundred journalists who had covered the referendum only about two dozen, mainly radio and print journalists, stayed. They had all moved to the Turismo, where a few activists also remained.

Two UN officers had come to the hotel to see if they could buy some food and water. Unamet had, it seemed, not made preparations for an influx of refugees, but also not for the possibility that its own people might need food and water. After a discussion they left without supplies but with Antero, who, we thought, might be safer in the Unamet compound.

Some of the journalists had decided to pay the Indonesian police to protect the hotel from the militia. Most of the time the policemen sprawled in the garden and dining rooms, guns at their feet, swilling big Bintang beers and devouring plates full of *nasi goreng*. They did not make me feel much safer. They wanted to draw up a list of who was staying in which room: not a bad plan, in other circumstances, but now something we tried to avoid at all costs. I was afraid that when the time came to attack the Turismo, the policemen would not protect us but would join the raid instead.

I went out to talk to the refugees in the nearby compounds of Bishop Belo and the ICRC. Thousands of people were camped out on plastic sheets. They had brought little cooking stoves and some food. While I was at the bishop's, a car belonging to the Salesian Brothers, who ran a large school in Comoro, brought in some young men. They said Aitarak were looking for all the activists and they could not protect them any longer.

But even with the bishop they were not safe. And Bishop Belo had asked Joanico Belo, the leader of Tim Saka, the Baucau-based paramilitary group largely made up of Falintil veterans, to come and rescue the people from his compound. Joanico had arrived in the middle of the night and had taken dozens of young men to the safety of Baucau.

When I returned to the Turismo I saw that another group of journalists was leaving the hotel on army trucks. TNI officers, they said, had warned that a militia attack was imminent. They had refused to be evacuated, and the army had agreed to bring them to the Unamet compound. But that day, to my surprise, Alex Samara, the owner of the Turismo, had turned up. He had come back because he was worried about his niece, who ran the place in his absence. With Alex back, his long-standing connections with the military made a surprise attack less likely, I hoped.

That night I stayed in Alex's quarters. The shooting was getting on my nerves. My room was facing the street and I was afraid to attract attention with lights. I also worried about flying glass (my desk was built into an alcove in front of the window) and I had started to do my radio interviews in the darkness, sitting under my desk. In Alex's office I was further from the road and close to the e-mail and telephone connections. We sat around his kitchen table, by the light of a candle, not daring to switch on the ceiling lights. Shooting sounded very near. An Australian journalist, who was still in the hotel, got a mysterious call that Falintil was on its way to pick him and me up and take us to Uaimori. It sounded far-fetched. The city was surrounded by road-blocks and Falintil would have to fight their way in, something I did not think they were prepared to do. From Jakarta, Xanana had appealed to people to remain calm. 'Let them burn our homes; it doesn't matter. Let them rob the things that individually we have sweated for; it doesn't matter.' And he appealed to the guerrillas to 'maintain their positions and not to react to all these things'.

We were sharing the biscuits and cheese Alex had brought from Surabaya when between all the calls from radio stations and human rights organisations, I received a courtesy call from the Dutch Embassy in Jakarta. The political attaché asked, in a tone as if he was inquiring about the weather, what the situation was like. We had to trust that the international community was 'doing everything to improve the situation'. And he added that fresh Indonesian troops were on their way to the island 'so we could rest secure'. Secure? Were they from Mars?

I went over to where the other journalists were to hear if there was more news. The UN had given us a walkie-talkie for use in emergencies and we listened to the traffic on it: militia blocking the road to the airport; streets impassable without armed escort; shooting around the UN; IDPs fleeing into the UN compound. We tried to make plans, discussing an escape route over the roof. Perhaps we could hide behind the water tank or jump into the garden of the Red Cross. The international staff of the ICRC were still in their offices. They had prepared for a large influx of refugees, and had enough food supplies to last them at least a month.

I looked around our odd little group: a few Irish and Australian activists, some freelance journalists and the former Australian consul to Portuguese East Timor, James Dunn. His room had become our gathering place. We had a small stock of beer, water and other supplies that had been left by fleeing journalists and that we had collected from their rooms. James Dunn recalled 1975 when he had also sat in the Turismo Hotel with journalists, drinking beer and listening to gunfire. He tried to keep our spirits up. 'It sounds worse than it is,' he kept saying, when another burst of gunfire shattered the silence of the night. 'It's still some streets away from us.' The gunbursts were bad but the worst and most ominous sounds, I thought, were the single shots. They sounded like executions.

§

The next day the family that ran the hotel restaurant were packing their belongings together. They wanted to get a ferry back to their hometown of Atambua. While I was taking my chance to buy up their last cigarettes, I noticed that the old waiter João had returned. With his wife and little daughter, he had slept for one night at the Unamet compound, but as the UN did not encourage Timorese to stay with them he had opted to go back to the hotel. Before Alex went to the airport, ostensibly to see his niece off, he gave João the keys to the hotel and told him to look after it. Alex did not return.

When, around midday, shots rang through the hotel, I still thought naïvely that they were just trying to scare us and that we could hide and try to stay put. But the shooting had a more sinister motive. They were pinning us down in the hotel so we could not see what they were doing at the house of the bishop and the ICRC. I was hiding with a dozen others in a bathroom on the wrong side of the hotel. From the other side a few journalists could see that soldiers and militiamen had surrounded the ICRC compound. The soldiers had started to shoot at the windows, over the heads of the refugees. At gunpoint they forced out screaming, terrified women and children. Bags were searched for ID papers, and on the beach road, family groups were separated. Some people were forced on to trucks, others herded along the beach.

In the meantime a group of soldiers had entered the hotel. I heard their boots stomping through the corridors. They knocked on every door. They came nearer and nearer. When they reached our room I hardly dared breathe. A key was turned. The bathroom door opened. We stood eye to eye with one of the receptionists, a small weasel of a man from West Timor – one I had always suspected of being *intel*. He looked up at the Indonesian soldiers with the smuggest smile I had ever seen.

The hotel was occupied by newly arrived marines. These were the purple berets who had played an important, and largely benign, role in Jakarta during the tense period around the fall of Suharto. There they had been supporting the forces that toppled the old dictator. Here they seemed to play a different role. 'Hurry up; you have to get out,' their officer barked at us, 'the militias are on their way to attack.' I had my doubts about this story, but realised there was no way we could stay any longer in the hotel.

The Australians had called their consul when the shooting started, more than an hour earlier. He was on his way but had come under fire near the governor's palace – no doubt to prevent him too from seeing what was going on in the ICRC, and in the bishop's compound, which had come under attack at the same time.

The soldiers wanted to load us on to their truck. But, afraid they would drive us to the airport, instead of Unamet, we decided to wait for the consul. When he arrived I was doing a radio interview from the reception telephone and the embassy staff, still jittery from their experience with the militias, had literally pulled Minka and me off the phone. When I got into the embassy car I saw old João standing at the gate. He stared at us, in a sad but not accusatory way. He had seen it all before. In 1975 he had also stayed behind in the hotel when everybody had gone and the army had moved in. His personal story, like Timor's history, was repeating itself.

From the car we could see the flames licking up through the roof of the bishop's residence. Hundreds of people filed along the beach. Behind them walked soldiers, their weapons raised.

CHAPTER 21

. . . .

A Sea of Flames

Madness is rare in individuals – but in groups, parties, nations, and ages it is the rule. (Nietzsche, *Beyond Good and Evil*)

§ THE first night in the Unamet compound, I slept, like the refugees, on a piece of cardboard on the concrete floor outside one of the buildings. Antero slept next to me, his head hidden under a blanket I had grabbed as we left the hotel. He was afraid he would be killed in his sleep by one of the Indonesian soldiers who patrolled the compound, or by one of the militia members who had infiltrated the refugees. Cocooned in the red blanket, his body stretched rigid, he looked like a corpse. I pushed that thought away.

Just before sunrise I woke up, cold to my bones from the pre-dawn chill, to the sound of bawling children. In front of the few outside toilets stood long queues of men and women with plastic bottles and jerrycans. These were the only toilets the refugees could use to get water to drink and to wash.

I found Tata in the offices of the political affairs department. She was still shocked by what she had witnessed on the night before I ended up in the compound. About 1,500 refugees were camped in the school next to the Unamet compound, as close as they could get, since Ian Martin did not want to let them in. The militias had opened fire on the school compound. It was like hell, she said: screaming women and children; shouting UN and Indonesian policemen; refugees frantically trying to squeeze through the narrow opening that separated Unamet from the school.

As part of their latest security measures, Unamet had put razor wire on the wall. Desperate mothers, who had hurled their babies over before scrambling over themselves, were bleeding from deep cuts all over their bodies. Unamet personnel, Tata said, were too scared to go into the school compound to help. The refugees, afraid and angry, took their feelings out on people like Tata, who, as UN staff, had been able to stay in the compound when they were not allowed in. Tata felt hurt by this, but with her friend Elisa had worked hard to help them. She had calmed them down, made a register of the families, allocated them floor space and found out who needed food.

In fact food supplies had become Unamet's biggest logistical problem. Many of the refugees had brought their own basic necessities, but Unamet was not prepared for a long siege. It did not, for example, have enough drinking water for its own staff, and very little food. Later that morning a convoy of UN vehicles ventured out to the UN's warehouse, escorted by two truckloads of Indonesian soldiers. They came back with next to nothing. When they had tried to load up their trucks with supplies, they had been shot at by militiamen. The army tried to shoo the militias away and urged the UN staff to return to the compound. But they did nothing to stop the militiamen smashing the windshields of the retreating cars with stones, nor to stop them looting the warehouse.

That day, Indonesia had imposed martial law. Three new Indonesian battalions had arrived, in addition to the two sent a week earlier, and the martial law commander, General Kiki Syahnakri, had vowed to stop the mayhem. The Indonesians' favoured explanation – 'it's only a handful of rough elements in the army' – still had adherents within the UN, including Ian Martin. But this incident dispelled even their hopes that things were going to change for the better. On the contrary, the violence seemed to have become even more blatant. Tension in the compound mounted. There were constant rumours of imminent evacuation. Cars loaded with duffle bags and suitcases stood with their engines running. By now almost all foreigners had been rounded up. They were taken to the main police station and from there to the airport to be put on planes. Unamet had allowed only the remaining twenty or so journalists and the head of the local office of the United Nations High Commissioner for Refugees into its compound.

Meanwhile, in Jakarta, Xanana was released from his prison house. It was not the triumphant walk to freedom he had dreamed of; no fist salutes or smiles; only a solemn statement: 'I promise as a free man to do everything to bring peace to East Timor and to my people.' We had heard rumours for some time that the Indonesians would release him in Dili, where he would, like us all, end up in the Unamet compound, before he would be somehow transported to Falintil in Uaimori. But Unamet refused to accept this responsibility. No one could guarantee his security in Timor. Instead of flying to Dili, he was whisked off under heavy police escort to the British Embassy in Jakarta.

§

On my third day in the compound, 8 September, I decided to go out to see what was going on in town. I thought I could no longer report truthfully on what was happening unless I could see it with my own eyes and, ideally, speak to some people. Unamet staff could not tell us what was happening: they had given up all attempts to venture out.

With Marie Colvin, of the *Sunday Times*, I set out early in the morning, before seven o'clock, hoping that the militia would still be sleeping, or, if they were awake, at least would not yet be drunk or crazed with drugs. We sneaked out through the adjacent high school compound where the Canossian sisters had set up camp with their refugees. The Indonesian security guards at the school gate looked weary when they saw us approaching. 'Just trying to get some of our clothes from the hotel,' we mumbled. Demonstratively we showed our empty hands to the soldiers. Hesitantly they let us through.

The neighbourhood around the UN compound looked like a war zone, with sad gaping holes in the façades of the buildings. Most in this part of town used to be government offices, built by Indonesia, which had maintained a startling number of departments for such a small province. Of most of these concrete monstrosities now only skeletons remained.

At a nearby crossroads a bunch of militiamen were hanging around, armed with sticks, knives and guns. To avoid being seen we went into one of the looted buildings. Carefully, we stepped over heaps of broken glass and other debris. Everything not fixed to the walls had been carried off. In some places the floor tiles had been meticulously smashed, as if someone had taken the trouble to hammer every single one of them into tiny pieces.

From behind a wall we observed the scene at the crossroads. A blue Kijang appeared. Out of one of its windows hung a man with long bushy hair. He pointed an automatic gun in the air, and the silence was shattered by long bursts of gunfire. Hugging the walls of burned-out buildings, we made our way through small back alleys in the direction of the central *mercado*. Two Indonesian soldiers on a motorbike came up behind us, making me jump. 'Is everything all right?' asked the one on the pillion, in good English. 'Oh yes, fine,' I replied sullenly.

Closer to the *mercado* we saw a few more people. Silently they walked past us, their eyes fixed on the ground, balancing bundles of clothes and sacks of rice on their heads. They looked shell-shocked. On a little square behind the market a few ramshackle buses stood piled up with boxes, bags and mattresses ready to depart – to Atambua, explained an old woman who, to my surprise, still operated a little noodle stall.

A man with a red-and-white bandanna had watched us suspiciously from under his pro-autonomy baseball cap. I smiled at him but he didn't smile back. His glare grew more intense, and I noticed how blood-shot his eyes were. 'If you go there,' he muttered, pointing the way we were heading, 'you get killed.' He made a cut-throat sign.

We had walked a further twenty metres or so when suddenly the English-speaking soldier appeared again. He stood in the doorway of a small dilapidated building. 'Come in, come in,' he beckoned us politely, adding softly: 'There are too many militiamen around here.' I hesitated. 'Only if you have coffee,' I said, half in jest, half embarrassed that I would indeed sell my soul for a cup of coffee and something cooked to eat. 'We have coffee, please come in.' He guided us to an old sofa and some chairs around a wooden coffee table.

The soldier, who was called Dendi Suryadi, didn't even ask whether we worked as journalists. I think he just assumed we did. As a first lieutenant he had 19 soldiers under his command. One of them brought some hot strong coffee and plates of steaming noodles with fried eggs. Greedily I wolfed it down. Our conversation only sometimes touched on the madness raging outside. We drifted in and out of the United States, his family in Kalimantan and East Timor. New York, yes, he hoped to be there one day. Perhaps his career as a professional soldier – he was 26 – would take him there. His ultimate dream was to study at the military academy at Westpoint.

Eight months ago he had been posted to East Timor. 'We came to win the hearts and minds of the people,' he said pensively, adding, without a trace of irony, 'I think we failed.' This was mind-boggling; had he really believed this possible after everything that had happened? He became defensive. 'It wasn't our fault as soldiers, the generals should take the blame for the mistake of invading East Timor. Moreover,' he added, 'the United States and Australia had pushed Indonesia to go ahead with the invasion. So shouldn't they carry some of the blame?'

Dendi had given the matter some thought. Personally, he believed that East Timor would be better off within Indonesia, but at the same time he had concluded that it was a separate country. 'The question for me', he said, 'is not that East Timor should be free from Indonesia but that Indonesia should be free from East Timor.'

So eager was he to be liked by us, the two Western women, that when we bade our farewells he got up and presented us with bottles of perfume. We politely declined. He was disturbed that we still wanted to go to the Turismo. 'Be careful!' he warned us, 'these militia are wild; they drink.' I sensed he was afraid too. He offered to take us there, adding, 'My orders are to protect the foreigners. But at the same time I'm also under orders not to intervene – whatever might happen.' This, I could see, posed a serious dilemma for our lieutenant.

While we waited for him to get ready and organise his men, I noticed small bits of broken crockery and children's toys in the back of his white pick-up. I wanted to believe that Dendi really was a decent guy, a professional soldier who had the dignity to stay clear of the carnage, pillaging and arson. But this was evidence that if not he himself, then at least his car had been involved in some looting.

As we drove through town with the lieutenant at the wheel and four heavily armed soldiers in the back, we got a sense of the scale of the destruction. In less than five days almost all public buildings, shops and hotels had been systematically looted and burned. Familiar shopping streets had been transformed into foul smoking piles of melted plastic, steel and shattered glass. Burned-out shop fronts gaped at us. Bits of plastic and paper whirled through the desolate streets.

'I don't mind them burning government buildings. They belong to Indonesia, so they can do what they like with them, but private businesses, I think that's unfair,' Dendi said. The only building still untouched was the governor's palace. It stood like a virgin bride between the black smouldering ruins. Under the arches a few families squatted with their belongings. Dendi looked uncomfortable at the scenes around us. 'It would be only for a little while longer,' he said mysteriously. Within the next two days he expected to get an order that would change things.

At the Turismo we were met by hostile-looking Indonesian soldiers, wearing balaclavas and bandannas. Dendi observed them warily. Quickly I ran around the hotel looking for João the waiter. A few rooms had been burned and Alex's office ransacked. In the servant quarters I softly called João's name, but didn't get an answer. Please let him not have been killed! I thought guiltily. I felt that we had abandoned him. He, after all, had come back from the UN compound to look after us.

Marie searched her room for clothes and returned with her flak jacket and a plastic bag. 'What kind of militias are these?' she scoffed indignantly. 'They steal my silk knickers but leave my flak jacket behind!' Dendi didn't laugh. He was growing increasingly tense. 'We have to go,' he kept urging us.

We drove along the beach road. A few army trucks were parked near the post office. A group of men ran out of the building and, seconds later, orange flames shot through the roof. 'Look carefully,' Dendi said, 'it is important that you remember this.' Without my camera, the unearthly images of the town became fixed in my brain as on film. I can still recall them: like evil in Technicolor. The blue sky contrasting with the ubiquitous red-and-white flags. The apocalyptic burning; the smouldering buildings. Police trucks packed with mixed groups of militiamen, police and soldiers, some raising their M-16s and madly shooting the sky, others slashing the air maniacally with long samurai swords. Men on motorbikes roaring down the road carrying television sets and waving homemade pistols. Militia groups, it seemed, had descended from all over Timor, and they were absorbed in a frenzy of looting and burning.

The headquarters of Eurico Guterres's Aitarak was buzzing with activity. The crowd was so dense that it blocked the street in front of it. Some wore black Aitarak T-shirts; others ran around in red-and-white tops, sporting brand-new red berets or blue baseball caps.

Across the street, in the port, four ships were moored: two passenger ferries and two navy frigates. Thousands of people crowded the docks and a number crawled over the ships. Among the people camping in the port, I would hear later, were Felis and his family. They were waiting for a ship that could take them to Bali.

The route Dendi had chosen to bring us back to Unamet took me by surprise. It was like a sightseeing tour of a war zone: the Mahkota Hotel, the *Suara Timor Timur* offices, Duta bank – all had been burned. When we sped past the turn-off for the Unamet compound I got suspicious. 'I don't know where the UN is,' Dendi explained curtly. This was odd – even the smallest child would have known the way. 'We have to go to Polda,' he continued. The UN would not be at the police headquarters, I protested. But Dendi persisted. 'All foreigners go there.' I began to worry. What if he left us with the police? They would try to deport us as soon as they could find a flight.

Polda was a sprawling compound near the airport. Still worried that we would be left behind, I remained in the car till a cranky police officer turned up. His name, stitched on his uniform, was Napoleon. 'ID cards!' he barked aggressively. While Napoleon scrutinised our passports for a while, we had time to look around. The police station seemed to be a popular gathering place for the militias. Groups of them, armed with an assortment of weapons, drifted in and out. Sometimes they were hanging on to trucks full of television sets, mattresses and other household items. Against a building near the entrance stood huge piles of boxes, guarded by some menacing-looking men dressed in red and white. Propped against another building sat a few women and children.

This police station was supposed to be a safe haven. Bishop Belo and some prominent pro-independence activists had been brought here for their own safety. Now, however, it looked like a depot for looted goods. Unable to conquer Timor, Indonesia was carrying it away.

Somewhere in this labyrinth of barracks, there was still a Filipino UN police officer. In the three months he had worked in Timor, he had built up good relationships with some of his Indonesian colleagues. This, however, did not help him much. He feared for his life and the lives of the people who had been brought over to the compound, such as Timorese human rights activists and other prominent members of the resistance. Several times Eurico Guterres and his band of fully armed militia had barged in looking for these activists. Aniceto Guterres, the director of Yayasan Hak, was a particular target, but managed to hide from Eurico and, with two colleagues, made a miraculous escape to Jakarta, because the militia at the road and airport checkpoints did not recognise him.

After half an hour we were on our way again, but Dendi still did not take us to the UN compound. He took us instead to army headquarters, a place that exuded a strange calm. The army, it seemed, had the situation firmly under control. We were taken to the office of the head of military intelligence. This was the last place I wanted to be. When we entered the room the commander got up from his desk and shook our hands politely. He did not ask us anything, not even our names, and moments later we were standing outside again. I don't know what he told his boss, but it was clear that Dendi had covered his back. As an ambitious officer, he apparently did not want to jeopardise his chances of promotion by being accused of doing the wrong thing.

§

Upon our return we found the compound again humming with rumours of an imminent evacuation. Ian Martin had been in a meeting with the UN head of security, who had concluded that the situation had become untenable. Despite martial law, despite the visit of a group of Indonesian cabinet ministers, despite the constant stream of reassurances, things kept getting worse. Morale among UN staff was very low. Some had been through traumatic experiences, such as evacuation under gunfire from district offices. Moreover, the compound was running out of food and drinking water. Ian Martin had agreed.

In UN terms the evacuation was euphemistically branded a 'relocation' of the mission to Darwin. This would, in theory, be short-lived. They would all return in a few days, when the security situation had improved. But whatever it was called it would mean all international staff pulling out, leaving behind the Timorese – both the local staff and the refugees. The task of informing the community leaders of the decision had fallen to the people from the political affairs office. One of them wrote later about his experience. 'Sitting on our wooden chairs in the drab office, surrounded by friends whom we were about to betray, we could scarcely find strength to speak. And as we spoke we wept.'[1] They had discussed two possible options for the refugees: to go to the police station or up the hill to Dare, to join the other refugees already there.

At that meeting was Madre Esmeralda, a tiny delicate-looking figure, dressed in the grey robes of the Canossian sisters. Her sparkling eyes and bubbly energy reminded me of her brother, Padre Jovito. The Canossian convent, a stone's-throw from the compound, had been attacked several times. But when the militias had arrived and told them that they had a choice between staying – and being burned to death – or going to Atambua, Madre Esmeralda had stood up to them. She did not want to leave East Timor and chose a third option: to take the refugees to Unamet, which was just 100 metres away. But the UN refused to allow them in, so the four nuns and novices settled with the families in the school building next door.

The meeting had lasted two hours and Madre Esmeralda had been given 20 minutes to speak. 'For 20 years, the Timorese people have not believed in anyone.' But Unamet had reassured them every day that whatever the outcome, they would stay after the vote. 'The people believed this,' she told me she had said. 'They voted. Now you'll leave us to die like dogs? We want to die like people.' When she finished she had asked them if she could contact Taur Matan Ruak to organise protection for the refugees.

After the meeting she ran up to the gallery where I was working. She looked flustered. She urgently wanted to call her mother superior in Rome. 'In twelve hours we're all going to be killed,' we heard her saying.

The local staff had been informed about the evacuation, and Antero had heard about it from Sebastião. He sat on the gallery writing his farewell letters. His pen moved slowly over the paper. Minka gave him her short-wave radio, so he could listen to the news when he was in Dare, she said. He accepted it without a word. The Filipino policeman, who had managed to get out of *polda*, watched the little scene. 'This is unbelievable, this cannot happen,' he said and picked the radio up from the table. 'You have to promise her that in a year's time you will give this radio back. You have to survive.'

A little later the evacuation plan was made public. I saw disbelief and despair on the faces around me. A woman begged in tears to use Marie's satphone to call her sister in Australia. A few men contemplated kidnapping Ian Martin, or the 'bald one' as they called him, but others calmed them. Women planned to put their babies in front of the departing UN trucks.

The Timorese had no illusions about what might happen to them after Unamet's departure. They had heard the rumours of killings in the church in Suai, where on 6 September, three priests and more than a hundred people, mainly women and children, had been slaughtered. But soon the angry outcry gave way to a mood of resignation. People quietly packed their bags. They headed for a hole in the fence and up the dark, rocky slopes of the hills behind the compound. They wanted to reach the coffee plantations of Dare, where, they understood, Falintil would protect them. In the chaos families were separated. A woman hysterically shouted the name of her husband. She had been packing when he had disappeared with their month-old baby, whom she was breast-feeding. 'How can my baby survive?' she wailed.

The escape route was no secret from the Indonesians. Among the refugees were members of the pro-Indonesia militia, and Kostrad troops armed with M-16s patrolled the grounds of the UN complex day and night, training their guns on the women and children sitting on the ground.

Soon shots rang out. Indonesian soldiers were taking pot shots at the refugees on the hill. The most vulnerable came back: a man with two toddlers, whose bare little feet and hands had been cut by the sharp stones; a woman with a baby who had seen two dead bodies on the hillside. In tears they told me they were prepared to die, if that was their fate. But they would rather die together in the compound than alone on the hillside. Others came back desperate, because there was no food in Dare.

At the foot of the stairs to Ian Martin's office a group of golden-skinned naked toddlers played in dirty sand. Their cheerful babble went right through my bones. I crouched down to play a bit with them and while they shrieked with glee, I felt miserable, and ashamed at being so powerless. A UN worker who saw me fighting back tears grabbed my arm. 'Pray for a miracle,' she whispered. 'Believe, they still happen!' Miracles, I thought bitterly, is that all they can come up with?

But the UN staff were doing something. After Madre Esmeralda's speech, political affairs officers had gone up to Ian Martin and told him that the decision was politically and morally wrong. Others went around with a petition, collecting signatures. By 10 p.m. a small majority of the UN staff had put their names on a list to volunteer to stay.

The UN is what the member states make it. But on the ground it's very much what its employees make of it. So the lessons of Srebenica and Rwanda had been taken to heart by individual workers more than by the organisation itself.

While I was waiting near Ian Martin's office for his reaction to the petitions of the journalists and the UN workers, I noticed how few Timorese were protesting or even making representations. Only two women with babies hung around the stairs. 'You promised us you would stay!' they wailed at one of the UN officials.

'We can't do anything here,' I heard a distraught UN worker say, 'the decision is taken in New York.'

But the decision had been taken in Dili; and it was also overturned in Dili. By midnight we heard that the evacuation was postponed for 24 hours.

CHAPTER 22

. . . .

Under Siege

§ IT felt like being in the eye of a giant storm. All around us the air exploded with the loud bursts of automatic gunfire and sometimes a few tracer bullets, a bit like firecrackers. The bullets were aimed above our heads and flew over the compound. After a few nights I had become so accustomed to the shooting that I found it more eerie when it suddenly became quiet.

Being virtually locked in the compound – since our trip into town no journalist had been allowed to go out – it was hard to know what was happening in Dili, let alone in Timor. I felt anger taking over again. What the hell was the international community doing? Why did it have to take so long before someone would intervene?

On the radio we heard that all over the world vigils and demonstrations were held. In Australia, the protests were huge. Portugal came to a halt on 8 September, when the prime minister himself took part in a kilometres-long human chain in Lisbon. Even the World Bank and the International Monetary Fund joined the chorus. The World Bank's president warned Habibie that Indonesia's aid donors' commitments were dependent on his honouring the outcome of the referendum. The IMF suspended a planned mission to Jakarta.

Our presence in the compound helped keep attention focused on the destruction. Working continuously for a week made my adrenalin flow. 'It's the most difficult story I have ever had to report,' I heard myself telling radio interviewers. I would answer their questions almost mechanically. When Europe went to sleep, America woke up and the other way around. The only sleep we got was between four and six in the morning. I hardly took time to eat, wash or change my by now quite smelly clothes. And I hardly had time to be afraid.

Outrage, my strongest emotion at the time, kept me going. I felt angry on behalf of the Timorese, who had calmly accepted that their trust had been betrayed. I was aware my anger would come through in the radio interviews. But I could not stop myself from feeling indignant about the way the international community and, to a lesser extent, Unamet, had behaved.

I felt it was the UN's moral responsibility to find a solution. I blamed Unamet for poor preparations. It had enough information at least to have anticipated an influx of scared Timorese, and after all the aggression against the UN in the last month, it should have expected to become a target too. But as so often in East Timor's history, the interests of its people seemed secondary to other international concerns. The West, in particular the United States, was wary of embarking on new peacekeeping ventures, feeling overextended already in the Balkans. And, still, there was the hypnotic allure that Indonesia, even now, seemed able to exercise: so important to nurture the 'progressive' forces there, and not to give 'hardliners' scope for a comeback; so vital to give its leaders the benefit of the doubt, so soon after its own democratic experiment, which was, after all, of so much greater global significance. Rumours circulated in Jakarta of a planned coup to remove Habibie.

§

The next day it was less crowded in the compound. The strongest among the refugees had quietly left for Dare. The weakest – mostly women with small children and the very old and sick – remained. The new plan was to evacuate the international UN staff, along with local employees, their direct family members, and other foreign passport-holders. Those Timorese who were excluded naturally took this badly. There was a nasty confrontation, with refugees accusing the local UN staff of betraying them. Aida, one of José Ramos Horta's younger sisters, who was in the compound, told Tata: 'You are digging our graves. We should go together or die together.'

An angry Sebastião had gone to Ian Martin with a delegation of local UN workers to beg him not to abandon the refugees. Aida took more drastic action. She and her five children lay down on the steps leading to Ian Martin's office. 'I have two hand-grenades,' she said. 'If we don't go together, I will blow us all up, so we will die together.'

All the UN's local staff had difficult choices to make. For Elisa, Tata and Sebastião the decision to go or to stay became one between life and death. Elisa was lucky enough to be able to discuss it with her family. Tata, however, had become convinced that her whole family had been killed and she didn't want to leave because she wanted to remain 'close to them'; Sebastião wanted to go out of the compound to rescue his family. Both were eventually persuaded by their UN colleagues to join the evacuation.

Elisa's whole extended family, of around a hundred people, was camping in the school compound next door with Madre Esmeralda, who was Elisa's aunt. When Elisa heard that she could evacuate to Darwin, along with her brother, who also worked for the UN, and his wife and children, she wept. She begged the UN to allow her to take her mother, but was told that, since she was single, she had to go alone. Her mother told her to go: 'If we die, our family can live on through you and you can tell our story to your children and your children's children.'

That night a Unamet information officer went around the compound with an evacuation list. 'You have 15 minutes to put your name on it,' he told us, adding, to encourage us to go, that anybody who still wanted to stay on would have to leave the UN compound and find a place outside. It was clear that they were trying to get the journalists out.

I had already made up my mind to stay, so I did not feel the pressure much, but for others it was a traumatic decision. Two journalists had already hiked up with the refugees to Dare, and my colleagues Minka Nijhuis and Marie Colvin, and an American writer and activist, Alan Nairn, had decided to stay. My decision was not well received in Europe. My colleagues thought I was insane. It sparked discussions at the radio stations I worked for, and one of the BBC programmes even contemplated boycotting my reports in the hope that this would take away my reason for staying.

§

Early in the morning of 10 September, a long convoy of army trucks appeared at the gate. On the open-topped backs stood unsmiling Kostrad soldiers. A UN officer called out names from a list and one by one the trucks filled up. Tata and Elisa, tears in their eyes, crouched among the others, between the legs of the Indonesian soldiers. I noticed some non-UN staff, including Aida and her children, among the people in the trucks but could not spot Antero, who had also been offered the chance to leave.

After the convoy had left, the atmosphere in the compound changed again. Virtually all the 80 UN workers who had stayed tried to make the best of it. The Latin Americans played salsa and danced with the children. A New Zealander taught little boys to play cricket and an Aboriginal-Australian and a Uruguayan exchanged jokes. But we, of course, were not supposed to linger in the compound any longer, as the UN's information officer solemnly re-minded us.

Minka, Marie and I did not have a firm plan. We knew we couldn't go to any of the convents or other places where refugees were still staying. That would make their precarious situation even more dangerous. So we thought we would borrow a dog from a refugee family and move to an empty house just outside the compound's main gate. If we were attacked, which seemed quite likely, we hoped at least to be forewarned and so maybe have time to run back to the UN.

Just as we stood with our bags in our hands, I noticed UN security per-sonnel, dressed in blue flak jackets, hovering around the side gate. They gestured agitatedly with their arms that we should stay away. A small group of men in militia T-shirts had entered the school on the backs of motorbikes driven by soldiers. They threatened the refugees with hand-grenades; then they stole a few cars and smashed up some others – all with the help of the Indonesian soldiers.

The refugees in the schoolyard panicked, and two of Elisa's old aunties threw themselves over the barbed wire into the Unamet compound. They were badly cut. Unamet's security guards watched the scene in growing anger and frustration. In the event of a militia attack they knew they could do nothing to defend the compound; they could not even defend themselves. This powerlessness was perhaps even more stressful for them than for the civilian staff. They were used to being armed to deal with these kind of situations. Without weapons, they felt impotent, 'like lame sitting ducks', as one of them said.

The attack made it again very clear that the 'fresh soldiers' from Jakarta were providing no protection. In this case, they were Kostrad troops, reputedly loyal to General Wiranto, and, unlike some other soldiers, not prey to an 'emotional relationship' that made it impossible for them 'to hurt the militia, that are like their distant brothers'.[1] After the incident at the school the security guards allowed the refugees, including Sister Esmeralda and Elisa's extended family, into the Unamet compound. And, rather reluctantly, the information officer told us we could stay as well – as long as we pretended we were not reporting from inside the UN compound. Ian Martin had not been happy about the journalists staying so close. In New York, after all, journalists could not wander around UN headquarters on their own. Now he felt intently scrutinised.

It was not clear what Ian Martin was doing at the time. After a short and chaotic press briefing he stopped talking to the journalists in the compound. Moreover he hardly spoke to his staff and did not even address the refugees once. The only time I saw him outside his office, he was running in a flak jacket and helmet to his Land Cruiser, his head bent, avoiding eye contact with the refugees around him.

We were still talking about what had happened in the next-door compound, when we heard a whizz through the trees followed by a sharp 'pok'. A bullet had perforated the roof of a car just a few metres from where we stood. It was the second bullet that had penetrated the compound, and like the first one, it was a spent, stray bullet, not a targeted shot. Nevertheless, it was enough to spark immediate panic. Something like an electric current went through the compound. 'Quick, quick, get on the radio, they want to evacuate again!' shouted a distraught UN worker. After a while, when it was clear the shot did not herald an outright attack, an uneasy calm returned, but in the coming days we would witness several more of these evacuation scares.

In the meantime we installed ourselves in a large classroom that the Portuguese diplomatic delegation, who had also stayed in the compound until that day, had left full of computers, sleeping bags and camp beds. Antero moved into one of the small offices off the main room. When he was not sweeping the floor, he sat behind one of the computers, still typing his project proposals.

During the days in the compound Antero had become a shadow of his old self. I would often find him sitting on his own against a wall staring wistfully into his lap. He looked very lonely and lost between the refugee families. He had once told me about his family. His mother had hated boys, and right after Antero's birth she had tried to swap him for a baby girl. His grandparents had intervened and taken him into their house. Antero was the second son his mother had abandoned. She gave birth to one more son, whom she also rejected, before the longed-for baby girl arrived. The girl died in the mountains during the war and his mother died giving birth to her second daughter, who had survived. It took me a little while to realise that he had now, perhaps unconsciously, adopted Minka and me as his family.

For days he had been lethargic and had only perked up for a while, when he took part in meetings with some community leaders representing the refugees. But soon he fell back into a kind of dream world that he seemed to have created to escape from reality. At the best of times he could be hard to follow. He would talk about abstract concepts, wandering off in esoteric directions, losing himself in trains of thought and cryptic language. Now it was hard to understand him at all.

His present plight had brought back memories of the war years, when he had lived high up the slopes of the Matebian, and these memories seemed to have paralysed him. He was not the only one. Many Timorese resembled Antero in never having left that mountain and the trauma of those years: the displacement, the loss of close family to war and starvation, the bombing, and then so many years of living in a climate of fear. They had seen it all before. This second time may have been even more intense: not only did they have to deal with what was happening now, they also had to cope with all that had happened in the past.

I saw it in Antero's eyes and in the haunted looks of others who had been children when they had fled with their families to the mountains. Fear and sorrow; hunger and pain; the misery of the wailing children; the horror of the tiny dead babies along the mountain path; all the immeasurable, un-stoppable torrent of grief of a lifetime of tears that is almost unbearable to keep holding back. Above all, I saw it in the eyes of old people. Exhaustion had deepened the lines in their faces. Their eyes were dull with the weariness not just of sleepless nights but of endless suffering. They had witnessed enough of it; they didn't want to see any more.

§

Hours felt like days; days felt like weeks. It was 11 September, a week since the result of the ballot had been made public, when the guns suddenly fell silent and the mobile telephone network started working again, at least for a while. This was a sign that important visitors had arrived. General Wiranto had flown in on a military jet, followed on another plane by a delegation of ambassadors from the UN Security Council in New York.

The international scandal that East Timor had become was the latest item in the charge sheet against the UN, accused of being an impotent bystander in the great horrors of our age: in Rwanda, in Bosnia, in Kosovo. The 'international community' was at risk of being forever caught between two stools. Do nothing, as in Rwanda, and the consequences were unthinkable. But start encouraging interventions without a UN mandate – as had happened in Kosovo – and who knew where it might end? Sadly for East Timor, it was the Rwandan precedent rather than Kosovo's that applied.

The Security Council would not authorise intervention without obtaining an invitation from Indonesia, and there was no regional grouping or individual country willing to intervene without such authorisation. The country that was ready and able to lead an intervention force, Australia, above all did not want to risk open confrontation with Indonesia. So the outside world behaved as the police often do when asked to intervene in a 'domestic': it stayed away and hoped not too much blood was spilt. Malaysia, one of the rotating members of the Security Council at the time, staunchly stood up for the interests of Indonesia, its big friend, neighbour and ASEAN partner. If there was one principle that united ASEAN, it was that of non-interference in a sovereign country's internal affairs. Russia and China, too, both permanent members of the Security Council, were adamantly opposed to setting a precedent for unsolicited intervention.

The delegation was a face-saving exercise, intended to show that the UN was doing something, while placating Indonesia's friends on the Security Council. Officially it was to report back to Kofi Annan, so that the UN could decide what to do. As one UN official later argued, it was not only an unnecessary exercise; it also delayed the Security Council's eventual decision – by three days in his estimate. The delegation came with some journalists in tow. The BBC's Jonathan Head had brought a very welcome bottle of whisky and a carton of cigarettes (we had all started to smoke like chimneys) and, curiously, a bottle of the HP sauce that, he said, he always packed when travelling, to make uneatable food palatable.

After the UN diplomats had their meetings and the journalists took their pictures and grabbed their soundbites, they were off again. Of course the delegation was horrified by the destruction and shocked by the stories of the refugees. But the mission's real achievement may have been to rub Wiranto's nose in the mess he had – wittingly or not – helped create. He toured the still-smouldering town with the delegation and, according to the diplomats, looked genuinely taken aback by the extent of the destruction. East Timor, he may already have realised, was to be his own undoing.

Only a day before, the UN ambassadors had been told by him, straight-faced, that they should trust him and give him more time. Now, in a sudden change of heart, he conceded that it was time for an international peace-keeping force. Had the presence of the UN ambassadors embarrassed Wiranto into making this statement, and in effect making a foreign policy decision on the hoof? President Habibie had, under pressure from Kofi Annan, already privately given his consent to an intervention force, although in public he continued to back his generals' insistence that they could restore order. It is hard to believe that Wiranto was really surprised by what he saw that day. It is almost inconceivable that Jakarta did not know exactly what was going on in Timor. Whatever the government's failings, it did boast, in some respects, an excellent intelligence apparatus.

A day later, at a party in Jakarta for retired army officers, Wiranto crooned Morris Albert's song 'Feelings' in a bizarre expression of support with pro-Jakarta forces in East Timor. He dedicated the song to foreign journalists saying: 'I hope you have feelings like me for East Timor.' 'F-e-e-l-i-n-g-s, wo-o-o, f-e-e-l-i-n-g-s, wo-o-o, feel you again in my arms,' he sang. 'Feelings, feelings like I've never lost you and feelings like I'll never have you again in my heart …' He even hit all the high notes.[2] Wiranto sought an alibi and found it in 'feelings'. These were the feelings that led his forces to refrain from controlling the militias, or from using the far-reaching powers martial law had given them. 'It is understandable', he said, 'that many of them find it hard to shoot the people who have been regarded as their brothers-in-arms.'

§

The afternoon after the delegation left, I noticed two men with big rice sacks over their shoulders staggering up the hill behind us. Soon, salvos of auto-matic gunfire rang out and I saw the men zigzag and duck behind a big rock.

We heard that soldiers had also launched an attack on Dare. Mana Lou had called. One person had been killed, she said. The soldiers had been visiting a Javanese priest who lived in Dare and had opened fire after they had felt provoked.

'Where are you?' she had demanded to know. 'We are waiting for you.' I promised her I would come as soon as I could. 'Come quickly; one child has already died,' she groaned and asked if I could bring some milk powder. She sounded urgent but still in command rather than in despair. I had been thinking about Mana Lou a lot. Two days before, I had found among a queue of people lining up to board trucks for evacuation Sister Anna, a brave 70-year-old nun from Australia. She had just come down from Mana Lou's institute. She said thousands of families were sleeping out there under the coffee trees. Mana Lou herself had been very busy in her usual fashion: trying to do many things at once. She fed the children and sick old people with the meagre food supplies she had left and at the same time was trying to galvanise the CNRT leadership into organising the refugees. She had prayed and meditated with them.

When they saw the city burning they had cried. She had told them: 'Just let the old Timor burn. We will build a new Timor.' Despite the tragedy I had to smile. I could picture the scene: Mana Lou, taking the moral high ground, bossily telling the political elite to get on with it.

§

The next day the formidable Madre Margarita came to the compound. She wanted to call her mother superior in Rome. She leaned heavily on my arm as we climbed the steps to our balcony where the satphone stood. Her head came not much higher than my waist. Being a bit hard of hearing, she shouted: 'Father Karim is dead!' She had just come from his funeral in the garden of the Jesuit House.

Father Karl Albrecht, or Father Karim, as the German Jesuit was known in Timor, was the director of the Jesuit Relief Service. He had, until that day, travelled around in his car trying to help the refugees in Dare with medicines and food. The night before, Father Karim had heard a noise and had gone outside with a torch. 'Who is there?' he had called, flashing his light in the darkness under the trees. A voice had answered: 'Turn off the light!' But Father Karim, who was old and a bit deaf, had not reacted. The intruders had shot him in the chest.

Madre Margarita had a long telephone conversation with her superior in Rome. In rapid Italian she explained the death of the priest, the ransacking of the town and the fear people were living in, and asked her to pray for Timor. 'If nothing is done, we will all die,' she concluded in a matter-of-fact tone.

At the time, all sorts of hysterical horror stories were circulating about what was going on outside the compound. Many made their way into the international media, giving a picture of widespread massacres and assassinations. There were 'eyewitness accounts' of bodies piled up in *polda*, heads on sticks along the road, many nuns and priests, including Madre Margarita, dead. Xanana's father was 'reliably' reported to have been killed, and so on. Many of these stories were exaggerated and impossible to substantiate, and some, such as the 'death' of Xanana's father, might have been manufactured to protect people.

I had been reluctant to report that a genocide was going on. But Madre Margarita's account, I knew, was purely factual. That made her forecast all the more chilling.

14. A mother with her child in the UN compound.

'Are you afraid to go back into town?' I asked her when I helped her down the steps. 'Afraid?' She snorted. 'I'm far too old to be afraid to die.' When all the sisters of her convent had packed and left for West Timor, Madre Margarita had, at the last possible moment, climbed off the lorry and stayed behind. She had always resented the fact that her order had made her evacuate from Timor in 1975. She did not want to leave again.

She was not the only one who was still moving around the burning town. Other courageous nuns and priests were also trying to do what they could. Some stayed with the people in the towns; others accompanied them into the hills, and to West Timor. They knew they enjoyed no immunity from the hatred of army and the militias. In Suai and later in Los Palos these priests and nuns paid with their lives.

Padre Jovito was one of those who stayed. In his white priest's robe he drove around Dili on a motorbike. Sometimes he would drop into the compound to see his parents and his older sister, Madre Esmeralda. After the attack on the house of the bishop, he said, almost all the priests and nuns had left. But he and Padre Francisco Pinheiro, with whom I had climbed Ili Manu, had refused to go. Padre Jovito remembered 1975, when his family fled into the mountains, and he had been determined not to flee again.

When the priests and seminarians had gone, he later recalled, he felt not fear, but a deep peace of mind. 'I felt free, really free,' he said. 'I felt the king of the place.' He went to see the police and the military, and he talked to the people who were still in town, 'to make them feel that they had not been abandoned'. Several times the army and the militia had come to the seminary. Once, when they tried to enter, Padre Jovito, standing in the doorway, had told them not to treat it like an electronics goods warehouse. 'This is a training institute. Go ahead, burn it if you like, but you'll have to burn me in it.' They took the motorbikes and cars that stood outside, but they brought a video-recorder back.

Something similar had happened at the Salesian convent further along Balide. The sisters had protected over a hundred refugees in the convent, mainly women and small children. I knew from the time when I often went there for a breath of sanity that it was a hiding place for some of Xanana's family. His sister Armandina, especially, would flee there in times of danger. And I suspected that they might be there this time as well.

From our balcony in the compound I could just see their big green roof and reassure myself that the convent had not been burned. Sometimes, when the mobile phone network worked, I would give them a quick call. Often I would get Sister Marlene, an American-Filipina nun who had worked in Timor for many years. The militias had burned the houses around them and they and the army had been at their door several times, she said. They had even gone inside but nothing had happened, although they took the refugees' motorbikes with them.

§

Later that Sunday evening, we tuned a short-wave radio to Indonesia's state radio. Habibie was expected to make a live broadcast. Crowding around the small receiver, everyone held their breath. I can't remember much of what he said but for the most important thing: that Indonesia would accept an inter-vention force. Ali Alatas would travel to New York to discuss the details. Where was the catch?

Over the weekend, the pressure on the UN to act had become irresistible. On the day of the Security Council mission's visit to Dili, Kofi Annan an-nounced that Australia, New Zealand, the Philippines and Malaysia had all indicated willingness to take part in an international peacekeeping force. Bill Clinton had said Indonesia 'must invite' the international community to assist in restoring security.

The UN could no longer even wait for the return of its mission before holding an open meeting of the Security Council. In a six-hour session, some 50 countries spoke, mostly condemning the violence, with only a few speaking in support of Indonesia. As the session wound up, Habibie had held a cabinet meeting, and informed it that he had called Kofi Annan to request UN assistance.

Now, he had to explain himself to the Indonesian public. Just as he spoke his last words, my mobile phone rang. It turned out to be Avelino, my resistance contact from 1994. I had not spoken to him for years. After his younger brother was arrested following a bombing incident, he had fled to the Austrian Embassy in Jakarta. With his wife and small children he had remained there for almost two years. Now he was calling from Dare. I told him what we had just heard on the radio and had to repeat it several times for all the resistance leaders to hear. The shouts of joy in the background became louder every time I repeated it.

Simultaneously, as the news spread around us, a huge collective sigh of relief went through the compound, as if a death sentence had been lifted. Smiles became full of hope again. Women came up to embrace us. 'Thank you,' they said in tearful voices, 'and please tell the world, thanks for saving us.'

The important question remained: when would the force arrive? For many months we had been told that more than two thousand Australian troops were on standby and could be deployed within 24 to 48 hours. But Australia did not want to go in alone, so it looked as if we still had to wait a lot longer until the multinational force would be formed. Every minute counted. As long as the army was running the show people's lives were in danger. Much more blood would be spilled before the first foreign soldiers set foot on Timor's soil.

Antero, too, had perked up, but after the first moments of ecstatic relief and joy he hurried back to his room and, with shining eyes, fanatically started to type on the keyboard, writing an article called 'Killing two birds with one stone'. East Timor would get its freedom, he explained, and the Indonesians would get rid of the hardliners in the army.

But the words that appeared on his screen made as little sense as other things he had been talking about lately. He seemed tormented by a combination of guilt and fear that made him teeter on the edge of insanity. In his sleep, he would scream: 'Don't kill my friends!' I observed him helplessly, and not for the first time I wondered if we had been right to take him out of the room that night. Maybe he would have found a way to be with his friends. But if he had not?

§

On the day after the announcement I could relax a bit. But we did not get much time to rest. In the afternoon we were told that there was a new evacuation plan. This time all the 1,500 people in the compound – the UN's international staff, the refugees, and us, the tiny press corps – would leave for Darwin. Never before had the UN taken refugees with them during an evacuation. The plan had to be kept quiet. The UN feared that if word spread to Dare, more people would try to join, jeopardising the whole scheme.

Why leave when help was on its way? One explanation was the fear that we might all become hostages. But of greater importance was a more banal reason: food. Unamet's staff had survived on modest army rations and a limited supply of bottled water. Most refugees were also beginning to see the bottoms of their bags of rice and corn, or had already run out of food. Babies were particularly at risk, lacking milk and food they could digest.

We had to make up our minds fast. Marie decided to follow the refugees to Darwin. Minka and I would go to Dare. I called Avelino, who promised to send *estafetas* down to guide us up the hill that night. The situation was growing desperate, Avelino said. 'People had started to eat the leaves from the coffee trees.' We quietly told Antero about the evacuation and he decided to come with us.

A few hours later we stood near the hole in the gate straining our eyes to see the contour of the hills. There was no moon and the hillside was pitch-black. A good sign. We had all dressed in black hoping to blend into the night. Antero wore my flak jacket and carried his laptop. After a reconnaissance trip, an *estafeta* came back, looking very concerned. He had never seen so many soldiers on the hill. The UN, it transpired, had moved the evacuation forward and instead of leaving at daybreak, they had decided to start at midnight. They had asked the Indonesian military to seal off the compound to prevent people from the hills joining. We were trapped.

After so many days of little sleep and food we were too weak to risk the hike. Unable to walk fast enough with our heavy backpacks, we might even endanger the lives of the Timorese accompanying us. I was not too sure what Indonesian soldiers would do if they saw us on the hill. I had seen the deep hatred in their eyes: hatred enough to kill us 'by accident'. Now, humiliated by the decision to let foreign troops in, they had even more reason to vent their anger.

So we stood there for what felt like a very long time, weighing our chances. The *estafetas* discussed the situation too, mystified by the presence of all these soldiers. They looked at us, loaded down with equipment and bags of food, and I saw they were very anxious. Just when I thought I ought to tell them the reason for the military presence, so that they were in a better position to decide what to do, there was a public announcement of the evacuation. The *estafetas* dropped the food bags and ran to join the queue that had formed near the assembly hall. We had lost our last chance to escape.

Two hours later I looked from the back of a truck at the spooky contours of the burned-out, silent town, faintly visible against the starry sky. On the floor of the truck women and children squatted on top of their few scant belongings. The refugees had been given an hour to get ready. In the nervous frenzy of those last moments a young man suffered an epileptic fit and fell from the stairs. His wife and children were already on a truck when he died on the spot and he was left behind, shrouded in a white sheet.

When the last truck filled up, Madre Esmeralda's small figure stood still among the rubble in the courtyard of the compound. She had stubbornly refused to leave and, finally, when the last lorry was preparing to leave, she had to be lifted up by one of the UN staff – still protesting – and put among the other evacuees. Only one person had stayed behind: Alan Nairn, who was led away by the Indonesian soldiers as soon as the last truck had left. He ended up in a prison in Kupang before he was deported.

The airport was swarming with Indonesian soldiers. One of the UN workers, a Brazilian woman, had persuaded a soldier she knew to help her retrieve some of her personal belongings. Triumphantly she returned with her suitcase. Minka, who had also left all her possessions, including many of her notebooks, behind in a house, tried to convince the same officer to take her back there. While she was talking to him, a soldier – who had overheard the conversation – peeled out of the shadows.

'Your house is burned, totally burned,' he informed her. And when she asked him if he was sure, he added maliciously: 'Everything, your notebooks are burned and your pictures are burned too.' We stared at him in disgust. He was one of the soldiers from a small army post near Minka's house. She remembered him. No doubt he had been there himself, and probably helped with the burning and looting.

I looked around the departure hall. Hundreds of people were packed on the filthy floor of the small, unventilated room. The smell of unwashed clothes and bodies, rotting food and human excrement was stomach-turning. Antero sat huddled in a corner resting his head on his laptop computer. He was consumed by guilt. He knew he should be with his friends in Dare helping organise the refugees. Instead he was boarding a plane for Darwin.

'Are you happy that you can leave with the UN?' I asked a woman who sat nearby. 'What do you mean, happy?' she replied indignantly. 'Of course I'm not *happy*. I don't know where my husband is, where my brothers are, or father and mother, how can I be happy to be leaving?'

The evacuation took the whole day. The planes had to fly back and forth. I had not yet given up hope of finding a way to stay. Perhaps we could persuade an Indonesian soldier to take us back to town, or we could wait till nightfall and make it to the hills. Talking about our options, we sat down on the conveyer belt hidden behind the check-in counter. The rubber was soft and we were so exhausted that when we lay down for a moment we soon drifted off into a deep sleep.

I was startled back to reality by an Indonesian soldier shaking my arm. 'Quick, get your things,' he chivvied me. 'The last plane is about to leave.'

They were not quite finished yet, and I felt regret that I could not be there to see what other evil plans they had in mind.

CHAPTER 23

Counting Bodies

There's no such thing as a hero – only ordinary people asked extraordinary things in terrible circumstances – and delivering. (Timothy Mo, *The Redundancy of Courage*)

§ 1 RETURNED to Timor in the cockpit of a Hercules. The country was still smouldering. Here and there columns of smoke rose from villages below, but otherwise there was no sign of human activity. Dili's airport, however, was buzzing. Australian army helicopters hovered over the tarmac like big insects. Heavily armed soldiers lay behind sandbags or in trenches.

The week I had spent in Darwin had been a frustrating wait for the deployment, and then an even more frustrating scramble to get back to Timor. Interfet, the International Force for East Timor, had accredited only a select group of journalists, almost all Australians, and all male.

It had taken nine days for Interfet to form and land in Dili. As intervention forces go this was a display of spectacular speed, but for East Timor each day, each hour counted. The urgency of the deployment meant that Interfet was not a blue-helmeted UN force. It was a 'coalition of the willing'. Its mandate from the UN Security Council went beyond peacekeeping, allowing the soldiers to 'take all necessary measures' to restore peace and security.[1] For Indonesia it was vital that Asian countries were included. To its intense irritation, however, Australian and British contingents formed Interfet's core and called the shots. In command was General Peter Cosgrove, an Australian.

When Cosgrove's troops landed, most of the militia had already moved out, and instead of an angry mob the soldiers had been met by a handful of journalists who had made their way from Kupang. While we waited in the ruins of the departure hall for some form of transport, an Australian soldier called us over to show off more than twenty weapons he had confiscated: a neat display of mainly crude handmade guns, unloaded of their ammunition of rusty nails and match-heads. 'Where are you from?' he inquired. 'The Netherlands,' I replied. 'I'm sorry, we just found your colleague,' he said. 'He is dead.' The soldier could not remember the name of the journalist.

Even before I got into the hotel I had heard the whole story. Everyone was talking about what had happened. Sander Thoenes, a correspondent for the *Financial Times* in Jakarta, had flown in from there the previous afternoon and taken a motorbike taxi to Becora. When his driver had spotted soldiers blocking the road, he had smelled trouble and turned his bike. Sander had been shot in the back. His mutilated body had been found that morning near the roadside.

Around the same time Indonesian soldiers had attacked the British journalist Jon Swain and his photographer. They had had a very lucky escape. Their interpreter, however, had been taken away by the soldiers and their driver beaten so badly he had lost an eye. When I heard the name of the interpreter, I had another nasty shock. It was Anacleto, one of Antero's brothers.

Once again, the Turismo had been appropriated by soldiers, this time Australians, who let us in only after a lot of trouble. They had made it their information office and reserved space for their handpicked group of accredited journalists. I found João, the old waiter, in the garden, hovering around with a broom. When he saw me, he flung his scrawny arms around me in a tight hug, tears running down his hollow cheeks. He had never left, he sobbed. When I had been looking for him he had stayed with Indonesian officers who had made their quarters in a house next door to the hotel. He proudly led me to the back of the hotel and showed me my bicycle. He had defended it from being looted.

'It was the military that did all the looting and burning here,' he said. They took all the journalists' belongings, and, curiously, all the mattresses. Only one room was completely burned out, the room I had stayed in for a few months, which was later taken over by John Martinkus, an Australian journalist who had, like me, lived in the Turismo for the past year. Written in the soot on the wall were the words: 'Lies was here'.

§

That afternoon, and over the next days, I wandered around the desolate town looking for friends and for people I knew and, I hoped, were still alive.

In the empty streets, between the fire-wrecked buildings, bits of charred paper that made up their owners' histories swirled around like autumn leaves in the ash-filled wind: birth certificates, ID cards, letters, a wedding portrait, snapshots of family parties, strips of negatives. The few people that had returned from the hills drifted like zombies through the ravaged city, still in shock. They found their houses destroyed, their families missing. Occasionally I saw a few men equipped with shovels and sticks rummaging through the rubble looking for usable bits and pieces. Others pushed carts laden with furniture and animals. Sometimes the stillness was broken by the roar of armoured personnel carriers that drove at high speed through the ghost town.

In the bishop's compound I found Madre Margarita dusting a sofa, part of a smart three-piece suite upholstered in a flowery pattern, which had somehow survived the looting and burning. It stood, complete with coffee table, forlornly in front of the blackened ruin of the bishop's residence. She took a glass jar off the crocheted tablecloth. 'Would you like a biscuit, perhaps?' she greeted me, as if I had popped in for a genteel tea-party.

On the beach in front of the bishop's house a shanty town had sprung up where children, goats and pigs fought over the same fodder. The city's walls, or what was left of them, spoke of war. The retreating militiamen and soldiers had scrawled graffiti everywhere, some smeared out in letters of excrement. 'UN go to hell'; 'TNI for ever'; 'Timor eat stones'. But there were other messages too, desperate and defiant: 'Help me' was written on one house; 'Indonesia is the devil'; 'Independencia'. And on the surface of the road, someone had written in English with white paint: 'Please forgive me'.

On major intersections Interfet soldiers were building huge forts of sandbags while the columns of smoke of new fires still climbed into the sky. When I arrived at the Salesian convent, Sister Marlene had just returned from her first trip outside 'to loot mangoes', as she called it, and offered me her booty in a bowl of fruit salad. On the wall behind her hung a whiteboard bearing the famous Second World War graffito: 'I believe in the sun even if it isn't shining. I believe in God even if He is silent.'

Like some of the others who had been through Dili's nightmare and lived to tell the tale, she was on a survivor's high. She talked non-stop. 'It is a real miracle that nothing has happened to us. Three times the militia and the military came to the convent. Every time they entered the courtyard, the children started to sing and pray. Even the smallest ones folded their hands and joined in the hymns.' 'Please go ahead, look inside!' the sisters would say in welcome to their attackers. 'We only have women and small children here.'

Two of Xanana's sisters and their families had been in the convent, but only for a few days. The nuns urged them to take their chance and hike up the hill to the relative safety of Dare. But they hid Xanana's parents, who were in their eighties and too frail for this hazardous journey, in the laundry room. While the militias had searched every room in the building looking for men and boys, the sisters had started to scrub the floor in front of the room and this had, miraculously, stopped the men from opening the door and finding the old couple. Sister Marlene took a jam jar off the shelf. It was full of cartridge cases. 'One day the children and I will do something creative with these.'

With Sister Marlene I went to Mana Lou in Dare to drop off a few boxes of high-protein biscuits. The coffee plantations still resembled a huge encampment. Many people would go down to Dili during the day but still sleep in the hills at night. 'Where were you?' Mana Lou greeted me, shaking her head. Like everybody else, Mana Lou had lost weight and looked tired, but her boundless energy seemed undiminished. She was full of plans. A new health clinic, a guesthouse, rebuilding the Sick House, distributing food to the refugees, and so on. But she was still upset too.

She showed me her rubbish-strewn gardens. She was annoyed with the people for destroying the banana trees, trampling through her vegetable gardens and bathing in her drinking-water well. 'They behaved as if they were on a picnic,' she snorted. They had shown no respect for the hard work that goes into nurturing plants, and they had not even helped her carry water up the hill for the soup she cooked for them.

She had given CNRT leaders and their families places to sleep in her buildings. Leandro Isaak and Xanana's sister Armandina and her family, who had climbed up from the Salesian compound, had slept on the floor in the dining room. They should have organised the people but everyone had been so afraid, Mana Lou said, that their fear had paralysed them. 'Their minds didn't work any more.'

It was the exactly the same phrase Madre Esmeralda had used to explain the inability of people in the Unamet compound to formulate a statement for the Security Council delegation. Fear and trauma helped explain the lack of leadership among the people not only in the short-lived community in the compound, but also in many other parts of Timor. Most people were, understandably, too busy saving their own skins, and in many cases were also too traumatised to do much.

Mana Lou borrowed my mobile to call Father Tom in Yogyakarta. She talked for a long time, and then started to sob. She was still shaking when she handed the phone back. She had told Father Tom how shocked she was by the hatred she felt for the Indonesians. 'The Indonesian army sees us as snakes, the worst of the vermin that you kill because it's a snake, not because they have done anything to harm you,' she burst out. 'I don't want to hate them, but I hate them so much for what they did to us.'

On the way back from Dare I went past Mana Lou's Sick House. The buildings had been looted and badly damaged by fire. While I looked around, an old man with a long grey beard emerged from a nearby house that had not been torched. 'Many people around here are still in their houses,' he said. 'We have no food.' He pointed at his stomach. 'I survived for weeks on two mangoes a day. It gives me cramps.'

A group of soldiers had come to his house just while he was taking a *mandi*. They pulled their guns, screaming and shouting abuse. But when they saw that he was very old they left him alone. 'You should look over there,' he said, pointing at a small banana grove. 'Around there are eight dead people, seven boys and a girl. The Indonesian soldiers killed them. The dogs and pigs had a feast.' His face contorted. 'I'm so old I have lived through four wars.

But this one was the worst. They have stolen and burned everything, they even killed our women and children.' His feverish eyes glowed with anger.

I walked over to the trees. The half-decomposed corpse of a young man lay down in a gutter. His body was covered in something black that, when I came nearer, disintegrated and turned out to be a swarm of flies. Covering my face with a scarf, I had a quick look round. The noxious sweet smell of death hung everywhere, and I did not have the stomach to look further. When I retraced my steps the old man was still standing in front of his house. 'Where are these foreign troops?' he demanded when I passed him. 'We've seen nobody yet.'

§

During its first weeks in Timor, Interfet did not move very fast. It secured the airport and port and flushed out a few militiamen who were still lurking in buildings in the centre of town. But it did not extend its control beyond Dili, a failure some British Gurkhas privately criticised, and blamed on Australia's unwillingness to risk the lives of its soldiers. 'If it was up to us we would have secured the country in a few days,' boasted one British commander, adding, not without some pride: 'We are used to taking casualties.' But there may have been other reasons for the delay. General Cosgrove had a delicate task. Indonesia was still regarded as being responsible for Timor, until the MPR ratified the result of the referendum. So it was essential that Interfet maintained close coordination with its army.

It may have been that Interfet simply did not have the manpower. To the press Cosgrove reported the force held around seven thousand, but it was hard to know how many were actually on the ground, since he deliberately inflated the numbers. Also, Dili was one of the ports from where thousands of Indonesian soldiers and police were leaving, and maybe Interfet felt the need to keep an eye on what they were up to in Dili.

Cosgrove later said he had other 'special intelligence' he could not reveal, which had made him decide not to venture out of the capital: a decision, he said, he had never regretted.

It was true that Australia's intelligence agencies indeed had a ringside seat. Their units listened in to telephone conversations and they had satellite pictures, including close-up images of massacres and the perpetrators. The bulk of this has not been released, as the way it was obtained makes it too sensitive. But one intelligence report dated 24 September warned that the TNI might engineer a very violent incident with Interfet to discredit Cosgrove and force Interfet to withdraw.[2]

But I had reason to be sceptical about whether Australia's intelligence on the ground – or its spies' ability to interpret it – was as good as it liked to claim. I remembered one evening in August in the garden of the Turismo,

15. People return to find their houses burned.

when an Australian diplomat stationed in Timor had berated me and two other journalists for going around the country and talking to people. He never ventured out of his office or spoke to people in the street, he said. The situation was too delicate for that.

In the port I ran into Dendi, the young lieutenant who had driven us around a burning Dili. He greeted me coolly. He was inspecting a group of soldiers who had gathered in the port ready to board a ship. Many of them carried birdcages with parrots, emerald doves and other colourful birds, or had pet monkeys on their shoulders. I could not read from Dendi's face how he felt. He said he had been involved in the search for Jon Swain and his photographer. This carried a subtle warning, and I had to think about what an Indonesian colleague had told me. Many of the Indonesian soldiers she had spoken to had told her they 'felt hot'. She had been worried. The Javanese have a word for it: the practice of *sampyuh*. A cornered man may lessen the humiliation of his defeat by taking down as many as possible of his enemies before his own death.

§

I had moved from the Turismo, having had enough of the militarised atmosphere. During one of the nightly briefings about security, an officer informed us about whistled codes that would tell us to either lie flat on the ground or to crawl on all fours to a meeting area. He also forbade accredited journalists from sharing their water and food with unaccredited ones. It all seemed so pompous and bizarre that I had to hide my grin behind my notebook. The Australian soldiers had killed the ginger cats, kicking to death the creatures they called 'vermin'. They were not badly missed, but their demise added to the strange atmosphere of the place. And after a night of sleeping on a balcony and waking up every hour to the heavy boots of patrolling soldiers near my head and their sinister shadows on the walls above me, I decided it was better to go elsewhere.

I moved to IPI, the educational centre for the Dili diocese. Most of the 'unaccredited' journalists were staying there and had nicknamed it 'the nunnery'. We had no protection there, but we could receive our Timorese friends. And we had electricity, water, more space, and above all, food. An enterprising Timorese woman with contacts in the Indonesian army had got hold of bags of rice. She improvised three meals a day from whatever she could find; in the first weeks this was mainly boiled unripe jackfruit.

One afternoon João Sarmento wandered in. I hardly recognised him. His eyes had sunk deep in his face, and his black curls were streaked with grey. He had come down from Dare to look for food and, typical of João, for his books. His love of books made his friends joke: 'We have friends, João has books.' His search had taken him to Minka's old house, where he and Antero had left some of their possessions. In the ashes he had found two novels and Antero's diary. His hands were still grey, and when he wiped his forehead he left smudges of ash. There was hunger in his eyes but he ate the rice and breadfruit we gave him painfully slowly. After many weeks of hardly eating at all, his stomach could not handle it. He did not talk about his own suffering. So many people in the hills had been ill and without food.

After his escape to Dare, João had stayed near the seminary. Some seminarians remembered him from when he had gone to school there, and gave him preferential treatment. He did not need to queue up for his food and got better portions. He had not approved of that, and moved on up the hill until he ended up at Mana Lou's institute, where he was treated like anyone else.

Mana Lou had distributed corn soup for people who had nothing and João had eaten it twice. He did not complain, but said that many people had turned their noses up at it. João remembered how furious she had been with the townspeople. 'This is my father's plantation. You have to show respect!' she had shouted in a way that had reminded him of 'Jesus in the temple'.

In bits and pieces, I heard the story of how João had risked his life for his books. As soon as they heard that Interfet was about to arrive and the militia had left, he and his friends had gone down to Dili. It was 17 September. João had been worried about his books. He lived in an Indonesian neighbourhood and was known by the militias as a student activist. He found his house and all his books burned. When he left, a militiaman emerged from a neighbouring house and shot at him. To his horror he saw the end of the road blocked by more militias. He had to duck and dive and then run for his life. As soon as he got back to Dare, the trauma of the narrow escape triggered a bad malaria attack. For three days he did not eat or drink. He thought he would die, he said, but when he heard that Interfet had at last reached Dili he recovered miraculously.

§

One of the first friends I met who was not so badly traumatised was Rosa Garcia, the young journalist from *Suara Timor Timur*. A Japanese news agency for which she had done some work had helped her escape to Jakarta, and she had returned as soon as there was a flight. She was in a vibrant mood. The horror and destruction seemed to have given her a new purpose. She had started to write her own newsletter called *Loro Foun Sae* (New Sunrise), a single photocopied sheet with an initial circulation of just five copies. But it was a start in a place that had no media left.

With her best friends, Isabel Fereira and Ivete de Oliveira – at the time respectively Sebastião's and Antero's girlfriends – she had set up a new human rights organisation called Comissão dos Direitos Humanos Timor Lorosae (East Timor Human Rights Commission). They had started to document the killings in Dili and, later on, in other parts of the country. Yayasan Hak, Timor's best-known human rights organisation, had not returned to Dili yet, and conducting investigations and collecting evidence were not among Interfet's priorities. Any serious investigations, they said, had to await the arrival of a UN forensic team, not expected until the end of the year. In the meantime Interfet, and especially the Australians, were suspected of destroying evidence and underplaying the extent of the killings for their own political purposes.

Rosa took me proudly to the office of the Comissão, as she called it, a large house in the centre of town. As we stood there a boy walked up and thrust a plastic bag in her hand. Curiously she peeked inside. 'A human tongue', she shrieked as she dropped it on the ground. 'We need to investigate if this is a tongue of an old or a young person,' the boy said. He picked the bag up and disappeared into the office.[3]

Rosa and her friends had to work fast. Returning families and neighbours tended to bury in their backyards the bodies that lay strewn around Dili. Other evidence was washed away by the rain. In total they documented more than a hundred killings. Among the dead they found young people, who, Ivete said, had no connection with politics. Victims were thrown into burning houses or cars. Just outside Dili stood a pick-up truck with the charred bodies of seven people.

The only leader they found murdered was Mau Hodu, the CNRT leader and former Falintil commander. He had stayed on in Dili for the first meeting of the Consultative Commission and for the visit of Wiranto on 5 September.

After that the military had taken him to Kupang, where he was seen in a hotel. A month later, on the border in Batugade, Ivete and an Australian doctor exhumed a body from a shallow grave. They identified it as that of Mau Hodu.

Neither Rosa, her friends, nor anybody else I met in those first weeks complained that the UN, the NGOs and the foreign press had fled the country. They saw it simply as a consequence of the war. It had taken 24 years but now the cuckoo had finally been thrown out of the nest. The nest was destroyed, but could always be rebuilt.

On my first day in Dili I had run into João da Neves, Sebastião's soft-spoken uncle, whom I had met on the Ili Manu pilgrimage. 'Thank God, you are still alive,' he had greeted me. This had become something of a standard greeting at the time, and when people met their friends and acquaintances in the street, they hugged and kissed. A reunion of survivors.

João da Neves was trying to find soap and cigarettes. There were no shops and of the old *mercado* only the Portuguese-style gate was still standing. On top a few forlorn red-and-white flags fluttered in the wind, the only colour among the desolate grey remains of the corrugated-iron roofs of the stalls, which looked as if they been trampled by a large herd of elephants.

He surveyed the destruction quietly. 'I think it was worth it,' he said suddenly, in answer to a question I had not asked. 'I guess it's zero hour. Our boats have been burned behind us. Literally.' He pointed around. 'Now we have not only to rebuild the buildings, but also our lives, our language, our culture. Everything is gone – but at least we are free.'

§

My first trip out of town took me to the east of the country. I travelled in a long aid convoy, escorted by a group of Gurkha volunteers. Whatever Cosgrove's reasons, the slow roll-out of Interfet from Dili had already had grave consequences for the starving people outside Dili. The many humanitarian aid organisations that had descended on Timor could not start their relief programmes before Interfet secured the areas they needed to go to. We drove through deserted, fire-ravaged villages: army barracks of which only the walls were still standing; schools that looked as if they had been bombed.

Manatutu had been, as its *bupati* had foretold before the ballot, 'a sea of flames': the whole town was destroyed; only the church was still standing. Along the road straggled a group of bony men. They were scouts. The rest of the town's population were still in the mountains. Some waved at the convoy, but most seemed just too weary and dazed. 'We are hungry, we have no clothes, no medicines,' a man shouted. But the relief supplies on the trucks were meant for Los Palos and they had to watch in astonishment as the aid convoy departed, leaving them only a bit of rice.

The ravaged landscape changed at Baucau. The town had hardly been touched, thanks in large measure to the role Bishop Basilio had played. He had always maintained good relations with the local military and militias. This now paid off. As he told me when I went to see him: 'I think my staying here saved the town.' At the height of the mayhem, he had been sitting in his house in Baucau watching television when he heard his name mentioned. A reporter said he had been wounded and fled to the mountains. But in fact he never left. While he was watching the news he could not get out of his head words uttered in May 1999 by Armindo Mariano, a pro-autonomy member of the provincial government: 'If the people reject autonomy the only sound we will hear in Dili, for the coming three years, is birdsong.'

Bishop Belo had been staying with him for a few days when, after the attack on his residency, he had been flown to Baucau by the police. Bishop Belo had feared for his life. 'There is a bullet out there that has my name on it,' he had told Basilio. He had joined the last evacuation flight from Baucau, but Bishop Basilio, arguing that at least one of them should stay behind, had remained. On 10 September, the day he heard that all the journalists had left, he counted 107 trucks full of 'war tools' passing his house. He got frightened: 'Without observers, they could do anything, just like in 1975.' Ever since the massacres in Alas and Liquiça, he had done his best to maintain a dialogue with the Indonesian security forces and the *bupati* of Baucau.

Another important factor was that the local militia groups, Saka and Sera, consisted of only local people. The bishop thought that the absence of outsiders had saved them a lot of trouble. The militias promised the bishop that 'as long as they were there, nothing would happen'. They had even fought off an attempt by Aitarak to enter their area. As soon as the militias left for West Timor the army became active. 'Over the next four days we could see what they were up to,' Bishop Basilio said. 'They would come in five separate groups. The first one shot in the air, the second told the people to get out and leave town, the third took everything they laid eyes on, the fourth would burn and the fifth, they would lament, "*aduh, aduh, kasihan*, oh dear, oh dear, poor you!"'

The bishop advised people not to resist when the soldiers came. 'Just let them take what they want.' This strategy appeared to have worked reasonably well, and apart from a few shops and businesses, nothing much had been burned or destroyed. 'It was only when the new Kostrad troops arrived, introducing themselves as the "peacekeepers", that the market and the barracks went up in flames.'

CHAPTER 24
. . . .
Valley of Tears

If you cannot have both reason and strength, always choose reason and let
the enemy have all the strength. In many battles strength can obtain the
victory, but in all the struggles only reason can win. The powerful can
never extract reason from his strength, but we can always obtain strength
from reason. (Sub-Comandante Marcos of the Zapatistas)

§ AS soon as I climbed down from the back of the lorry, I could see that Taur
Matan Ruak was in a bad mood. He greeted us without his usual exuberance
and walked briskly back into his headquarters. He was agonising about the
refugees. Thousands had stayed with them in the Uaimori cantonment site
and another 50,000 in the wider area under Taur's command. Now, more than
ten days after its arrival, Interfet had still not moved into the east of the
country and aid could not reach the starving population. The forest, in the dry
season, shrivels up, and even the jungle grasses are too dry to eat. Children
had started to die. Airdrops of food eventually started on 17 September, after
Indonesia gave clearance for Australian planes to fly in. This was a disaster
too. A child was crushed to death by one of the bags, and the high-protein
biscuits had been too rich to digest and had given the people diarrhoea.

When a UN official accompanied by a military observer arrived in Uaimori,
Taur had made it clear that he was not impressed by Interfet's performance.
'They are like tourists on holiday,' he told his astonished visitors. 'Give me
3,000 armed men and I'll do it in two days, and on the third day I'd liberate
West Timor as well.' He laughed his familiar laugh, but it sounded hollow.
His mood had not been improved by the way Interfet had treated the independence fighters. When the foreign forces had arrived, Falintil had expected to
be able to work with them. Since they did not provide security in every
village, Taur had been more than willing to help. Through his intelligence
network he knew that only a few isolated pockets of militiamen remained,
and that they were, with the TNI out of the way, no match for his guerrillas.
He even offered unarmed Falintil soldiers to escort food convoys.

Falintil had proved its point in Com, where a handful of armed militiamen had taken a large group of people hostage. Interfet commandos twice failed to arrest them; the men hid by mingling with their hostages. Falintil finished the job, flushing out the militiamen, pursuing them into the forest and detaining them.

But Interfet stuck to its mandate: to disarm all armed groups apart from the TNI. So they treated Falintil fighters in the same way as they did the militias: they disarmed them by force and took them to prison in handcuffs. This was a great humiliation for the proud fighters, who thought they were merely doing their best to ensure security in areas Interfet had not reached. In Cairui, the village nearest the cantonment site, for example, Falintil had refused to hand over its weapons unless Interfet established a permanent presence there.

'Interfet did not come because of crimes against humanity committed by Falintil,' Taur pointed out. 'So they have no reason to confiscate our arms without consultation.' Xanana, in Portugal at the time, had been furious too. Falintil should not be treated as bandits, he said, but as a liberation army. L7, too, was bitter. He blamed Unamet for people being killed. It was the saddest he and his men had felt, he said, in 24 years. What should have been Falintil's moment of triumph had ended in bitter tears and recriminations. Its fighters were conquering heroes, but enjoyed no triumphal march. They knew that instead of cheering their victory, people were grumbling about them: 'We have fed them, brought them medicine and money, but when we needed them they weren't there.'[1]

Taur had been under a lot of pressure ever since the army and militias had gone on their vengeful rampage. On 4 September Falintil soldiers in Uaimori had watched the announcement of the referendum results on their televisions. For an hour they had danced around, emptying their guns in the air. But then, as they saw the pictures of the destruction, joy had turned into anger and grief. And as more refugees arrived with horrific stories, begging them to do something, the guerrillas wanted to leave the compound to defend the people and save their families.

On the phone from his sanctuary in the British Embassy in Jakarta, Xanana had screamed and wept, pleading with his commander not to fight back. Taur had shouted at him that he could not hold his men back much longer, that it had all become too much to bear. 'How can you ask us to stay calm, how can you stay quiet when we are being killed?'

Asking Falintil not to fight had been one of the most difficult decisions Xanana had ever had to make. He would later say that he was crying because 'we had not been able to avoid the very worst outcome'. But if he had not stopped Falintil, the Indonesian army would have had an excuse to kill even more people. 'We knew the strategy of the Indonesian generals, and we wanted to avoid falling into their trap. They wanted to show that East

Timorese were fighting each other, so no UN intervention would have come.'[2]

After Madre Esmeralda called Taur from the Unamet compound, he proposed sending 200 armed men to protect the refugees. Xanana had not given his permission. Taur called the UN military liaison officer and told him that either 'you go all together or you die all together'. After they had heard that an intervention force was coming but still nothing had happened, the feeling of frustration had become too much. Taur could no longer restrain his troops from leaving the cantonment site. Some of the commanders, including L7, had gone to Manatutu and Laleia to help the people there, and prevent those places from being destroyed. They were too late.

They decided to ambush the notorious TNI battalion 745 from Los Palos, as it retreated to Dili. Its soldiers had destroyed Los Palos town and many other villages and killed scores of people. But Falintil had been betrayed. When the Indonesian soldiers reached the ambush (on 21 September), they had clearly been forewarned, and had come on foot instead of in their trucks. A fierce firefight broke out, and the guerrillas barely managed to escape with their lives. Some were seriously wounded. The Indonesian soldiers, pumped up by the battle, went on to Dili. They were the ones behind the attacks on foreign journalists, including the murder of Sander Thoenes and Antero's brother, Anacleto.[3]

In L7's sector Bisoi and Veronica welcomed me back with tearful hugs. Veronica had turned into a bony bundle of despair. She had convinced herself that her whole family had been killed and that she was all alone. Bisoi had, I knew, lost her little daughter. I had seen her once already, in a Falintil-protected area in the hills near Dili. In her makeshift tent she had offered me a drink from an impressive collection of bottles of brandy, rum and gin, that somehow had ended high on this mountain slope.

This time her tears were not only for her missing daughter. 'Agus is dead,' she wept. Agus Mulyawan, an Indonesian journalist and Timor activist, had stayed with them in September. 'We all begged him to stay,' she said. But Agus had left with a priest for Baucau. There, on 25 September, he had joined a group of nuns and seminarians for Los Palos. Their car had been ambushed by militiamen from Tim Alfa and they had all, including a 68-year-old Italian nun, been killed.[4]

The atmosphere in the camp had been depressing. And it didn't get better when the newly arrived press assistant of Taur, an Australian woman (a former aide to José Ramos Horta), started trying to rewrite history, denying things Taur had said. Worse, my notebook disappeared. I went up the chain of command in my attempts to get it back and was every time told that Falintil did not steal. 'If the thief is a Falintil soldier, I will kill him.' Taur had left for Laga and at headquarters I could not get a straight answer, but it became apparent that it had been the new press assistant who had taken my notebook to 'check it for security reasons'. I had to wait several days to get it back. I felt like a hostage. Was this a foretaste of what the new nation would be like?

§

As soon as I arrived back in Dili I joined an Australian doctor and two human rights activists on a trip to Suai. Interfet had not gone into the mountains yet. Along the road, burned-out villages and towns were mostly deserted; people were still hiding. Ainaro town lay in ashes, including the hospital and the houses of the priest and nuns. In Cassa only Cansio's brick house was still standing, as if he had left it untouched, ready for his return. Further west the penetrating stench of rotting corpses lingered in the air; a smell that seemed to cling to my skin and hair.

One night we camped in a dry riverbed. We heard footsteps rustling on the wooded bank, and a dog barking, but saw nobody in the darkness. Our interpreter called out: 'Please show yourselves. We come to do no harm.' He called it again and again, every time with more desperation. He was in tears because the people were too terrified to come to us.

In Suai we met a group of a dozen or so people who had returned from the hills. They took us to the large compound housing a school and two churches that had been a sanctuary for thousands. In the afternoon of 6 September, a group of a hundred army, police and militia had opened fire, killing at least a hundred people, mainly women and children and the three priests who had sheltered them.

In a big classroom we found a few men searching, with vacant eyes, through layers of charred papers, photos, clothing, tufts of human hair. They pulled a couple of ID cards from the debris and scrutinised them closely. Lifting up the blood-soaked clothing, I saw a thick layer of black congealed blood, so thick you could scrape it away. In the stairwells of the steeple in the still unfinished cathedral, blood had dripped down the stairs. From the marks, it looked as if bodies had been dragged across the landing and thrown out of the windows.

There were no bodies. A man who witnessed the massacre hiding in an oil drum told us they had been loaded on to trucks and taken to West Timor. A few months later three mass graves were discovered there with 26 bodies, including the three priests and three children.

§

Suai was the scene of one of the largest massacres that took place after the referendum. It had top priority for the serious crime unit of the UN in Timor, but at the time of writing a court case is still pending.

With four other journalists and photographers I rented a bemo to go to Maliana, another place where many people died. We were joined by a Timorese human rights lawyer and Filomena da Silva, a mother of one of the students of the Student Solidarity Council.

Filomena stared silently out of the window of the *bemo*. It was hot. The black dress she wore made her sweat; little beads trickled from her forehead. Sometimes she pushed an unruly lock of hair back under her black headscarf. Erna, the youngest of her eight children, sat next to her. She was eight, but did not speak or smile during the five hours it took us to drive from Dili to Maliana.

It was All Souls' Day – the day Roman Catholics remember their dead. Filomena had just returned from West Timor and was on her way back to Maliana hoping to find some remains of her husband, Lorenzo. When we came closer to the border with West Timor again the road and surrounding landscape emptied. In the ghostly villages we saw no people, no dogs, not even chickens, just a few blackened beams of what once were homes. This was the militias' heartland, the home villages of the Tavares and the Gonçalves clans.

Late in the afternoon we reached Maliana. From the church a small procession of men, women and children filed in the direction of the graveyard. They carried baskets full of blossoms. At the cemetery, people sat around the graves of their relatives, saying prayers and burning candles. Filomena started to cry. She wanted to find her dead husband, so that she too would have a grave to visit and lay flowers on. The place she started her search was the UN, in the hope that they knew something about her husband.

She and her husband Lorenzo had worked for Unamet during the referendum. But when she climbed the steps to the porch, an armed guard brusquely shooed her away. Bewildered, she turned around. These were her colleagues, the people she had seen as friends. Then one of the women in the office recognised her and she got a warm welcome after all.

Unamet's international personnel had left the town on 3 September, leaving behind many of their local staff. They had told Filomena and Lorenzo, who had stayed to help with the ballot papers, to go with their family to the police headquarters – Unamet officials had made an agreement with the local commander that they would take care of security. There were some 200 people at the police station, including CNRT leader Manuel Magalhaes, who felt he could not abandon the people in their hour of need.

In most other places in Timor, CNRT members had immediately left after they cast their vote, but in Maliana, persuaded to do so by Unamet, some leaders had stayed in town. Unamet had told them that they would stay with them after the ballot, so they should not worry.

By the time the UN left the people in the police station had been trapped: the town was surrounded. Five days later the militias and the army attacked but the police did nothing to protect them – they joined in. Forty-seven men and boys were killed.[5] Eight men, among them Manuel Magalhaes, managed to escape and hide in a swampy lagoon. They were betrayed and killed a day later. Filomena, who had heard all this, did not accuse Unamet; she did not even complain. All she cared about at that moment was to find her husband. The stories she had heard did not give her much hope: the bodies had been burned and thrown into the sea.

The next day Filomena and her daughter went to the police station. We walked around the burned-out barracks. On some walls people had scribbled messages: 'Help us! Why has everybody forsaken us?' Filomena was looking for the room she had seen her husband being dragged into. She found the little office full of rubble and broken glass. Near the back door she saw a large bloodstain. 'Here is where they stabbed him,' she cried. She lit a few candles and put some flowers on the rubble. Her daughter watched her with big, frightened eyes, cupping her little hands carefully around a candle flame, shielding it from the wind.

A man who had watched the little ceremony exchanged a few words with Filomena. He took us through a side entrance, through a little river and over a tapioca field, until we reached a white wall. On it, black soot had formed the silhouette of a human body. Quietly she started to search around and found the remnants of a burned shirt. Only the pocket had survived. Gingerly she peeled the fabric apart and pulled out a rosary with a little cross. The blue beads had broken. She looked around and found a second one. She kissed the crucifixes, whimpering softly: 'God help me.' One was the rosary she had given her husband the day before he died.

Lorenzo had had enough strength to run away after he was stabbed, but he had got no further than this wall. His pursuers must have caught up, killed him, and set fire to his body before dumping the remains in the sea. Erna prodded in the ashes with a little stick. She found a toenail. Filomena too, along with a few other people who had joined us, sifted systematically through the scorched earth. It was as if they had done nothing else in their lives but identify bone splinters. 'This is part of a middle finger and that is a piece of the arm,' said a man with the authority of a forensic scientist. The others agreed. After 24 years probably everybody in Timor is expert in identifying body parts, even eight-year-olds. Filomena put everything she found in a plastic carrier bag, cradled it to her chest, wiped away her tears and went to look for a priest, so that she could organise the funeral.

On the coast road back to Dili the *bemo* had a flat tyre. Filomena took her shoes off. 'I love the sea,' she said, and waded into it. She stood there quietly, for as long as it took to change the tyre, looking at the small waves that played around her ankles, as if she was looking for comfort in water that had engulfed the bones of her husband. When we were sitting in the bus again, she said: 'I feel closer to him now.'

§

The whole country was waiting for Maun Boot Xanana to come home. When he did at last, on 21 October, two days after the MPR in Jakarta had officially ratified the outcome of the referendum, it was not a triumphant homecoming. For security reasons, he made a quiet arrival under cover of darkness on an Australian airforce plane. The next day cars with loudspeakers went around announcing his arrival. Within an hour Timorese from all over town and nearby villages were streaming to the governor's palace to welcome their hero.

He stood on the balcony in his army fatigues, flanked by Taur Matan Ruak and Leandro Isaak and surrounded by Interfet bodyguards. His voice broke with emotion when he spoke, and many people wept as they listened. 'They tried to kill us, but we are still here, crying and suffering, but still alive ... from today nothing can stop us.' Sorrow mixed with joy. Among the tears, some people were dancing and singing. 'We can leave our suffering behind,' he promised. 'We will be independent for ever.' He asked people to look forward, not back. 'All of us must let go of the bad things they have done to us, because tomorrow is ours.'

Xanana came home a demi-god, a saviour and a healer. He was the little white moth left, after all the evil had come out from Pandora's box: in Padre Jovito's words 'the embodiment of people's hopes.'

But Xanana soon came to hate the atmosphere in Dili. He felt his people had been colonised again, this time under the UN flag. He moved to Remexio, one of Falintil's historic bases in the hills near the capital, where Taur and his men had moved to, and started to travel around in the eastern part of the country.

When I next saw him he was sitting in front of a large crowd in his birthplace, Laleia. This was supposed to be a 'dialogue' with local people, but he was the only one speaking. The villagers sat in quiet awe, listening patiently, while he, still in his army fatigues, screamed and shouted and pounded his fists on the table. He explained his vision of the future. He told the crowd they had to learn to stand on their own feet, not holding their hands out for food. 'We need a change in mentality and have to all work very very hard for our future.' But then he smiled and joked, the tension evaporated and every-one smiled and loved him.

After his initial joy at being back in his country, Xanana felt devastated. The situation was worse than he had imagined. Many people had no shelter, and often no food either. The task he saw in front of him overwhelmed him. But his trip around the country had given him new hope, he said. 'Slowly, when I met my people, I got a new confidence, a new determination to fight.' As if to bolster him for the new struggle ahead he wore his Falintil uniform wherever he went. When I asked him about the uniform and his dual role as commander of Falintil and head of the CNRT, he said: 'I feel more a guerrilla leader than a politician. I was arrested as a guerrilla fighter, I return as a guerrilla fighter.' And although his mannerisms recalled Fidel Castro, in his words he resembled Mandela: he consistently stressed the need for reconciliation.

Xanana had returned in time to see the Indonesian flag lowered and to bid farewell to the Indonesian commanders who left as he had arrived, in the middle of the night. He was also in time to welcome the United Nations Transitional Administration in East Timor, UNTAET, which was established by the Security Council on 25 October. UNTAET was a mission with an unprecedentedly broad and ambitious mandate. It was not only a peacekeeping exercise, it was responsible for administration and security until East Timor's independence. And it had to rebuild the country from scratch.[6]

It was the first time in its history that the UN held such complete sovereignty over a country: holding responsibility for the legislative, executive and judicial branches of government. This put the UN's transitional administrator, the special representative of the secretary-general, Sergio Vieira de Mello, a Brazilian, in a position 'comparable with a pre-constitutional monarch'.[7] When he arrived, on 16 November, Xanana was not at the airport to meet him. By then the honeymoon period between the Timorese people and the UN was already over, and Xanana himself was feeling resentful towards the UN and Interfet.

Aware of this, the first thing de Mello did after he arrived was to make contact with Xanana. The second was to declare that all public buildings belonged to UNTAET, to put an end to the practice of 'building grabbing', which had become a real problem. De Mello had, he said, arrived with 'a bunch of generalists, people I knew and literally recruited in the corridors of New York and brought with me, but who had no experience with actual government ... There was no instruction manual attached to the mandate,' de Mello lamented.[8] And he would later write that he had no clear conception of how to 'exercise fair governance with absolute power', other than to seek a model for 'benevolent depotism'.[9]

Most of the staff he brought into the mission he knew from Kosovo. 'An inner circle from the Balkans, whose members projected a blunt, bullying style' was how one disaffected colleague described them.[10] They seemed to treat East Timor as an intellectual exercise, not as a country with real people.

So the Timorese soon felt marginalised. As Xanana had put it: 'We don't feel very comfortable with some people acting like kings of East Timor, coming here to impose their models ... We are strong enough to expel anybody from East Timor.'[11] Relations reached an all-time low on 19 November when, to make a point, Xanana took armed Falintil guards into the UN compound.

He was annoyed with the UN for not consulting the CNRT. But he was also annoyed with aid agencies, which he saw as taking away from him the money earmarked for the development of the country for their own expensive pet projects. In one meeting with some of them in Aileu, Xanana broke down in tears, pleading with them to work with the people and not to destroy Timor by creating a begging-bowl mentality.

After de Mello mended fences with Xanana, the UN agreed to set up a National Consultative Council, including seven CNRT members, to advise de Mello on important political issues.[12]

For weeks Xanana and Sergio travelled together all over the country in UN helicopters. In effect Xanana was being used to introduce and endorse the new, temporary leader of East Timor. Xanana called on the people to be patient. His long orations were now accompanied by speeches by de Mello. In one of these speeches he apologised for the failure of the UN to predict and prevent the violence in September. 'I am not ashamed to ask you to forgive us. I would be ashamed not to acknowledge what happened,' de Mello grovelled.[13] De Mello's rather cold, schoolmasterly delivery, however, was received politely but without much enthusiasm or even interest. People wanted to see results, not hear a lot of talk; and they wanted not just food parcels, but assistance to set up their lives again.

§

Waiting in a Dili sports hall for one of these gatherings to begin, I saw Xanana consoling a woman and a little girl. He was talking softly to the mother while hugging the crying child on his lap. I had not noticed that Felis was there, until he sat down next to me. He was unusually quiet. Pointing the scene out to him, I asked who they were. 'My mother and sister,' he said. Felis's father Mateus had been missing since 8 September. Militiamen had turned up at the front door of their house, and Mateus had gone to meet them. He refused to be afraid or to run away. Felis's mother ran out of the back door and managed to reach her parents' house, where her children had taken shelter.

Felis was bitter at the lack of support they had had from Falintil. 'When they needed us for money and medicines they always knew how to find us,' he said. And although Xanana had come to his house and had wept, and Xanana's girlfriend had given them a couple of hundred dollars, he felt that this had been just a token. Felis's friend Fernãu had also lost his father. Cancio's militiamen had set fire to his house in Cassa. When his father ran out they shot him. Fernau had buried his father at the spot where he died, in the courtyard near the front door.

In many families I knew, somebody had been killed or had gone missing. By the time of writing, January 2002, it is still not clear how many people died in East Timor in September 1999. The true extent of the destruction across the country, and the number of lives lost, may never be known. Once again, countries such as Australia, whose intelligence apparatus might have gathered enough evidence to make a reliable estimate, have chosen to stay silent. Their relations with Indonesia are seen as more important. And the UN's serious crime unit did not have the capacity to make a comprehensive investigation.

The pattern I found, on extensive travels through the countryside in the autumn of 1999, was that in most villages the Indonesian security forces and militias had killed an average of four people, either as reprisals, or to force the rest of the people to join the mass deportation, or both. This adds up to a total of roughly two thousand. In the border districts of Bobonaro and Kovalima, and the enclave of Oecussi, the death toll was much higher. In Maliana and Suai alone the numbers reached well into the hundreds.

But there were also other places, such as Laga and Baguia, where the militias were never strong. In Baguia, local priests negotiated with Falintil to grant safe passage to the Indonesian army unit there. Falintil would let the sixty or so soldiers withdraw peacefully if they did not burn, loot, harass or kill. The scared and trapped Indonesians were only too happy with the bargain. Other areas with a strong Falintil tradition likewise escaped destruction. In Soibada and Laclobar students staged patrols of their own with wooden replicas of guns. The Indonesian army had watched from a distance, mistook them for Falintil, and left them alone.

§

Bishop Belo ordered the journalists out of the 'nunnery' and I moved to Rosa's house. Her mother had stubbornly stayed behind when the militias had ordered her to leave Dili and, apart from a smashed mirror, the house was intact. Most of Rosa's family was still in West Timor. Apart from her mother, she shared the house with two sisters – her brother and nephews slept in the garage. The house had quickly become a refuge for all her girlfriends whose houses had been burned and who had nowhere else to go. While Dili's streets became more crowded with the people who had returned from the hills and West Timor, Rosa's house filled up too. By now Rosa and her friends slept six to a double bed, diagonally. A tent was pitched in the garden for the others.

Every time more friends and family arrived there were new tears, hugs and more stories. One of her returning friends was quite cheerful. She said she had been rescued by Eurico Guterres, who had protected the convoy she was travelling with from attacks from other militia groups and from the army. Yet another friend had been 'made a girlfriend' – raped, in other words – by a militiaman in Kupang.

I was never sure how many people were staying in the house at any given time. They came in and out like tides. At night the living room changed into a dormitory: mats, cushions and mattresses were spread over the floor. Sometimes, when I got up to fetch some water, I had to step carefully over sleeping bodies and I would come across people in the kitchen I never saw in the daytime.

These tidal waves sometimes washed up people I had come across before. The cheeky Falintil soldier who had turned up his head in defiance when L7 had punished him turned out to be one of Rosa's many cousins. And early one morning as I staggered out of my bedroom after an all-night *festa*, looking for coffee, I saw the dwarf from the airport, standing in the middle of the living room. 'Wartawan!' (Reporter!) he shouted when he saw me. My impulse was to run back into my room, but I stood there, feeling silly in my night-clothes. Rosa spotted my anxiety. 'Yes, he used to have to look after the journalists,' she laughed. 'But he's okay; he's also family of Taur Matan Ruak.'

Rosa's family had a backlog of celebrations to work through. One of her brothers had married but never had a wedding party; a friend who was staying wanted to celebrate her birthday; a cousin had had her wedding in Kupang but wanted to have another party.

At the all-night parties, we would dance the *tebe tebe*, the wild circle dance that Timorese have been dancing as long as they can remember. They danced it long before the Portuguese arrived, they danced it during the Japanese occupation and danced it during the Indonesian invasion. The songs that used to be chanted with it were epic poems recounting the history of a village or a king. Now they told the story of the struggle:

'O Hele Oh, Oh Hele ole, Lei O Hele La,
Timor oan namakari fila ita rai
Timor oan hamutuk tane ita rai.
Inan aman maun alin feto nan oan sira.
Mai ita hamotuk Timor ukun'an.

(East Timorese who were separated, went back to our land
East Timorese, together, raise up the country.
Father, mother, brothers, sisters and children.
Come together and reign over our country.)[14]

Singing and dancing helped release the stress, and maybe ease the suffering of not just recent weeks, but of the past few years. But beneath the gaiety and festivity of newfound freedom lurked uncertainty. A quarter of the population were still trapped in camps in West Timor. While they were still there, no one could fully enjoy any celebrations. And as long as lists and portraits of children looking for their parents hung at the local hospital, no one could forget the pain of separation.

By the end of 1999, the refugees in West Timor were one of the most urgent and complicated issues the UN and the Timorese leadership had to deal with. Mass displacements had been one of the Indonesian army's tactics to create the impression that a civil war was raging. It also suited the secession plans that pro-autonomy leaders had been talking about for the west of the country. Perhaps most important, having 'hostages' with them gave the militia leaders a sense of power and provided them with a bargaining chip to try to wrest concessions from the UN and the CNRT: for amnesty, land, protection and even political power.

Rosa often thought about her brothers. They and their families had not come back from West Timor yet. She missed all three, but especially the middle one, who had taken care of her like a father after their father died. Rosa's family, like many families in Timor, had a politically complicated background. Her father had been a Fretilin central committee member, and her mother was the sister-in-law of David Alex, the legendary Falintil commander. But in the photograph of her favourite brother, hanging over the sofa, he stood in a nice suit and tie next to Frederico Almeida da Costa, the Apodeti leader, who had not cut his hair since his sons went missing after Santa Cruz. Rosa's brother Agostinho had, like da Costa, supported autonomy. After the looting and burning had started he had taken a large group of pro-autonomy families on a boat to Kupang.

Politics, however, had not divided Rosa's family. Before Rosa's father died, he had called on his children to stay united and take care of each other, whatever happened. For a long time Rosa's brother had provided for his younger siblings' upbringing and education. Now Rosa was the only bread-winner in the family, and she in turn took care of everyone. She had talked to leaders of Falintil and the CNRT about Agostinho's security after his return and they promised to 'receive him back'. And she had made a plan to go to Kupang to persuade him to return before Christmas.

§

I travelled with Rosa and her friend Santos, who was trying to find her sister, to Kupang. In my bag I had a list of names of missing people given me by friends. Madre Margarita still had all her family in the West. Mana Lou's mother had left with one of her daughters and a group of grandchildren with Eurico Guterres, because she wanted to spread the risk, so that at least part of the family would survive. Mana Lou was anxious about them, but also about four members of her institute who were still working in Atapupu. And Bisoi had written her daughter's name on a piece of paper that she had slid into my pocket. Although large groups of people had started to return, the militia had also stopped many people from leaving. There were still around 140,000 East Timorese in West Timor. We found Rosa's brother and his family in a small rented house. They were lucky not to be in one of the miserable camps.

The camps near Kupang were similar to the ones I had seen across the border in Atambua, which I had visited with Ivete in November. Some looked like shanty towns built from rusty sheets of corrugated iron, others looked like poor villages with bamboo huts, while others were long purpose-built barracks that stood in orderly rows between high walls. Some were more notorious than others. UNHCR officials had been denied access to, or had even been attacked in, camps where a hard core of the militia and Timorese ex-soldiers lived. People in other 'camps' were less aggressive, but there were always a few militiamen around to keep an eye on everyone. In October a convoy of 200 people who wanted to return to East Timor was set upon. Since then the numbers of returnees had fallen.

The refugees I found when visiting camps in Atambua and now again in Kupang were often too scared to speak to us. Or they told us they had not made up their minds about going home, but were 'waiting for their leaders to make the decision'. Some were defiant. 'We don't want ever to have to run into the hills again. I did it in 1975 and I still have nightmares,' a woman in one camp shouted. These feelings were fanned by the media in West Timor, which reported that a war was raging in the East. 'After people went back Interfet would separate men from women, kill the men and rape the women.' They even produced interviews with people who told about their 'terrible experiences'.

After being disappointed in the UN, which had promised to stay after the referendum, people did not know what to believe any more. Some were angry with Unamet for abandoning them, and said they could never trust their words again. And however much Ivete in Atambua or Rosa and Santos in Kupang reassured them that it was safe to return, they would say that they would believe it only when they saw it with their own eyes.

Santos did not locate her sister that time, but Rosa's brother, Agostinho, came home before Christmas. Xanana had made it clear that people who had supported autonomy peacefully were welcome back. But on New Year's Eve, some Timorese told the UN police that a militiaman had returned. The police, as a show of force, took Rosa's brother away and locked him up. Rosa, furious, went to the UN. Her brother had no blood on his hands, and he was soon released.

EPILOGUE
. . . .
The Crocodile Returns

After climbing a great hill, one only finds that there are many more hills to climb. I have taken a moment here to rest, to steal a view of the glorious vista that surrounds me. To look back on the distance I have come. But I can only rest for a moment, for with freedom comes responsibility, and I dare not linger, for my long walk is not yet ended. (Nelson Mandela, *Long Walk to Freedom*)

§ THE crocodile returned. Just a couple of weeks before Timor's first experience of democratic elections, on 30 August 2001, one was seen in the tidal canal near the Turismo. A crowd gathered on the bridge and threw sticks and stones into the water to draw it to the surface. An excited boy screamed, 'It killed a pig!' mimicking its snapping jaws with his hands and pointing at something floating in the rubbish in the dirty canal water.

News of the sighting, the first since 1998, spread fast. It added to the nervous, rather febrile atmosphere that hung over the city. Some Timorese saw it as an auspicious sign: their ancestor had returned. But also, as in 1998, many saw in the crocodile's return an ominous political message. It heralded more warfare.

Perhaps, some thought, the crocodile wanted to guard Timorese culture and protect it from loose foreign morals. Women had offended Christ by bathing under the gaze of his giant statue in skimpy bikinis, or even naked, at Areia Branca, which had become a popular weekend haunt for foreigners. Now a large sign was erected with big red letters: 'WARNING: DANGER, Crocodiles'.

But the foreigners were also protecting the crocodiles. The one in the Motael church was among the first residents of Dili to be rehoused. Australian Interfet soldiers had spotted that it was in a bad way. They wanted to take it to Australia, but 'realised that it was some sort of totem', so they alerted a famous Australian crocodile hunter, who built a state-of-the-art crocodile enclosure costing tens of thousands of dollars.[1] This was Timor under UNTAET: grappling to come to terms with its own past, and to rescue its traditions and values from the centuries of foreign domination, while being helplessly dependent on foreign goodwill, and uncertain that freedom would mean peace.

For most of my friends, this was a time of hope, but also of frustration and impatience that everything took so long and was so complicated. Daily life was still a struggle, if of a different order from that endured under Indonesian occupation. But they also had to come to terms with what it meant to be Timorese. Having for so long defined themselves by reference to what they were not – Indonesians – they had to decide what they were. And that could be a confusing and unsettling process.

One day over lunch in one of over a hundred new restaurants, Sebastião noticed the music churning out of a loudspeaker. He had just returned from Ireland where, when he felt homesick, he would listen to the very same singer for some solace. She was an Indonesian pop-star. A generation of Timorese had grown up, albeit unwillingly, as part-Indonesian: Indonesian pop culture formed their mental landscapes; the language they felt most at home in was Bahasa Indonesia; Indonesian politics circumscribed and defined their own.

Examining their own culture and history, many Timorese also had to come to terms with a record of persistent ugly violence. They were used to seeing this as imposed from outside, as heroic resistance to brutal repression, and to rejecting the Indonesian caricature of themselves as destined, without outside intervention, to perpetual civil war. But they also had to admit that many of their nation's troubles were self-inflicted; that, as far back as history related, the Timorese had been fighting each other as well as foreign invaders. Now that they had their freedom, would they start fighting again? 'The Timorese people, by nature, are peaceful and tolerant,' Xanana wrote once. But even he added that 'what defines the character of the Timorese people is their aggressiveness when reacting'.[2]

To build a Timorese society where people could live together in harmony meant finding a path between the conflicting demands of truth on the one hand and, on the other, of peace. Truth and justice, obviously, were important. The culture of impunity that the Indonesians had helped create was one reason for the cataclysm that had happened. But to build a new nation required a break in the cycle of violence and retribution, and an end to the endless saga of vengeance. In one way or another, most of my friends were struggling with how to achieve these competing aims, a battle that had come to be wrapped up in a distant and elusive goal: 'reconciliation'. As João Sarmento put it: 'My country is a puzzle. I don't know where to put the pieces.'

§

The students who had evacuated with Unamet to Australia had returned. They had done quite well: Tata and Elisa were training to become diplomats and Sebastião had benefited from a scholarship to study in Dublin. Antero had also clawed his way back from despair and breakdown to realise his dream: he had set up a community research centre, which, among other things, worked on informal education for villagers and conflict resolution.

João had been elected leader of the Students' Solidarity Council, a post that he, like Antero before him, had accepted reluctantly. The Council's library had become his home. Stacks of books covered the floor, and his laptop was almost buried under piles of papers. He slept amid this chaos on three wooden chairs that he would push together at night, using a book as a pillow. His personal belongings could still fit in the small backpack that I had left him in 1999. But at least he was near his beloved books. His eyes were red with tiredness. As long as I had known him, he had never slept very much, but now that he had three jobs he hardly slept at all. At night he worked as a journalist at *Suara Timor Lorosae*.[3] In the morning he taught at the university, and in between he ran the Student Council.

The student movement was struggling to decide what role it should play in the new Timor. The young people felt they had made many sacrifices, and many of them had died, but now, in the reconstruction of their country, they felt left out. Language had become the issue that defined their alienation. The older generation wanted, for cultural reasons, to reintroduce Portuguese, which most young people could not understand, having been educated in Bahasa Indonesia.[4] 'We have fought because we want to have our own culture, not because we want to become Portuguese again,' said one of the students.

§

In the struggle to find a national identity, there were still of course foreigners from whom Timorese could distinguish themselves. This time, most of the outsiders meant well, but their help was often badly directed. The crocodile lovers, who rehoused a reptile while people were still homeless, did at least give some money to the Motael clinic in the end, hoping it might encourage people to look after the beast.

But many Timorese waited in vain for the economic benefits of the latest foreign invasion. The $552 million earmarked for the reconstruction went in large part into the UN mission and its salaries and logistical needs. Some of these salaries in turn ended up in the pockets of foreign hotel and restaurant owners. And even before the Timorese were provided with food and shelter, the streets were clogged with new Toyota Land Cruisers, jeeps, minivans, rental cars – most of them with licence plates from Darwin. After the car dealers came the construction workers, and so on. Prostitution and HIV/Aids followed in their wake, as did pornography, which small boys peddled on DVDs in front of 'Hello Mister', the first supermarket to open.

After a while, the welcome for the influx of foreigners, flaunting, as it seemed, their wealth of money and opportunities, while more than four out of every five Timorese were jobless, turned to resentment and even unrest. Stones were thrown at UN cars, and at a UN recruitment drive fights broke out. The streets had again become unsafe after dark, but now the ones who had to be careful were the foreigners.

§

The challenges in building a country from scratch were extensive and hydra-headed. Once UNTAET had tackled one, two new ones would appear.

Schools were rebuilt and even a modest university had opened again; teachers were recruited and a curriculum, based on the Indonesian one, was developed. But the quality of the education was not much better than under Indonesian rule and still only half of the pupils in the fourth year could read, write and do simple arithmetic.

UNTAET had helped Timor to secure a deal with Australia about sharing the revenue from developing the oil and gas reserves in the Timor Gap, but the deal was held up by a dispute with the oil companies over tax. Revenues that were expected to start flowing in 2003 would now not materialise before 2005, at the earliest.

Land rights were an unsolved and potentially dangerous issue. Conflicting claims derived from assumed traditional rights and those granted by successive colonial rulers.[5] The chaos that followed the mass displacement of the early years of Indonesian occupation and the scorched-earth campaign in 1999 further complicated matters.

Three district courts were operating, but they were severely underfunded and the Timorese judges and lawyers had very little, if any, experience. The UN's chief prosecutor resigned in disgust at what he saw as 'political interference, incompetence and mismanagement'.[6] Of ten cases of serious crime the UN had pledged to take on, only one had been prosecuted and the target had to be lowered to four.

§

UNTAET was to measure the success or failure of its mission above all by the conduct and outcome of the elections. These were not to be the simple celebration of independence many Timorese had hoped for. Most had assumed that this would be their chance to endorse *Maun Boot* Xanana as the leader who had carried their hopes through all the years of darkness, and the one whom they could now follow into the light. They would have been happy for him to be a benign dictator, and trusted him to pick a good team to run the new country.

But the elections were not for a national president; they were not even for a parliament. Rather, people were asked to choose delegates to a constituent assembly that would draft a constitution. Confusingly, this assembly had the power to decide to turn itself into a new government and set out the rules for future elections, including the one for a president.

In the run-up to the elections, I travelled for weeks through the country, hitch-hiking on trucks and pick-ups. Burned-down traditional wooden houses with thatched roofs were replaced by clusters of structures with identical shiny corrugated-iron roofs the UN agencies had distributed. Some people had left these villages and moved higher up the mountains, to live in tiny hamlets on their ancestral lands.

The students had again gone back to their villages to educate the people about democracy and the elections. They met with little enthusiasm. In one place, people had even berated João for not telling them that this would happen; if they had known, they might not have voted for independence.

Very few Timorese were that cynical, but many were suspicious about the political elite in Dili, people they saw as pursuing position or status; 'looking for their chairs', in the graphic Tetum phrase. In 1975 the formation of parties had led to civil war and ultimately to the Indonesian invasion; in 1999 voting had cost many people their houses, crops and everything they owned. The UN welcomed the emergence of a large number of parties – 16 in all – as a sign of vibrant pluralism. For many Timorese, however, it was proof of a growing division between the people and the leadership. If the leaders had really understood what the people wanted, they would have found a way to agree among themselves.[7] 'When the leaders fight it is the small people that die' was a typical comment.

The enthusiasm for simply handing Timor's troubles to Xanana and asking him to solve them was not shared by my student friends in Dili. While no one doubted that he had the best intentions for the Timorese people, many questioned the motives of his inner circle, and criticised his style of leadership as opaque, even undemocratic. He felt hurt by the criticisms, and after a row about how to conduct a consultation on the constitution, he offered to resign from the National Council.

Xanana's personal life had also dented his image a bit. He had married Kirsty Sword, an Australian activist who had worked as his secretary and *estafeta* during his last years in prison. She was one of the assistants I had seen in Jakarta. It was his first church marriage. Kirsty was pregnant with their child, Alexandre. Many of my Timorese friends were disturbed about the wedding. Not because she was pregnant – it is not uncommon for couples to live together after a traditional ceremony and marry in church when the bride is pregnant – but they felt Xanana had not dealt properly with his former marriages. The women he had lived with during his time in the jungle had not been consulted, and one was planning to take him to court. But above all, my friends seemed to take Xanana's choice of a foreign rather than a Timorese bride as a collective insult.

But, despite the muttering about Xanana, there was only a small, if noisy and sometimes violent, opposition to him and the UN process to which he was lending his charisma. It was a political movement that called itself the 'People's Commission for the Defence of the Democratic Republic of East Timor' (CPD-RDTL).

'A coalition of the disgruntled', João Sarmento had dubbed it. What its members had in common was opposition to Xanana, the CNRT and UNTAET. Their objection to the transitional process was based on the argument that East Timor was already an independent nation, following the declaration made in 1975.

One person who had been linked to the group was Avelino. Whenever I saw him these days, he was carrying works by Lenin or Marx under his arm. He himself had started to resemble a portrait of Marx. His bushy beard was still raven-black, but had grown in a wide triangle covering his neck. He was the leader of the PST, the Timorese Socialist Party. It held on to purist Marxist-Leninist doctrines. As soon as he had come down from Dare, he had set up education projects and agricultural cooperatives, in the style of the old Fretilin of the 1970s.

Most of the original Fretilin leaders had perished in the jungle. The new leadership was dominated by returned exiles such as Marí Alkatiri, Ana Pessoa and Estanislau da Silva, who had come back from Mozambique and Angola. But the chairman was Lu-Olo (Francisco Guterres), who had spent 24 years in the jungle.

Other familiar faces had reappeared on the political stage. Fretilin's first president, Francisco Xavier do Amaral, returned from house arrest in Indonesia and re-established his old party, the ASDT. The return of the Carrascalão brothers, João and Mário, resulted in a split in the UDT: João remained UDT leader, while Mário set up the Social Democratic Party (PSD). José Ramos Horta, the Nobel laureate, and many many more had returned.

I had seen them sitting in the front rows at the CNRT congress in August 2000 – the first time that the leaders of the Timorese diaspora had conferred in Timor with the grassroots clandestine front. The congress was marred by tension and mistrust. Those who had carried on the struggle in the villages were suspicious of the exiled political elite. There were tantrums and walk-outs. The exiles were accused of power-grabbing without having shared in the suffering. They even spoke a political language the locals could not follow. 'We have not suffered for 24 years to be killed by politics,' lamented one of the village women.

§

Facing the challenges of civilian politics was hard for everyone. But it was hardest of all, perhaps, for the proud warriors of Falintil. When I had seen

Xanana in April 1999, he had dreamed about a country that, after so many years of warfare, would be demilitarised. It could even, he thought, do without an army. But this was unrealistic in the face of the threat the militias still posed, and the National Council agreed to form the 'East Timor Defence Force'.[8] Its initial 650 members were recruited from Falintil, and it was, in effect, a continuation of the old guerrilla army.

On 1 February 2001, in an emotional ceremony, the former rebels lowered their flag and replaced it with the blue-and-white banner of the UN. They had fought for independence, yet now they were swearing loyalty to a bunch of foreigners, whom some saw as being no better than earlier invaders.

Taur had cut his hair short; the epoch of guerrilla struggle was over for him at last. But he did not take off his uniform and set up a charity as he had planned. 'We cannot always realise our dreams,' he said. He had become a brigadier-general. It was his duty 'to consolidate peace and democracy', and he added that it was 'a lot easier to fight in the jungle than to rebuild a country'.[9] But he did start a family; he married Isabel Fereira, a human rights activist and friend of Rosa.

For L7, too, it had long been over. He had left Falintil in May 2000, disgruntled. He had taken off his red gloves, as he had vowed to do when the war was over, but he had not yet cut his hair, which he wore clasped at the back of his head in a neat knot. When I had seen him in December 1999, in the Falintil cantonment in Aileu, L7 had been living in a small house on a windy ridge. On his door could still be read in big red letters: 'Otonomy Yes!' Inside I found Bisoi, lying in bed under a pile of rags with a high fever, whimpering that her daughter was still missing. Veronica entered. Her sleek shoulder-length hair was hanging in dirty strings around her face. Self-consciously she sighed: 'Xanana tells us to wash. But how can we wash if we have no soap or shampoo?' On the dining table stood a pan of low-grade rice. Embarrassed, Veronica offered me a plate of this with a spoonful of watery soup. Falintil received no food or other aid. The UN and aid agencies were bound by their mandates not to feed armed groups. It was odd to see them between these concrete walls. It brought out the sadness of their existence far more than the jungle ever did. In the jungle, the harshness of their life evoked respect. Now I just pitied them.

Within six months, L7 had had enough of life in Aileu. The war was over, and as a fighter he had become redundant. Nor did he get from the other commanders the respect he aspired to as Falintil's spiritual leader. So, with 30 of his armed men, he left Aileu and went home to Laga. In September 2000 I looked him up there, in the house where he was living with his family on top of a little hill, next to the market. He had put on a little weight, probably because he drank and smoked less. Supplies of beer and cigarettes had dried up, he grumbled. But he was not unhappy. He was among his clan and people still called him *Comandante*. He had no good words for other Falintil commanders, who, he said, were lusting after power, while his only wish was to help the community and to provide a living for his family.

His activities – such as setting up road-blocks – were watched with rising alarm by the UN and Timorese leaders in Dili. Their worst nightmare was the emergence of a rival warlord. Fuelling suspicions, L7 was perceived as part of the CPD/RDTL and, like his brother Mauk Muruk, loyal to Abilio Araújo, the ex-Fretilin leader, who was close to the Suharto family and General Zacky Anwar.[10] Xanana had ordered L7 to report to him, or face a charge of defection. But he did not respond until Ramos Horta persuaded him. 'He is a good man. He slept here in my house.' L7 pointed proudly at the bare concrete floor of his empty room.

In Laga, L7 was a local hero. When Ramos Horta eventually cajoled him into accompanying him to Dili, the entire community surrounded the cars and refused to let them through. Women and children were crying. They feared that L7 would be taken prisoner in Dili and punished. Some even thought he would be killed.

Using his powers of persuasion to the full, Ramos Horta at last got the convoy, which had grown to include ten cars, on its way to Dili. There members of the RDTL joined in. The crowd swelled to several hundred, and it was not a friendly one. A potentially ugly confrontation was avoided by a meeting between L7 and Xanana, at which Xanana appointed him his 'special security adviser' for the eastern part of East Timor.[11]

Bisoi had left Falintil too. She ran a tiny shop in the market at Maubisse. Her daughter had eventually returned safely with the Carmelite sisters, and was still staying with them, because Bisoi was too poor to take care of her. Unlike other Falintil veterans who left the force, she had not been given financial help to reintegrate into civil society. Commander Falur did not pay anything towards the upbringing of their daughter, either. She had tried to go home to her relatives, but they had not recognised her at first, and when they did, they demanded that she get Falur to acknowledge his daughter. She would take him to court, she said bitterly. The feelings of abandonment triggered the memory of an experience she could not forget. She hesitated to tell me it. She had been told not to share her story with outsiders because 'it would not be good for Falintil's reputation'.

When she was seven months pregnant, Indonesian soldiers attacked her unit. Bisoi was shot in her leg and her abdomen and was left behind. It was January, and the rain was pouring down. She lay on her side with her head on a stone in the wet forest, and chewed leaves to dress the wounds. When, after a few days, the guerrillas found her, the wounds were crawling with maggots. She pulled her shirt up and showed me a nasty deep scar in the left side of her abdomen. Two months later Lekas Susar was born, alive, but with a bullet in her arm. When Bisoi saw the doubt on my face, she said: 'Go and look for yourself.'

§

Everyone carried their own scars from the years of warfare. Church leaders tried to heal them. Bishop Basilio worked tirelessly at building bridges between politicians in East Timor and militia leaders in West Timor.

Mana Lou, of course, had her own ideas about reconciliation. Above all, she wanted to stop it becoming a 'project', a term to which she had become even more allergic after a year of meetings about 'reconciliation' and 'nation-building' initiatives in Dili. In December 1999 Xanana had persuaded her to go with him to the border for talks with the militias. She had agreed to join him, but on the night before her planned departure, one of her assistants died and another fell seriously ill. She saw this as a bad omen, a sign that it was the wrong time for her to go, and that she should stay with her group and give her attention to them.

A year later, in early 2001, she did visit West Timor, on her own terms, and paying her own way. The militias were suspicious of her at first but when she explained she had not come to persuade them to go back, just to offer spiritual guidance at a time that she knew was also difficult for them, she gained their confidence and spent six weeks travelling from one camp to another, drawing big crowds.

Reconciliation needed personal transformation and this, she knew, 'had to come from the inside'. She had returned with the resolve to concentrate on educating her *aspirantes*. Breaking the cycle of violence, she felt, needed to start in villages, in the families.

Mana Lou had become more focused. Her ideas had matured. She developed a new curriculum and taught subjects such as psychology and early childhood development to her women as well as to her growing number of male candidates, so they would understand children better and could become role models of non-violent behaviour. With her fast-growing numbers she was hopeful that in 20 years' time life in the villages would change and that it would be better than in the towns.

One afternoon when I arrived in Dare, Mana Lou was preparing a wedding ceremony. She wanted to devise a ritual without the Portuguese and Catholic imported symbols, and she and her group were inventing new words for the union between husbands and wives. She was not only reinventing culture; she also wanted to prepare young couples for a life of mutual respect and so hoped to stop violence in the family.

Domestic violence in Timor had always been a problem, but combined with the effects of post-traumatic stress and high unemployment, the problem had become even more widespread. Timor's orphanages were full of children.

Some were there because they had lost family in the violence following the referendum, but more came from broken, violent homes.

Mana Lou's institutes also had more little ones. One was Veronica's son Apai, whom I had seen running around with guns in Uaimori. Veronica had found her family, whom she had presumed dead, all unhurt, and had found herself a job.

Mana Lou had installed two solar panels at Dare, so, at least in the dry season, they had electricity, and they now had a television set in the dining room. She and her members would watch every night, when the election candidates were given airtime. They found it all amusing: 'Look at him,' they would scoff. 'Who would vote for him?' She insisted, with a naughty grin, that she was not going to vote, and nor would her members. 'The politicians just talk, talk, talk, but what does it all mean? We have to see what they deliver, then perhaps in the next elections we might know who to vote for.'

But, when polling day came, she and her members trooped off to vote anyway – for Fretilin. Mana Lou explained that it was Fretilin that had inspired her and others to work for their country. 'If you love Timor, you love Fretilin.'

§

Most of Mana Lou's compatriots did as she did. In the constituent assembly elections Fretilin won 55 of the 88 seats. The party's leader, Lu Olo, said that their victory meant that 'all their suffering had not been in vain'.

The high turnout of 91 per cent and the calm that surrounded the voting, the counting and the announcement of the results came as a great relief to UNTAET. The outcome was welcomed too: decisive enough for Fretilin's rule to be secure, but not so totally overwhelming as to allow it to ride roughshod over its opponents – although its leaders were quick to point out that under many electoral systems, such as the British, they would have enjoyed almost total dominance.

Five seats short of the number needed to pass the new constitution single-handed, it would have to learn the art of coalition politics and could perhaps sidestep the pitfalls that befell other liberation movements that turned into ruling parties and entrenched themselves in power. In Timor the hope is that the Democratic Party, the PD, which, with 8.7 per cent of the vote, was second only to Fretilin, will prevent that. It is the party of youth, whose motivation in contesting the election was precisely to challenge Fretilin's dominance.

There seemed to be two main reasons why people voted Fretilin. One was summed up by my driver: 'If we don't have one big party, then they will fight again.' But, more importantly, Fretilin was seen as the bearer of the flag, the *bandeira nacional* that was, as Timorese like to say, 'steeped in the blood of Timor's people'. People had voted not for the promises made for the future but for their feeling about the past. The black, red and yellow flag with the white star, for which so many people had sacrificed their lives, had become a sacred symbol. The party that carried that flag, and had stayed with them during all these years of suffering, had, through its determination, won their freedom. Now it was its turn to finish the historic mission that had started in 1975.

I remembered that on one of my visits to the Martins family in the hills, Francisco Martins had come into the room carrying the Timorese *bandeira* in his outstretched hands. He unwrapped it with the tenderness owed a precious and fragile heirloom and held it in front of him. 'Please take a photo now,' he had said. 'I'm ready to die if I have to, but I want the world to remember what I stood for.'

§

When we climbed Ili Manu, Padre Franciso said independence would heal all wounds. It did not, nor could it make all victims forgive their persecutors. At times Xanana seemed to want even more than this: to skip forgiveness and move straight to forgetfulness. In spring 2001, he even appeared with Prabowo on a podium at a symposium in Jakarta, hugging his former enemy, as if, all being fair in love and war, bygones could be bygones.

But not everybody could share this generosity of spirit.

A year after the massacre in Maliana, I travelled back there to attend a meeting on reconciliation organised by the Students' Solidarity Council. Most of the town's residents had returned by now, but the militia leaders and their supporters were still in West Timor.

A group of twelve women, all dressed in black, set huddled together on wooden benches. When the students asked people what they thought about reconciliation, one of them stood up. 'What is reconciliation?' she asked. 'With whom? Going back to when?' They did not want reconciliation on the South African model, granting amnesties to torturers and murderers. Their constant refrain was that they wanted reconciliation 'with justice'.

I had to think of what Filomena had said when she clutched the plastic bag that contained the little that remained of her husband. For her it had been simple enough: 'If I meet the men who are responsible for his death, I'll kill them.'

With Regina, the widow of Manuel Magalhaes, Filomena had set up a widows' support group. Filomena complained that although her husband had died because he had worked for Unamet she had never received any support from the UN. But the support they were looking for with each other was more emotional than economic. They met every day to share their stories, and, as Regina said, 'to serve history'. One woman, who had lost her husband and two young sons, had no doubt that if she saw their murderers she would beat them up. Another said she sometimes wished the killers dead. But on the whole they did not dream of revenge; although they needed to see justice done before they could think of reconciliation.

Yet it seems unlikely that Timor's widows will ever receive the sort of justice they are seeking. UN investigators recommended the establishment of an international tribunal. But the Security Council, thinking such a proposal would in any event be vetoed by China, accepted Indonesia's offer to set up a special human rights court and deal with the war crimes themselves. Indonesia has refused to extradite any of its soldiers or officers who are charged with war crimes and crimes against humanity in East Timor's courts. And up till now they have brought only a few lower-level thugs and murderers to trial, and given them ridiculously light sentences.

Eurico Guterres had turned into something of a folk hero, a defender of Indonesia, and after serving a mock sentence he became prominent as a member of PDI-P, President Megawati Sukarnoputri's own party, and leader of an 'anti-communist alliance' that burned 'communist' books in Jakarta.

In January 2002, after many delays and much international pressure, Megawati had at last named twelve judges who would sit on the *ad hoc* human rights court she promised when she came to power. The cases against the 18 suspects have been ready for ages.[12]

But Megawati's close relationship with the army makes many question the ability of this court to deliver justice; and, valued as a moderate leader of the world's most populous Muslim nation, she is likely, in the climate that followed the 11 September 2001 attacks on America, to be given the benefit of the doubt in Washington.

In the week when she inducted the judges for the human rights court, the Timorese themselves set up a body to deal with their violent past. Seven persons 'of high moral character, impartiality and integrity' have been chosen and sworn in as commissioners who will sit on the panel of the Commission for Reception, Truth and Reconciliation (CRTR). Based loosely on the South African model, it aims to reconcile the East Timorese, and facilitate the return of the militias and their families still in West Timor. But it will have no power to grant amnesties. Criminals who confess to serious crimes will be referred to state prosecutors. Less serious crimes, such as arson, theft and the killing of animals, will be handled by the commission through customary forms of punishment, such as community service. For example, someone who burned down a house might be required to rebuild it.

The commission will also seek to establish the truth about human rights violations that occurred in Timor between 1974 and 1999: an ambitious project that involves examining the role of foreign governments – and their responsibilities for the crimes against humanity in Timor.

Xanana's constant theme is that people should forget the past. As early as

April 1999, in his prison house, he told me that the South African format would not suit the East Timorese. He had had experience with reconciliation, he said. During his time in the jungle he would tell the people who had lost their families that they, as Falintil, shared their suffering and that it was 'the consequence of the liberation struggle'. Vengeance, he said, would demean all the sacrifices made.

But he also recognises that Timor's future is written in its past: that only when people have answers to their questions about the past can healing begin. In the words of a Timorese priest: 'Without justice we will not have reconciliation, and without reconciliation we'll not have peace.' Xanana, however, would add that there will be no justice without amnesty. Even before the ballot in 1999, he personally promised an amnesty for all the crimes committed before the referendum. Even now, he argues that people who have committed serious crimes should be pardoned after they are sentenced. Not surprisingly militia leaders such as the brothers Cancio and Nemesio have said that, on this basis, they would be ready to face trial.

At the time of writing, the constituent assembly has still not adopted a new constitution, but it had set a date for presidential elections – another precondition for East Timor's independence. Xanana has agreed to run for president, giving in to the pressure exerted on him, not only from his people and the political parties but also from the 'international community'. He still insists that he is not the right person for the job and has made it a condition of his candidacy that all parties nominate him.

§

Over the years I have spent working on this book I have often thought about what the future for Timor holds – that big question Antero put to me so baldly one afternoon in London. Having been so close for so long to those who risked their lives to make the dream of independence come true, I am bound to be susceptible to their sense of anticlimax, disillusionment and frustration. Watching the birth was bad enough; I do not enjoy the growing pains.

Inevitably, the images that stick hardest in my mind are those of pain and fear: the trembling old ladies in the church in Liquiça; the empty, hollow eyes of the women in the UN compound when they heard Unamet was leaving them behind; Erna poking around in the ashes in search of pieces of her father she could bury. But I also remember courage, pride and perseverance. Mana Lou's soaring, magical soprano, singing songs of reconciliation quivering in the cricket-filled nights in the hills; the ex-guerrillas in their crisp uniforms with new stripes on their shoulders; a student leader in Maliana whose first child was born on the morning of the first gathering of his long-planned reconciliation meeting. He called his new son Reconciliano and hoped that he would later carry on his work.

I am also haunted by Padre Jovito's words: 'The dark forces are still alive.' He had meant not just that the old Indonesian generals and their East Timorese stooges were still around, but that the old mentality of mistrust, hatred and vengeance still clouded the future. 'If they fight again I'll be out of here, for good,' Padre Jovito had said. In the years I had known him I had seen him often struggling with his disillusionment. Like many priests of his generation, his calling was to serve God, serve his people and to help liberating his homeland – sometimes in a different order. Now his country was about to be independent he needed to examine his role again. He looked tired and felt sick. 'I've been to ten doctors,' he said, 'but nobody could find anything physically wrong with me.' He, like many other Timorese, seemed to be suffering from post-traumatic shock.

But once, when I was depressed about the infernal politics of it all, he corrected me. He had just returned from a long tour around the countryside, where he had talked with people about the new constitution. He had come back more optimistic than I had seen him for a long time. 'You forget', he said, 'that the people in the villages feel freer than they have ever felt.'

In January 2002, as I write these closing words, Padre Jovito has been sworn in as one of the commissioners of the Commission for Reception, Truth and Reconciliation. He sees reconciliation in theological terms and believes that, for countries as for people, there is always the chance of a new start. As Padre Jovito says of his new role: 'We'll just give them an opportunity to choose to remain in the past or to liberate themselves to a new future.' Every dawn, however bitter, holds the hope of a better day.

Chronology

1600s

Portuguese set foot on East Timor and set up trading post.

1859

Portugal and the Netherlands divide the island of Timor into East (Portuguese) and West (Dutch).

1942–45

Japanese invasion and occupation.

1974

25 April: 'Carnation revolution' in Portugal overthrows 48-year-old Portuguese dictatorship.

20 May: Fretilin founded.

1975

11 August: UDT stages a coup and takes over strategic parts of Dili.

20 August: Falintil founded.

September: Fretilin gains control of the country.

October: Indonesia begins attacks across the border from West Timor.

16 October: Five foreign journalists killed by Indonesian troops in Balibo.

28 November: Fretilin declares the 'Democratic Republic of East Timor'.

6 December: US President Gerald Ford visits Suharto.

7 December: Indonesia launches full-scale invasion of East Timor.

1976

31 May: Indonesia annexes East Timor as its 27th province.

1983

March: Ceasefire between Indonesian troops and Falintil.

August: Kraras massacre, ceasefire breaks.

1987

The National Council of Maubere Resistance (CNRM) is established.

1988

Suharto visits East Timor.

1989

October: Pope John Paul II visits East Timor.

1991

2 November: Santa Cruz massacre. Indonesian troops fire on mourners in Dili, killing hundreds of people.

1992

November: Xanana Gusmão captured, and sentenced (in 1993) to a life sentence, later reduced to 20 years.

1996

November: Nobel Peace Prize awarded to José Ramos-Horta and Bishop Carlos Ximenes Belo.

1997

South African President Nelson Mandela meets Xanana Gusmão.

1998

April: CNRM changes its name to the National Council for Timorese Resistance (CNRT) – umbrella organisation for pro-independence individuals and organisations.

18 May: Suharto forced to step down. B. J. Habibie succeeds him as president of Indonesia.

8 June: Students establish East Timor Student Solidarity Council (ETSSC) in Dili.

27–30 June: Visit of European troika, mass demonstrations in Dili.

10–11 September: Reconciliation meeting in Dare between independence leaders and supporters of integration with Indonesia.

9 November: Killing of Indonesian military spies and the attack on an arms depot in Alas lead to massive operation against the local population.

20 December: UN envoy Jamsheed Marker is airlifted out of East Timor.

1999

27 January: President Habibie announces that East Timorese will be granted choice of autonomy or transition to independence.

February: Xanana moved from prison to house arrest.

4–6 April: Massacres in Maubara and Liquiça. More than fifty people killed in church compound of Liquiça.

17 April: Militia go on rampage through Dili and attack Manuel Carrascalão's house, killing 30 people.

21 May: Wiranto brokers 'peace agreement' between militias and resistance. KPS is established.

5 May: Portugal, Indonesia and UN sign agreement that paves way for 'popular consultation' on status of East Timor.

4 June: UN flag raised in Unamet compound.

25–30 June: Dare II, reconciliation meeting in Jakarta.

4 July: Militiamen attack humanitarian convoy in Liquiça.

16 July: Voters' registration for referendum starts.

27 July: Unamet visits Falintil cantonment for the first time.

6 August: Registration closes with 451,792 voters registered.

12 August: Falintil complete cantonment at four sites.

14 August: Start of campaigning.

28 August: Falintil and militia leaders agree to lay down arms.

30 August: Polling day, 432,287 people (98.4 per cent of eligible voters) turn out to vote. Three UN staff are killed in Ermera.

1 September: Militia violence in Dili, journalists attacked.

3 September: Unamet leaves Maliana.

4 September: Election results; 78.5 per cent of votes cast for independence.

5 September: Wiranto and Alatas fly to Dili. Refugees enter UN compound.

6 September: ICRC's and Bishop Belo's compounds attacked, refugees forced out. Massacre in Suai.

7 September: All Unamet staff withdrawn from the districts.

8–9 September: Maliana massacre.

9 September: Massacre in Oecusse.

10 September: UN international and Timorese staff evacuate to Darwin.

11 September: Security Council delegation visits Dili.

12 September: President Habibie announces he has invited UN peacekeepers to restore peace and security in Timor.

15 September: Security Council mandates Interfet.

14 September: Last UN staff evacuate, taking refugees with them to Darwin.

20 September: First Interfet troops land in East Timor. Unamet starts returning.

25 October: Indonesia formally resigns its authority over territory. UN Transitional Administration in East Timor (UNTAET) established.

27 October: Xanana returns to East Timor.

30 October: Last Indonesian military leaves East Timor.

December: National Consultative Council (NCC) established in East Timor.

2000

28 February: Interfet hands over security responsibility to UNTAET.

July 2000: Establishment of cabinet-style East Timor Transitional Administration, ETTA.

21–30 August: CNRT congress.

6 September: Three UN refugee agency workers killed by pro-Indonesian militia gangs in Atambua. UN evacuates all its staff from West Timor.

October: NCC replaced by 36-member National Council (NC).

2001

1 February: Falintil formally disbanded; 650 of its members recruited to form new East Timor Defence Force.

9 June: CNRT abolishes itself.

30 August: Election of 88-member Constituent Assembly, to write and adopt constitution before East Timor's independence.

September: New all-Timorese transitional cabinet established.

2002

17 January: Seven panel members sworn in for Commission for Reception, Truth and Reconciliation.

14 April: Date set for presidential elections.

20 May: Date set for independence.

Notes

Prologue

1. General Zacky Anwar, quoted in *Tempo*, 27 December 1999.

1 The View from the Ditch

1. Years later, Jill wrote a book about this incident: *Cover-up: The Inside Story of the Balibo Five*, Melbourne: Scribe Publications, 2001.

2. 'Avoid taking photographs showing torture in progress [such as when] people are being subjected to electric current, when they are stripped naked, etc. Remember do not have such photographic documentation developed outside East Timor which could be made available to the public by irresponsible elements.' Instruction Manual No. PROTAP/01-B/VIV, 1982, *Established Procedure for Interrogation of Prisoners*, Military Report Command, 164 Wira Dama, 8 July 1982.

2 Distant Glimmers

1. Not his real name.

2. *USA Today*, 3 December 2001.

3. According to the Australian linguist Dr Geoffrey Hull, East Timor has 16 distinct indigenous languages, which can be sub-divided into 35 dialects and sub-dialects.

3 The Past Casts its Shadow

1. John G. Taylor, *Indonesia's Forgotten War: The Hidden History of East Timor*, London: Zed Books, 1991.

2. Ibid.

3. James Dunn, *Timor: A People Betrayed*, Australia: Jacaranda Press, 1983.

4. Jill Jolliffe, *Cover-up: The Inside Story of the Balibo Five*, Melbourne: Scribe Publications, 2001.

5. On 6 December 2001 declassified documents confirmed that the Indonesian government launched the invasion of Timor with the concurrence of Ford and Kissinger. William Burr and Michael L. Evans (eds), *National Security Archive Electronic Briefing Book No. 62*, George Washington University.

4 Requiems

1. Constâncio Pinto and Matthew Jardine, *East Timor's Unfinished Struggle: Inside the Timorese Resistance*, Cambridge, MA: South End Press, 1996.

2. Amnesty International, *East Timor: Continuing Human Rights Violations*, London, 1995. After close examination many of the names were duplications arising from confusion of Indonesian and Timorese spelling, and many on the list later surfaced.

3. Mario Carrascalão in interview with author, June 2001.

4. Pinto and Jardine, *East Timor's Unfinished Struggle*.

5. Adam Schwarz, *A Nation in Waiting*, London: Allen & Unwin, 2000.

5 *Underground*

1. Arnold S. Kohen, *From the Place of the Dead*, New York: St. Martin's Press, 1999.

2. Coffee farming in Timor dates back to the beginning of the twentieth century, when the Portuguese started to plant Arabica. It was part of the drive to make the colonies profitable for the motherland. Soon it had become Timor's most important cash crop and export product. During colonial times the Portuguese trading company SAPT sold the coffee on the world market. After the Indonesian invasion the lucrative trade came under control of the Indonesian military and SAPT became P.T. DENOK, a company with strong links to the Suharto family. For a few years, however, the American organisation NCBA, sponsored by USAID, the American government aid agency, had managed to organise the farmers and buy direct from them, paying the world market price. It became so successful that they in effect cut out middlemen and, more importantly, P.T. DENOK, and so broke its monopoly on the coffee trade. The quality is said to be superb and the coffee is marketed internationally as 'organic', since it grows more or less wild and the small coffee farmers don't have the money to use fertilisers or pesticides.

3. The Internal Political Front (FPI), the National Security Service (SNN), the National Security Information Service (SISN) and the Civil Security Service (Seguranza Civil, mainly operating in Dili and Baucau.

6 *The Bishop on the Mountain*

1. Richard Tanter, Mark Selden and Stephen R. Shalom, *Bitter Flowers, Sweet Flowers: East Timor, Indonesia, and the World Community*, Oxford: Rowman and Littlefield, 2001.

7 *Timor's Joan of Arc*

1. The thesis has been published in East Timor by Yayasan Hak and the Sahe Institute for Liberation.

2. *Annual Health Report 1996*, Regional Health Department, East Timor.

3. Jill Jolliffe, *East Timor: Nationalism and Colonialism*, St Lucia: Queensland University Press, 1978.

8 *The Crocodile Bares its Teeth*

1. David Boyce, *East Timor: Where the Sun Rises over the Crocodile's Tale. A Collection of Environmental, Historical and Cultural Notes*, Dili, 1999.

2. The ICRC can make information public only when its host country agrees. In this case, the ICRC's information served Indonesia's interests.

3. Robert Lowry, *The Armed Forces of Indonesia*, London: Allen & Unwin, 1996.

4. Peter Baretu, 'The militia, the military and the people of Bobonaro district', in Damien Kingsbury (ed.), *Guns and Ballot Boxes: East Timor's Vote for Independence*, Monash Papers on Southeast Asia, Monash Asia Institute, Victoria, Australia.

9 The Dam Breaks

1. For full letter see Tim Fisher, *Seven Days in East Timor*, St Leonards, NSW: Allen & Unwin, 2000.

2. Ian Martin, *Self-Determination in East Timor, United Nations, the Ballot and International Intervention*, London and New York: Lynne Rienner Publishers, 2001.

3. Martin, *Self-Determination in East Timor.*

4. BBC World Service, 11 February 1999. http://news.bbc.co.uk./hi/english/

5. Dino Djalal later became the spokesman for Indonesian Task Force for the Implementation of the Popular Consultation in East Timor, a task force led by former military intelligence chief General Zacky Anwar.

10 Big Brother Xanana

1. Ian Martin, *Self-Determination in East Timor, United Nations, the Ballot and International Intervention*, London and New York: Lynne Rienner Publishers, 2001.

2. Xanana Gusmão, *To Resist is to Win*, Australia: Aurora Books, 2000.

11 A Difficult Time Never to be Forgotten

1. Xanana Gusmão, *To Resist is to Win*, Australia: Aurora Books, 2000.

2. Interview with author in Dili, May 2001.

3. Ramos Horta, *Funu: The Unfinished Saga of East Timor*, New Jersey: Red Sea Press, 1987.

4. The United States had provided Indonesia with the Bronco, the OV-10, a American plane manufactured by Rockwell International, designed for counter-insurgency operations and equipped with infra-red detectors, rockets, napalm and machine-guns. These planes were specially designed for close combat support against an enemy without effective anti-aircraft capability – in short, an enemy precisely like the Timorese resistance.

5. Britain first sold Hawk ground attack aircraft to Indonesia in 1978. They were used to bomb the population in the mountains of Timor.

6. There are many claims that napalm and Agent Orange were used by the Indonesians. George Aditjondro, an Indonesian scholar who did a lot of research on this time, supports the claims of the Timorese that both napalm and Agent Orange were used in the bombings. America did not deny that Indonesia used napalm, just that it came from America. It suggested that the Indonesians had made it themselves.

7. Interview with author.

8. Conversation with author, May 2001.

9. It assumed it would have grown by 2 per cent a year, and would have reached 750,000 by 1980. Indonesian census figures showed that 550,000 people were living in Timor that year. The census figures are unreliable and the missing 200,000 could also have meant that in these terrible times, the natural population growth rate fell anyway. So the only conclusion that can be drawn from these figures is that Timor had been deprived of 200,000 people: either killed by war or hunger, or never born. See Dunn, *A People Betrayed.*

10. John Pilger, *Distant Voices*, London: Vintage, 1994.

11. Gusmão, *To Resist is to Win.*

12. George Aditjondro, *In the Shadow of Mount Ramelau: The Impact of the Occupation of East Timor*, Leiden: Indoc, 1994.

13. Interview with Mario Carrascalão, June 2001.

14. Dunn, *A People Betrayed.*

15. John Pilger's questions sent to Xanana in 1994.

16. Abílio Araújo was one of the hard-line communist members of Fretilin's Central Committee, who lived in exile in Portugal. He had been Xanana's successor as Fretilin's president until he was suspended over a fundamental disagreement and replaced by a leadership troika of Lu-Olo, Mau Hudo and Ma' Huno.

12 No Sanctuary

1. Garda Paksi, a vigilante group of pro-Indonesian youth set up in 1994 by Prabowo's SGI (the military intelligence unit of Kopassus) as a response to the pro-independence youth organisations, which had become increasingly well-organised in the towns in Timor. They operated under SGI's command (and had Kopassus members among them) and were widely believed seen as responsible for the *ninja*, which terrorised the independence supporters with their nightly attacks.

13 'Fear is the Parent of Cruelty'

1. James Anthony Froude, 1877.

2. Damien Kingsbury (ed.), *Guns and Ballot Boxes: East Timor's Vote for Independence*, Monash Papers on Southeast Asia, Monash Asia Institute, Victoria, Australia.

14 Blood Rites

1. Damien Kingsbury (ed.), *Guns and Ballot Boxes: East Timor's Vote for Independence*, Monash Papers on Southeast Asia, Monash Asia Institute, Victoria, Australia.

15 Asking the Fox to Guard the Chickens

1. UN Security Council Briefing, June 1999.

16 Dancing with Falintil

1. Ian Martin, *Self-Determination in East Timor, United Nations, The Ballot and International Intervention*, London and New York: Lynne Rienner Publishers, 2001.

2. Ibid.

3. Press release, CNRT, 18 June 1999.

4. Martin, *Self-Determination in East Timor.*

17 Life in Uaimori

1. Seventy guerrillas at Atalari (Region 1), 260 guerrillas in Uaimori (Regions 2 and 3), 153 at Poetete and 187 at Aiassa (both Region 4).

2. Ian Martin, *Self-Determination in East Timor, United Nations, the Ballot and International Intervention*, London and New York: Lynne Rienner Publishers, 2001.

3. The scale and importance of a party in Timor is often measured by the number

of *karau*, water buffaloes. For example, for a wedding, the family of the groom has to provide *karau* as a present for the bride's family, and at least one *karau* will end its life as the main dish of the wedding banquet.

18 Party in the Jungle

1. Peter Bartu, 'The militia, the military and the people of Bobonaro district', in Damien Kingsbury (ed.), *Guns and Ballot Boxes: East Timor's Vote for Independence*, Monash Papers on Southeast Asia, Monash Asia Institute, Victoria, Australia.

2. Ibid.

19 Kings of Cassa

1. ABC TV, Australia, *Licence to Kill*, 1999.

2. *Reconciliation Dare II*, press release, 30 June 1999.

3. The agreement was signed on 28 August in Baucau and made public on 29 August, one day before the ballot.

4. Ian Martin, *Self-Determination in East Timor, United Nations, the Ballot and International Intervention*, London and New York: Lynne Rienner Publishers, 2001.

20 The Price of Freedom

1. Total turnout of voters 432,287.

2. Damien Kingsbury (ed.), *Guns and Ballot Boxes: East Timor's Vote for Independence*, Monash Papers on Southeast Asia, Monash Asia Institute, Victoria, Australia.

3. UN press briefing, 30 August 1999.

4. Ali Atalas: 'Up to the balloting, the reports we got from our own people, of the pro-integration people, including Lopes da Cruz, and so on, is that we were going to win.' *Jakarta Post*, 2 November 1999.

5. UN press briefing, 31 August.

6. Garnadi, 'General Assessment if Option 1 Fails', 3 July 1999.

7. Desmond Ball, 'Silent witness: Australian intelligence and East Timor', *Pacific Review*, Vol. 14, No. 1, 2001.

8. Ian Martin, *Self-Determination in East Timor, United Nations, the Ballot and International Intervention*, London and New York: Lynne Rienner Publishers, 2001.

9. *The Report of the Panel on United Nations Peace Operations*, also known as the *Brahimi Report*, states that: 'the Secretariat must not apply best-case planning assumptions to situations where the actors have historically exhibited worst-case behaviour'.

10. Filomeno in interview with author. The family also features in Carmela Baranowska's film *Scenes of an Occupation*.

21 A Sea of Flames

1. Geoff Robinson, 'With UNAMET in East Timor – an historian's personal view', in Richard Tanter, Mark Selden and Stephen R. Shalom, *Bitter Flowers, Sweet Flowers: East Timor, Indonesia, and the World Community*, Oxford: Rowman and Littlefield, 2001.

22 Under Siege

1. Interview with Major-General Theo Syafei, *Jakarta Post*, 8 December 1999.

2. John Gittings, 'The shock that led to peace hope', *Guardian*, 13 September 1999.

23 Counting Bodies

1. Security Council Resolution 1264, 15 September 1999, 'authorises the establishment of a multinational force under a unified command structure, pursuant to the request of the Government of Indonesia conveyed to the Security Council with the following task: to restore peace and security in East Timor, to protect and support Unamet in carrying out its task and, within force capabilities, to facilitate assistance operations, and authorises the States participating in the multinational force to take all necessary measures to fulfil this mandate.'

2. Desmond Ball, 'Silent witness: Australian intelligence and East Timor', *Pacific Review*, Vol. 14, No. 1, 2001.

3. Later it would transpire that it was actually a dried-up sanitary napkin.

24 Valley of Tears

1. Soon rivalries surfaced between political parties and clandestine organisations within the CNRT. Members of these groups, such as Frente Politica and Falintil, were now looking for their 'rewards'. Some were made village and hamlet chiefs, while others became linked to gangs that operated in Dili and Baucau, where they ran extortion rackets, threatening especially the overseas Chinese businessmen who had made a tentative comeback. In Dili this had lead to confiscation of houses and land, cars and motorcycles. Their nick name soon became *milisi-ke-dua*, the second militia.

Another point of long-term friction within the resistance was the rivalry between the Feraku and the Kaladi. Feraku and Kaladi were derogatory nicknames the Portuguese had bestowed on the people from the Eastern and Western part of East Timor. The Kaladi, from the west, were characterised as the easygoing ones, the people who, when they given orders 'would just look at them and keep silent'. The Feraku, the Makasai for friend, 'would not listen but turn away'. They are the people who always want to win. For example, all Falintil commanders were Feraku. And people such as L7 claimed the Feraku had fought harder and sacrificed more during the war than the Kaladi.

2. *Time* magazine, 20 March 2000.

3. The Timorese members of Tim Alfa were convicted in Dili district court on 11 December 2001 and received long prison sentences. Indonesia did not allow the extradition of the Kopassus officer involved, who was, at the time of writing, still at large in Indonesia.

3. *Christian Science Monitor*, 23 September 1999, http://www.csmonitor.com/atcsmonitor/specials/timor/backgrnd/back6.html

5. Captain Andrew Plunkett, a senior military intelligence officer, said in the SBS Australia television documentaries *Australia's Secret* (9 May 2001) and *See No Evil* (16 May 2001) that 59 people were killed in and around the police station, and that the death toll, including what his unit had found in surrounding areas, came to 300.

6. According to Resolution 1272 (1999), UNTAET has a mandate to: a) provide

security and maintain law and order throughout the territory of East Timor; b) establish an effective administration; c) assist in the development of civil and social services; d) ensure the coordination and delivery of humanitarian assistance, rehabilitation and development assistance; e) support capacity-building for self-government; f) assist in the establishment of conditions for sustainable development.

7. Jarat Chopra, 'The UN's kingdom of East Timor', *Survival*, Vol. 42, No. 3, Autumn 2000.

8. Interview with the author, June 2001.

9. Sergio de Mello, 'How not to run a country: lessons for the UN from Kosovo and East Timor', unpublished paper, June 2000.

10. Chopra, 'The UN's kingdom of East Timor'.

11. Unpublished interview with Norwegian journalist Torgeir Norling, November 1999.

12. Reuters, 30 December.

Epilogue: The Crocodile Returns

1. 'Save the sacred crocodiles', *Scientific American*, www.sciam.com/explorations/2001//032601croc/box7.html.

2. Xanana's speech at the symposium on 'Reconciliation, Tolerance, Human Rights and Elections', Dili, 12 February 2001.

3. *Suara Timor Timur* had changed its name in 1999 to *Suara Timor Lorosae*, but was still printed mainly in Bahasa Indonesia, since that was the most widely read language in Timor.

4. The constitutional assembly compromised and made both Tetum and Portuguese official languages.

5. During the late Portuguese colonial period, 3,000 land titles were issued. The Indonesians issued another 1,400.

6. Carlos Vasconcelos in a briefing to the annual conference of the International Association of Prosecutors, Sydney, 2–7 September 2001.

7. See also Elizabeth Traube, 'Producing the people', unpublished paper, Wesleyan University.

8. See also the *Independent Study on Security Force Options and Security Sector Reform for East Timor*, Centre for Defence Studies, King's College, London, 8 August 2000.

9. Interview with the author, September 2001.

10. Hamish McDonald, 'Magic man ruffles Gusmão's vision', *Sydney Morning Herald*, 20 January 2001.

11. The affair set a malign precedent. To placate L7's supporters, Ramos Horta threw his weight around, intervening with the UN's judicial branch to secure the release of an RDTL member detained for a 'grenade incident', seen as an attempt on his life and that of Xanana.

12. Among the 18 suspects are Indonesian generals Muis and Suratman (who had been promoted in the meantime) and Timor's former police chief, Timbul Silaen. Zacky Anwar's name was conspicuously absent and so was Wiranto's although on her first day in office in June 2001 Megawati had called Wiranto in to warn him that he and his colleagues would not enjoy immunity from prosecution for crimes in Timor.

Bibliography

Aditjondro, George Junus, *In the Shadow of Mount Ramelau: The Impact of the Occupation of East Timor*, Leiden, Netherlands: INDOC, 1994.

Amnesty International, *Power and Impunity: Human Rights under the New Order*, London: Amnesty International Publications, 1994.

Ball, Desmond, 'Silent witness: Australian intelligence and East Timor', *Pacific Review*, Vol. 14, No. 1, 2001.

Boyce, David, *East Timor: Where the Sun Rises over the Crocodile's Tale. A Collection of Environmental, Historical and Cultural Notes*, Dili, 1999.

Budiardjo, Carmel and Liem Soei Liong, *The War against East Timor*, London: Zed Books, 1984.

Carey, Peter and G. Carter Bently, *East Timor at the Crossroads: The Forging of a Nation*, Social Science Research Council, London and New York, 1995.

Centre for Defence Studies, King's College, London, *Independent Study on Security Force Options and Security Sector Reforms for East Timor*, 8 August 2000.

Chopra, Jarat, 'The UN's kingdom of East Timor', *Survival*, Vol. 42, No. 3, London: IISS, Autumn 2000.

CIIR/IPJET, *International Law and the Question of East Timor*, Catholic Institute for International Relations and International Platform of Jurists for East Timor, 1995.

Dunn, James, *Timor: A People Betrayed*, Australia: The Jacarandra Press, 1983.

Gusmão, Xanana, *To Resist is to Win*, Australia: Aurora Books, 2000.

Hainsworth, Paul and Stephen McCloskey (eds), *The East Timor Question: The Struggle for Independence from Indonesia*, London: I.B.Tauris, 2000.

Hill, Helen Mary, 'FRETILIN: the origins, ideologies and strategies of a nationalist movement in East Timor', MA thesis, Monash University, Australia, 1978.

Inbaraj, Sonny, *East Timor: Blood and Tears in Asean*, Thailand: Silkworm Books, 1995.

Jardine, Matthew, *East Timor: Genocide in Paradise*, USA: Odonian Press, 1995.

Jolliffe, Jill, *East Timor: Nationalism and Colonialism*, St Lucia: Queensland University Press, 1978.

— *Cover-Up: The Inside Story of The Balibo Five*, Melbourne: Scribe Publications, 2001.

Kingsbury, Damien (ed.), *Guns and Ballot Boxes: East Timor's Vote for Independence*, Monash Asia Institute, Australia, 2000.

Kohen, Arnold S., *From the Place of the Dead*, New York: St. Martin's Press, 1999.

Lennox, Rowena, *Fighting Spirit of East Timor: The Life of Mattinho da Costa Lopes*, Australia and London: Pluto Press and Zed Books, 2000.

Lourdes Martins, Maria de, *Kelompok Gerejani Basis*, East Timor: Yayasan HAK and Sahe Institute for Liberation, 2001.

Lowry, Robert, *The Armed Forces of Indonesia*, London: Allen & Unwin, 1996.

Martin, Ian, *Self-Determination in East Timor, United Nations, the Ballot and International Intervention*, London and New York: Lynne Rienner Publishers, 2001.

Martinkus, John, *A Dirty Little War*, Australia: Random House, 2001.

Mo, Timothy, *The Redundancy of Courage*, London: Chatto & Windus, 1991.

Nijhuis, Minka, *De erfenis van Matebian*, Amsterdam/Antwerp: Uitgeverij Contact, 2000.

Pilger, John, *Distant Voices*, London: Vintage, 1994.

Pinto, Constâncio and Matthew Jardine, *East Timor's Unfinished Struggle: Inside the Timorese Resistance*, Boston, MD: South End Press, 1997.

Ramos-Horta, Arsenio, *The Eyewitness: Bitter Moments in East Timor Jungles*, Singapore: Usaha Quality Printers, 1981.

Ramos-Horta, José, *Funu: The Unfinished Saga of East Timor*, Trenton, NJ: The Red Sea Press, 1987.

Schwarz, Adam, *A Nation in Waiting*, London: Allen & Unwin, 1999.

Tanter, Richard, Mark Selden and Stephen Shalom (eds), *Bitter Flowers, Sweet Flowers: East Timor, Indonesia, and the World Community*, Oxford: Rowman & Littlefield, 2001.

Taylor, John G., *Indonesia's Forgotten War: The Hidden History of East Timor*, London: Zed Books, 1991.

— *The Indonesian Occupation of East Timor 1974–1989: A Chronology*, London: Catholic Institute for International Relations, 1990.

Traub, James, 'Inventing East Timor', *Foreign Affairs*, Vol. 79, No. 4, New York, July/August 2000.

Traube, Elizabeth, *Cosmology and Social Life: Ritual Exchange among the Mambai of East Timor*, Chicago: Chicago University Press, 1986.

— 'Producing the people', unpublished paper, Wesleyan University, USA, 2001.

Turner, Michele, *Telling: East Timor, Personal Testimonies 1942–1992*, Australia: New South Wales University Press, 1992.

Websites

http://www.timor.org/

http://www.timor.com

http://www.gov.east-timor.org

http://www.un.org/peace/etimor/etimor.htm

http://www.easttimor-reconciliation.org/

http://tapol.gn.apc.org/

http://www.solidamor.org/english/english.html/

http://www.indonesia-ottawa.org/news/Timtim/

http://www.uc.pt/timor/netret.htm

http://etan.org/

http://www.timoraid.org/timortoday/index.htm

http://www.easttimorpress.qut.edu.au

http://www.geocities.com/easttimor_bitterdawn/index.html
http://www.ease.com/~lourdes/who/
http://www.etrs.ip.com.au/index.html/
http://goasiapacific.com/specials/etimor/default.htm
http://www.vicnet.net.au/news/east_timor.htm
http://etan.org.ifet/
http://etan.org.lh/
http://www.iidnet.org/adv/timor/overview.htm
http://www.tip.net.au//wildwood/
http://homepage.esoterica.pt~cdpm/frameI.htm
http://www.memorialforsander.org/

Index